ReFocus: The Films of Paul Leni

ReFocus: The International Directors Series

Series Editors: Robert Singer, Stefanie Van de Peer, and Gary D. Rhodes

Board of Advisors:
Lizelle Bisschoff (University of Glasgow)
Stephanie Hemelryck Donald (University of Lincoln)
Anna Misiak (Falmouth University)
Des O'Rawe (Queen's University Belfast)

ReFocus is a series of contemporary methodological and theoretical approaches to the interdisciplinary analyses and interpretations of international film directors, from the celebrated to the ignored, in direct relationship to their respective culture—its myths, values, and historical precepts—and the broader parameters of international film history and theory. The series provides a forum for introducing a broad spectrum of directors, working in and establishing movements, trends, cycles and genres including those historical, currently popular, or emergent, and in need of critical assessment or reassessment. It ignores no director who created a historical space—either in or outside of the studio system—beginning with the origins of cinema and up to the present. *ReFocus* brings these film directors to a new audience of scholars and general readers of Film Studies.

Titles in the series include:

ReFocus: The Films of Susanne Bier
Edited by Missy Molloy, Mimi Nielsen, and Meryl Shriver-Rice

ReFocus: The Films of Francis Veber
Keith Corson

ReFocus: The Films of Jia Zhangke
Maureen Turim and Ying Xiao

ReFocus: The Films of Xavier Dolan
Edited by Andrée Lafontaine

ReFocus: The Films of Pedro Costa: Producing and Consuming Contemporary Art Cinema
Nuno Barradas Jorge

ReFocus: The Films of Sohrab Shahid Saless: Exile, Displacement and the Stateless Moving Image
Edited by Azadeh Fatehrad

ReFocus: The Films of Pablo Larraín
Edited by Laura Hatry

ReFocus: The Films of Michel Gondry
Edited by Marcelline Block and Jennifer Kirby

ReFocus: The Films of Rachid Bouchareb
Edited by Michael Gott and Leslie Kealhofer-Kemp

ReFocus: The Films of Andrei Tarkovsky
Edited by Sergey Toymentsev

ReFocus: The Films of Paul Leni
Edited by Erica Tortolani and Martin F. Norden

edinburghuniversitypress.com/series/refocint

ReFocus:
The Films of Paul Leni

Edited by Erica Tortolani and Martin F. Norden

EDINBURGH
University Press

Edinburgh University Press is one of the leading university presses in the UK. We publish academic books and journals in our selected subject areas across the humanities and social sciences, combining cutting-edge scholarship with high editorial and production values to produce academic works of lasting importance. For more information visit our website: edinburghuniversitypress.com

© editorial matter and organization Erica Tortolani and Martin F. Norden, 2021, 2022
© the chapters their several authors, 2021, 2022

Edinburgh University Press Ltd
The Tun—Holyrood Road
12 (2f) Jackson's Entry
Edinburgh EH8 8PJ

First published in hardback by Edinburgh University Press 2021

Typeset in 11/13 Ehrhardt MT by
IDSUK (DataConnection) Ltd

A CIP record for this book is available from the British Library

ISBN 978 1 4744 5451 3 (hardback)
ISBN 978 1 4744 5452 0 (paperback)
ISBN 978 1 4744 5453 7 (webready PDF)
ISBN 978 1 4744 5454 4 (epub)

The right of the contributors to be identified as authors of this work has been asserted in accordance with the Copyright, Designs and Patents Act 1988 and the Copyright and Related Rights Regulations 2003 (SI No. 2498).

Contents

List of Figures	vii
Notes on Contributors	ix
Chronology	xiii

1. Introduction   1
   Erica Tortolani and Martin F. Norden
2. Exploding the Cosmopolitan and Treating the Foreigners' Foreignness: Paul Leni's *The Diary of Dr. Hart*   36
   Jaimey Fisher
3. The Unnatural in the Natural: Leopold Jessner and Paul Leni's Early Weimar Film *Backstairs*   52
   Jason Doerre
4. Cinema Panopticum: Wax, Work, *Waxworks*   69
   Erik Born
5. The Proto-Horror-Comedy: *Waxworks*   82
   Joel Westerdale
6. Intersectional Avant-Garde: Paul Leni's *Rebus-Film* Series and the Confluence of Experimental Visual Styles   97
   Erica Tortolani
7. Bravura Beginnings: Paul Leni and the Art of the Prologue   116
   Martin F. Norden
8. Paul Leni's *The Cat and the Canary*: Adaptation into Genre   140
   Rebecca M. Gordon
9. Specters of the Mind: Ghosts, Illusion, and Exposure in Paul Leni's *The Cat and the Canary*   158
   Simone Natale

10	Misfitting in America: Paul Leni, Conrad Veidt, and *The Man Who Laughs* *Gábor Gergely*	172
11	Masculinity and Facial Disfigurement in *The Man Who Laughs* *Bruce Henderson*	189
12	Cinematic Space and Set Design in Paul Leni's *The Last Warning* *Bastian Heinsohn*	203
13	*The Last Warning*: Uncertainty, Exploitation, and Horror *Shawn Shimpach*	219

Filmography	239
Index	254

Figures

1.1	A signed Leni self-portrait from 1913, taken from a Berlin caricaturists' club program of the same year	4
1.2	Leni's cover design for a 1914 issue of *Die Illustrierte für Gross-Berlin*	5
1.3	Leni's cover design for a special issue of *Das Plakat*, October 1920	7
1.4	Poster announcing The Gondola at Vienna's Roland theater, September 1, 1923	15
2.1	Fireworks at spa anticipate the exploded world	42
2.2	Invaders create a public health emergency that Dr. Hart then has to confront	45
2.3	Windmill before, charming landmark tending to the landscape	46
2.4	Windmill after, now exploded	47
3.1	Henny Porten (Housekeeper) and Fritz Kortner (Postman)	54
3.2	Henny Porten (Housekeeper) in the back stairwell	62
5.1	Ivan the Terrible (Conrad Veidt) as a "living icon"	87
5.2	The flirtatious caliph (Emil Jannings)	92
6.1	Mr. Rebus ("Herr Rebus") greeting the audience	101
6.2	One visual clue for "Paris"	108
7.1	Opening night for *Outside the Law* and "The Police Sergeant's Story"	117
7.2	Berlin's Palast-am-Zoo Theater	121
7.3	Leni's design concept for the *Varieté* prologue	123
8.1	Laura La Plante as Annabelle West in the 1927 *The Cat and the Canary*	144
8.2	Paulette Goddard as Joyce Norman in the 1939 remake of *The Cat and the Canary*	154

10.1	Conrad Veidt, in Jack Pierce's make-up, as Gwynplaine on stage	176
10.2	Olga Baclanova as Josiana drinking in Gwynplaine's performance	182
12.1	Hidden corridors and trap doors	207
12.2	Character placements in confined spaces	210
13.1	A poster designed by Paul Leni, director of *The Last Warning*	226
13.2	A natural for exploitation	229
13.3	Jury ballot to be given to patrons	230
13.4	The look, the horror	234

Notes on Contributors

Erik Born is an Assistant Professor in the Department of German Studies at Cornell University. His research and teaching focus on relations between old media and new media, and particularly on questions of mobility. Drawing on insights from the fields of media archaeology and the study of cultural techniques, his current book project examines the emergence of wireless technology in Germany around 1900. Erik is also the co-editor of a volume on the figure of the neighbor in German modernity, and he is the author of articles on medieval media theory, the pre-history of television, avant-garde film, and early German science fiction, as well as translations and book reviews on topics in film and media studies.

Jason Doerre is a Visiting Assistant Professor at Trinity College in Hartford, Connecticut. While a PhD candidate, he was awarded a Fulbright Fellowship to Germany to complete research on the German naturalist author Hermann Sudermann that became the basis of his dissertation. He has authored publications that deal with nineteenth- and twentieth-century German film and literature. At Trinity College, Jason teaches a wide variety of courses on German culture and history and has recently focused on the films of the Weimar Republic.

Jaimey Fisher is Professor of German and Cinema & Digital Media and director of the UC Davis Humanities Institute at the University of California, Davis. He is the author of *Treme* (2019), *Christian Petzold* (2013), and *Disciplining German: Youth, Reeducation, and Reconstruction after the Second World War* (2007). He edited the volume *Generic Histories of German Cinema: Genre and its Deviations* (2013) and has also co-edited *The Berlin School and its Global*

Contexts: A Transnational Art Cinema with Marco Abel (2018); with Brad Prager, *Collapse of the Conventional: German Film and its Politics at the Turn of the Twenty-first Century* (2010); with Barbara Mennel, *Spatial Turns: Space, Place, and Mobility in German Literary and Visual Culture* (2010); and, with Peter Hohendahl, *Critical Theory: Current State and Future Prospects* (2001). His current book project analyzes war films in Germany from 1914 to 1961.

Gábor Gergely is a Senior Lecturer in Film Studies at the University of Lincoln, UK. He has published *Foreign Devils: Exile and Host Nation in Hollywood's Golden Age* (2012) and articles (e.g. "The Nature of the Exile," 2012 and "The Jungle is my Home," 2017) on émigré stars and Hollywood representations of exile and displacement. He is currently preparing a monograph on the accented cinema of Arnold Schwarzenegger.

Rebecca M. Gordon is a Research Associate with Archive/Counter-archive Canada and a degree candidate in Ryerson University's Film Preservation and Collections Management program. She has taught cinema studies and literature at Oberlin College, Reed College, and Northern Arizona University, and was recently a Fulbright Fellow in Managua, Nicaragua. She is the author of articles on actor–director collaboration, international auteurs, and studies of how audiences' responses to film and television aesthetics shape new modes of spectatorship. She is currently preparing a monograph on cuteness and Latinidad. Her work has appeared in *Film Quarterly*, *Film Philosophy*, *The Journal of Cinema and Media Studies*, and various collections.

Bastian Heinsohn is an Associate Professor of German at Bucknell University and an affiliated faculty member in Film/Media Studies. His main areas of interest are the representation of urban spaces in German and European cinema and the examination of the role of graffiti in cities in transition. Among his publications are essays on Weimar cinema, on film pioneer and Universal Studios boss Carl Laemmle and his affidavits for immigrants from Germany, and on the portrayal of postwar cities in German cinema in the 1950s. His current book project examines the language and meaning of urban graffiti texts in contemporary European cinema.

Bruce Henderson was Professor of Communication Studies at Ithaca College, where he taught for over three decades and from which he retired in May 2020. He has a PhD in Performance Studies from Northwestern University and a PhD in Disability Studies from the University of Illinois at Chicago. He is author/co-author/co-editor of four books, including two performance studies textbooks, a collection of essays on disability studies and performance studies, and a textbook on queer studies. He is past editor of *Text and Performance*

Quarterly and *Disability Studies Quarterly*, and has published on such topics as the writers Marianne Moore and Flannery O'Connor, children's literature, and film and television "clowns."

Simone Natale is Senior Lecturer in Communication and Media Studies at Loughborough University, UK, and Assistant Editor of the journal *Media, Culture & Society*. Simone is the author of two monographs, *Supernatural Entertainments: Victorian Spiritualism and the Rise of Modern Media Culture* (2016) and *Deceitful Media: Artificial Intelligence and Social Life after the Turing Test* (forthcoming), and co-editor of two edited volumes, *Photography and Other Media in the Nineteenth Century* (2018) and *Believing in Bits: Digital Media and the Supernatural* (2019). His research has been funded by numerous international organizations including the AHRC, the ESRC, the Humboldt Foundation and Columbia University's Italian Academy.

Martin F. Norden teaches film history and screenwriting as Professor of Communication at the University of Massachusetts Amherst, USA. He has more than one hundred publications to his credit and has presented his film research at dozens of professional conferences across North America and Europe. His edited books include *Lois Weber: Interviews* (2019), *Pop Culture Matters* (2019), and *The Changing Face of Evil in Film and Television* (2007). He is the author of *The Cinema of Isolation: A History of Physical Disability in the Movies* (1994) and consulted on the documentary films *CinemAbility: The Art of Inclusion* and *Be Natural: The Untold Story of Alice Guy Blaché*.

Shawn Shimpach is an Associate Professor of Film and Media Studies in the Department of Communication at the University of Massachusetts Amherst where is also the Director of the Massachusetts Multicultural Film Festival. He is the author of *Television in Transition: The Life and Afterlife of the Narrative Action Hero* (2010) and editor of *The Routledge Companion to Global Television* (2020). His research interests include the social and institutional constructions of the media audience, the cultural history of film and television, screen genres, and screen industries.

Erica Tortolani is currently a doctoral candidate (ABD) in Communication with a concentration in Film Studies at the University of Massachusetts Amherst, USA. She earned her Master's degree in Communication at the University of Rhode Island, and has been featured in *Film Matters* and *Interdisciplinary Humanities* journals. Her essay "Horror's Founding Mothers: Women in Proto-Cinema, Visual Avant-Gardes, and the Silent Era" will be appearing in the forthcoming edited volume, *Bloody Women! Women Directors of Horror* (eds. Victoria McCollum and Aislinn Clarke; Rowman and Littlefield). Erica received the first prize (shared) in the juried 7th annual Graduate Film Certificate paper competition with her essay "Sound, Pleasure, and the Uncanny: An Analysis of Martin Arnold's *Alone. Life Wastes Andy Hardy* (1998)." Her research interests include silent cinema, horror films, German Expressionist film, and avant-garde and experimental film.

Joel Westerdale is an Associate Professor in the Department of German Studies at Smith College, where he teaches literature, film, and intellectual history. His writings on film have appeared in *Film History*, *German Quarterly*, and *Filmblatt*, as well as in *A New History of German Cinema* (2012) and *The Many Faces of Weimar Cinema: Rediscovering Germany's Filmic Legacy* (2010). His current research project examines the myth of the "dark German soul" and its role in the development of the early Weimar cinema canon.

Chronology

1885 Born Paul Josef Levi in Stuttgart, Württemberg (now Baden-Württemberg), Germany, on July 8 to Moses Hirsch Levi and Rosa Mayer Levi.

1900s After graduating from high school in Stuttgart, he works as an apprentice draftsman in an ornamental ironworks company while developing his skills as an avant-garde painter and costume designer on the side. Around 1902, shortly after the death of his father, he moves to Berlin and enrolls in Berlin's Academy of Fine Arts (Akademie der bildenden Künste) for a degree in painting.

Around 1908, he starts receiving his first professional assignments as a graphic artist, poster artist, caricaturist, and stage designer. He begins calling himself "Paul Leni" but does not legally change his surname. Among the posters he designs in 1908 is one for a Berlin cinematograph exhibition; it is his first film-related work in any medium.

1910 He designs an advertisement for a Polish tea and biscuit company ("Herbata Marka Herbatnik"), a commercial illustration so striking that it eventually finds its way into the Museum of Modern Art's collection. He designs the title page for the film periodical *Lichtbildbühne* and eventually does the same for other film journals such as *Die Projektion* and *Kunst im Kino*.

1911 His circle of associates in the worlds of graphic design and theater expands to include such future film luminaries as Ernst Lubitsch,

F. W. Murnau, and Conrad Veidt, who work in various capacities for Max Reinhardt's theater company in Berlin. In collaboration with Ernst Deutsch and Josef Fenniker, Leni creates posters for the company.

1912 He designs a promotional poster and the décor for the Lichtspielhaus Wittelsbach am Bayrischen Platz, one of Berlin's first luxury film theaters. He also designs a poster announcing the opening of the Union Theater in his hometown of Stuttgart. In addition, he designs movie posters for Diskus-Film productions, including *The Mark of Their Past* (*Das Brandmal ihrer Vergangenheit*) and *The Poison of Love* (*Das Gift der Liebe*).

In 1912, and for several years thereafter, numerous German trade journals and directories devoted to poster design, graphics, lighting, architecture, and theater arts frequently mention Leni and his work. They include *Moderne Bauformen, Innen-Dekoration, Die Scene: Blätter für Bühnenkunst, Arena, Deutsche Kunst und Dekoration, Die Schaubühne, Dekorative Kunst, Neuer Theater-Almanach, Licht und Lampe: Zeitschrift für die Beleuchtungsindustrie*, and *Das Plakat*.

In October, he joins the staff of Weilwerke GmbH, a business equipment manufacturing company in Frankfurt am Main. His responsibilities include oversight of the company's illustrations and advertising campaigns. The contractual relationship does not work out and he returns to Berlin the following year.

1913 Under the direction of Rudolf Bernauer and Carl Meinhard, he works as an artist in the Technical Department of the Berliner Theater on Charlottenstrasse and becomes a key player on the theater's décor and costumes team. He works for other Bernauer–Meinhard theaters, including the Komödienhaus, the Hebbel-Theater, the Theater am Nollendorfplatz, and the Theater on Königgrätzerstrasse, and teaches classes in theater painting and stage design through these theaters. His settings for *Macbeth* at the Königgrätzerstrasse theater are among his outstanding designs during this period. He also serves as secretary for an illustrators' group in Berlin called the "Caricaturists' Club" (Club der Karikaturisten EV).

He designs posters for Vitascope films such as *The Tango Queen* (*Die Tangokönigin*), *The Berlin Range* (*Die Berliner Range*), *The Waters Are Silent* (*Die Wasser schweigen*), and *Passion* (*Leidenschaft*) as well as ones for Vitascope stars Hanni Weisse and Toni Sylva.

He designs the sets for what is believed to be his first film assignment: *An Outcast, Part 1: The Young Boss* (*Ein Ausgestossener, 1 Teil: Der junge Chef*), directed by Joe May and released on March 14. The film marks the beginning of a long professional relationship with May.

1914 He designs the sets for four films in the "Stuart Webbs" detective mystery series, all directed by Joe May.

He joins the German military near the start of World War I, soon reaching the rank of corporal.

1915 He is among the artists who contribute illustrations to *The German Soldiers Book* (*Das Deutsche Soldatenbuch*), published by Verlag der Deutschen Bibliothek in Berlin in June.

1916 While serving in the military, he begins developing plans for a wartime film that would eventually become *The Diary of Dr. Hart* (*Das Tagebuch des Dr. Hart*).

1917 With the support of the German Photo and Film Office (Bild- und Filmamt, also known as Bufa), a propaganda unit created in January by the German Supreme Army Command, he begins filming *The Diary of Dr. Hart*. Shot largely in German-occupied Brest-Litovsk, it is his first film directorial assignment. Censorship-related delays ensue, however, and the film goes unreleased.

After his military discharge, he designs the sets for *The Ring of Giuditta Foscari* (*Der Ring der Giuditta Foscari*) and *The Blouse King* (*Der Blusenkönig*), both released late in the year. The latter film is directed and co-written by Leni's close friend Ernst Lubitsch, who also stars.

In December, Leni completes two films that he started after commencing work on *The Diary of Dr. Hart*: *Prima Vera* (*Die Kameliendame*) and *Sleeping Beauty* (*Dornröschen*). They are the first films directed by him to play in theaters. He also designs the promotional poster for the latter film.

1918 In January, *The Diary of Dr. Hart* is released. That same month witnesses the debut of another Leni-directed film, *The Mystery of Bangalor* (*Das Rätsel von Bangalor*). Promoted with another poster designed by Leni, *The Mystery of Bangalor* is the first of several notable collaborations with renowned stage and screen actor Conrad Veidt.

1919 He signs a contract with Gloria-Film GmbH to direct and design films. His first production under this agreement is *Prince Cuckoo* (*Prinz Kuckuck: Die Höllenfahrt eines Wollüstlings*), starring Conrad Veidt and released in late September. While under contract to Gloria-Film, he develops projects for other companies on a freelance basis. The most prominent are his set and costume designs for Richard Oswald's production of *Lady Hamilton* in 1921.

1920 During the making of the Gloria film *The White Peacock* (*Der weisse Pfau: Tragödie einer Tänzerin*), he meets Leonore "Lore" Sello, a professional dancer and actress. They marry within a year.

He designs the cover image for a special film issue of the poster magazine *Das Plakat*, published in October.

1921 He co-directs and designs the sets for *Backstairs* (*Hintertreppe*), a *Kammerspielfilm* co-produced by Gloria-Film and Henny Porten Filmproduktion.

His design work is displayed at the Great Berlin Art Exhibition (Grosse Berliner Kunstausstellung) in a section devoted to stage sets and film set design.

He purchases the rights to fellow Stuttgarter Wilhelm Hauff's 1825 story "The Tale of the Ghost Ship" ("Die Geschichte von dem Gepensterschiff") for Gloria-Film. He plans to direct and design its settings. He lines up Carl Mayer and Hans Janowitz, the screenwriters for *The Cabinet of Dr. Caligari* (*Das Cabinet des Dr. Caligari*), to write the script. Gloria-Film begins advertising Leni's *The Ghost Ship* (*Das Gespensterschiff*) as a "monumentalfilm," but for unclear reasons the film is not made.

1922 Perhaps as a result of the *Ghost Ship* project's failure, Leni declines to follow the terms of his contractual agreement with Gloria-Film after having completed nine productions for the company. He elects instead to develop his own film projects. He founds his own company, Paul-Leni-Film GmbH, but produces no films under that company title.

1923 In June, he and film composer Hans May co-found "The Gondola" ("Die Gondel"), a cabaret theater funded by Alexander Kwartiroff and other Russian émigrés. Leni designs some of the shows' sets, working with such creative collaborators as Kurt Tucholsky, Hans Brennert, and Walter Trier. The cabaret, located on Bellevuestrasse near Potsdamer Platz in Berlin, remains active until 1926.

CHRONOLOGY xvii

He reunites with Joe May and designs the sets for two of May's films in the fall.

1924 He strikes a deal with Neptun-Film AG, a film company owned by the same Russian émigrés who financed "The Gondola," to create *Waxworks* (*Das Wachsfigurenkabinett*). Co-directed with Leo Birinski and produced under an extremely tight budget, *Waxworks* is released in November. It becomes his most famous film to date.

1925 He is among a cohort of German directors invited to participate in the Paris Film Congress in June. Others included Lupu Pick, Joe May, Fritz Lang, Karl Grune, F. W. Murnau, and Robert Wiene.

In early September, he designs the settings for *Look Out! Wave 505!* (*Achtung! Welle 505!*), a musical revue staged at Berlin's Theater im Admiralspalast to critical acclaim.

In late October, several newspapers report that Leni seeks to produce a film based on Gilbert and Sullivan's famed light opera *The Mikado* in a "lacquer work style" (i.e. as a Japanese art film). The film is not made.

The management team of the Palast-am-Zoo, the largest movie theater in Berlin controlled by Universum-Film Aktiengesellschaft (Ufa), hires Leni to design live stage acts called prologues as lead-ins to the films exhibited in that venue. His first is for the E. A. Dupont film *Varieté*, which opens on November 16 at the Palast-am-Zoo. Critics uniformly praise Leni's work.

His prologue for Ernst Lubitsch's Hollywood film *Forbidden Paradise* debuts at the Palast-am-Zoo on December 4. His follow-up prologue for Herbert Brenon's *Peter Pan* opens at Ufa's Mozartsaal theater on December 17.

He designs the cover illustration for Rudolf Kurtz's *Expressionism and Film* (*Expressionismus und Film*). The book, published by Verlag der Lichtbildbühne the following year, becomes a landmark text on German Expressionist cinema.

He founds Rebus-Film GmbH, a company through which he creates eight short crossword puzzle films in collaboration with writer Hans Brennert and cinematographer Guido Seeber. The first *Rebus* film is released in December, the next six on an irregular basis throughout 1926, and the final one in January 1927.

1926   He completes the prologue for Buster Keaton's *The Navigator*, which opens at the Palast-am-Zoo on January 4.

On February 5, *The Lost World* opens at the Palast-am-Zoo, with Leni once again providing the designs for the prologue. That same month, film-related design drawings by him go on display at London's Mayor Gallery. Anthony Bertram, critic for *The Saturday Review of Politics, Literature, Science and Art*, pronounces them "extremely amusing and executed with dash and distinction."

He designs the sets and costumes for *Manon Lescaut*, directed by Arthur Robison. It opens on February 15 at the Palast-am-Zoo.

Universal Pictures president Carl Laemmle, in Berlin at the beginning of the year for financial negotiations with Ufa, learns about Leni and his expertise as an illustrator, set designer, and director. He invites Leni to come to the US and join Universal.

On March 19, Leni and his wife Lore Sello are issued visas. They sail from Hamburg on board the steamship *Hamburg* on April 9. On the ship's non-immigrant manifest, he lists his name as Paul Levi and his occupation as a stage manager. They arrive in New York City on April 20, and he immediately begins work on his first Universal project: a prologue for the Tod Browning–Lon Chaney film *Outside the Law*. The trade press reports in April that Laemmle has hired Leni to design sets for Universal's big productions and establish and take charge of a "mechanical presentations department" at Universal City.

Outside the Law opens in revival at Manhattan's Colony Theater on May 9, and Leni's work as the creator of the film's prologue, titled "The Police Sergeant's Story," draws considerable critical praise.

Outside the Law closes on June 5, and Leni remains in New York City to design a prologue titled "Tremendous Trifles" for the Universal comedy *Rolling Home*, the next film to be shown at the Colony.

He departs Manhattan for Los Angeles during the *Rolling Home* run, arriving on or around June 17. He soon begins working on his first US film: *The Cat and the Canary*, an adaptation of the hit stage play by John Willard.

The Los Angeles-based Photoplay League honors the recently arrived Leni by sponsoring a weeklong exhibition of *Waxworks* at the Sherman

Theater in Sherman, California, beginning on July 12. Actor-director Robert Vignola introduces him to the League's highly appreciative audiences.

1927　In March, speculation circulates in the trade press about other projects that Leni may direct for Universal following *The Cat and the Canary*. The potential films include *He Knew Women* and *Polish Blood*, both of which would be starring vehicles for the internationally acclaimed actress Lya de Putti. Leni ends up directing neither of these films.

The Cat and the Canary opens on September 9 and becomes a huge worldwide success. He follows it up in October with *The Chinese Parrot*, an early "Charlie Chan" movie.

1928　*The Man Who Laughs*, an adaptation of the Victor Hugo novel and perhaps Leni's most ambitious film, is released on April 27. It is the last of his collaborations with Conrad Veidt.

On May 31, he fills out and signs a "declaration of intention" form to become a US citizen. Once again, he lists his legal name as Paul Levi.

Hoping to capitalize on the success of *The Cat and the Canary*, Universal releases what would be Leni's final film on December 25: *The Last Warning*, an adaptation of the mystery novel by Wadsworth Camp and the play by Thomas F. Fallon.

1929　In February, Universal begins announcing different projects that Leni may direct. The potential films include adaptations of Philip Gibbs's *A Bargain in the Kremlin*, Owen Davis's *Tonight at 12*, and Molière's *The Imaginary Invalid*.

Around June, Leni contracts severe blood poisoning resulting from an infected, ulcerated tooth. He becomes critically ill, and his condition deteriorates over the next few months. By the end, his illness leaves him paralyzed and unable to speak.

Leni dies of sepsis and heart failure on September 2 in Los Angeles at the age of forty-four. His remains are cremated two days later. At the request of his widow, a probate court judge appoints Ernst Lubitsch as executor of Leni's estate.

CHAPTER 1

Introduction

Erica Tortolani and Martin F. Norden

In the decades since silent-film director Paul Leni's untimely death on September 2, 1929, at the age of forty-four, the landscape of the film industry witnessed many categorical shifts. From the widespread use of synchronized sound and the transition from monochrome to color film to the evolution of numerous genre categories, styles, and global cinemas, the cinematic medium matured into a full-fledged economic, cultural, artistic, and social force.

Though Leni did not have the chance to participate fully in these changes in the industry, he was among the European directors—Germans, especially— who heavily influenced the international film industry during the 1920s and beyond. In the US, Britain, and other countries, film critics were quite aware that Leni and other *deutsche* filmmakers were cultivating a particularly rich cinema during the post-World War I years. For example, New York-based writer Bushnell Dimond argued in 1926 that "the Germans are doing more distinguished work than we in the cinema." Dimond, little known today but praised by public intellectual Gilbert Seldes in 1924 as "the best actual critic of the movies,"[1] had just attended the American premiere of Leni's film *Waxworks* (*Das Wachsfigurenkabinett*) and had come away highly impressed. Using *Waxworks* as a case in point, he elaborated on the differences he saw among German and American films and filmmakers:

> This picture emphasizes, somewhat pitifully, the paucity and meager conventionality of the great bulk of our native directors. "Sweetness and light," even luxury and display, the four essentials of our American product, are all very well in their way, but when the first two degenerate into glucose and bathos, it is time for a little redeeming morbidity to

step in. [The German filmmakers] have a fuller, riper, more varied and plastic sense of existence—they realize that drama is not achieved by putting a pretty woman into a costly frock and getting some well-paid hack to revamp the Cinderella theme around her "personality."[2]

Leni was a key figure among the host of filmmakers referenced by Dimond; indeed, the critic described Leni as "the astonishing motion picture director whose [*Waxworks*] first electrified London intellectuals with its fresh and graphic power."[3] There is little question that Leni was at the forefront of German directors whose stylistically daring and narratively innovative films were garnering international acclaim and who soon found themselves heavily recruited by Hollywood studios.

The growing acclaim that Leni received in the 1910s and 20s for his work as a director, set designer, and graphic artist might lead one to conclude that he has been suitably recognized for his lasting contributions to the cinematic medium, just as his fellow German émigrés have been. Unfortunately, this has not been the case. Bushnell Dimond lamented in 1926 that "the name of Paul Leni is not one that rings with illustrious persistence in American ears,"[4] and his observation aptly, if sadly, characterizes most ensuing film scholarship on Weimar cinema, 1920s Hollywood cinema, and the silent-film era as a whole. Though this scholarship has been saturated by careful analyses and rich, historical narratives of a number of German and German-turned-Hollywood directors, Leni has been largely ignored save for some passing references. Though some recent analyses have begun to pay attention to Leni, they have tended to dwell only on his Hollywood films, such as his most famous contribution, 1927's *The Cat and the Canary*. This slight uptick in Leni scholarship, while laudable, nevertheless fails to account for Leni's lengthy career in Germany, transition from Weimar to Hollywood filmmaking, experiments with narrative and non-narrative films, and rise to fame during the transition into synchronous-sound filmmaking. Leni's fascinating career trajectory is worthy of critical and popular attention but has, for unclear reasons, been mostly ignored.[5]

ReFocus: The Films of Paul Leni picks up where most silent-film scholarship has left off. The first volume in English on the life and career of Paul Leni,[6] it covers the scope of the German director's multifaceted career and offers new perspectives on his films, both well-known and obscure. It examines many never- before explored dimensions of Leni's professional creativity, including his early visual- arts and theatrical work in Germany during the 1910s, collaborations with contemporaneous filmmakers, career in and experiments with set and stage design, and transition from German to Hollywood filmmaking. To do so, our book engages with new historical, analytical, and theoretical perspectives on Leni's most influential films from both his German and American careers. As a result, it fills in crucial gaps in existing research on the director, the artistic and cultural "scene" in Germany during the 1910s and 20s, and Hollywood filmmaking during the late silent and early sound years.

One of the most important pieces of the much larger puzzle of Paul Leni involves his early life and work in the visual arts in his native Germany. Born Paul Josef Levi on July 8, 1885 in Stuttgart to banker Moses Hirsch Levi and his second wife Rosa Mayer, Leni entered the world in a period of creative, intellectual, and spiritual development across the nation, prompted in part by the growth of Germany's Jewish community during the nineteenth century.[7] While very little survives on his formative years, historians generally agree that Leni, upon leaving secondary school, defied his parents' wishes and became a metal draftsman's apprentice at an ornamental ironworks company. During his late teenage years, Leni faced simultaneous loss and accomplishment, with the death of his father in 1901 coinciding with the growth of his career in the plastic and performing arts.

As Hans-Michael Bock has observed in his German-language anthology *Paul Leni: Grafik, Theater, Film*, Paul Leni eventually settled in Berlin, the booming heart of the arts in Germany, with his widowed mother. Berlin address book records of the time list Leni under his birth name, Paul Levi, and indicate his profession as a painter. In a 1929 interview with the *New York Herald Tribune*'s Marguerite Tazelaar, Leni recalled one of his first gigs as a teenager: designing and painting scenery for Berlin's Lessing Theater. With very little formal artistic training guiding his work, the youthful Leni essentially just followed his creative impulses. "I had nothing to lose," he remembered. "I was getting [the equivalent of] about five dollars a week and knew that I would probably be fired, no matter how the scenery turned out, so I just went ahead and carried out my ideas."[8]

Leni's reputation as a free-spirited jack-of-all-trades in the graphic arts and theatrical design fields began around this time. Accepted into Berlin's Academy of Fine Arts, Leni created painterly work that led to numerous other projects: poster designs for a local cinematographers' "Kino-Ausstellung am Zoo" exhibition in 1908–9 and Berlin's Metropol Theater in 1910; cover art for publications like *Lichtbildbühne*; and set and costume designs for the theatrical venues controlled by producers Carl Meinhard and Rudolf Bernauer, including the Berliner Theater, the Komödienhaus, the Theater am Nollendorfplatz, the Hebbel-Theater, and the Theater on Königgrätzerstrasse.[9] Though these early projects were not films, they reflected Leni's growing interest in all things cinema. A brief comment by art critic Robert Breuer illuminates an example. Writing on theatrical innovations during the 1912–13 season, Breuer suggested that Leni's promotional design work for a small Berlin theater built by Alfred Wünsche and Max Pechstein had a playfully cinematic touch: "Paul Leni, a successful poster designer and aspiring decorator of the stage, has achieved . . . through whimsical applications of colored fabrics on a colored background, the psyche of a grotesque movie projector."[10] The aesthetic qualities of Leni's theatrical and, later, cinematic poster designs served as the basis for the unique visual language and keen attention to detail that he became known for during his eventual turn behind the camera.

As Bock has noted, Leni was distinctive in his frequent use of bold typeface graphics and modernist, geometric shapes, particularly in his advertisements for companies like the Duskes GmbH and Vitascope, while his more conservative contemporaries employed classical compositions, recycling images of garlands, braided ropes, and intricate tendrils.[11] At the same time, Leni often demonstrated a flair for the dramatic, experimenting with curved and organic lines, architecturally influenced designs, and, at times, Eastern-inflected motifs in his poster designs for theater productions in Berlin. Leni's frequent oscillation between the modern and the traditional proved to be his calling card within the Berlin arts scene.

Leni's gravitation towards the graphic arts also led him to a successful career as an illustrator and cartoonist. In addition to serving as secretary for the "Caricaturists' Club" (Club der Karikaturisten EV) in prewar Berlin,[12] Leni took his skills for drawing to several different arts organizations and events across Germany, including the Free Association of Advertising Art

Figure 1.1 A signed Leni self-portrait from 1913, taken from a Berlin caricaturists' club program. The image not only shows Leni's flair as a "Karikaturist" but also suggests the way he saw himself at the start of his movie career: rather world-weary at age twenty-seven.

Figure 1.2 Leni's cover design for a 1914 issue of *Die Illustrierte für Gross-Berlin*.

and Science, the festival of the Cooperative German Stage Workers, and the Union of Cinema Directors.[13] Though he moved frequently between these and other circles within the Berlin arts scene—from industrial organizations supporting cinema and theater to leisurely drawing clubs, and even underground radical arts groups—his perspective as a visual artist, honed during his forays into poster design, always shone through.

An example is Leni's design for the restaurant-lounge "The Queen" in 1912: an illustration of a modern group of socialites sitting in a nondescript lounge setting, a sleek champagne stand accompanying the group as they chat amongst themselves. Contrasting these slim, cartoonish figures is the poster heading, featuring the location and ownership of the "Original American Grillroom and Bar" in a flourished serif font.[14] Another design from around 1914 for the short-lived magazine *Die Illustrierte für Gross-Berlin* is a more resonant display of Leni's impulse towards dynamic graphic design. With an illustration of the Berlin city skyline in the cover's background, the primary focal point is a top-hatted gentleman (a common visual used by Leni), pad and pen in hand, gazing wide-eyed at his surroundings. Deviating from realistic, anatomical proportions—the man is pear-shaped, his head and limbs seemingly suspended in mid-air—Leni accompanied his illustration with text conveyed in a childlike way, contrasting the stylized objects of the poster with a more commercial, approachable heading. Leni's 1921 design for the small-format publication *Kunst im Kino* exemplifies some of his more experimental, boundary-pushing designs, which he revisited in his cover art for Rudolf Kurtz's pioneering book *Expressionism and Film* (*Expressionismus und Film*) in 1926. Vividly designed with a color palette of yellows, reds, and greens, the *Kunst im Kino* design illustrates an abstract depiction of a movie set, shot on location in the jungle. Collapsing the foreground and background into one flat space, the tiny filmmakers run away frantically from the focal point of the poster—a gigantic elephant, angrily flinging its trunk into the air. The magazine's title, written in blocky lettering, cleverly spews from the elephant's tusk, spraying into the sky above the scene. Experimental, playful, and keenly attentive to even the smallest of details, Leni's graphic design circulated around the Berlin cultural milieu, earning him a living for the better part of the 1910s.

Around 1913, the Berlin-based Continental-Kunstfilm GmbH took notice of Leni's talents in the visual arts and asked him to join the studio as an artistic advisor on a number of films. It was at this point that Leni entered into the first of his many collaborations with established film directors, prefiguring his own career behind the camera in the years to come. Leni began working with Continental's star director, Joe May, as a set designer for the first installment of his *Outcast* film series, *The Young Boss*, thereby establishing his first major credit in the film industry in 1913. He continued his working relationship with May with a series of prize-mystery films (*Preisrätselfilme*) during the mid-1910s that encouraged audience participation in the solving of mysteries by the cunning fictional detective, Stuart Webbs.[15] May eventually broke with Continental due to internal conflicts and started his own production company, May-Film GmbH, for which Leni frequently offered his creative expertise as a set designer. Their collaborative projects included *Veritas Vincit* in 1919, *The Tragedy of Love* (*Tragödie der Liebe*) in 1923, *The Love Letters of Baroness von S . . .* (*Die Liebesbriefe der Baronin von S . . .*) in 1924, and *Somebody's Son* (*Der Farmer aus Texas*) in 1925. These productions not only helped diversify Leni's cinematic portfolio but also offered valuable insight into the painstaking measures the nascent director needed to make to ensure historical accuracy, mood and tone, and artistic innovation on these and other productions. In a 1924 editorial piece for *Der Kinematograph* titled "Architecture in Film" ("Baukunst im Film"), Leni stated that his role as set designer (or, in the parlance of the day, "film architect") was to make the world of the film believable for the audience. Though he argued that the set designer "is now considered an independent creative artist, one who makes a substantial contribution to film's characteristic style," he also noted that the designer's contribution must heighten and support the creative vision of the director. "The architect is of course not free to do whatever he pleases," he remarked, adding that "his charge and the restrictions he must respect in his work are handed to him by the director, who always

Figure 1.3 Leni's cover design for a special issue of *Das Plakat*, a leading poster-art magazine based in Berlin. The issue, published in October 1920, was devoted to film posters.

remains the master on set." Leni used a then-recent example of his work on a Joe May film, *The Tragedy of Love*, as a case in point:

> A scene set in a small train station with an arriving train was produced in the studio. The impression we were charged with creating was that of a small train station on a cold, frosty winter's night. Had we shot the scene in a real train station, we would have undoubtedly ended up with an image that appeared thoroughly natural and realistic, but we would never have been so wildly successful in conveying that particular impression—a combination of loneliness, the country, the winter's night, the frost, and the squalor—that the studio allowed us to create. It is here in the studio that the angle of view, lighting technique, and decor can all be precisely coordinated with each other.[16]

This testimony alone reflects the point that Leni took his work as set designer—establishing a distinct, wholly immersive cinematic environment and bringing the creative vision of the director to life through architecture, costuming, and prop usage—quite seriously. Leni's creative aptitude served to his advantage on a host of other visually sumptuous, often historically minded, films. His notable work on the 1915 period piece *The Catwalk* (*Der Katzensteg*) directed by Max Mack is one such example, in which the Prussian backdrop of the film is taken to new levels with true-to-life military costuming and paraphernalia. Leni's designs for Ernst Lubitsch's 1917 comedy *The Blouse King* (*Der Blusenkönig*)—the first of several collaborations with Lubitsch prior to the latter's emigration to the United States in 1922—are other valuable examples of his extravagant stylings as set designer, this time taking inspiration from the contemporary garment industry by featuring lush fashion designs and busy Berlin city streets. Frequent collaborations with E. A. Dupont on postwar films such as *The White Peacock* (*Der weisse Pfau: Tragödie einer Tänzerin*, 1920) and *Wally of the Vultures* (*Die Geierwally*, 1921), with their intricate sets representing the flashy dance halls of London's East End and the vast, stark landscapes of the Alps, respectively, are further evidence of Leni's visual versatility.

His work on the 1921 Richard Oswald feature *Lady Hamilton* was his most grandiose experiment with stage design yet, one that illustrates his acute ability to create realistic, historically motivated scenic environments while staying true to his artistic point of view. Based on the Heinrich Vollrath Schumacher novels of the same name, *Lady Hamilton* takes place in the luxurious locale of eighteenth-century European society. Due to Leni's masterful design of the vivid, period-specific scenery, the setting practically becomes a third character in the tumultuous love affair of the titular character and Lord Nelson. *Lady Hamilton* marked Leni's first time abroad as a set designer, and he worked closely with other members of Oswald's team as they filmed in such locations as London, Venice, Naples, and Rome. His contributions included the creation of the interior architecture and decor of the homes of the European nobility featured in the film, and he worked to assure consistency between these fabricated interiors and their on-location exteriors. The effect Leni achieved in his ambitious *Lady Hamilton* design work, which featured gold-adorned ballrooms, extravagant water fountains, walls covered in fine portraiture and sculptures, and nods to maritime culture, was not lost on critics upon the film's release in 1921. Echoing what many critics observed at the time, *Variety*'s C. Hooper Trask opined that, while the plot and pacing of *Lady Hamilton* suffered in many spots, the film's shining light was its set design. "The interiors designed by Paul Leni achieve much beauty and can even compare with the exteriors taken on the historic locations in Italy itself," he asserted. A critic for the journal *Der Film* offered that "there are scenes that look like Hogarth engravings or Teniers paintings come to life," implicitly suggesting Leni's creative talents and abilities to recreate the historical. Ludwig Brauner of *Der Kinematograph* extended this idea, noting that Leni, working closely with set builder Hans Dreier, took on the "remarkable" task of replicating objects and locations unique to the time period in which *Lady Hamilton* is set. Brauner further observed that "where an actual 'on the spot' item was lacking, Paul Leni (design) and Hans Dreier (execution) created an effective substitute" that added to the film's vivid environment.[17] Predating his collaboration on Arthur Robison's 1926 film *Manon Lescaut*, another powdered-wig period piece based on a popular novel, *Lady Hamilton* ultimately solidified Leni's status as a distinctive creative force who could work just as effectively alone as with established German directors.[18]

Leni's career as a film director, which developed concurrently with his celebrated work as a set designer, was born under extraordinary circumstances: in the midst of his military service during World War I. While serving briefly in the German army as a non-commissioned officer, Leni had the opportunity to direct his first film, *The Diary of Dr. Hart* (*Das Tagebuch des Dr. Hart*). Funded by the German Supreme Army Command's propaganda unit, the Photo and Film Office (Bild- und Filmamt, also known as Bufa),[19] and produced in collaboration with Paul Davidson's Projektions-AG Union film company, *Dr. Hart* was designed to advocate for peaceful relations between Germany and Poland and push for the latter's re-establishment into the German Empire. An early example of Leni's attention to detail, *Dr. Hart* is unique due its successful integration of documentary footage showing the frontlines of war in Poland. This hybrid fiction–documentary film focuses not only on the social and political turmoil of World War I but also on the intimate, interpersonal relationships amongst its central characters: the titular Dr. Robert Hart (Heinrich Schroth), Jadwiga Bransky (Dagny Servaes), and the Russian Count Bronislaw Krascinsky (Ernst Hofmann). The scenes portraying this love triangle are interspersed with others that depict the overall compassion held by members of the German military for their Polish compatriots; their humanitarian work is at the center of the film's action, with the German leads shown as being diligent, kind, and eager to help at the frontlines of war, even in the face of personal or ideological conflicts.

Though *Dr. Hart* was delayed in its release until January 1918, after Leni had returned to civilian life, it ultimately led to two significant developments, one in the much broader industrial landscape of German cinema and the other in Leni's career. Firstly, impressed by Leni's artistic ingenuity in his directorial debut and the film's success in Germany and abroad, Universum-Film AG (Ufa)—the organization that absorbed Paul Davidson's company following the film's premiere—was motivated to make a string of propaganda films. These productions, such as Georg Jacoby's *Unatonable* (*Unsühnbar*, 1917) and May's *The Sacrifice* (*Das Opfer*, 1918), attempted to combat international anti-German sentiment with images of the caring, philanthropic German, therefore aiming to appeal to audiences outside of the national context.[20] None, however, matched the success of *Dr. Hart*.

Secondly, it launched Leni's long-term working relationship with Hans Brennert, a multi-talented actor, playwright, screenwriter, journalist, and lyricist. Brennert, who wrote the script for *Dr. Hart*, went on to collaborate with Leni on numerous other film and theater projects during the 1910s and 20s. Indeed, he wrote the screenplay for Leni's next film as director and the first to be publicly exhibited: *Prima Vera*, released in December 1917. An adaptation of a novel by Alexandre Dumas *fils*, the film centered on a tragic romance set during the mid-nineteenth century. With Leni serving as both director and set designer, the Brennert-scripted *Prima Vera* prefigured the elaborately stylized period pieces of the postwar years such as *Lady Hamilton* and *Manon Lescaut*.

Leni's next feature as director, *Sleeping Beauty* (*Dornröschen*), as well as his collaborative work with Ernst Lubitsch as set designer on the aforementioned *The Blouse King*, and with Alfred Halm on *The Ring of Giuditta Foscari* (*Der Ring der Giuditta Foscari*), all released in 1917, further placed the director in the forefront of Germany's film scene. Critics acknowledged his talent, hailing him as a "painter-director" who brought exotic settings to life on screen.

Leni followed up these early works with what was arguably his first true critical success: the action-adventure film *The Mystery of Bangalore* (*Das Rätsel von Bangalor*), co-directed with Alexander von Antalffy for the newly formed Pax Film GmbH. Debuting in Hamburg and Berlin in the early half of 1918, *Bangalore* garnered unanimous praise across all audiences. The "sensation of 1918" was indeed a sensational cinematic experience for audiences, who were transfixed by the film's fast-paced narrative and continent-hopping protagonist, Archie Douglas, played by Harry Liedtke.[21] Reviewers were quick to point out Leni's extraordinary scenic design, as was typical of his contributions in films leading up to *Bangalore*. For example, press from the *Hamburgischer Correspondent* focused on the film's captivating "wonderful scenery," in which Leni

> brings greatness to three of the most beautiful and interesting parts of the world. The skyscrapers from the land of unlimited possibilities, the splendid Japanese landscapes, the palaces of Indian princes bursting with golden splendor, the mysterious Japanese tea houses entice the beholder into a spell that he can no longer escape.[22]

A reviewer for *Der Kinematograph* extended the applause for *Bangalore*'s scenic design, asserting that Leni's "fine-crafted artistry" elevated the film to new levels:

> The Indian palace, the glittering cosmopolitan refinery, the flower-covered Japanese city, all these are images, full of romance and yet full of real life. Here German art showed that it is able to endure and fight the competition . . . The presentation was excellent.[23]

The response to *The Mystery of Bangalore* is a clear example of the growing critical fanfare for Leni's work in a career otherwise defined by sweeping historical epics and an impressive capacity for replicating classical, romanticized locales.

What made *The Mystery of Bangalore* different from Leni's previous films, however, was the fact that it was praised equally for its visual *and* narrative dimensions; his films rarely received such accolades during the earliest stages of his directorial career. A reviewer for the *Neue Hamburger Zeitung*, for instance, observed that the film is "equally powerful and equally interesting" due to the fully fleshed-out structuring of each adventurous segment which, as opposed to working wholly separately from each other, instead work cohesively together, bound by the unifying thread of the "Indian romance novel." Berlin's *Der Film* described *Bangalore* as a "monumental, extremely effective film show," its power lying in its ability to guide the viewer "not only to the mysterious dark corners of the ancient Indian city, but half way through the world to finally witness how love and energy win over cunning, revenge and intrigues."[24] A *Lichtbildbühne* reviewer exclaimed that "the Pax Film Company has had an extraordinary success in its first work" and continued:

> The painter Paul Leni has conjured images on the canvas with assured taste and artistic sensitivity, as they are hard to find in similar splendor and authenticity . . . Alexander von Antalffy's work worthily rounds out the production, the text for which was cleverly written by Rudolf Kurtz

and Paul Leni in accordance with the needs of such an extraordinary feature film . . . Once again, we must pay tribute to Paul Leni's great art of set design, which with taste and instinct has given the film a décor that promises a significant future for *The Mystery of Bangalore* in the struggling world market.[25]

The films that Leni directed during the late 1910s and early 20s formed an expansive body of work that proved a relatively modest commercial success, at best, in his native Germany. Several of these films, including *The Platonic Marriage* (*Die platonische Ehe*, 1918), *Prince Cuckoo* (*Prinz Kuckuck: Die Höllenfahrt eines Wollüstlings*, 1919), and *The Genoa Conspiracy* (*Der Verschwörung zu Genua*, 1921), received mixed reviews from critics; they were disappointed by the narrative content of the films yet thoroughly impressed by Leni's aesthetic choices. *Prince Cuckoo*, which reportedly caused a furor in Berlin with its use of atmospheric settings,[26] is a case in point. A review of *Prince Cuckoo* in the January 1919 issue of *Der Kinematograph* praises the visual and technical accomplishments of Leni behind the camera but little else in the overall assessment of the film. "At first glance, one looks at this picture as a puzzle; only slowly does one see beyond the surface to the artistic truth," wrote the reviewer, continuing:

> What we do *not* have is a screenwriter's manuscript, which is rearranged for motion pictures by a director before being recorded on film by a photographer . . . Here, everything gives way to the vision of one prodigious personality, in whom the creator and the adaptor meld seamlessly. This man is Paul Leni, the Artist/Director.[27]

This reviewer further opined that *Prince Cuckoo* is a well-acted, thought-provoking film in places but that Leni's visualizations were the things that truly made the film worth watching.[28]

Reviews for his later films, such as the 1920 drama *Patience* (sometimes listed with a subtitle, *The Cards of Death*, or *Die Karten des Todes*), further mirrored this sentiment. A *Berliner Börsen-Courier* reviewer stated that, despite the director's ability to "elevate the banal everydayness of material into an attractive work of art," Leni ultimately fell short in his portrayal of a "very sentimental and not completely enlightening action," with images too quickly strung together for the audience to make sense of them. "This is undoubtedly a mistake of the direction for which Paul Leni is responsible," a *Film-Kurier* reviewer noted, "which could have been avoided with some serious effort." Commenting on *The Genoa Conspiracy*, critic Herbert Ihering criticized Leni's directorial output even further, characterizing the film as "effective only when it functions as a pictorial composition set apart from its theme. And the pictorial composition is most successful when it focuses on presenting the intrigue separated from all content." A Berlin-based reviewer for *Moving Picture World* commented that *Genoa* "will without a doubt be the most picturesque film of the season" but diplomatically declined to discuss the film's story.[29] The response to Leni's films of the immediate postwar period remained relatively consistent; the critics praised the director's visual stylings but often faulted his approach to storytelling.

Perhaps prompted by the uneven critical reaction to his post-*Bangalore* films, Leni began experimenting with a different approach, one indebted to the Expressionist movement then underway in film, theater, and the visual arts. This new strategy led to the creation of *Backstairs* (*Hintertreppe*, co-directed with Leopold Jessner), a 1921 film that essentially merges a Naturalistic narrative with chiaroscuro lighting and angular, exaggerated scenery to represent a grim love triangle between a housekeeper (Henny Porten), her lover (Wilhelm Dieterle), and a disabled postman (Fritz Kortner). As Leni's close friend and frequent collaborator Rudolf Kurtz observed, *Backstairs* stakes an immediate claim in the realm of Expressionism since "the expressionist element can be seen whenever the director is aiming for something more than pure entertainment."[30] In other words, since the resulting effect of the Leni–Jessner film was to highlight the emotional trauma and interpersonal conflicts taking place amongst the three star-crossed lovers—rather than merely providing something to excite or entertain the audience—*Backstairs* successfully entered the canon of German Expressionism. Though he erred in attributing the film's direction solely to Leopold Jessner, Kurtz explained his perspective:

> The set is certainly not expressionist; but without Expressionism, it is unthinkable. The style in which the light is divided, splitting the visual space into abrupt, arbitrary spaces; the thrusting of the walls toward and away from one another so that all sounds are muffled; these cannot deny their parentage. And Jessner has visibly tried to transfer forms of expressionist set design to the film. The psychological expression of the gestures is truncated into intense, economical motions. He insinuates instead of letting things die away, only to have them erupt again in moments of concentration.[31]

Leni's successful stylistic and thematic experimentation in *Backstairs* enabled him to have more creative freedom with his subsequent films. To be sure, he continued to design sets for conventional films like E. A. Dupont's *Children of Darkness* (*Kinder der Finsternis*) films of 1921–2 and *The Countess of Paris* (*Die Gräfin von Paris*), co-directed by Dimitri Buchowetzki and Joe May in 1923. Yet Leni, who had long been attuned to the world of modern art and its limitless possibilities, was eager to move his film career in a new direction. He took his greatest chances as a director during the mid-1920s, leading to some of his most influential films.

In the midst of this transitional period, Leni gave himself an artistic recharge of sorts by returning to the realm of live theater; he formed the cabaret "The Gondola" ("Die Gondel") with Hans May, Kurt Tucholsky, Hans Brennert, and various Russian émigré artists and financiers like Alexander Kwartiroff. The Gondola opened on Bellevuestrasse in Berlin on June 1, 1923 and had a steady presence with humorous, satirical productions during the mid-1920s. It proclaimed itself "eccentric theater" ("exzentrisches Theater") in its advertising, and it more than lived up to that billing. Max Herrmann, a reviewer for *Der Kritiker*, had high praise for The Gondola. He suggested that "the stylish cabaret," a type of theatrical enterprise that he characterized as a "harmless evil" and "based on Russian models, is best represented by The Gondola." He noted that the evening's entertainment consisted of rebellious, satirical, and grotesque numbers, including Hans Brennert's edgy ballad "The Galley" ("Die Galeere") and scenes from *Dancing Girls, Ham and Eggs, Wumba-Wumba, Decorate Your Home!* (*Schmücke dein Heim!*), *Cuban Corso* (*Cubanischer Corso*), and *1001 Nights* (*1001 Nächte*). Opining that "everything is really tastefully, carefully arranged," Herrmann concluded his review by lauding the performers ("Every actor seems to be participating with gusto and love"), Hans May's music, and Leni's stage designs.[32]

Information on the set designs for the various Gondola productions is limited, but, based on surviving historical fragments, it is clear that Leni brought his creative genius back to the theatrical realm. An extant illustration for the Gondola production of *The Coachmen* (*Droschkenkutscher*) underscores his visual mastery. Drawn in a markedly Cubist style—made evident by the fragmentation of basic human forms, as well as the distinct use of geometric shapes framing each of the characters—the stage tableau vividly depicts three large, grotesque male figures standing outside of what appears to be a residence. Standing inside of a series of crooked, geometric frames is a female character, drawn in a more Naturalistic style, despite her lower torso blending into an abstract collage of gray shapes. The background of the scene is made even more disorienting by letters that float across the space and spell the word "Tingeltangel" (slang for German-style vaudeville/burlesque) coupled with painted backdrops that give the illusion of chiaroscuro lighting. Stills from the live iteration of *The Coachmen* are unavailable; however, Rudolf Kurtz noted that Leni's *Coachmen* sets were "unusually skilful at conforming to the public's tastes." Hans Reimann, a critic for *Die Weltbühne*, praised the production, noting that it "prompted frenetic applause" and was "the best scenic performance I have seen in a German cabaret."[33] He elaborated on its final number:

> This is called "The Street Song" (words: Theobald Panter [pseudonym for Kurt Tucholsky], music: Hans May, set design: Paul Leni). The hunger of society's "little man" for the good, the true, and the beautiful has taken tangible shape here, as the deep longing for *Tingeltangel* is met

in the form of three troglodyte-like coachmen; it is phenomenal. Thank you very much, you brave souls. It was very beautiful.[34]

A photograph from the Brennert-directed Gondola performance of *1001 Nights* (also known as *Arabian Nights*) illustrates another example of Leni's achievements in set design. Published in a 1924 issue of the lifestyle magazine *Die Dame* and featuring a sultan (Paul Christoph) attended by two mistresses (Gertrud Päch, Iwanka Jana Kiewa), this publicity shot displays a large, Middle Eastern-style couch, adorned with embroidered flowers, tufted headboards, and tasseled pillows. The roundness of the furnishings is echoed by the sultan's exaggeratedly unraveling turban and by the painted backdrop of the scene: a cluster of spherical, crescent-topped buildings, punctuated by two minarets and standing out against a nondescript black background. Contrasted against the fanciful Middle Eastern costuming and décor, Leni's semi-abstract setting is yet another example of his skill at blending the experimental with the whimsical. His visions could ultimately be translated onto paper, the screen, and the stage, making him a triple threat in German artistic circles.[35]

Figure 1.4 The Gondola (Die Gondel) was such a successful cabaret that Leni and his colleagues soon took it on the road. This poster announces the arrival of The Gondola for a guest performance at Vienna's Roland theater on September 1, 1923, three months after it had opened in Berlin.

Leni's design work for *1001 Nights* at The Gondola was intimately connected to what soon became his most celebrated German film: *Waxworks*. Featuring Middle Eastern sets and costuming in one of its three narratives, *Waxworks* had actually been in development prior to The Gondola's formation. Leni had begun the *Waxworks* project in 1920, eventually creating about 500 preliminary design sketches in preparation for the film's production through his newly created company, Paul-Leni-Film GmbH. When the company failed in 1922, however, Leni managed to secure significant backing from the same Russian financiers—most notably Alexander Kwartiroff—who later bankrolled The Gondola.[36] Kwartiroff, who had caught the movie bug in 1922 while serving as a cinematographer for *Escape in the Marriage: The Big Flirt (Die Flucht in die Ehe: Der grosse Flirt)*, worked with his associates to form a company specifically for Leni's film: Neptun-Film AG. To save on expenses, Leni leaned on his colleague Joe May and got permission to shoot the film at May's studio in Berlin's Weissensee district. Leni faced significant financial problems while filming but did receive a payoff of sorts at the end; Ufa, Germany's largest film company, agreed to distribute the film.[37]

Debuting nationally on November 13, 1924, *Waxworks* was the collective effort of Leni, who was the driving force behind the aesthetic look and feel of the film; Leo Birinski, who worked directly with the actors; and screenwriter Henrik Galeen, who had previously contributed scripts for such Expressionist films as Paul Wegener's *Der Golem* (1920) and F. W. Murnau's *Nosferatu* (1922). Galeen's dark, Expressionistic touches came through in the film's narrative: a young freelance writer finds employment at a wax museum sideshow, where he is commissioned to write backstories for three notorious, sinister figures of the past (the Caliph of Baghdad, Ivan the Terrible, and Jack the Ripper/Spring-Heeled Jack).[38] However, these stories came alive through Leni's visual virtuosity.

With a nod to Robert Wiene's landmark Expressionist film, *The Cabinet of Dr. Caligari (Das Cabinet des Dr. Caligari*, 1920), the framing story of *Waxworks* takes place in an amusement park. The setting features the dizzying, speedy movement of carnival rides in the background; angular exteriors, with the wax museum's eerie tent as the focal point of this landscape; and the blurring between the past and present, with the modernity of Weimar Germany cast alongside the antiquated scenery and technology characteristic of the fairgrounds. The "tales" of the three historical figures further exemplify Leni's reputation, honed throughout his collaborations and individually directed films, as a "directorial genius," to borrow from a 1926 article in the *Los Angeles Times*.[39] Leni's creation of the three historical-fictional tales housed in the film's main narrative accomplishes the task of both expressing distinct storylines, ranging from the comedic to the dramatic and suspenseful, as well as constructing distinct aesthetic choices, with each tale taking on a unique look and feel that are, at face value, markedly different from one another. Leni's tendency towards ornate historical replications comes to mind here, but the way that he combined them with modern, Expressionistic visuals arguably catapulted his film to worldwide success. The rounded, stylized interiors of the Caliph's Arabian palace, harkening back to Leni's set design for *1001 Nights* at The Gondola, are followed narratively by the literally and figuratively cold interiors of Ivan the Terrible's palace, made even more horrifying with its jagged, angular doorways and dimly lit dungeon. These images are then followed by the mysterious, abstract haunting of the main protagonist by the specter of Jack the Ripper.[40] In 1924, Leni remarked on his creative process for making the film:

> The creation of believable natural objects is especially important to the success of films that take place in an unreal world. In my film *Waxworks*, I sought to create an architecture that was so thoroughly stylized that it would completely preclude any thoughts of reality as such. I constructed a fairground that was entirely devoid of details, conveying instead a nearly indescribable ambience produced by lights, moving bodies, shadows, lines, and curves. The camera does not capture reality, but rather the reality of our experience. This is so much deeper, more potent, more gripping than what we look at every day with our eyes, and I really believe that film can effectively reproduce this enhanced form of reality . . . I cannot emphasize enough how far the film architect must really turn away from that world we see before us every single day in order to put his finger on that pulse beating just below the world's surface.[41]

Leni concluded his essay by arguing that the film designer is not prevailed upon

> to construct "pretty" spaces. He is asked to penetrate beyond the surface to reach the heart of the matter. He ought to create a mood, even if the only tools at his disposal are those simple, everyday objects we can all see lying around us. And this is precisely what makes him an artist. Were this not the case, there would be no need for an architect in film in the first place and no reason whatsoever why a talented apprentice carpenter could not replace him.[42]

Journalist Heinz Michaelis, who visited the *Waxworks* set and reported his observations in a piece published in *Film-Kurier* in August 1923, underscored Leni's work ethic: "Paul Leni works with tireless artistic energy on every detail until the scene fully corresponds to his vision of it," he wrote. He suggested that Leni's vivid combination of disparate styles and compositions in each of the tales, all housed in a much larger Expressionistic framework, eventually resulted in "a wonderful third world that crystalizes out of dream and reality." Michaelis's positive impressions of *Waxworks*, in fact, became widely shared among German audiences. It was a surprise hit of sorts that, despite its similarities to earlier Expressionist films, was met with relatively enthusiastic reviews. A writer for *Die Bildwart*, for example, highlighted the film's Ivan the Terrible episode, calling it "a masterpiece, as it shows the rich expressive possibilities of the film. It has an impressive unity and ever-increasing dramatic force . . . The actor and scenery meld into one."[43] In a review for *Lichtbildbühne*, Georg Victor Mendel observed that Leni's vision resonated throughout *Waxworks* despite the film's relatively simplistic and "almost worthless" storyline. "The whole thing is an artist's caprice," wrote Mendel, who continued:

> [It is] a charming and spirited play in which the picturesque is by far the main consideration . . . Here the material is transferred with a virtuosity to that most rewarding realm of the unreal fairytale in a way that is unparalleled even in *Caligari* and *Shadows*. We have seen the most successful fairytale films, but they were not all "fairytales" precisely because they did not know how to match this naïve-grotesque, magical-fantastic style. Here is his very own film area; Leni should continue to build here![44]

Waxworks premiered in the United States on March 18, 1926, with audiences equally drawn to the film's combination of compelling storylines and the overall visual feats accomplished by Leni and his team. Describing *Waxworks* as a "fantastic film [consisting] of three weird tales," Mordaunt Hall of the *New York Times* commended the narrative intricacy and flow of the film, remarking on the skill with which Leni and his actors portrayed the equally grotesque and captivating historical characters. In *Motion Picture Classic*, columnist Matthew Josephson described *Waxworks* as "the highly impressionistic German film which has created a sensation wherever it goes," placing the film front and center as an example of the American public's demand for more high-brow cinema.[45]

The distinction granted to *Waxworks* as being both intellectually stimulating and entertaining is underscored in several international reviews, an indication of its lasting success outside of the German context. Noting the film's inclusion in the first program of London's newly formed Film Society, British-based *Photoplay* contributor Edwin Severn described *Waxworks* as "a brilliantly produced and acted, extremely modern fantasy" and "creepy and eerie."[46] A reviewer for the *Times* of London concurred, noting that the grouping and movement-design are beautiful indeed, and the acting, particularly of Mr. Conrad Veidt as Ivan and Mr. Emil Jannings as the Caliph, has both power and decorative significance. The uses of photography in conveying a rapidly varying succession of mental states are brilliantly illustrated in the dream.[47]

A reviewer for Vienna's *Die Filmwoche* also offered positive feedback on *Waxworks*, remarking that "Paul Leni has created a highly stylized picture à la *Caligari* . . . The film will receive the highest praise from people greatly interested in the arts."[48] Robert Trévise, critic for the Parisian film journal *Cinéa-Ciné pour tous*, wrote that *Waxworks* is an "ingenious pochade [i.e., study or sketch] made especially worthy by its technique and aesthetics" and went on to say that

> this phantasmagoria is worthwhile for its very curious experiments with stylized and distorted sets much superior, it seems to me, to those of *Caligari*. The film is admirably played by three of the best performers of German art, Werner Krauss, Emil Jannings, Conrad Veidt and by Olga Belajeff.[49]

Mordaunt Hall of the *New York Times* was so impressed by the film that he penned a second review. "Not only is the fantastic character of the narrative quite absorbing, but the settings are remarkably well-suited to the [film's] fables," he wrote, adding that "this picture contains the spice of originality from the first chapter to the last." Such literary notables as George Bernard Shaw, James M. Barrie, and H. G. Wells were likewise impressed and added their voices to the growing international acclaim for Leni's art-entertainment hybrid.[50]

Most importantly for Leni, *Waxworks* drew particular attention from Universal Pictures head, Carl Laemmle, himself a German immigrant who came to the United States in 1884 and had success as a film producer. Around the time of Leni's international breakthrough with *Waxworks*, Hollywood was experiencing its first major wave of European emigration, importing cinematic talents from Germany, Austria, Scandinavia, and the Balkans in order to build up a competitive edge in the expanding, international film distribution market. As Graham Petrie explains in his study of Hollywood filmmaking during the silent era, executives from major studios scouted directors and offered them lucrative contracts that provided sufficient incentive to stay in the US, "before such countries as France, Italy, and Britain, the traditional suppliers of films to these areas before the war, had a chance to re-establish themselves."[51] Partnerships such as Lubitsch with Paramount and the Swedish director Victor Sjöström with Goldwyn are just some of several major contractual pairings during the first wave of European emigration during the 1920s.

Perhaps seeing this activity as a competitive threat to Universal Pictures, and doubtless impressed by *Waxworks* and Leni's general multi-media artistry, Laemmle asked Leni to join Universal in the mid-1920s. Contracts between Universal and Leni are no longer extant, but it was widely reported across trade magazines of Leni's affirmative response to Laemmle's invitation around 1926. Leni "is the latest member of the Hollywood screen colony," wrote one columnist from the *Los Angeles Times*, "having been signed on a long-term contract by Carl Laemmle . . . As an artist, he finds much to interest him in this new country."[52] *Motion Picture News* also offered more information on the business transaction between Leni and Laemmle, noting that Laemmle, while on a visit to Europe,

> was attracted to Leni's art. He invited him to come to America and produce the prologues for Universal productions. It was quite natural that the genius of Leni would not long be satisfied with the settings of prologues, and it was just as natural that Laemmle would not be long in giving him his opportunity to develop in the American film his unique decorative talent.[53]

Leni, accompanied by his wife, professional dancer Leonore "Lore" Sello, came to the US at Laemmle's request initially to direct a string of live theatrical introductions ("prologues") to Universal films and design sets for feature films directed by others. In Berlin, Leni had directed prologues for numerous films, including Lubitsch's *Forbidden Paradise* (1924), Herbert Brenon's *Peter Pan* (1924), and Dupont's *Varieté* (1925). Leni's vast experience in theatrical production clearly transferred over to the realm of live prologues in Berlin, in that they featured the same elaborate staging, performances, and costuming that had become hallmarks of Leni productions. These prologues had the unique distinction, however, of aligning with the cinematic medium, becoming live, three-dimensional lead-ins to what viewers watched on-screen. These spectacles appealed to Laemmle, who commissioned Leni to produce prologues for several Universal films: *Outside the Law* (1920; re-released 1926) and *Rolling Home* (1926). Leni's American prologues propelled him more deeply into the spotlight, leading Laemmle to select him as the director for the upcoming Universal feature film, *The Cat and the Canary*.

Leni began preparing for his directorial work on *Cat* immediately upon his arrival at Universal City in July 1926. Based on the 1921 John Willard stage production of the same name, *The Cat and the Canary* began production in the early half of 1927, inspired by Laemmle's efforts to capitalize on earlier, relatively successful comedy-horror films. Given Leni's reputation as a director in Germany, news that he would helm *Cat* spread across multiple publications.

"Paul Leni recently finished this production," a *New York Times* scribe wrote in June of 1927, adding

> [he] is an interesting figure to watch in action. His first care is the angle from which his scene is to be shot, and, inasmuch as the great majority of scenes were shot with the camera on the floor, his own efforts to be in direct line with the camera eye added a touch of quaintness to his rather robust figure and his method of obtaining his results. He achieves these with the count system. These counts are almost analogous to a beat of music, and he increases or decreases them with the tempo which he is striving to achieve in a certain scene or sequence.[54]

Critics and audiences appreciated the results of Leni's directorial strategies, lauding his use of Expressionist-inflected film techniques, a thrilling plot, and the skillful combination of horror and comedy. A critic for the *Washington Post*, for instance, noted that

> there are a number of sequences where the action is entirely visualized through the play of gigantic shadows on the walls of the fantastic, bizarre sets which were, of course, impossible of execution in the stage presentation of the play. Leni has not neglected comedy relief, utilizing three comedians who can be depended upon to carry ideas to the full.[55]

Echoing the *Post*'s glowing review of *Cat*'s visual style and approach to genre, a reporter for *Motion Picture News* noted that the "forbidding, deserted mansion" at the crux of the film proved to be wildly popular amongst local audiences, where "matinees went strong and nights even stronger," to the extent that the film was kept on screen for another week. Describing *Cat* as "a masterpiece of ingenious directing," *Photoplay* praised Leni's directorial prowess in creating a film "so full of illusion and bewildering action that it may be described as one continuous thrill."[56] The *Chicago Tribune*'s resident film critic, "Mae Tinée," proclaimed *The Cat and the Canary*

> one of the best mystery pictures that ever was filmed. Because—it manages to stay mysterious throughout . . . So well is the mystery "atmosphere" maintained by means of clever scenic arrangements, that you can fairly smell the mustiness of the old corridors and when a dust eaten curtain flops—your heart flops with it.[57]

Picture-Play Magazine's Norbert Lusk wrote that *The Cat and the Canary* was "the most successful mystery story the screen has yet offered" and suggested that "the spectator is made to feel that he is actually in the musty home of the dead millionaire" but that, "curiously enough, the proceedings seem real, probably because interest is kept at such a high pitch that there is scant opportunity to sit back and analyze the rather conventional labyrinth of the story." Lusk concluded his review by sharing the widely held view that one "can't get away from the fact that the director—and his camera—are really the stars" of the film.[58]

Leni's overall success with *The Cat and the Canary* had major implications for Hollywood filmmaking. It was the first film in the "thriller-chiller" and "old dark house" subgenres of the then-nascent horror genre, inspiring a host of copycat films like Danish émigré Benjamin Christensen's *House of Horror* in 1929. Moreover, *Cat*'s success led Universal to extend Leni's contract, and he was commissioned to direct three additional films within a two-year time span: *The Chinese Parrot* in 1927, *The Man Who Laughs* in 1928, and *The Last Warning*, also in 1928.[59]

Universal had high expectations for *The Chinese Parrot*; not only was it Leni's immediate follow-up to the wildly successful *Cat*, but it was only the second Hollywood film to center on Earl Derr Biggers's popular fictional detective, Charlie Chan. Based on Biggers's 1926 serialized novel of the same name, *The Chinese Parrot* featured Kamiyama Sôjin, Marian Nixon, Hobart Bosworth, and, in a small but important role, Anna May Wong.[60] With Leni's high-profile involvement and audiences' familiarity with the source material, the film seemed destined for success.

The Chinese Parrot, however, was not the critical and commercial hit that the studio hoped for; it received decidedly mixed reviews. "Locked doors, mysterious knockings, uncanny screams, and a disappearing pearl necklace, all furnished by Earl Derr Biggers' plot, might have made an exciting mystery picture," wrote *Educational Screen*'s Marguerite Orndorff, "but director Paul Leni has succeeded only in making a sort of jigsaw puzzle in which the pieces don't fit." The *Film Spectator*'s Welford Beaton praised Leni for his visual artistry ("he composes and lights his scenes superbly") but nevertheless opined that "Leni has not made as good a picture out of *The Chinese Parrot* as he did out of *The Cat and the Canary*. He has used weird shots until they lose their effectiveness by their frequency." John S. Cohen of the *New York Sun* found the film "a rambling and somewhat uncoordinated account of stolen jewels, creeping Chinese servants, and Nordic principals attired in evening clothes, and it isn't especially diverting."[61]

Other critics, however, found much to praise. "The success of the film lies perhaps with the acting, perhaps with the story, but most probably with the direction of Paul Leni, to whose lot seems to fall all of Universal's mystery plays," wrote a reviewer for the *Los Angeles Times*, who continued:

> Leni handles the situations with unusual skill. Most noticeable is his attention to detail . . . the glint of an embroidered dragon's eye . . . an

unusual shadow design upon a wall [creating] an atmosphere truly eerie. The skillful use of double exposure is another device employed to lend to the supernatural quality.[62]

A critic for the *Washington Post* called *The Chinese Parrot*

> one of the most unusual pictures to have flickered hereabout in some time. Paul Leni, one of Universal's imported directors, is responsible for the cinema version of this story by Earl Derr Biggers and, in consequence, the picture is presented in as bizarre a fashion as one might reasonably hope for. Many of the tricks of the German school of the cinema are utilized in the filming of *The Chinese Parrot* and the general effect of the whole production is one of cleverness.[63]

A reviewer for the Paris-based European edition of the *New York Herald Tribune* echoed this perspective, writing that "in San Francisco's Chinatown, the plot develops in a drama atmosphere rather 'caligariesque,' so dear to German producers, keeping one in suspense and thrilled."[64] A *Nottingham Evening Post* writer described several specific moments:

> For certain "shots" Leni has used gaps in hedges, half open doorways, half open windows and half drawn curtains as focusing points. In some instances he has cleared the stage of moving figures and used a chair, a flickering candle, a window swayed curtain, or a blazing fire, to convey an air of mystery. His lighting effects are weird. . . . He uses a parrot with amazing effect. The bird merely moves its head to one side, opens his wicked beak, or extends a grasping talon, but the movement is timed to the fraction of a second and is an integral part in the construction of the plot.[65]

Considered a lost film as of this writing, *The Chinese Parrot* remains a significant and tantalizing gap in our knowledge of the Leni oeuvre.

Leni's third US film, *The Man Who Laughs*, had considerably more fanfare surrounding it. Leni, who as a student had studied the works of Victor Hugo, embraced the opportunity to adapt the titular Hugo novel, and news of his involvement spread rapidly in major news outlets around the world.[66]

Like *The Chinese Parrot*, *The Man Who Laughs* did not initially meet the expectations that Leni had established with his first Hollywood feature. While some critics leveled harsh criticism at the film (for example, British film critic Paul Rotha, then only twenty-three, condemned *The Man Who Laughs* as "a travesty of cinematic methods"), many responded favorably to Leni's overall vision for the film and, in the words of a *Close Up* reviewer, "the old Germanic power of atmosphere" that he brought to the production. Writing for the Viennese *Mein Film*, for instance, Julius Siegfried Seidenstein lauded the director for his ability to maintain the "beauty, richness and novelty" of his source material, while T. O. Service of *Exhibitors Herald and Moving Picture World* declared that *Man* was "undeniably better than *The Hunchback of Notre Dame*," given its rich locales coupled with the masterful performance of Conrad Veidt. Leni himself was so pleased with the work of Veidt and co-star Mary Philbin that he planned to reunite them in a film adaptation of an opera based on Victor Hugo's 1832 play *Le roi s'amuse*: Giuseppe Verdi's world-famous *Rigoletto*. It was an unrealized project.[67]

Leni's fourth and final film, *The Last Warning*, was praised for its thrilling performances and cinematography but criticized for its lackluster storyline.[68] Despite Leni's attempts towards technological innovation (such as incorporating recorded sounds into the film, as he did with *Man*) and audience engagement (by inviting viewers to solve the film's mystery via an interactive game), *Warning* generally missed the mark for magazines like *Screenland*, the reviewer for which bluntly stated that the story "loses its speed and compactness when transferred to the screen." Nevertheless, in a trend common across Leni's career, critics such as Mordaunt Hall of the *New York Times* applauded Leni for his "finely directed passages" in addition to the "impressive" set pieces of the film, which were shot in an intricately replicated Broadway theatre.[69] In a review published in the *New York Herald Tribune*'s European edition, a critic went as far as to compare Leni to a famed French playwright known for his terror-inducing productions:

> Paul Leni is the André de Lorde of the American motion-picture. You all have heard of André de Lorde, that playwright who writes plays for the Grand-Guignol and whose nickname is "Le Prince de la Terreur." Useless then to tell you that if you like mystery plays you will enjoy every minute of [*The Last Warning*]. There are threats of deaths, disappearances, mysterious disasters with a thrilling but rather surprising climax. The sense of suspense, weird people and impressive shadows create the necessary atmosphere under Leni's skilful direction.[70]

Given the large amount of press that surrounded Leni's films, there was no shortage of opportunities for the director to express his thoughts on acting, lighting, and directorial techniques. For instance, he praised Laura La Plante, an actress who starred in two of his four American films. "I was impressed with her winsomeness, her facial mobility in registering emotions and her obvious charms," he said. "She is one of the very few screen personalities who has the faculty of reading the director's mind, almost literally speaking."[71]

Importantly, a common thread through many of Leni's interviews was his emphasis on the future of cinema, on the ways in which the medium had developed, and its capacity for development in order to achieve the most desirable artistic effects. "The day is past when the conveying of human emotions requires 'wild gestures' of the hands and arms, as was the custom of earlier dramatic expression," Leni remarked on developments in cinema acting. "Perfect expression can be conveyed by the simplest movements of the hands and arms, but I believe the eyes and the facial muscles will always be the most effective media. Motion picture expression is now being concentrated on these scientific facts."[72] In an interview initially published in the *New York Evening World* and reprinted in *Universal Weekly*, Leni shared similar progressive ideas regarding film's innate potential to excite, engage, and entertain audiences. "What is the use in presenting situation after situation, if there is no reaction from the audience?" he asked, continuing:

> It is terrible to see the situation so carefully served go so far over the heads of the audience, or strike so low, that no return is possible. Making pictures is just a game that I like to have the audience win, because it makes them feel good—which is the reason they came to see your pictures.[73]

In the majority of his public statements during his US career, Leni acknowledged the artistic capacity of the cinematic medium, of which he was both student and teacher. "It took the motion pictures to 'come to the rescue,'" the director [Leni] points out," as a *Los Angeles Times* correspondent recounted,

> and thus the public is now conversant with the world's greatest literature of the past not only through the silent dramas, but through newspaper and magazine criticism of these pictures and various news stories relating to activities in the literary departments of the various studios.[74]

In early 1929, Leni remarked on his future in the industry, optimistically stating, "But for my next picture? It will be different, I am looking over every play in New York now and hope I may take one back with me."[75]

Early in 1929, Universal began announcing numerous projects that Leni might direct. The potential films included adaptations of *Rigoletto*, noted above; Philip Hamilton Gibbs's 1924 short novel *A Bargain in the Kremlin*; Owen Davis's 1928 play *Tonight at 12*; and Molière's *The Imaginary Invalid* (*Le Malade imaginaire*, 1673). The rumored films also included one that would be originally written for the screen: *The Return of the Phantom*, a sequel to *The Phantom of the Opera* with Mary Philbin and Conrad Veidt slated to star. Most intriguing of all the possibilities was a screen version of *Dracula*, a film that

Leni had hoped would be another showcase for longtime collaborator Veidt. Universal shelved the project upon Leni's death on September 2, 1929, and Veidt's return to Germany that year, but the studio ultimately revived it under Tod Browning's direction in 1931. Influenced to an important extent by Leni's bi-continental work, *Dracula* launched the Universal horror-cycle that would dominate screens worldwide during the early 1930s.[76]

The legacy that the German director left on early filmmaking was clear to those who worked with him. Rudolf Kurtz remarked that Leni, throughout his career, had "discovered for himself the life of light, the immense power of the play between lightness and heaviness, semi-darkness and shadow."[77] Writers for American trade journals were equally touched by Leni's work. "Creators of merit are found too infrequently and so, this industry in Leni's death suffers a loss," wrote *Film Daily* editor Maurice Kann in a piece published two days after Leni's passing, continuing:

> Schooled in Europe and mellowed in the art centers of the Old World, this German, in turning from the Berlin stage some years ago brought to motion pictures a fruitful knowledge. His film work in this country always has been a reflection of that intelligent experience.[78]

We fully agree with this perspective; indeed, it heavily informed the shaping of *ReFocus: The Films of Paul Leni*. We see this book as a celebration of Leni's rich experiences and believe it sheds considerable light on the work and decades-long influence of one of the film world's most underappreciated talents of the 1910s and 20s. Relying on rare historical documents and extensive scholarship from a variety of perspectives, this volume takes a close look at the German director's life in film from his days in Germany through his emigration to Hollywood.

Beginning with one of Leni's earliest films, Jaimey Fisher in "Exploding the Cosmopolitan and Treating the Foreigners' Foreignness: Paul Leni's *The Diary of Dr. Hart*" explores the titular film as an important historical document that chronicles both the changing institutional context of German cinema and the "disheartening denouement of the 'war to end all wars.'" As Fisher offers, *Dr. Hart* "is tellingly transitional, perhaps even transformative, for Leni's emergent career and in the wider landscape of German cinema during World War I." Combining a thorough production history of the film with early cinematic trends, such as the popularization of cinematic–medical discourses and "late nineteenth- and early twentieth-century cosmopolitanism," Fisher illustrates the ways that Leni's debut demonstrates "how a combination of genres could be deployed to remake the dynamically forged war genre and how such genres were already evolving—invoked, manipulated, hybridized—at this early moment in German cinema history."

The discussion of Leni's early German work continues in "The Unnatural in the Natural: Leopold Jessner and Paul Leni's Early Weimar Film *Backstairs*" by Jason Doerre. Analyzing the influence of literary Naturalism on German Expressionist cinema as reflected in Leni's 1921 film, Doerre asserts that *Backstairs* is "an example of early Weimar cinema that blends together seemingly disparate styles and themes in order to reflect a society still reeling from the impact of the Great War." In his analysis, Doerre notes that while Leni's film demonstrates an Expressionistic impulse (as scholars such as Lotte Eisner have astutely observed), other aspects including milieu and story are clearly leftovers of the literary Naturalism of the prewar period. Using *Backstairs* as a case in point, "The Unnatural in the Natural" counters the overemphasized focus on Expressionism broadly in the films of the Weimar Republic by highlighting the multivalent styles present throughout this period, "telling the story of a familiar world that has become alienating" after the war.

Erik Born in "Cinema Panopticum: Wax, Work, *Waxworks*" begins the discussion on Leni's most famous and influential German film by situating it in the context of popular wax displays in the Weimar Republic. As Born explains, Leni's anthology film is valuable in its updating of "expressionist tropes of wax effigies, mechanical automata, and living puppets with a more realistic setting at a modern funfair-cum-workplace." Consequently, the film both supersedes and absorbs the visual techniques present in the antiquated wax museum, transforming them into unique, immersive displays. "Cinema Panopticum" illustrates how Leni's *Waxworks* can ultimately be considered an "artistic statement about wax, work, and waxworks," bypassing a more traditional farewell to a dying medium and instead "speaking to the multiple afterlives of presumably 'dead media' after their own metempsychosis."

Continuing the *Waxworks* discussion, Joel Westerdale in "The Proto-Horror-Comedy: *Waxworks*" looks at how Leni's film can be conceptualized not only as "metonymic shorthand for early Weimar cinema as a whole" but also, through its substantial comedic aspects, as an example of a genre oftentimes pushed to the margins of Weimar scholarship. Westerdale illustrates how the Harun al-Rashid episode in the film uses comedy as its "dominant modality," employing elements such as "irreverent intertitles and a slapstick chase scene" to diffuse the film's otherwise threatening tone. For Westerdale, *Waxworks* "provides a glimpse into Weimar film culture both by participating in the dark, mysterious filmmaking considered characteristic of early Weimar cinema, and by going beyond it, pointing to the rich generic diversity of this era's films that is now beginning to receive sustained scholarly attention." Westerdale's "Proto-Horror-Comedy" chapter therefore presents a shift in current discourses on Leni's film, reconsidering how Leni's film can be categorized and underscoring the director's adept reinterpretations of genre in the Weimar era.

The next chapter, "Intersectional Avant-Garde: Paul Leni's *Rebus-Film* Series and the Confluence of Experimental Visual Styles" by Erica Tortolani, turns to Leni's foray into experimental filmmaking in the midst of his expanding career in the German film industry. Focusing on Leni's eight-part short film series, Tortolani situates the series alongside various artistic movements and cinematic styles developed at the beginning of the twentieth century, such as Cubism, Futurism, and Dada. Illustrating Leni's interactions within and alongside experimental arts circles in Berlin, Tortolani argues that the *Rebus-Film* series "shows a more complicated web of connections in [Leni's] own films and across the art movements in Europe during this period," encapsulating the dialogic nature of varying experimental arts scenes across Europe. Leni's short films offer a glimpse of his careful attention to detail in all aspects of the visual arts and how he consistently had his finger on the pulse, so to speak, of trends in both mainstream and experimental film styles.

Leni's subsequent transition from German to American cinema is reflected in Martin F. Norden's "Bravura Beginnings: Paul Leni and the Art of the Prologue," which provides a detailed overview of the often overlooked artform of the cinematic prologue. Norden defines prologues as live exhibition events that often consisted of brief plays, song and dance numbers, orchestral music, or some combination thereof, designed as lead-ins for late silent-era films. Leni, whom Norden describes as having been specifically recruited by Universal Pictures' Carl Laemmle to direct prologues, eventually became known for his "technical expertise" in creating these accompanying performances, ultimately securing his role as director of four Universal pictures. "Bravura Beginnings" demonstrates how Leni was both "comfortable working within very different genres" and "adept at mounting productions with flair and flamboyance," resulting in his successful adaptation to the American film industry.

Rebecca M. Gordon's chapter "Paul Leni's *The Cat and the Canary*: Adaptation into Genre" is the first of two chapters illustrating Leni's ultimate acclimation into the Hollywood industry by way of his first American film, *The Cat and the Canary*. Tracing contemporaneous reviews of the film alongside its production history and aesthetic influences, Gordon demonstrates how *Cat* created "a visual and aural iconography still essential to film and televisual 'old spooky house' narratives and creates a rhythm that remains the hallmark of horror-comedy." As Gordon suggests, Leni's influential film included stylistic innovations that became identifiable as parts of a pattern by the end of the 1930s. Gordon thereby posits that Leni was responsible for developing a new film formula, underscoring his importance in early Hollywood filmmaking.

A second approach to Leni's most notable Hollywood film comes from Simone Natale, in "Specters of the Mind: Ghosts, Illusion, and Exposure in Paul Leni's *The Cat and the Canary*." Exploring the film's status within the broader trend of ghost movies in which the ghost "is ultimately refused and relegated to the realm of human imagination and trickery," Natale posits that Leni's film can be framed in a variety of ways, "within the tradition of spiritualist exposés, to the characterization of ghosts as creations of our mind, to the use of superimposition effects, and to the question of sound." Combining a historical overview of the role of spiritualism in American culture with an analysis of the function of the ghost in early horror cinema, Natale positions *Cat* as a unique example, at least within the context of Hollywood filmmaking, of "the contradictory power of our relationship with the occult," subsequently counting among "successful instances of supernatural fiction in the history of film."

Gábor Gergely in "Misfitting in America: Paul Leni, Conrad Veidt, and *The Man Who Laughs*," the first of two chapters that analyze Leni's successful adaptation of the Victor Hugo novel of the same name, interprets the film's portrayal of physical difference as a much broader metaphor of the "trauma of displacement" experienced by émigrés to the United States. Noting the "complex dynamic of absence and presence" that the film adopts in engaging with this unique type of trauma, Gergely sees the portrayal of protagonist Gwynplaine, played by German expatriate Conrad Veidt, as key to understanding the real-life ways in which Hollywood studios situated their European émigré stars in the years following World War I. "Misfitting in America" situates Leni's film discursively in regards to how the outlier body is positioned within society, offering an "interpretive framework for the films of exile and émigré actors in Hollywood in the sound era."

Bruce Henderson in "Masculinity and Facial Disfigurement in *The Man Who Laughs*" examines Leni's film through the lens of disability studies in film. Henderson offers a reading of *Man* that addresses the creative liberties that Leni took when adapting the Hugo novel to the screen and that accounted for the "effects that may get lost within Hugo's labyrinthine prose," the most important of which is the representation of physical disfigurement. As Henderson asserts, the cinematic representation of Gwynplaine's disability, in contrast to that in the novelization, "restores a kind of lost masculinity to Gwynplaine, reminding us, in ways the novel never quite does, that Gwynplaine's body was as 'fit' as any other man's." Henderson's chapter thus reconceptualizes Leni's adaptation as "offering a positive vision for disability," finding equilibrium between Gwynplaine's contrasting characteristics of masculinity–femininity, ability–disability that are absent in both the novel and other films in this era.

Bastian Heinsohn's "Cinematic Space and Set Design in Paul Leni's *The Last Warning*" analyzes Leni's fourth and final Hollywood film as exemplary of Universal's "new beginning . . . at the brink of a new decade and the ascendency of sound film." As Heinsohn notes, Leni fully utilized the lavish sound stages created by the studio as a tool for expressing the uncanny and suspenseful tone of the film. According to Heinsohn, the fundamental spatial characteristics of the Hollywood sound stage during this era "allowed Leni one last opportunity to create a stylized, eerie mystery story that could combine his distinct Expressionist cinematic style" and lent themselves well to the "predominantly ghostly themes with Universal's emerging flair for producing horror films and using lavish theatrical sets." Consequently, "Cinematic Space" posits that Leni's directorial efforts in *Warning*, through his use of expansive sound stages, appealed "to the taste of an American audience that expected and appreciated a mix of horror and entertainment," expanding the trends that he and Universal became known for in the latter half of the 1920s.

Concluding this discussion of Leni's Hollywood career vis-à-vis *The Last Warning*, Shawn Shimpach in "*The Last Warning*: Uncertainty, Exploitation, and Horror" explores the exhibition practices that Universal adopted upon the release of the film in American theaters. Looking at Universal's relationship with its audiences at the end of the silent period of Hollywood cinema, Shimpach highlights the ways that Universal promoted the film to exhibitors and advertised it to the public, suggesting how Universal imagined the audience for this film and its strategies for connecting the film's narrative to this imagined audience during the transitional period to synchronized sound. Adopting the trend of audience participation through devices like surveys, puzzles, and games (coincidentally explored in Leni's earlier *Rebus* series), Universal, according to Shimpach, therefore engaged in a creative and playful approach to making the film experience more interactive, albeit in a decidedly low-tech way. Shimpach therefore posits that Universal imagined a specific, rather sophisticated type of audience engagement, investing time and money into Leni's final feature film.

As a means of concluding this Introduction, we return to the words of Leni's close friend and colleague Rudolf Kurtz. Upon Leni's premature death, Kurtz published a lengthy and moving tribute to his friend in *Lichtbildbühne* in which he discussed the growing acceptance of film as an art and Leni's place within the film world. He ended his eulogy with these thoughts:

> The film is a young art form, and gradually the spiritual has to infuse the space in which it lives. And if today the artist has become more prominent, it is proof of the wonderful make-up of humanity, despite its ceaseless demand for entertainment. It is less likely now that the people at the beginning—the pioneers, the trailblazers—who cultivated the film field with clear instincts and strong "elbow work" will be forgotten. Then, in a future history of cinematic art, at the forefront of those who viewed art and film as one, will appear the figure of Paul Leni—a fighter, an expert, a creator—a man who took film seriously, who used his brain and flexed his muscles to assert his will in a difficult, reluctant, and doubtful world. That will be Paul Leni's memorial.[79]

It is our immodest hope that readers will find *ReFocus: The Films of Paul Leni* to be precisely the type of tribute that Kurtz had envisioned so many years ago for this world-class filmmaker.

NOTES

1. Bushnell Dimond, "*Waxworks* Film Thrills Gotham as It Did London," *Lincoln* (NE) *Sunday Star*, April 11, 1926; Gilbert Seldes, *The Seven Lively Arts: The Classic Appraisal of the Popular Arts* (New York: Harper & Brothers, 1924), 9.
2. Dimond, "*Waxworks*."
3. Dimond, "*Waxworks*."
4. Dimond, "*Waxworks*."
5. This neglect has not been limited to Leni's film career; his work as a graphic artist has similarly received minimal attention. For example, one would think he would loom large in a book titled *Expressionism and Poster Design in Germany* 1905–1922, knowing that he designed countless posters in Germany during the first decades of the twentieth century and was associated with the Expressionist movement. Though this volume includes a discussion of *Waxworks*, the only acknowledgment of his poster design work is a single sentence: "Leni was well-known as a graphic artist and set designer for theater and film." Similarly, the encyclopedic and lavishly illustrated *The Book Cover in the Weimar Republic*, which includes sections on film- and theater-related designs, does not mention Leni's work save for an incidental reference: a facsimile of the back cover of an issue of *G: Material zur Elementaren Gestaltung*, a 1920s avant-garde arts journal. This back cover, which announces the publication of Rudolf Kurtz's seminal *Expressionism and Film* (*Expressionismus und Film*), simply lists Leni as the book's cover designer. This same passing reference is reproduced in miniature on *The Book Cover*'s back cover. See Kathleen G. Chapman, *Expressionism and Poster Design in Germany 1905–1922: Between Spirit and Commerce* (Leiden: Brill, 2019), 323; and Jürgen Holstein (ed.), *The Book Cover in the Weimar Republic/Buchumschläge in der Weimarer Republik* (Cologne: Taschen, 2015), 210.
6. And only the third book in any language, following Swiss historian Freddy Buache's forty-page *Paul Leni 1885–1929*, Anthologie du Cinéma, no. 33 (Paris: Avant-Scène Cinéma, 1968) and Hans-Michael Bock's edited volume, *Paul Leni: Grafik, Theater, Film* (Frankfurt am Main: Deutsches Filmmuseum, 1986).
7. Bock, *Paul Leni*, 12–13; Kerstin Rech, "The Director Paul Leni: The Man with the Gifted Look" ("Der Regisseur Paul Leni: Der Mann mit den genialen Blick"), *Stuttgarter-Zeitung*, July 8, 2015, available at <https://www.stuttgarter-zeitung.de/inhalt.der-regisseur-paul-leni-der-mann-mit-dem-genialen-blick.75fc77a2-c1b9-45e8-9761-9a9291ee4e53.html>.
8. Bock, *Paul Leni*, 13; Leni quoted in Marguerite Tazelaar, "Paul Leni, Master of Atmosphere, Is a Genial, Adventurous Soul," *New York Herald Tribune*, reprinted in *Universal Weekly*, January 19, 1929.
9. Bock, *Paul Leni*, 13; Paul Westheim, "Deutsche Plakat-Kunst," *Deutsche Kunst und Dekoration* 26, no. 9 (June 1910): 196; Rech, "The Director Paul Leni."
10. Robert Breuer, "Kunstgewerbe," *Arena* 29, no. 3 (1912–13): 1818. Ever the multi-modal artist, Leni designed movie-themed posters throughout the remainder of his career. His stark poster for *The Last Warning*, his final film, was posted on a billboard in the heart of Universal City and is reproduced in "Exploitation," *Universal Weekly*, November 24, 1928.
11. Bock, *Paul Leni*, 15.

12. The Leni self-portrait reproduced in the text originally appeared in a program for a circus-themed event sponsored by the Club der Karikaturisten in March 1913. It is accompanied by the following bit of doggerel: "Das ist der Paule Leni / An ihm ist nichts zu weni' – / Im Klub ist er Berater / In Sachen – Theater." With no attempt at matching its rhyming scheme, the poem translates as: "That's Paul Leni / There's nothing too little about him – / In the club he is a consultant / On things – theater." See *März 1913 Programm: Ball im Circus* (Berlin: Club der Karikaturisten EV, 1913), 4.
13. Bock, *Paul Leni*, 15.
14. Bock, *Paul Leni*, 14, 47.
15. Interestingly, May's prize-mystery films predated Leni's *Rebus-Film* series by nearly a decade and could be argued as one of Leni's main inspirations for creating the series.
16. Paul Leni, "Baukunst im Film," *Der Kinematograph*, August 4, 1924, reprinted as "Architecture in Film," in *The Promise of Cinema: German Film Theory 1907–1933*, ed. Anton Kaes, Nicholas Baer, and Michael Cowan (Oakland: University of California Press, 2016), 500.
17. C. Hooper Trask, "German Picture News," *Variety*, December 23, 1921; review of *Lady Hamilton*, *Der Film*, October 23, 1921, reprinted in John T. Soister, *Conrad Veidt on Screen: A Comprehensive Illustrated Filmography* (Jefferson, NC: McFarland, 2002), 142; Ludwig Brauner, review of *Lady Hamilton*, *Der Kinematograph*, October 30, 1921, reprinted in Soister, *Conrad Veidt*, 142–3.
18. In addition to these collaborations, Leni also worked with a handful of other filmmakers and producers, including (but not limited to) Karl Grune, Leopold Jessner, Guido Seeber, and Mihály Kertész (birth name Manó Kaminer), later known as Michael Curtiz.
19. Bufa was created in January 1917.
20. See Peter Jelavich, "German Culture in the Great War," in *European Culture in the Great War: The Arts, Entertainment, and Propaganda, 1914–1918*, ed. Aviel Roshwald and Richard Stites (Cambridge: Cambridge University Press, 1999), 40.
21. See the collection of reviews, advertisements, and general notes related to *The Mystery of Bangalore* at <http://filmhistoriker.de/>.
22. Review of *The Mystery of Bangalore*, *Hamburgischer Correspondent*, reprinted in *Hamburger Echo*, January 22, 1918.
23. Review of *The Mystery of Bangalore*, *Der Kinematograph*, February 13, 1918.
24. Review of *The Mystery of Bangalore*, *Neue Hamburger Zeitung*, reprinted in *Hamburger Echo*, January 22, 1918; review of *The Mystery of Bangalore*, *Der Film*, February 16, 1918.
25. Review of *The Mystery of Bangalore*, *Lichtbildbühne*, January 26, 1918. Some essays, like this one, attribute the film's direction solely to producer Alexander von Antalffy (also known as Alexander Antalffy) instead of jointly to Leni and von Antalffy. However, most historians agree with Conrad Veidt's assertion that both men directed the film. See Veidt's comments in "My First Film—What the Stars Reveal" ("Mein erster Film—Was Stars verraten"), *Der Kinematograph* (anniversary edition), December 1931/January 1932.
26. "What Were They Doing in 1918?" *Film Daily*, May 24, 1928.
27. Review of *Prince Cuckoo*, *Der Kinematograph*, January 1, 1919, reprinted in Soister, *Conrad Veidt*, 79.
28. Review of *Prince Cuckoo*.
29. Erwin Gepard, review of *Patience*, *Berliner Börsen-Courier*, April 18, 1920, reprinted in Bock, *Paul Leni*, 264–5; review of *Patience*, *Film-Kurier*, April 18, 1920, reprinted in Bock, *Paul Leni*, 264–5; Ihering quoted in Klaus Kreimeier, *The Ufa Story: A History of Germany's Greatest Film Company, 1918–1945*, trans. Robert and Rita Kimber (Berkeley: University of California Press, 1999), 90; "Germans Due to Finish *Anne Boleyn*," *Moving Picture World*, January 22, 1921.

30. Rudolf Kurtz, *Expressionism and Film*, ed. Christian Kiening and Ulrich Johannes Beil, trans. Brenda Benthien (New Barnet: John Libbey Publishing, 2016), 86.
31. Kurtz, *Expressionism and Film*, 86.
32. Max Herrmann, "Berliner Kabaretts," *Der Kritiker: Zeitschrift für Wirtschaft, Politik und Kunst*, September–October 1924, 17–18. The word "Wumba" was an acronym for Waffen- und Munitionbeschaffungsamt (Weapons and Ammunition Procurement Office), a military bureau during World War I. Its repeated use in a Gondola performance piece's title may have been a playful reference to Leni's wartime service. See Kurtz, *Expressionism and Film*, 7; and Chapman, *Expressionism and Poster Design*, 330–1.
33. Kurtz, *Expressionism and Film*, 49; Hans Reimann, "Exzentrisches Theater," *Die Weltbühne* 19 (1923), 707.
34. Reimann, "Exzentrisches Theater." For additional perspectives on *The Coachmen* and a reproduction of the described image, see Kurtz, *Expressionism and Film*, 49–50.
35. About a dozen still photographs from various Gondola productions are viewable online at <https://www.gettyimages.ca/photos/die-gondel>.
36. B. Bertram, "Artists as Film Designers," *Drawing & Design* 5, no. 11 (April 1926): 362. On November 16, 1922, Leni wrote a check for 150,000 marks to acquire the world filming rights to Gustav Meyrink's 1908 novella, *Das Wachsfigurenkabinett*. A facsimile of the check is available at <https://www.filmportal.de/en/node/9515/material/678566>.
37. Heinz Michaelis, "*Das Wachsfigurenkabinett* (Drehbericht)," *Film-Kurier*, August 29, 1923, available at <https://www.filmportal.de/en/node/9515/material/678568>. As is widely known, budgetary issues forced Leni to truncate the "Jack the Ripper/Spring-Heeled Jack" episode and eliminate another: a story centering on Rinaldo Rinaldini, a "robber captain" made famous in a 1797 penny-dreadful novel by Christian August Vulpius. In the film's framing story, the wax statue of Rinaldini is still visible inside the proprietor's fairground tent.
38. Galeen's *Waxworks* script and supplemental information are included in Henrik Galeen, *Das Wachsfigurenkabinett: Drehbuch von Henrik Galeen zu Paul Lenis Film von 1923* (Munich: Edition Text + Kritik, 1994).
39. "West Seen as Land of Joyous Hue," *Los Angeles Times*, June 27, 1926.
40. The order of the three episodes appears to have changed when the film was brought over to the US. As Graham Petrie has observed, the Harun al-Rashid sequence was shown first in Germany but last in the film's New York premiere. In a March 19, 1926 review of the film, Mordaunt Hall of the *New York Times* indicated that the Harun al-Rashid sequence occurred last. In a follow-up review on March 28, he repeated this point and added that the Ivan the Terrible sequence was shown first and the Jack the Ripper sequence second. See Graham Petrie, *Hollywood Destinies: European Directors in Hollywood, 1922–1931* (London: Routledge & Kegan Paul, 1985), 168; Mordaunt Hall, "The Screen," *New York Times*, March 19, 1926; and Mordaunt Hall, "Fine Character Studies in Fantastic Picture," *New York Times*, March 28, 1926.
41. Leni, "Baukunst im Film," 501.
42. Leni, "Baukunst im Film," 500. For an alternative translation, see Lotte H. Eisner, *The Haunted Screen: Expressionism in the German Cinema and the Influence of Max Reinhardt*, trans. Roger Greaves (Berkeley: University of California Press, 1969), 127.
43. Michaelis, "*Wachsfigurenkabinett*"; review of *Waxworks*, *Die Bildwart*, December 1925, reprinted in Soister, *Conrad Veidt*, 160.
44. Georg Victor Mendel, review of *Waxworks*, *Lichtbildbühne*, November 15, 1924, available at <https://www.filmportal.de/en/node/9515/material/678570>.
45. Hall, "The Screen"; Matthew Josephson, "The Rise of the Little Cinema," *Motion Picture Classic*, September 1926.

46. Edwin Severn, "Sunday Film Exhibits," *Photoplay*, February 1926, 119.
47. "Film Making as an Art," *Times* (London), October 26, 1925.
48. Review of *Waxworks*, *Die Filmwoche*, November 26, 1924, reprinted in Soister, *Conrad Veidt*, 160.
49. Robert Trévise, "Les présentations de la quinzaine," *Cinéa-Ciné pour tous*, December 1, 1924, 22.
50. Hall, "Fine Character Studies"; Marc T. Greene, "Classics of the Cinema in Revival," *China Press*, July 18, 1926.
51. Petrie, *Hollywood Destinies*, 7.
52. "West Seen as Land of Joyous Hue."
53. "Biographical Sketch," *Motion Picture News*, October 1927.
54. "Art of Light and Shadow in Motion Picture Making," *New York Times*, June 12, 1927. The cinematographer for *The Cat and the Canary*, Gilbert Warrenton, would corroborate this report in an interview with Kevin Brownlow: "Leni was sitting by the camera thinking what he should do and setting up his cymbal board . . . He used a three foot Chinese cymbal to startle the actors when he wanted a particular effect, 'Vell now, venn I hit mein cymbal . . .' He beat that thing worse than the Salvation Army beat a drum." Leni was also said to burrow into the studio floor "to get exaggerated angles," as well as installing multiple sets of additional lights to get a more contrasted, shadowy effect. See Kevin Brownlow, "Movement in Moving Pictures: An Interview with Gilbert Warrenton, ASC," *Film History: An International Journal* 24, no. 3 (2012): 329.
55. "Trick Shots Tell Story," *Washington Post*, September 25, 1927.
56. "Key City Reports: Detroit," *Motion Picture News*, September 2, 1927; "Laura La Plante in a Great Mystery Play," *Photoplay*, July 1927.
57. Mae Tinée, "These Film Dramas Are All Bellringers," *Chicago Tribune*, November 6, 1927.
58. Norbert Lusk, "The Screen in Review," *Picture-Play Magazine*, December 1927, 60.
59. *The Last Warning* had a limited release in December 1928 and was exhibited widely in January 1929 and thereafter. In our Introduction and Filmography, we refer to the film as a 1928 release since this year marks the film's US debut. In an acknowledgment of *The Last Warning*'s international exhibition the following year, the two chapters in this volume that analyze *The Last Warning* use 1929 as its date.
60. Leni coincidentally created prologues for two films in which Wong had appeared: *Peter Pan* (1924), which featured her as Tiger Lily; and *Outside the Law* (1920; re-released 1926), in which she played an uncredited background character. See Martin F. Norden's chapter in this volume.
61. Marguerite Orndorff, "The Theatrical Field," *Educational Screen*, September 1927, 327; Welford Beaton, "*Chinese Parrot* Is Not Leni's Best," *Film Spectator*, June 11, 1927; John S. Cohen, "The New Photoplay," *New York Sun*, January 5, 1928.
62. "*Chinese Parrot* Is Weird," *Los Angeles Times*, October 8, 1927.
63. "Rialto," *Washington Post*, October 24, 1927.
64. "In the Cinema World," *New York Herald Tribune* (European edition), January 10, 1928.
65. "The Footlights and Picture Shows," *Nottingham Evening Post*, April 21, 1928.
66. "An Artist and Stage Settings: Paul Leni Seeks to Reflect Character Even in Black and White Designs for *The Man Who Laughs*," *New York Times*, November 6, 1927; "Color Motifs to Dominate *The Man Who Laughs*," *China Press*, November 12, 1928.
67. Paul Rotha, *The Film Till Now: A Survey of the Cinema* (London: Jonathan Cape, 1930), 204; "English Releases," *Close Up*, February 1929, 101; Julius Siegfried Seidenstein, review of *The Man Who Laughs*, *Mein Film*, January 18, 1929, reprinted in Soister, *Conrad Veidt*, 203; T. O. Service, "Service Talk," *Exhibitors Herald and Moving Picture World*, October 13, 1928; "Cinema Notes," *New York Herald Tribune* (European edition), July 8, 1928.

68. Several secondary sources suggest that Leni's last film was actually a 1929 sync-sound experimental short simply titled *Puzzles*. No corroborating evidence could be found to support this assertion, however. See Georges Sadoul, *Dictionary of Film*, trans. and ed. Peter Morris (Berkeley: University of California Press, 1972), 186; David Quinlan, *The Illustrated Guide to Film Directors* (Totowa, NJ: Barnes & Noble, 1983), 183; and "Paul Leni—The Forgotten Master," *The Missing Link*, available at <http://www.classichorror.free-online.co.uk/leni.htm>.
69. "Let's Go to the Movies!" *Screenland*, April 1929, 76; Mordaunt Hall, "Who Is the Killer?" *New York Times*, January 7, 1929.
70. "News of Cinema World," *New York Herald Tribune* (European edition), March 4, 1929.
71. Leni quoted in "European Training Beneficial," *Los Angeles Times*, October 23, 1927.
72. Leni quoted in "Movie Pantomime Better," *Sunday Star* (Washington, DC), October 23, 1927.
73. Leni quoted in James Hood MacFarland, "Leni Likens Film Game to Spirited Tennis Tilt," *Universal Weekly*, January 26, 1929.
74. "Classics Not as Popular, Director Says," *Los Angeles Times*, November 13, 1927.
75. Leni quoted in MacFarland, "Leni Likens Film." Leni's post-*Last Warning* plans were not clear. He had signed a five-year contract with Universal in 1926, but the *Exhibitors Herald and Moving Picture World* reported in August 1928 that Universal had just renewed it. Adding to the confusion, this latter periodical, now retitled *Exhibitors Herald-World*, reported in late January 1929 that Leni was leaving Universal that month upon the expiration of his contract. See Sumner Smith, "Leni Learns the Lingo," *Moving Picture World*, January 29, 1927; "Leni Renews with U," *Exhibitors Herald and Moving Picture World*, October 19, 1928; and "Leni Leaves Universal," *Exhibitors Herald-World*, February 2, 1929. The latter article is datelined January 29.
76. "Paul Leni—The Forgotten Master."
77. Kurtz quoted in Christian Kiening and Ulrich Johannes Beil, "Afterword," in Kurtz, *Expressionism and Film*, 155.
78. Maurice Kann, "The Great Beyond," *Film Daily*, September 4, 1929.
79. Rudolf Kurtz, "Gedächtnisrede auf Paul Leni," *Lichtbildbühne*, September 21, 1929, reprinted in *Rudolf Kurtz: Essayist und Kritik*, ed. Rolf Aurich, Wolfgang Jacobsen, and Michael Wedel (Munich: Edition Text + Kritik, 2007), 121.

CHAPTER 2

Exploding the Cosmopolitan and Treating the Foreigners' Foreignness: Paul Leni's *The Diary of Dr. Hart*

Jaimey Fisher

INTRODUCTION: GENRE AND CINEMA CULTURES OF WORLD WAR I

Despite lengthy battle sequences throughout *The Diary of Dr. Hart* (*Das Tagebuch des Dr. Hart*, 1916/1918), the two main German trade publications at the time avoided labeling Paul Leni's directorial debut a war film in their reviews. This approach of both *Der Kinematograph* and *Lichtbildbühne* is particularly surprising because the genre of the "Kriegsfilm" or "Kriegspielfilm" was well established by this late-war moment, as contemporaneous advertisements from these same trade journals confirm. Since the genre had already consolidated and *Dr. Hart* offers multiple combat sequences—including a nearly twenty-minute single battle in the approximately seventy-minute film—the failure to invoke the war genre in their notices is all the more remarkable. This surprising generic (non-)designation manifests at least two telling aspects of the film: first, that *Dr. Hart* proves intriguing not only as Paul Leni's directorial debut but also as a historical document of its changing institutional context, and, second, that the film, initiated in 1916 but premiering in 1918, spanned watershed years arcing toward the disheartening denouement of the "war to end all wars." As I shall explore herein, both of these aspects of *Dr. Hart* underscore how the film is tellingly transitional, perhaps even transformative, for Leni's emergent career and in the wider landscape of German cinema during World War I.

Exploring the genres of a little-discussed, even little-known, film may seem an exercise in obscurity, but such an approach is revealing not solely for the above historical reasons, but also because it comports with important trends in the study of early cinema. Such complex generic figurations of this period highlight how the generic hybridity usually traced to a much later period was already in operation in cinema's first decades.[1] In this way, despite exotic or "primitive" appearances, the films and their makers met familiar industrial challenges early on; they found and appealed to savvy audiences holding developed generic preferences and distastes. More nuanced investigations of such mechanisms have helped normalize this period, especially in illuminating the sophistication of works that look strange at times; they also elucidate how the films were thoroughly, and intriguingly, both products of and engaged with the cultures of their historical moment.[2] Elsewhere I have explored how the early travel or cultural film was absorbed by the war film emerging around this time, but herein I focus on how Leni's debut engaged several constitutive elements of the "explosion film," the medical drama or "doctor film," and the espionage thriller into its staging of territorial conquest, in a way revealingly transformative for the early war genre. Before investigating these aspects of the film, however, I would offer more about how *Dr. Hart*'s curious production history can open up the institutional–industrial context of its troubling time.

DR. HART'S CHECKERED PAST: A COMPLEX PRODUCTION CONTEXT

The reviews in *Lichtbildbühne* and *Der Kinematograph* revealingly term *The Diary of Dr. Hart* a "Propagandafilm." At this early point in cinematic propaganda, such a designation was more of a matter-of-fact assessment than a condemnatory one. The trade journals identified what seems particularly noteworthy in the film; not, of course, that it would end up ushering in the directorial career of one of Weimar's (and then Universal's) most celebrated auteurs,[3] but that it was born of a watershed institutional change related to the war and Germany's rapidly declining fortunes in it. Around this time of increasingly failed offensives and sagging spirits, military officials were reconsidering how best to depict the war and increasingly called for fiction over documentary films. This deliberate departure from documentary signals a notable change in strategy that anticipates the emphases of the 1917-founded Bild- und Filmamt (Bufa) and the Universum-Film Aktiengesellschaft. Following the checkered development of Bufa, Ufa famously arose from the growing disagreements between the military and corporate leadership of the German film industry and eventually incorporated Gen. Erich Ludendorff's argument, in a letter that came be known as "Ufa's birth certificate," that it was "absolutely necessary for a successful conclusion to the war that film be put to work with the highest priority everywhere where German influence is still possible."[4] Such was the increasingly desperate cultural and political context of Leni's work on *Dr. Hart*. But even before Ufa's much better-known emergence, Bufa was already under the Supreme Army Command and the military division of the Foreign Office, running 900 "front cinemas" as well as film teams to document ongoing combat operations. Bufa had reportedly received 18 million marks annually from the war ministry, with another 492,000 marks from the foreign ministry's military desk.[5] *The Diary of Dr. Hart*, as Klaus Kreimeier has suggested in his influential history of Ufa, was among the most important of Bufa's longer-form features, and it has been similarly praised by Sabine Hake.[6]

Another peculiarity of *The Diary of Dr. Hart* is that it counts as Leni's initial directed film but not as his first directorial effort to open in theaters. His first "civilian" film, *Prima Vera*, actually premiered in December 1917, while *The Diary of Dr. Hart* ended up debuting in early 1918 despite Gerhard Lamprecht's dating it as a 1916 film in his influential multivolume cataloguing of German silent cinema.[7] This stuttering production history reveals much about the film and the debates about German propaganda in these years as well as about Leni's somewhat confusing early biography. According to the account in Hans-Michael Bock's catalogue—understandably modest on the beginnings of Leni's career—Leni was drafted in 1915 and by 1916 was quartered with a Polish family, where the German Jew developed a fascination with Polish Catholicism and the iconographic figure of the Virgin Mary in particular. He apparently dreamt of projecting Mary onto the sky in hopes of inspiring all to put down their weapons. Perhaps because of these surprisingly wide-ranging interests, he was brought back to Berlin to work on Polish subjects in the propaganda department, and *The Army Doctor* (*Der Feldarzt*), as *The Diary of Dr. Hart* was initially called, was part of this work. The eventual delay in the film's release likely had to do with the reworking that Leni's film had sustained. Although archival/documentary evidence is—as with much of Leni's biography—scant, one can imagine that Bufa elected to refashion a war-emphatic title like *The Army Doctor* into a more civilian, softer sounding *Diary of Dr. Hart* at this late and disappointing point in the war. *The Diary of Dr. Hart* provides, in this and the above ways, a fascinating historical document bridging these stages of the evolution of the early national German film industry.

The film is also noteworthy because its personnel list reads like a compendium of early German film history, as Thomas Brandlmeier has also noted.[8] First and foremost was Leni himself, who had worked primarily as a graphic artist and set designer in both theater and film until that point. His signed work could also be seen regularly on the cover of *Lichtbildbühne*, so the whole industry presumably knew his name well before his first film. In addition to serving as Leni's directorial debut, *The Diary of Dr. Hart* involved other key figures accomplished at the time and then in the subsequent Weimar period.

For example, the screenwriter Hans Brennert co-wrote the screenplay for the 1938 *Heimat* (*Magda*) among a huge number of other scripts. Leni's assistant director, Hanns Kräly, became Ernst Lubitsch's preferred screenwriter, including on *Madame DuBarry* (1919) and *Anna Boleyn* (1920); he specialized in love triangles and rectangles of the sort with which *Dr. Hart* flirts. And the film's cinematographer, Carl Hoffmann, shot some of the most celebrated films of Germany's best-known period, including Fritz Lang's *Dr. Mabuse the Gambler* (*Dr. Mabuse der Spieler*; 1921–2) and *Die Nibelungen* (1922–4), E. A. Dupont's *Varieté* (1925), and F. W. Murnau's *Faust* (1925–6). Some of the brightest threads of Weimar film history are woven through this early propaganda-combat film about a doctor from near Baden-Baden mobilized to the eastern front.

EXPLOSIONS IN THE SPA, LOOKING BACKWARD AND FORWARD

For the purposes of early(ish) cinema, what is an explosion? Pansy Duncan has argued that early-cinema explosions transcended the mere "cinema of attractions" that Tom Gunning has influentially explored for the alternative—or diminished—narrative mode of many early films.[9] For Duncan, the use of explosions did not so much mimic modern fragmentariness or astonishment, as Gunning, following thinkers like Simmel and Benjamin, has suggested.[10] Rather, the genre manifested a clear form of monstration, inquisitiveness, and curiosity. Duncan posits a different set of audience perspectives than that presented in earlier theories that highlighted the intersection of attraction and astonishment. For her, early cinema, as manifested in its explosion genre, was not so much a matter of astonishment at spectacle as it was a "device of curiosity" akin to scientific investigation. This was likewise true of the complex of phenomena that Giorgio Bertellini has theorized with the early-cinema interest in seismic activity, especially volcanic eruption;[11] certainly this interest is, but is simultaneously more than, mere spectacle and attraction. These early-cinema explosions proved themselves more effective (and affective) than telescoping, or microscoping, shots that were also commonly deployed at that point in the same investigative spirit. According to Duncan, these explosion films blew stuff up not to only to shock and awe but also to comprehend those self-same objects, both to evoke and satiate viewers' curiosity about them.[12]

It is notable that many of the early explosion films (as with the volcano films discussed by Bertellini) detonate their explosions in the quotidian economic contexts of the presumed audiences, such as in the kitchen, in the photography laboratory, or in the factory, all of which were familiar social spaces from the Lumière brothers' influential works.[13] The explosive interest in both photography and motorcars manifests, for example, the curiosity, and concerns, about what the economy was producing with its rapidly innovating technologies. But *Dr. Hart* sets its first explosions in the form of fireworks in a resort town, Bad Oos near Baden-Baden, where the title character lives. In this way the mechanisms of monstration and curiosity are unfolding in one of Germany's most famous tourist destinations, offering a window into a different socio-economic world than that inhabited by most audiences. The explosion film that Duncan charts is thereby brought into concert with travel or cultural films; the monstration and curiosity of the explosion here divulge the social ensemble of the tourist destination and its upcoming transformation. If the good doctor starts the film in this famous spa town, he shall travel far, indeed, in his literal and figurative mobilization to the east.

As David Blackbourn argues, such spa towns were a revealing crossroads for myriad nineteenth-century sensibilities: the intersection of the aristocracy and the rising middle class; the concern with health and the perils of illness; and, befitting the generic transformations I am charting, the ever-widening circles of travel and tourism.[14] In her comprehensive history of the prewar travelogue, in fact, Jennifer Lynn Peterson analyzed a 1911 German film, *Life and Times in the Bohemian Baths of Marienbad, Karlsbad, Franzensbad* (*Leben und Treiben in den böhmischen Bädern Marienbad, Karlsbad, Franzensbad*) as well as a satirical perspective on such curious tourist mores by Edwin S. Porter's 1904 *The European Rest Cure*.[15] This filmic interest in a formerly aristocratic form underscores sociological changes at work in nineteenth-century travel and tourism; by the later nineteenth century, border-crossing leisure travel was no longer the sole purview of aristocratic grand tours. Despite Dr. Robert Hart's nostalgic carriage ride back to Bad Oos, the train was instrumental in this transformation of an earlier socio-spatial form. A spa town like Baden-Baden, for relevant example, went from around 1,000 visitors per annum in 1800 to 56,000 per annum by 1870, according to Blackbourn.[16] The presence of a middle-class doctor like Robert only underscores this mélange of old-world aristocrats and modern physicians: such new-fangled bourgeois doctors proved central to the appeal of these spa towns, emblematic of the intersection of traditional aristocratic genteelness and modern health and hygiene. As Blackbourn has noted, "taking the waters" of the spa were, in fact, seen as the very modern "antidote to the diseases of 'civilization'" prescribed by the very embodiment of that ever-advancing civilization, the medical doctor.[17]

Despite such very modern underpinnings for these resort towns, Blackbourn emphasized how spas, rather like the train stations analyzed by Wolfgang Schivelbusch, looked backward as well as forward;[18] despite the overtures of modern hygiene, they were careful to cultivate the nostalgic aura of an earlier era. The neo-baroque architecture, the geometric gardens, and the endless diversions all invoked a court idyll rapidly withering on the ornamental vine. A key aspect of this antiquated court charm was the old-world cosmopolitanism of the spa, where aristocrats of various nations (often related to one another in some convoluted way) could gather and cavort. This is certainly the case in *Dr. Hart*. Bad Oos is used to introduce the other lead characters from a range of nations, including Polish Count Bransky, Russian Count Bronislaw Krascinsky, the French Vicomte Latour, and Robert's second love interest, the Polish Jadwiga, the daughter of Bransky. In fact, the film stages the subterfuge of spa flirtation and then jealousy in a love triangle among Jadwiga, Robert, and Bronislaw, a plot bespeaking a bygone, border-busting cosmopolitanism that the film will soon renounce in its nationalist remapping.

In this way the first reel of the film emphasizes how Robert exists and, indeed, embodies late nineteenth- and early twentieth-century cosmopolitanism. It also underscores how, even in the era of high and eventually pernicious nationalism, social interactions were already transnational. The film invokes this mode of cosmopolitanism to recast it with the war, an altogether new form of cosmopolitanism. Throughout the first act, *The Diary of Dr. Hart*'s ensemble cast provides for the positive but also fading potential of cosmopolitanism—a term usually deployed to mean something like a "citizen of the world," whereby one belongs to some kind of global civil (here spa) society.[19] This sense of belonging and membership means that cosmopolitans can belong as citizens of "their immediate political communities, and of the wider regional and global networks which impacted upon their lives," in David Held's words.[20] The war will soon foreground such "immediate political communities," but for now the transnational network of spa life still predominated. I would underscore how this sort of modern cosmopolitanism in the twentieth century relied upon an increase in mass mobility that Leni highlighted throughout *The Diary of Dr. Hart*. This cosmopolitan setting and its transnational romance—along with cinematic spectacles building on and complicating early-cinema visual attractions (fireworks!)—return to an era when most of what appeared on German screens was not German. And even the content that had been produced locally tended to downplay nationality in favor of border-crossing export potential.

Prewar Bad Oos cosmopolitan *modus vivendi* sketches an alternative sort of citizenship, an alternative to being in the world of segmented nations. With such a plot approach, *Dr. Hart* seems unusual for a combat film because, with its doctor protagonist, it foregrounds a pre-existing sort of German cosmopolitan: ethnic Germans living and working in transnational contexts, presumably speaking multiple languages, with friends and defenders from these countries that quickly turn Germany's enemies. By differentiating such modes of cosmopolitan mobilities, Zygmunt Bauman explores how the kinds of citizenship regimes could already be taken "as the metaphor for the new, emergent, stratification," laying bare the fact "access to global mobility . . . has been raised to the topmost rank among the stratifying factors."[21] *Dr. Hart* foregrounds both the mobility and stratification in the cosmopolitanism that it conjures. Indeed, Robert embodies precisely the elite worldliness of which Bauman wrote and that the film goes on to dismantle.

It is into this world that the film's initial explosion tellingly erupts. The fireworks are carefully anticipated in the interactions of Robert and Jadwiga; as viewers watch the good doctor going about his doctorly "Tagewerk" in his drawing-room office, Jadwiga and Count Bransky come by for medical attention. On their way out of the medical examination, Jadwiga asks if they will see the doctor at the fireworks, pointing at a poster in his office that displays a conspicuous image of the explosions to come as well as the "fateful" date of August 1. Of course, focusing on that single day, or even those few weeks, obscures the broader political context and Germany's decisive role in it.

The next scene picks up on that day, with the international spa-goers in black tails and tie. Robert sits with Jadwiga and the Count chatting, and shortly after Bronislaw enters and looks jealously at the two. "Despite the jealousy of Bronislaw," the intertitles inform viewers, Jadwiga asks Robert to accompany her to the terrace to watch the fireworks. The fireworks literally illuminate this spa world that has been proffered to viewers while also anticipating its destruction. It is the "single punctual moment of release" of which Duncan writes

Figure 2.1 Fireworks at spa anticipate the exploded world.

and anticipates a world that becomes catastrophic, convulsive, out of joint, all in ways that will engage and interest the viewers.[22] It recalls, as Schivelbusch has suggested, that "film is closer to the fire than to the theatre."[23] That this explosion is transitional becomes clear moments later when Leni matches the fireworks' explosions to a parallel eruption at the beginning of the war, with newspapers thrown dramatically above the panicking spa guests, signifying the effective end of this world. This was certainly the function of eruptions in the films that Bertellini analyzes; for their viewers at a northern remove, the spectacle of explosions opens a window into a faraway social world in transition.

DR. HART PUSHING THE BOUNDARIES MILITARILY AND MEDICALLY

Doctors and the medicine they practice have long played an important role in German self-understanding generally and in German cinema specifically. For instance, many scholars have observed the significance of assorted images of doctors in films made during the Nazi period as well as in the postwar period.[24] Films such as Hans Steinhoff's *Robert Koch: Der Bekämpfer des Todes* (1939) with Emil Jannings in the title role or G. W. Pabst's *Paracelsus* (1943) with Werner Krauss rendered the doctor as Germany's Führer-evoking "genius" shortly before and during World War II. These Nazi-era "genius films" elevated certain personalities as embodying the nation and its putatively existential struggles,[25] and it is telling that medical doctors could be imagined as functioning so centrally in the national imaginary. But long before those nefarious works under the Nazis, World War I propaganda had already made Germany's medical prowess a central part of national self-understanding. In fact, various industry professionals called for medicine-focused films early in World War I, as Germans were forced to adjust to the new and uncertain political realities and to the remade film-industrial market post-1914. Until 1914, as noted above, the majority of films playing on German screens were not made in Germany, so with the advent of war and boycotting of key producing countries like France, new content and, indeed, whole genres were needed. Films foregrounding Germany's relatively modern medicine were one of the much-mentioned fashions, itself symptomatic of medicine's relevance to national self-understanding as well as to wartime anxieties; such representations could doubtless help assuage the understandable fears about the wounded and dead.

Although not as prominent in films like *Robert Koch* and *Paracelsus*, a work like Max Kimmich's *Germanin* (1943) points to a central aspect of this cinematic–medical discourse: namely, the role that doctors and medicine could play in Germany's explorations and aggressions outside of its borders. As Laura Otis has argued, the discursive construction of the German nation in the late nineteenth century consistently built upon biological and medical deployments, for example, in the pairing of "hygiene" exhibits with those advocating colonialism.[26] She observed that "So intense and interrelated were the imperial and bacterial drives [like Robert Koch's] in the 1880s that they expressed themselves in each other's languages."[27] Amid the microbial era that Koch had helped usher in in the 1880s and 90s, Otis noted that scientists and doctors abroad were often ascribed the heroism of soldiers serving overseas as forgers and defenders of the growing German empire. For instance, Koch arrived in Berlin in 1880 for a position at the Imperial Department of Health before his appointment, five years later, as the chair of hygiene at the University of Berlin (today, Humboldt University). He took numerous trips to Africa between 1890 and 1910 representing the German government and its interests abroad. In this capacity, he even compared himself explicitly to explorers for the empire searching for gold, in this case "scientific gold," as he put it. Although he was at times critical of certain aspects of imperialism, he nonetheless worked to make the colonies safe for white Europeans and understood the colonial character of such an endeavor, for example, in occupying an increasing amount of territory as malaria is conquered.[28]

This intersection of Germany's medical capacities with its political agenda, and even foreign policy, becomes clear in Robert's first foray abroad. After the fireworks detailed above, viewers watch the spa-town doctor rapidly remade for the purposes of the war-mobilized nation, first by donning a uniform and then celebrating with comrades before deployment. The film suddenly jumps from this convivial carousing with newly minted cadets to his first deployment, as viewers watch German forces venture abroad into—as an abrupt intertitle declares—"Polen!" At this point, however, there was no country called Poland; it was a longed-for but still imaginary territory. *Dr. Hart*'s depictions transpire at a historical moment when the Central Powers' commitments to Poland looked more promising, that is, when they "liberated" many Poles from the Russian dominion of Russian Poland and the Russian army's early invasions of Austro-Hungarian and Prussian territories. It is notable that three images convey this territorial conjuring in quick succession: first, a hillside from which German commanders look out, presumably into the imaginary Poland, via binoculars; then the expansive landscape at which they look; and, finally, an advancing German troop column marching in the direction of their gaze and that targeted landscape. It is the war that conjures this longed-for territory into existence and, as detailed below, will convert the region's older social forms into a new kind of cosmopolitanism forged by explosions to replace those of the spa town in *Dr. Hart*'s first reel.

The intersection of medicine with foreign adventurism is confirmed soon thereafter in Robert's first encounter with local Poles as well as enemy forces in a small village—a sequence that makes the "tip-of-the-spear" of the German

Figure 2.2 Invaders create a public health emergency that Dr. Hart then has to confront.

advance into Polish territory not only its cavalry but also its medical professionals. This sequence is actually the first time that viewers watch the enemies of Germany, who, revealingly, immediately wage a kind of biological warfare against non-combatants by poisoning a small-town well. The German cavalry arrive to drive the enemy "Cossacks" off, but effectively helping the locals requires Robert's skills; he tests the well water, declares it poisoned, and then treats a villager who was wounded as he tried to prevent the poisoning. In World War I, there was a fundamental fear of "defeatism" spreading like a bacterial infection among German forces and populations, an infection that a doctor-protagonist is well suited to treat. Later, in the hut of the bedridden villager, Robert sees, among the icon-like images on the hut wall, a portrait of Jadwiga, who he learns is living in her family's castle nearby. This sequence would seem to resonate with that described by Bock of Leni's own quartering in the homes of Polish farmers and being impressed with their dedication to Mary materialized in an icon. The medicine man's intimate interaction with a civilian abroad—in fact, that he could visit this wounded farmer at home—allows the plot to thicken in a most cinematically satisfying way.

RECASTING THE EXPLOSION AND THE DOCTOR: OF WINDMILLS AND CASTLES

After departing this village, Robert is studying a map when the advancing German troops, per the diagrammed arrows, are suddenly shelled. Newly sensitized to the intensified spaces on the map, he realizes that a scenic windmill is, through the positioning of its massive blades, secretly signaling coordinates to the Russian forces to attack the oncoming German troops. This surprising plot development after Robert's small-town house call invokes another genre, although largely to negate it: the spy film. There were a good number of films, even in the prewar period, that played upon the intrigue and excitement of espionage,[29] but this particular espionage ploy invokes real events of the world outside the filmed events, as Russian spies did indeed encode the positioning of windmills to convey German troop positions.[30] As with Robert's map replacing the village above ("Alarm!"), the film's increasing use of abstract military codes (troop positions, artillery coordinates) refigures older forms like the scenic and seemingly harmless windmill. The apparent idyll of the countryside village and broad landscape with its pastoral windmill have been remade and reframed by the abstract codes of war and then the doctor's map-enabled reading of it. As Henri Lefebvre notes of cartographic representation—which he weaves into the longer-term modern production of abstract space—mapped objects alternate with carefully selected nature on the surface of the map in ideological fashion.[31] The map's relatively few objects (river, forest, spy-infested windmill) direct the film's increasingly geopolitical action and its overcoming of older, nature-oriented, landscape-dotted spaces.

Robert and his comrades quickly apprehend the Russian spy and then blow up the entire windmill with a spectacular explosion. One wonders why, if the troops are marching by and the spy has been caught, it is strategically necessary to blow up the windmill, but nonetheless it provides another visual highlight of the film. The enormity of the explosion revisits the film's use of fireworks in

Figure 2.3 Windmill before, charming landmark tending to the landscape.

the spa in *Dr. Hart*'s first ten minutes; both exemplify the visual attractions that Gunning famously highlights in early cinema. However, the spectacular destruction of the windmill, the importance of which is mapped by Robert onto the larger Polish plans of the German forces, has also been carefully woven into the film's longer narrative-territorial arc, per Duncan's analysis of such explosions. If the first-reel spa fireworks do astonish or astound the viewer, as Gunning put it,[32] they also give a window into the now lost social world that the war has so radically disrupted. The clearly echoing explosion of the windmill stages an astonishing attraction while also suggesting the remaking of rural ways of life. Here, too, the parallels to the exploding catastrophe films that Bertellini foregrounds seem relevant; such films provided a window into a different social order but also highlighted the precarity of these more "primitive" ways of life. As with the exploded spa above, the (literal) destruction of the antiquated building/machine signals another departure from an earlier spatial ensemble while simultaneously remaking the landscape for military action, clearing both the troops' route and the commanders' sightlines. This remaking of the mapped terrain permits the German forces to march on to the more important target, the Russian-held but Polish Castle Bransky. Robert's first-reel contemplation of the countryside and cosmopolitan spa life has turned into map-driven, calculated actions to produce homogenized spaces useful for this military he tends.

Figure 2.4 Windmill after, now exploded.

The estate's trajectory from aristocratic Polish castle to Russian fortification to German military hospital is revealing for the modernizing transformations of war that *Dr. Hart* foregrounds with its deliberate hybridization of the explosion, medical, and espionage genres. Military historian John Keegan observes that one of World War I's central "advances" was the increasing abandonment of traditional fortifications, that is, of large-scale architecture deployed for defensive purposes.[33] This surprising development—after millennia of being the literal cornerstone of defensive strategy and much urban life—transpired quickly because of World War I's decisive technological innovation: namely, the precision use of heavy, long-distance artillery. Because such artillery could obliterate any above-ground fortification and was increasingly mobile, sitting back in one's castle and waiting the enemy out was no longer a viable tactic. On the one hand, military planning focused increasingly on "temporary" redoubts like trenches, which due to the new artillery were often deeper and more warren-like than generally imaged in films. On the other hand, such planning highlighted as well the mobile fighting forces that could move troops and the fortification-obliterating artillery, which proved altogether more cinematic. With its dramatic explosions and mobile doctor, *Dr. Hart* advances quickly on to Count Bransky's estate.

This significant shift is hinted at in the final conversion of Castle Bransky, but with a telling revision; the kind of mobility sketched here is medically, not militarily, modern. Here, too, the film deliberately transforms the train, much as it transformed the prewar travelogue landscapes above. One finds in *Dr. Hart* not only the train's mobilization of the doctor for fighting in "Poland" but also a later, transformed train deployed at a narratively milestone moment. The crosscutting of the later film brings viewers briefly back to Germany, where Robert's original love interest, Ursula von Hohenau, is herself mobilized in an explicit, if belated, parallel to his first-reel mobilization; she likewise heads to the train station, dons a uniform there, boards a train as crowds cheer, and heads determinedly east. Notably, however, her heading east comes after, and in the wake of, Robert's mobilization. The train has now been remade by the increasingly important medical genre; it sports compartments rendered to medical beds, gleaming white wash basins, crisply folded linens, and all the latest medical technologies crammed into the confined but highly mobile spaces.

The entire final act, the film's post-combat last twenty minutes, focuses on this converted space of Castle Bransky, the rehabilitated war, and the transformed social order occupying both the castle and the broader combat zone. The arrival of von Hohenau's train completes the take-over of the Castle by converting it into a circulation space. As Schivelbusch notes of the train's impact on fixed locations, linkages via rail turned those kinds of rooted places into a point of circulation underscored by the train arrival of von Hohenau herself, the subsequent arrival of wounded troops in the long line of ambulances, and the departure of the sick back home,[34] all parallel to the circulating entity of the hillside replacing the landscape in the film's first act. The old, fixed castle—the cornerstone of aristocratic identity and cosmopolitanism in the film's first act—becomes a circulation point for the wounded masses and those tending them. Among those wounded arriving by ambulance is the stricken Bronislaw, whom the Russians' Cossacks had seized from Robert's care. Bronislaw now returns to the castle not as a military commander but on a stretcher, and not to fight on but to be treated by the film's hero, Robert. In the climax of the medical plot—in one of the final act's only dramatic moments—Robert treats him behind closed (but stately) doors, saving him. It is a newly forged transnational solidarity, a novel form of cosmopolitanism, set in the old castle but medically forged in the most modern way.

CONCLUSION: ABIDING NOSTALGIA FOR EARLIER EXPLOSIONS AND THE COSMOPOLITANISM THEREIN

The Diary of Dr. Hart's conclusion underscores recast cosmopolitanism among its Russian, Polish, and German characters, remaking the first act's idyllic but idle spa-town cosmopolitanism that I foregrounded above. The film's series of explosions have, in effect, both illuminated and demolished the older ways of life in order to replace them. In the film's last sequence, *Dr. Hart* revisits and reinforces the different moments of explosive and medical transformation that I have highlighted throughout Paul Leni's directorial debut. After a cross-cut and parallel assertion of the film's two couples—a post-operation reconciliation between Jadwiga and Bronislaw and then a romantic garden walk for Ursula and Robert—viewers abruptly find the film's principals assembled around the remade Castle Bransky's hearth. Surrounded by old Bransky and the recovering Bronislaw as well as Jadwiga and Ursula, the hearthside Robert leafs through his eponymous diary, reviewing the stations of, apparently, the film's greatest plot import via flashback. It is notable, I think, that the doctor's many military comrades do not conclude the film, but instead the principals from the spa reconvene amid refigured circumstances. After a brief image from the film's opening of Ursula von Hohenau working in her orphanage, the sequence's longest flashback revisits the evening of fireworks at Bad Oos detailed above. Viewers are returned to the spa shot of the jealous Bronislaw as he watches Robert and Jadwiga awaiting the show, and then they re-witness the actual fireworks above the fountain. In the extant film copy, the imaged fireworks and explosion are actually more elaborate and spectacular than those earlier in the film.

From that climactic first-act explosion, however, Robert's diary flashback sequence remarkably jumps over the second act entirely to a third and final shot, one of the surgery that Robert has just performed on Bronislaw—meaning that the flashback's reviewing of plot foregoes most of the film's lengthy battle sequences, including the twenty-minute advance at the core of Act II. As with its spa and windmilled landscape, *Dr. Hart* has deployed its explosions to transform the depicted war itself, along with the film's antiquated spaces. Its narrative point, especially by the depressing late-war moment of 1918, is beyond mere combat and victory. German-led, train-mobilized, and explosion-forged, the wartime maneuvers have, most importantly in the logic of the film, transformed the old-fashioned castle into a spatialized new world order, a spatial transformation changing the characters and their cosmopolitan relations as well. Although the "Kriegsfilm" and "Kriegsdrama" was already well established by 1916, Paul Leni's debut demonstrates, in both its production and it content, how a combination of genres could be deployed to remake the dynamically forged war genre and how such genres were already evolving—invoked, manipulated, hybridized—at this early moment in German cinema history.

NOTES

1. See Janet Staiger, "Hybrid or Inbred: The Purity Hypothesis and Hollywood Genre History," in *Film Genre Reader III*, ed. Barry Keith Grant (Austin: University of Texas Press, 2003), 185–299; and Rick Altman, *Film/Genre* (London: British Film Institute, 1999).
2. See Pansy Duncan, "Exploded Views: Early Cinema and the Spectacular Logic of the Explosion," *Screen* 58, no. 4 (Winter 2018): 405.
3. See Gerd Gemünden, "Parallel Modernities: From Haunted Screen to Universal Horror," in *Generic Histories of German Cinema: Genre and Its Deviations*, ed. Jaimey Fisher (Rochester, NY: Camden House, 2013), 31; and Kris Vander Lugt, "From Siodmak to Schlingensief: The Return of History as Horror," in Fisher, *Generic Histories of German Cinema*, 157.
4. Ludendorff quoted in Klaus Kreimeier, *The Ufa Story: A History of Germany's Greatest Film Company, 1918-1945*, trans. Robert Kimber and Rita Kimber (New York: Hill & Wang, 1996), 23.
5. Hans-Michael Bock (ed.), *Paul Leni: Grafik, Theater, Film* (Frankfurt: Deutsches Filmmuseum, 1986), 17.
6. Kreimeier, *Ufa Story*, 21–3; Sabine Hake, *German National Cinema* (London: Routledge, 2002), 23.
7. Gerhard Lamprecht, *Katalogisierung der deutschen Stummfilme aus den Jahren 1903-1931* (Berlin: Deutsche Kinemathek, 1970).
8. Thomas Brandlmeier, "Die polnische Karte: Anmerkungen zu Paul Lenis Film *Das Tagebuch des Dr. Hart*," in *Studien zur Kulturgeschichte des deutschen Polenbildes, 1848-1939*, ed. Hendrik Feindt (Wiesbaden: Otto Harrassowitz Verlag, 1995), 156–64.
9. Tom Gunning, "An Aesthetic of Astonishment: Early Film and the (In)Credulous Spectator," in *Viewing Positions: Ways of Seeing Film*, ed. Linda Williams (New Brunswick, NJ: Rutgers University Press, 1995), 114–33.
10. Duncan, "Exploded Views," 402–3.
11. Giorgio Bertellini, *Italy In Early American Cinema: Race, Landscape, and the Picturesque* (Bloomington: Indiana University Press, 2010), pp. 7, 28–9.

12. Duncan, "Exploded Views," 404.
13. Duncan, "Exploded Views," 408.
14. David Blackbourn, "Fashionable Spa Towns in Nineteenth-Century Europe," in *Water, Leisure and Culture: European Historical Perspectives*, ed. Susan C. Anderson and Bruce H. Tabb (Oxford and New York: Berg, 2002), 9–21.
15. Jennifer Lynn Peterson, *Education in the School of Dreams: Travelogues and Early Nonfiction Film* (Durham, NC: Duke University Press, 2013), 222, 194–6.
16. Blackbourn, "Fashionable Spa Towns," 13.
17. Blackbourn, "Fashionable Spa Towns," 12.
18. Wolfgang Schivelbusch, *Railway Journey: The Industrialization of Time and Space in the 19th-Century* (Berkeley: University of California Press, 1986), 174.
19. Ulrich Beck, *The Cosmopolitan Vision*, trans. Ciaran Cronin (Cambridge: Polity Press, 2006).
20. David Held, *Democracy and the Global Order: From the Modern State to Cosmopolitan Governance* (Cambridge: Polity Press, 1995), 233.
21. Zygmunt Bauman, *Globalization: The Human Consequences* (Cambridge: Polity Press, 1998), 87.
22. Duncan, "Exploded Views," 405.
23. Wolfgang Schivelbusch, *Disenchanted Night: The Industrialization of Light in the Nineteenth Century* (Berkeley: University of California Press, 1995), 221.
24. See Udo Benzenhöfer and Wolfgang U. Eckart (eds.), *Medizin im Spielfilm des Nationalsozialismus* (Tecklenburg: Burgverlag, 1990).
25. Eric Rentschler, *The Ministry of Illusion: Nazi Cinema and Its Afterlife* (Cambridge, MA: Harvard University Press, 1996), 181–2.
26. Laura Otis, *Membranes: Metaphors of Invasion in Nineteenth-Century Literature, Science, and Politics* (Baltimore: Johns Hopkins University Press, 1999), 32–4.
27. Otis, *Membranes*, 31.
28. Otis, *Membranes*, 32.
29. Philipp Stiasny, *Das Kino und der Krieg, Deutschland 1914–1929* (Munich: Edition Text + Kritik, 2009), 50–7.
30. Alexander Watson, *Ring of Steel: German and Austria-Hungary in World War I* (New York: Basic Books, 2014).
31. Henri Lefebvre, *The Production of Space*, trans. Donald Nicholson-Smith (Oxford: Blackwell Publishers, 1992), 233.
32. Gunning, "Aesthetic of Astonishment."
33. John Keegan, *The First World War* (New York: Alfred A. Knopf, 1999).
34. Schivelbusch, *Railway Journey*, 197.

CHAPTER 3

The Unnatural in the Natural: Leopold Jessner and Paul Leni's Early Weimar Film *Backstairs*

Jason Doerre

"The rear entry of the boarding house," reads the opening intertitle of *Backstairs* (*Hintertreppe*, 1921). Cut to a shot at the bottom of an empty, rickety stairwell with accented contrast between the light and dark from the lighting. A quick cut brings the viewer up the stairs to a door at which an iris shot focuses in on a white bell-pull handle, which in another close-up shot reveals the word *Rechnungsrat* or auditor. A fade-out and fade-in places the viewer into the room where a woman sleeps in a narrow bed. This opening sequence lasts only about thirty seconds, but it adeptly introduces the tone and setting of Leopold Jessner and Paul Leni's film. Not only does it establish the atmosphere with the desolate but eerily lighted staircase of the boarding house, it also foreshadows that which puts the dramatic events of the story into motion. A careful reading of this sequence also reveals certain markers of the disparate artistic styles of Naturalism and Expressionism. The environs of a boarding house squarely locates the narrative in a lower-class setting, a typical milieu for narratives of the Naturalist tradition, while the chiaroscuro lighting in the stairwell is a classic technique of filmic Expressionism. While the year 1919 typically marks the emergence of the Expressionist film in Germany, *Backstairs* shows that this new post-World War I direction in filmmaking did not necessarily replace older styles such as those that belong to Naturalism. By challenging understandings of German Expressionism of the early postwar years, this essay seeks to posit *Backstairs* as an example of early Weimar cinema that blends together seemingly disparate styles and themes in order to reflect a society still reeling from the impact of the Great War.

When *Backstairs* debuted on December 11, 1921, Germany was still reeling from the economic, political, and social instability as a result of the fallout after its loss in World War I. Only three years before, Imperial Germany and its allies had surrendered to its foes after four years of devastating warfare that brought with it unprecedented loss of life on the battlefield, but also starvation on the home front. Aside from the pervading sense of war weariness at the end of the hostilities, a harsh peace was dealt to the Germans via the Versailles Peace Conference, whose mission was to place all blame for the hostilities on the Germans and demand hefty reparations. The result was a crippling of the economy, producing a lasting political instability throughout the 1920s, as well as a compounding sense of national humiliation. Still, the Weimar Republic, which replaced Imperial Germany in 1919, grew to be a liberal democracy that ensured freedoms that rivalled any other Western democracy, and it was a time in which creativity flourished.

While Germany was facing the wrath of its foes in the aftermath of the war, its innovation in filmmaking was garnering international acclaim. The release of Robert Wiene's *The Cabinet of Dr. Caligari* (*Das Cabinet des Dr. Caligari*) in 1920 spurred broad critical commendation that lauded the film as an example of cinema's artistic potential. The international enthusiasm for German cinema grew in the wake of *Caligari*, making the film an anomaly for things "made in Germany" at the time. Although the appeal of films from the Weimar Republic was mostly due to their variety, technological innovation, and overall quality, the narratives from two post-World War II works—Siegfried Kracauer's *From Caligari to Hitler* (1947) and Lotte Eisner's *The Haunted Screen* (1952)—came to dominate our understanding of German cinema of the 1920s. Kracauer's work stressed the demonic, authoritarian features of the films that appealed to the collective mentality in the Weimar Republic and anticipated the coming of Hitler. Eisner's narrative focused on the artistic style of Expressionism as the defining feature of the cinema of this time. Certainly, these two works played a significant role in the two dominant discourses concerning German film of the 1920s: filmic Expressionism and Weimar cinema. As Thomas Elsaesser has astutely pointed out,

> "Expressionist film" and "Weimar cinema" continue to signal ready-made, self-evident identities, the former slanted towards the artists that produced the films, and the latter focusing on the society that consumed them—two halves of a whole that to this day spells Germany's national cinema.[1]

In recent decades, however, there has been a plethora of scholarship that upends the dominance that these two works have held over the discourse of cinema.[2] One result of this is that the term "Expressionism," with regard to Weimar Republic cinema, has been a contentious and crowded debate. In reaction to Eisner's sweeping generalization of ascribing Expressionist traits to the entirety of Weimar cinema, some authors have even sought to confine the number of Expressionist films to figures as low as six.[3] While Eisner's categorization of the totality of Weimar cinema as Expressionist is ostensibly exaggerated, limiting the discussion of Expressionism by canonizing a select few titles seems equally heavy handed. Is it possible that some films, while not Expressionist in totality, bear some characteristics of filmic Expressionism? Dietrich Scheunemann wrote:

> The expectation that a particular period has one dominant style that affects more or less, although in different ways, all art and literature production of this period is a rather unfortunate convention of the historiography of art and literature of the past century.[4]

Unlike the continuing debate about film Expressionism in postwar Germany, there has been little written about the influence of the earlier style of Naturalism in this era. One of Lotte Eisner's pitfalls in *The Haunted Screen* was her failure to adequately consider the existence of styles other than Expressionism in Weimar cinema, such as Naturalism. Even though she occasionally acknowledged the coexistence of Naturalism along with what she views as Expressionism, she de-emphasized its ability to produce meaning. Using Kasimir Edschmid's juxtaposing of Expressionism to Naturalism, she wrote:

> Expressionism sets itself against Naturalism with its mania for recording mere facts, and its paltry aim of photographing nature or daily life. The world is there for all to see; it would be absurd to reproduce it purely and simply as it is.[5]

Figure 3.1 Henny Porten (Housekeeper) and Fritz Kortner (Postman).

This essay posits Leopold Jessner and Paul Leni's *Backstairs* as a case in point of an early film that exhibits a hybridization of styles and techniques to create meaning. The film is not only a work of Weimar cinema in its *Weltanschauung* (worldview), but it also infuses its Naturalist setting with specific Expressionist markers. Using intertitles only at the beginning of the film to establish the setting, *Backstairs* uses its stylistic formalism to narrate a story about a housekeeper played by Henny Porten, who is happily in love with a humble workman played by Wilhelm Dieterle. Fulfilling her housekeeping duties by day, she is able to find joy in the embrace of her lover, whom she meets nightly in the rear courtyard of her upper-class employer's building. Little does she know that the crippled postman (Fritz Kortner), who secretly desires her, has been watching them. One evening her lover does not appear at their usual rendezvous point, and the next day there is no letter from him. Then one day a letter expressing his love for her does come. Enraptured by the clarification, she decides to pay a visit to the postman in order to thank for him bringing the welcome news. In the postman's basement apartment, she realizes that the letter was in fact written by him to console her and not by her lover. Touched by the perceived act of kindness, and under the impression that her lover had ghosted her, a romance springs between the two. One evening as the two are settling down to dinner to celebrate what appears to be their engagement, the workman suddenly returns. He reveals that an injury had kept him away and that his letters were sent back to him in the hospital because the postman had intercepted them. A dispute between the two arises, culminating in the postman's slaying of his rival. This scandal spells a precipitous downfall for the housekeeper, who immediately loses her job and place to live. Overwhelmed by the unfortunate chain of events, the broken woman climbs to the roof of the building, plunging to her death in the rear courtyard.

Backstairs not only featured Germany's first film star, Henny Porten, it was also an experimental film. The actress had already by this time a firmly established reputation as the embodiment of German womanhood, and her image was widely distributed in fan and cinema magazines, film posters, and postcards.[6] Beyond Porten's star presence, *Backstairs* incorporated a number of heavyweights from the film and theater world of Max Reinhardt. Leopold Jessner and the set designer Paul Leni handled the direction of the picture, while the already touted Carl Mayer, the scriptwriter for *The Cabinet of Dr. Caligari*, wrote the screenplay. While the casting of Henny Porten would suggest a Naturalistic picture, the names of Jessner, Leni, and Mayer were already associated with Expressionism through their work in film and theater. *Backstairs* is an example of the challenge that early cinema posed to the traditional bourgeois conception of art insofar as it begs the question of authorship. While Henny Porten's name was most prominently featured in most advertisements,[7] the writing of Mayer, the co-direction of Jessner and Leni, as well Leni's set design also carried considerable weight.[8]

Upon its debut in 1921, anticipation for *Backstairs* was already inflated. Negotiations regarding an early exit of contract between Henny Porten and Universum-Film AG (Ufa) had just been completed in March 1921, making way for her to form her own production company, Henny Porten Filmproduktion. As she would later state, her motive for leaving Ufa was not financial but rather came from the notion that she wanted more liberty to exert her own artistic inclinations.[9] *Backstairs* followed the company's first successful film *Wally of the Vultures* (*Die Geierwally*), which had appeared in September of 1921. *Wally of the Vultures* positioned itself for success by lining up E. A. Dupont, an established name in German cinema, to handle the direction. Paul Leni filled the role of set designer, while Porten and Wilhelm Dieterle played the main roles as lovers just as they went on to do in *Backstairs*. The film's financial success enabled Porten's company to take the financial risk of producing an experimental piece of cinema. Unlike its predecessor, *Backstairs* was intended to make its mark on film history as opposed to making big gains at the box office. As Porten recalled, "We decided in late summer of 1921 to take the risk of an artistic experiment and the founding of a new form for film. It was to be a film that forgoes the use of intertitles."[10] Leopold Jessner was pulled away from his position as director of the Berlin State Theater to direct his first film, while Paul Leni assisted him in the direction and oversaw the set design. Leni's integral role in the film can be gauged by his earnings of 100,000 marks as opposed to Jessner's 50,000.[11]

Despite the film's star-studded cast and experimental form, historians have regarded *Backstairs* as a failure due to its poor performance in box office sales. The contemporary film historian and critic Oskar Kalbus suggested that the film's simplicity was a prohibiting factor: "Nobody wanted to keep seeing the backstairs, the courtyard, the kitchen, a bourgeois parlor. They did not want to see hundreds of meters of film showing how dishes are cleaned in the kitchen."[12] Siegfried Kracauer attributed the film's failure to its thematic content: "The public was rather annoyed by such an accumulation of violence and misery."[13] Nevertheless, the initial reviews for the film were optimistic, showering the filmmakers with praise for their innovativeness and expressing excitement for what they viewed as the cinema's ascendance to high art. A reviewer for the magazine *Der Film* speculated on the impact such an experiment might have on German film:

> How far the general public will go along with it remains to be seen. But this should not hold one back from explaining that German cinematography can be proud of a work like this one, and be proud that there are companies that consider it their duty of honor to create works of artistic merit without concern for commercial resonance.[14]

In a similar sentiment, Kalbus wrote "that is not just 'the movies' anymore, that is art."[15] Even Alfred Kerr, famous for his witty but harsh criticisms, penned an overwhelmingly positive review of the film. He wrote, "This film is un-expressionist; psychological; and wonderfully restrained."[16] Much like that of other critics, Kerr's admiration for the film was based on its unconventional choice to forgo the intertitles and rely on film language to tell the story. The magazine *Der Kinematograph* declared that this artistic choice was "a milestone upon the way to a new composition of film."[17] Two years later, however, Hans Pander pointed to what he believed to be a divide between the critical praise of the *Kammerspielfilm* (chamber play film) and its lack of intertitles, such as *Backstairs*, and the public's reception of the film. He wrote:

> Critics have showered these chamber films with praise and recognition. Theatergoers were certainly more reserved; indeed, one had the impression that they—at last the vast majority of them—were left cold and were only able to follow the events on the screen with difficulty.[18]

In terms of the narrative, *Backstairs* relies on some rudimentary dramatic motifs or, as Kracauer put it, "a veritable excess of simplicity."[19] At its heart is a love triangle. The opening scene, described above, introduces a housekeeper played by Henny Porten, whose stardom represented the quintessential wholesome German woman. Surely, this weighed on the directorial choice of not assigning names to the figures because Porten already fulfilled preconceived expectations. The playfulness of the first scene with the alarm waking her from the comfort of her slumbers and her setting the clock back a few minutes in order to snooze a few minutes longer is formalistically articulated through an iris in and out. Techniques such as this rather than the use of intertitles are used to narrate the story, which can be attributed to the film's experimental style. The narrative is so simple that only the establishing title at the beginning of the film is needed; everything else is articulated through acting, editing, framing, *mise-en-scène*, and so on. This is what separates *Backstairs* from other films of the time; it relies on film language to tell the story. This speaks not only to the maturity that formalistic techniques of cinema had reached by this time but also to the sophistication of the cinema-going public to understand the intended meaning.

One integral component in producing meaning in *Backstairs* is the stage design and setting. The film belongs to a genre of film called the *Kammerspielfilm* or chamber play film, which was a popular German film genre throughout the Weimar Republic. The origins of this genre came from theatre, where Max Reinhardt coined the term *Kammerspiel* to label the theatrical genre of the chamber play. This genre is an outgrowth of late nineteenth-century Naturalism that sought to reinvent the German stage to make it more modern and relevant for

German society at the turn of the century. The depiction of the lower classes was one way in which Naturalism separated itself from bourgeois realism. Out of this arose the *Kammerspiel*.[20] The *Kammerspiel*, often called "intimate theater," required a smaller stage and audience and relied on the gestures of the actors in order to be understood. Lotte Eisner wrote of the *Kammerspiel*, "With dim lights and warm-toned wood panelling, [. . .] an élite (not more than 300 spectators) could feel all the significance of a smile, a hesitation, or an eloquent silence."[21] Since Max Reinhardt is considered the creator of the *Kammerspiel*, it is no surprise that this genre made its way to film considering how many of those he trained in the theater eventually transitioned to film.[22] Oskar Kalbus argued that the *Kammerspiel* aspired to develop cinema into an art form through its augmentation of film's means of expression. Therefore, the acting and *mise-en-scène* take on a more significant role in providing meaning in the *Kammerspielfilm*. He wrote, "Thus, it logically eschews the familiar intertitles and allows the plot to take place silently without intertitles and interpreter on the screen."[23] In a close analysis of the generic contours of *Backstairs*, Karen Risholm posed it as "the prototypical *Kammerspielfilm* of the Weimar era."[24] The use of space, Risholm wrote, is the key aspect that separates the *Kammerspielfilm* from the *Kammerspiel* of the theater:

> The spectator in the *Kammerspiel* theater was encouraged to sit back and enjoy the play on stage from a fully constituted subject position with a clearly delineated perspective augmented by a fixed point of view. The cinematic medium, on the other hand, opens up new challenges to the positioning of the spectator in relation to the text, and narration is the key interface.[25]

The *Kammerspielfilm*, much like its theater counterpart, bears many of the markings of Naturalism. What is widely considered the first instance of the genre, *Shattered* (*Scherben*), debuted in 1921. Another film that uses only one intertitle, *Shattered* makes heavy use of symbolism through acting and *mise-en-scène*. The film is set in the everyday life of a lower-middle-class railway lineman's family, echoing the background of Gerhart Hauptmann's 1888 classic work of literary Naturalism, *Lineman Thiel* (*Bahnwärter Thiel*). *Backstairs* carries all of the markers of the *Kammerspiel*: lower-class setting, Naturalistic acting, quotidian plot, and limited use of space. Unlike a quintessential example of the genre such as *Shattered*, however, *Backstairs* is imbued with common markers of Expressionism, such as ethereal set design, as well as exaggerated acting and makeup that produce meaning and thereby enhance the simple story. This film is therefore experimental in its combination of the two seemingly disparate styles of Naturalism and Expressionism. For Lotte Eisner, the mixing of these two styles led to the film's aesthetic failure. She wrote, "Probably it is on account of a fundamental opposition between the Kammerspiele—intimate, psychological—and the techniques of Expressionism that this work [. . .] today appears disappointing."[26] The problem with Eisner's assessment here lies in her assertion that the aesthetic style must remain pure. She made no attempt to locate any possible meaning arising from the combination of styles. Patrice Petro has also countered Eisner's dismissal of *Backstairs* by understanding it as a melodrama. She argued, "The stark contrast between visual styles and gestural support not only provides [*Backstairs*] with a melodramatic 'look' but also with a contemplative mode of looking almost demanded of the spectator."[27]

While the *Hinterhaus* (rear house) setting is a classic theme of literary Naturalism, the *mise-en-scène*, gesticulated acting (especially Kortner's), and lighting provide the Expressionist flavor. These areas reflect the authorship of Paul Leni most visibly in the film. Even though Lotte Eisner minimizes Leni's mark on *Backstairs*, early reviewers were quick to credit him for the film's memorable visual style.[28] A critic for *Der Film* noted how quotidian objects are instilled with meaning:

> Paul Leni as pictorial designer created display-worthy objects of artistic composition and design. Noteworthy is the unique and meaningful role objects play without obtrusive symbolism. An alarm clock, a hand bell, a bell pull, even the everyday work in the kitchen, aid the picture.[29]

Even more interesting than the objects mentioned in this review are the backstairs in the film. The film's title immediately connotes *Hinterhaus* or rear house, a locale that carries a heavy association with German literary Naturalism. In 1889, Hermann Sudermann ushered in the Naturalist theater with his breakthrough drama *Honor* (*Die Ehre*), based upon the inter-class encounters of the *Vorderhaus* or front house and the *Hinterhaus*. The class constellation is based upon architecture in Berlin where wealthier upper-middle-class families occupied the apartments facing the street, while the lower classes lived in the spaces facing the courtyard.

Backstairs brings nuance to a Naturalist setting with its use of Expressionism. The establishing shot of the staircase in the opening sequence of the film orientates the audience in this space before any of the anonymous figures are introduced. Staircases are frequent settings to scenes in Weimar cinema. In *The Haunted Screen*, Lotte Eisner explored the significance of staircases in German film. For her, the architectural design of the staircases caused actors to create certain movements that she argued were Expressionistic. She attributed this "movement-restricting architecture" to Paul Leni, who used it in his 1924 film *Waxworks* (*Das Wachsfigurenkabinett*) and later in his American film *The Man Who Laughs* (1928).[30] Moreover, spaces such as hallways and staircases are ideal for the chiaroscuro lighting so heavily associated with filmic Expressionism.

Staircases for Eisner, however, had a deeper, mystical meaning in German culture. She wrote, "Remembering the German fascination with *Werden* (becoming) rather than *Sein* (being), it could perhaps be granted nevertheless that their staircases represent an upward movement, the degrees of which are represented by the stairs themselves."[31] Leopold Jessner was known for the use of staircases in his theater productions, and he brought this association to his *Backstairs* directorial debut. The so-called "Jessner stairs" ("Jessnertreppen") have been interpreted to contain symbolic meaning, representing the psychology of the figures or signifying social differences.[32]

In the case of *Backstairs*, the staircase is the architectural component that indicates social divisions among the characters, but it also orients the spectator into the lower-class milieu. As opposed to the front stairs that were used by the owners of a residence, the backstairs were designated for the servant staff to be unseen in their coming and going. In the opening sequence, an establishing shot of the staircase is followed by a cut to a door at the top of it, before another shot shows the sleeping Henny Porten. Although the profession of Porten's character, a *Dienstmädchen* or housekeeper, situates her among the lower classes, her employer is of the haute bourgeoisie. Porten is shown preparing and cleaning up after lavish dinner parties that are held by her employer. Her social separation from her employers is stressed through spatial configurations and framing techniques. The housekeeper is relegated to the kitchen quarters at work while her employers indulgingly entertain their guests in an adjoining room. The identification with the lower-class housekeeper provides a Naturalist grounding to the story. Reversely, the lack of focus on the wealthy employers inhibits identification with them. The film employs certain techniques to alienate the audience from them; they are seldom present in the frame, and, when they are actually shown, their ghoulish makeup gives them a ghost-like appearance directly at odds with the housekeeper's wholesome look.

Beyond its sociological purpose in the film, the staircase also has a narrative function. While the housekeeper resides with her employer in the upstairs apartment, the postman inhabits a dingy courtyard-side basement apartment. From his abode he can secretly set his gaze upon the housekeeper when she comes out onto the rear balcony. In order to deliver mail to the wealthy bourgeois apartment, he must climb the stairs. The staircase, therefore, separates him from his object of desire. The wholesome nature of the housekeeper, who is often shown diligently performing her tasks in well-lighted rooms, provides a contrast to the postman, whose dark and crippled appearance is articulated through Fritz Kortner's body movements and facial expressions.[33] The staircase therefore spatially presents a chasm between the two contrasting figures in a hierarchy where the Naturalistic and virtuous is located spatially above the dark, Expressionistic and evil-minded.

While the acting in the film can generally be credited to Leopold Jessner, there is no doubt that the visual setting of *Backstairs* is a clear product of Paul Leni. A writer for *Der Kinematograph* noted, "Paul Leni supports [Jessner] through the somewhat expressionist architecture and the rear houses, together forming the courtyard, make an especially deep impression."[34] It was Leni who took the Naturalist setting of the *Kammerspielfilm* and imbued it with a certain Expressionistic aura. The quotidian story of the film, as well as the rear-courtyard milieu, would more readily suggest that the film would require a realist backdrop. Leni's design, however, upends these expectations with the architecture in the film that deliberately aims to create an otherworldly mood rather than attempting to reconstruct reality.

The design of his next German productions, such as *Waxworks*, went even further in this direction. In early film, set design rose to prominence, attracting audiences with the spectacle of elaborate sets. However, by the late 1910s, Hollywood began to implement techniques in order to subdue the cluttering of sets for the purpose of narrative clarity. German film, by contrast, continued the practice of producing elaborate sets long after. As Kristin Thompson noted, "In Germany, attractive sets, whether they were used for epics or ordinary locales, remained the ideal."[35] Therefore the prioritization of set design in Germany allowed filmmakers such as those like Paul Leni who specialized in film architecture to earn a reputation for their work. The recognition of these artists can be seen by their inclusion in the Great Berlin Art Exhibition (Grosse Berliner Kunstausstellung) in the early 1920s.

In 1924, Leni penned an essay in which he explained his conception of how set design functions in film. This short piece has the programmatic tone of a kind of manifesto of film architects for the primacy of studio films and their set designs. According to Leni, the public recognition that film architects were receiving was evidence that set design had finally reached the point at which they were publicly recognized as artists rather than studio craftsmen, who put their own aesthetic mark on the film's character and style.[36] Summing up the task of the film architect, Leni wrote:

> It is clear, then, that what is asked of the film architect is certainly not to construct "pretty" spaces. He is asked to penetrate beyond the surface to reach the heart of the matter. He ought to create a mood, even if the only tools at his disposal are those simple, everyday objects we can all see lying around us. And this is precisely what makes him an artist. Were this not the case, there would be no need for an architect in film in the first place and no reason whatsoever why a talented apprentice carpenter could not replace him.[37]

Although set design played an increasingly important role in Leni's films, his definition of what a set designer ought to add to a film is readily apparent in *Backstairs*. Not only are objects that play a role in the film, such as those of a clock and staircase, everyday, they play a significant role in setting the mood and helping to narrate the story. In order to do this, techniques must be employed such as lighting technology that allows for the creation of such things as cityscapes in studios. The key for Leni was not to produce a perfect one-to-one image of reality, but rather the film architect must "accentuate and give shape to the most essential and characteristic features of a natural object in such a way that they lend the resulting image a particular style and tone."[38] Leni did not mention Expressionism in this essay, but he did write that "the creation of believable natural objects is especially important to the success of films that take place in an unreal world."[39] For Leni, then, a mixture of the natural and the unnatural had the greatest potential for film.

In using the familiar, Naturalistic setting of the *Kammerspiel*, aspects of the unnatural are incrementally introduced in *Backstairs* that take on greater significance as the film culminates in tragedy. From the Naturalistic, well-lighted opening scene of the housekeeper comfortably sleeping in bed to her suicide at the end of the film, the Naturalistic scenes and settings give off a sense of equilibrium and harmony, while the unnatural elements disrupt this feeling. By the end of the film things are literally shown in a different light. Using chiaroscuro lighting, people who did not seem significant are presented in

Figure 3.2 Henny Porten (Housekeeper) in the back stairwell.

such manner as to enhance the mood. This is seen when the postman slays the returned lover in his lower-level apartment. Moments before, the postman's apartment was a space in which the housekeeper and her new love interest sat down to an intimate dinner. Following the return of her lover, she is locked out of the apartment. The neighbors come to aid the lover in the ensuing struggle between the two, but the next cut shows the postman behind the frame of the opened door, wielding an axe with the slain lover on the ground. In this tableau composition, the disembodied hands in white shirt cuffs extend from the sides of the heavily lighted frame, grabbing the murderer, who is dressed in black. Likewise, a cross-cut during the struggle reveals the appearance of the housekeeper's employers, who are watching the happenings in the rear courtyard from their upstairs apartment. Their ghost-like appearance further adds to the mood of horror at the end of the film. This shot cuts to another tableau of the housekeeper against the wall of the building, visibly traumatized by the events. The space of the otherwise empty courtyard is now populated by many who threateningly gaze upon her as she must cross it in her trance-like state in order to access the backstairs to her abode. The architecture of the set design in this shot takes on new meaning that adds to the newly unfolded events. With faces in the windows and others occupying its space, it suddenly seems claustrophobic. As the housekeeper reaches the backstairs and ascends them one final time, they appear to be vastly more frightening and detailed than when they were first shown in the opening sequence. The shot this time is taken from the landing below the level inhabited by her employers. The shot begins with her face at the bottom of the frame as she slowly climbs the stairs, bracing her shaken self along the way. She gradually becomes whole with her shadow cast upon the wall. A high angled shot of the door to her living quarters shows her employers stepping out to throw her belongings down the staircase, signaling her loss of job and home. A long take shows her upon the landing with the wall in the background. The strange coloring of the stairwell—an almost swirling pattern of dark and light—makes for a near-perfect metaphor for her confused and troubled state. Another medium close-up shows her tormented face directed upward at her former employer's door, a further indication of her psychological condition. With nowhere to go and nobody to whom she can turn, she continues her ascent of the stairs past her employer's door to the top of the building. Her somnambulistic pace and the jagged, geometric architecture at the top of the building readily call to mind the dream-like world that Expressionist artists Hermann Warm, Walter Röhrig, and Walter Reimann created in the most famous of all Expressionist films, *The Cabinet of Dr. Caligari*. With the housekeeper now perched on the edge of the roof, the shot cuts to the courtyard and its inhabitants below. As they all bend in one sudden and synchronized motion, it is apparent that she has jumped from the building to her death.

In the final sequence of *Backstairs*, Leni's set design, Carl Mayer's storyline, and the acting work together to produce a general sense of "The Uncanny," a concept that Freud examined in his famous 1919 essay of the same name. At the beginning of the film, we are introduced to the humble environment in which the housekeeper lives and works; she does not own much, but she has steady employment and is content in her relationship with her workman lover. She feels abandoned when he disappears without a trace. Only later do we learn that the lover had written to her from the hospital but the postman intercepted the letters. Her state of sorrow and heartbreak is soon replaced by a sense of normalcy when the postman fills the role of her missing lover. The latter's return shatters this false sense of equilibrium. Freud believed that the uncanny "is an actual repression of some content of thought and a return of this repressed content."[40] An otherworldly, Expressionist aesthetic replaces the familiar Naturalistic world of the rear courtyard when the vanished lover returns. Freud explained that the meaning of the German word *unheimlich* (uncanny) is the opposite of *heimlich* (homely) and equates to that which is not familiar.[41] The homely atmosphere of the housekeeper's world takes on an unfamiliar and alienating aura with the return of her original lover. In the sequence following the return of her lover, *mise-en-scène* and acting work to emphasize her shattered state of mind upon this revelation. In the rear courtyard she is confronted by her lover, who seemingly pleads with her to hear him out. Their state of mind in this encounter is emphasized by their shadows cast upon the wall behind them. She slowly approaches him as if to embrace, but then stops only to hang her head in sorrow. The use of shadows accentuates the space that remains between them and the difference in size stresses her reduced feelings of self-image with her head turned downward.

This melodrama takes a nightmarish turn in a subsequent scene with the final fight between the jealous postman and the lover. With the door to the postman's apartment locked, the housekeeper is unable to intervene. A cut to a long shot shows the housekeeper in a state of panic in the dark and empty space of the rear courtyard, which calls the attention of her employers, whose makeup gives them a supernatural appearance. Curiously, this is the first time that we see them acknowledging the housekeeper's existence. In previous scenes the housekeeper performs her duties in spaces apart from the employers and their social gatherings. We see her preparing refreshments for them in the kitchen and cleaning up after a dinner in the dining room. It is if they exist on two separate planes of reality, and the Naturalistic look of the housekeeper compared with the spectral appearance of her employers heightens this. By summoning their attention in the final sequence, the housekeeper has crossed the divide of class and reality. A medium iris shot provides a portrait of the family of three, who appear perturbed by this interruption from the housekeeper—an ominous indication of what is in store for the housekeeper.

Backstairs begins with the mundane but harmonious life of Henny Porten's figure, but her everyday existence is transformed into a nightmare due to circumstances out of her control. Other masterpieces of early post-World War I German cinema, such as Wiene's *Dr. Caligari* and F. W. Murnau's *Nosferatu*, are also about a disruption of reality. In 1921 moviegoers could certainly relate to the theme of one's world being turned upside down by a traumatic event. World War I was a caesura of unprecedented proportions that shook all facets of German society. New aesthetic forms were required to represent a new reality that was littered with the carnage and aftermath of the war. *Backstairs*, while bearing traits such as Naturalism and the star power of Henny Porten that predate the war, also makes use of postwar styles such as that found in the Expressionistic set design of Paul Leni which destabilizes the atmosphere, providing an element of horror to an otherwise mundane setting.

Among many challenges, the returning home of soldiers, dead or alive, was a ubiquitous subject during the war years and immediate postwar years. If what Freud argues is true – that the concept of the uncanny goes beyond the mere notion of that which is unfamiliar and can also pertain to that which is familiar – then the uncanny certainly abounded in the early years after the war. Soldiers returned home to find that the familiar had become foreign. Divorces soared as the separation and experiences turned husbands and wives into strangers. Husbands returned home from the field to find that their wives had moved on from them in their absence, while wives, not hearing from their husbands, repressed the memory of their thought-to-be-dead husbands. Film scholar Anton Kaes wrote in his landmark study of the impact of World War I on Weimar cinema, "The home front was often ambivalent about the sudden return of a soldier believed to be dead."[42] Divorce records from the time show the toll that the war exacted upon families and relationships.[43] Many literary texts and films dealt with the issue of the return of a soldier who finds that the home he knew was no longer the same. Leonhard Frank's 1926 novella *Karl und Anna*, made into a film in 1928 by Joe May titled *Homecoming* (*Heimkehr*), tells such a story. In the film Richard and Karl are prisoners of war. During their long days together Richard tells Karl everything about his beloved wife Anna and how he longs to be with her again. The two decide to escape together and while doing so Richard is recaptured. Karl makes it back to Germany where he meets Anna. Feelings begin to develop between the two, so much so that, when Richard finally returns, he realizes that this is no longer his home.

Backstairs, with its thematization of homecoming and the unnatural, is also certainly a reference to the soldier's experience after the war even though it makes no mention of it. As Kaes put it, "The film does not specify the nature of [the lover's] accident, but it did not have to: in 1921 a long absence and severe injury alluded to the war."[44] The housekeeper's ability to move on after her lover's absence suggests her coming to terms with the fact that he had perished. For many who went missing in the field, families held out hope for their survival and eventual return, "but for most people such hope faded rapidly."[45] The crippled state of the postman can also be read as a trace of the damage that the war had exacted upon society. One need only think of the Expressionist painter Otto Dix's many works depicting the abstract, deformed bodies of former soldiers in the postwar years. Likewise, Fritz Kortner's twisted and jerky motions suggest a body that had become un-whole, unnatural—an aspect of the uncanny, to be sure. Add to this his twisted psychology, desire to be loved despite his deformed physical appearance, and his jerky movements, one might furthermore be inclined to interpret this as a sign of shell shock, a discourse that was born out of World War I. As the World War I historian Jay Winter wrote, "Whatever the degree of disability they suffered, and however they were cared for, the presence in towns and villages, in cities and on the land, of thousands of shell-shocked men raises important issues for our understanding of the war."[46] Traumatized men returned home after the war forever altered by their experience. As the home front became aware of the horrors that soldiers were exposed to, the public wondered not only what these men had seen but also what they had done. If one had killed on the battlefield, surely they could kill again. In many ways, Fritz Korten's depiction of the postman is a nightmarish confirmation of this suspicion.

In conclusion, the film *Backstairs* is an example of Weimar film in which the styles of Naturalism and Expressionism work together to produce meaning. The *Kammerspiel*, with its typical lower-class milieu, realistic décor, Naturalistic acting, and sober story, relies on many of the factors that constitute the style of Naturalism. In Leopold Jessner and Paul Leni's *Backstairs*, however, this atmosphere is interrupted by the unnatural with the inclusion of specific aspects of Expressionism such as the set design and the acting. The stylistic intrusion of the unnatural into an otherwise natural setting assists to propel a film that forgoes the use of intertitles, telling the story of a familiar world that has become alienating. When *Backstairs* appeared in 1921, the world for many had become otherworldly due to the mass-scale devastation of human life and the disappearance of the world that existed before the war.

NOTES

1. Thomas Elsaesser, *Weimar Cinema and After: Germany's Historical Imaginary* (London: Routledge, 2000), 21.
2. For more on the legacy of Eisner and Kracauer, see Elsaesser, *Weimar Cinema and After*; Dietrich Scheunemann (ed.), *Expressionist Film: New Perspectives* (Rochester, NY: Camden House, 2003); and Anton Kaes, *Shell Shock Cinema: Weimar Culture and the Wounds of War* (Princeton, NJ: Princeton University Press, 2011).

3. Dietrich Scheunemann, "Activating the Differences: Expressionist Film and Early Weimar Cinema," in *Expressionist Film*, 2.
4. Scheunemann, "Activating the Differences," 4.
5. Lotte H. Eisner, *The Haunted Screen: Expressionism in German Cinema and the Influence of Max Reinhardt*, trans. Roger Greaves (Berkeley: University of California Press, 1969), 10.
6. For more about Porten's film star status, see Joseph Garncarz, "The Star System in Weimar Cinema," in *The Many Faces of Weimar Cinema: Rediscovering Germany's Filmic Legacy*, ed. Christian Rogowski (Rochester, NY: Camden House, 2010), 116–33.
7. "Eine Wohltätigkeitsaufführung," *Der Film* 50 (1921): 58.
8. Film-Kritik, "*Hintertreppe*: Berliner Erstaufführung," *Film-Kurier*, December 12, 1921.
9. Helga Belach, "Die Produzentin," in *Henny Porten, der erste deutsche Filmstar, 1890–1960*, ed. Helga Belach (Berlin: Haude und Spener, 1986), 72.
10. Belach, "Die Produzentin," 74. This and all subsequent translations are my own unless marked otherwise.
11. Helmut Regel, "Zur Produktionsgeschichte der Filme *Die Geier-Wally* und *Hintertreppe*," in Belach, *Henny Porten*, 78.
12. Oskar Kalbus, *Vom Werden deutscher Filmkunst: Der stumme Film* (Altona-Bahrenfeld: Cigaretten-Bilderdienst, 1935), 73.
13. Siegfried Kracauer, *From Caligari to Hitler: A Psychological History of the German Film* (Princeton, NJ: Princeton University Press, 1947), 97.
14. A. F., "*Hintertreppe*," *Der Film* 51 (1921): 48.
15. Kalbus, *Vom Werden deutscher Filmkunst*, 73.
16. Alfred Kerr, "Aufstieg im Film," *Berliner Tageblatt*, December 12, 1921.
17. "Hintertreppe," *Der Kinematograph*, January 1, 1922.
18. Hans Pander, "Zwischentitel," *Der Bildwart: Blätter für Volksbildung* 1 (January–February 1923), reprinted as "Intertitles," in *The Promise of Cinema: German Film Theory 1907–1933*, ed. Anton Kaes, Nicholas Baer, and Michael Cowan (Oakland: University of California Press, 2016), 489.
19. Kracauer, *From Caligari to Hitler*, 97.
20. Ellen Risholm, "Formations of the Chamber: A Reading of *Backstairs*," in *Peripheral Visions: The Hidden Stages of Weimar Cinema*, ed. Kenneth S. Calhoon (Detroit: Wayne State University Press, 2001), 125–6.
21. Eisner, *Haunted Screen*, 177.
22. The theater of Max Reinhardt had a heavy impact on Weimar cinema as a whole. Some notable film figures who trained with Reinhardt before making their way to film include F. W. Murnau, Wilhelm Dieterle, Paul Wegener, Werner Krauss, and Emil Jannings to name but a few.
23. Kalbus, *Vom Werden deutscher Filmkunst*, 73.
24. Risholm, "Formations of the Chamber," 121.
25. Risholm, "Formations of the Chamber," 132.
26. Eisner, *Haunted Screen*, 179.
27. Patrice Petro, *Joyless Streets: Women and Melodramatic Representation in Weimar Germany* (Princeton, NJ: Princeton University Press, 1989), 175.
28. Petro, *Joyless Streets*, 175.
29. A. F., "Hintertreppe," 48.
30. Eisner, *Haunted Screen*, 119.
31. Eisner, *Haunted Screen*, 121.
32. Eisner, *Haunted Screen*, 122.
33. A comparison to the appearance and unsteady movement of the postman can be found in the figure of the cashier in Karlheinz Martin's classic Expressionist film *From Morn to Midnight* (*Von morgens bis mitternachts*, 1920). This character also commits a crime.

34. "Hintertreppe," *Der Kinematograph*.
35. Kristin Thompson, *Herr Lubitsch Goes to Hollywood: German and American Film After World War I* (Amsterdam: Amsterdam University Press, 2005), 57.
36. Paul Leni, "Baukunst im Film," *Der Kinematograph*, August 4, 1924, reprinted as "Architecture in Film," in Kaes et al., *Promise of Cinema*, 499.
37. Leni, "Baukunst im Film," 501.
38. Leni, "Baukunst im Film," 500.
39. Leni, "Baukunst im Film," 500.
40. Sigmund Freud, "The Uncanny," in *The Standard Edition of the Complete Psychological Works of Sigmund Freud, Volume 17 (1917–1919): An Infantile Neurosis and Other Works*, ed. James Strachey (London: Hogarth Press and the Institute of Psycho-analysis, 1955), 248.
41. Freud, "The Uncanny," 219.
42. Kaes, *Shell Shock Cinema*, 117.
43. The set of records at the Landesarchiv Baden-Württemberg in Ludwigsburg shows various reasons for divorce during and directly after the war. Some records show that after several years separated by war, the couples had simply drifted apart, while other records give infidelity as a reason for divorce. One record even specifies that the wife had begun a relationship with the husband's brother while he was in the field. Divorce Papers from the District and Regional Court of Ellwangen. E 337. II. 602–55.
44. Kaes, *Shell Shock Cinema*, 118.
45. Jay Winter, *Sites of Memory, Sites of Mourning: The Great War in European Cultural History* (Cambridge: Cambridge University Press, 1995), 22.
46. Jay Winter, *Remembering War: The Great War Between Memory and History in the Twentieth Century* (New Haven, CT: Yale University Press, 2006), 54.

CHAPTER 4

Cinema Panopticum: Wax, Work, *Waxworks*

Erik Born

The wax museum <*Panoptikum*> a manifestation of the total work of art. The universalism of the nineteenth century has its monument in the waxworks. Pan-opticon: not only does one see everything, but one sees it in all ways.[1]

In 1924, when Paul Leni's long-awaited film about a collection of wax effigies finally premiered after three years of production delays, one of the few places left to view waxworks in Berlin was in the cinema.[2] *Waxworks* (*Das Wachsfigurenkabinett*) presents cinema as the legitimate heir to the city's moribund waxworks tradition, which was exemplified by the closing of Castan's Panopticum (1869–1922) and the Passage-Panoptikum (1888–1923). In anticipation of the Berlin premiere, there was even an "invitation to visit Paul Leni's *Waxworks* in the Ufa Theatre at Kurfürstendamm on Thursday, 13 November 1924, 7:00 pm."[3] Patterned after beloved guidebooks for wax museums, the document provided a very concise "guide to Paul Leni's waxworks" with small vignettes of a romantic pair (Wilhelm Dieterle, Olga Belajeff) next to drawings of three wax figures: Ivan the Terrible (Conrad Veidt), Jack the Ripper (Werner Krauss), and Harun al-Rashid (Emil Jannings).[4] To reanimate their well-known stories, Leni's historical anthology film updated Expressionist tropes of wax effigies, mechanical automata, and living puppets with a more realistic setting at a modern funfair-cum-workplace. As an allegory of media change, *Waxworks* suggests that film not only superseded waxworks but also absorbed its visual techniques and transformed them into its own immersive displays.[5]

Conceptualized in 1920, shot in 1923, and released in 1924, *Waxworks* coincided with the German film industry's brief flirtation with Expressionist cinema and its turn to a mode of realism known as New Objectivity.[6] Upon its initial release, the now-canonical film received mixed reviews and was dismissed by some as a belated attempt to cash in on the success of the only marketable exemplar of Expressionist cinema. "*Waxworks* is Paul Leni's *Caligari* film," Herbert Ihering asserted in one widely cited review. "A latecomer. A *Stilfilm*."[7] A range of factors made comparisons unavoidable: the allusion to *The Cabinet of Dr. Caligari* (*Das Cabinet des Dr. Caligari*, 1920) in the original German title; the celebrity status of Werner Krauss (Dr. Caligari, Jack the Ripper) and Conrad Veidt (Cesare, Ivan the Terrible); the abstract set design, comparable fairground setting, deployment of a frame narrative, and crucial scenes featuring a wax figure as a deceptive stand-in for one of the main characters.[8] Seminal interpretations from Rudolf Kurtz, Siegfried Kracauer, and Lotte Eisner solidified *Waxworks*' position in the Weimar film canon, though they also made it seem like a nostalgic farewell to a dying tradition.

In this essay, my reading of *Waxworks* in the context of popular wax displays in Late Imperial Germany and the Weimar Republic seeks to correct this constitutive blind spot of the film's reception. At the time, several critics lamented the filmmakers' failure to explore the depths of their chosen topic, and, in subsequent years, few scholars have rectified this misperception.[9] At first glance, the film's evocation of the waxworks tradition may seem like an unpersuasive attempt to insinuate itself into the classical tradition of Pygmalion aesthetics, thereby elevating the wax figure and, by extension, film itself to the level of Romantic art. However, I argue that juxtaposing the decline of waxworks with the rise of Germany's national cinematic styles reveals another aspect of Leni's project. The fairground setting recalls the early cinematic discourse of "living images," and the creation of large-scale atmospheres through small-scale set designs returns the increasingly monumental medium of cinema to an earlier tradition of "small art" (*Kleinkunst*) in modernist theater and experimental cabaret.[10] Ultimately, the waxworks tradition provided many productive topoi for *Waxworks*' exploration of stillness and motion, surface and depth, and relations between foregrounds and backgrounds. It also raised questions about the collective labor of filmmaking, the distinction between manual and intellectual contributions, and the presumed undesirability of people and objects still in good working order.

Widely credited as either the last German Expressionist film or the first feature-length wax museum horror film, *Waxworks* needs to be understood as both a local product of Berlin film culture and part of a more global tradition of visual display. According to the period's terminology, Leni's achievement was understood as an "episodic film" (*Episodenfilm*), a popular form of early narrative cinema that presented distinct episodes within a unifying narrative frame. In particular, the framing narrative about an obsolescent fairground attraction updates the Pygmalion myth, *1001 Nights*, and German

Romanticism for film-obsessed modernity. When an aspiring poet (Wilhelm Dieterle) gets hired by a waxworks proprietor (John Gottowt) to write "startling stories" about a makeshift chamber of horrors, the author increasingly falls in love with his creation until it comes to life and threatens to destroy him. Simulating the no-longer-attainable wax museum experience, *Waxworks* creates immersive episodes featuring exemplary figures of pre-modernity, which are presented in succession with maximum variety, crisscrossing space and time. The first episode is a fantasy tale about Harun al-Rashid; the second a costume drama about Ivan the Terrible; and a planned third segment would have been an adventure about the brigand Rinaldo Rinaldini. However, the short concluding episode explodes the anthology form with the intrusion of Jack the Ripper into the narrative frame, thereby threatening the author who was composing these very stories in pursuit of the owner's daughter (Olga Belajeff). What started out as a leisurely night at the fairground quickly turns into a night at the office, followed by a night spent trapped in the wax museum, which ultimately resolves in a strange sort of "date night."

Ever since its original release, *Waxworks* has challenged categorical understandings of genre, authorship, cinematic style, and media change. Like many *Autorenfilme*, Leni's artistic, proto-auteur film continued the emerging industry's efforts to persuade the middle class to accept cinema as legitimate art. During production, Leni's constructions were exhibited at the Great Berlin Art Exhibition (Grosse Berliner Kunstausstellung), promoting the practice of set design as a modern art rather than a traditional handicraft. In anticipation of the premiere, advertisements repeatedly referred to the film's status as an artwork, and underscored Leni's "complete artistic direction" ("gesamte künstlerische Leitung").[11] Reinforcing the message from publicity materials, contemporary reviews foregrounded only one aspect of Leni's multifaceted background, subsuming his previous work in illustration, advertising graphics, and interior design under the reductive label "the painter Leni."[12] At the same time, however, the filmmakers' own attempt to credit their collective production—with technical direction (*Regisseur*) attributed to Leni and direction of the actors (*Spielleiter*) to Leo Birinski—had an unintended effect. Eager to identify a single authorial figure, critics including Joseph Roth and Walter Gottfried Lohmeyer created mocking portmanteaux of their names and credits: "Mister Lenibirinski, together with Mister Birinskileni (the former the *Regisseurspielleiter*, the latter the *Spielleiterregisseur*)."[13]

In recent years, many of these assumptions about *Waxworks* have been revised in scholarship addressing the film's difficult categorical fit within Weimar Cinema.[14] Still, these productive, revisionist readings of the film, which tend to emphasize its self-reflexivity as an artistic statement about media change, could be connected further to conventions governing the waxworks tradition. The longstanding debate about *Waxworks*' status as a "horror film" would clearly benefit from considering the fact that only some wax effigies elicited fear, while many others provoked laughter, desire, and a wide range of emotions.[15] In a wax museum, the juxtaposition of historical figures who, like those in *Waxworks*, would not otherwise belong together was another proven technique for making different moments present simultaneously.[16] Lastly, viewing *Waxworks* through waxworks should nuance now-dominant readings of the film as an allegory of media competition:[17] while the combatants in the *Kino-Debatte* of the 1910s–20s were literature, theater, and cinema, *Waxworks* negotiates a different vernacular tradition of carnivalesque advertising, the artisanal construction of lifelike figures, and their mediated display with both visual techniques and oral narrations.[18]

Before the emergence of cinema, one of the most popular attractions of European modernity was the public display of wax effigies, which were initially shown in itinerant show booths and eventually institutionalized into the permanent space of the wax museum.[19] Like the tradition of *tableaux vivants*, the wax tableau was usually staged around one particularly poignant moment in a well-known narrative, which seemed to suggest the entire backstory. In a wax museum, multiple wax effigies were exhibited in thematic rooms dedicated, for instance, to famous royals, nude female bodies, ethnographic collections, anatomical figures, and, almost without exception, a gallery of criminals commonly known as the "chamber of horrors." To some extent, the Victorian logic of repression determined the subjects of wax sculptures—putting on display what was excluded from polite bourgeois society, whether the sacred aristocratic body, the abject sexual body, the abnormal criminal, or the exoticized other. With eclectic displays of wax effigies alongside mechanical automata, historical replicas, patriotic mementos, medical curiosities, ethnographic objects, and optical devices, the wax museum was truly, as film historian Mark Sandberg puts it, a "school for voyeurs."[20] In particular, the wax effigies in a chamber of horrors demanded physiognomic scrutiny, since the displays did not depict crimes but rather their perpetrators. Ultimately, the uncanny atmosphere of a wax museum, like that of *Waxworks*, encouraged spectators to enter into an immersive environment constructed out of costumes, architectural designs, and narrative context.[21]

Around 1900, there were many parallels among waxworks and cinema before the younger medium parted ways with the older one over the course of the interwar period.[22] Although they were initially a favored site for the exhibition of cinematic technology, wax museums gradually failed to attract visitors for a variety of reasons.[23] To be sure, the decisive factors for the closing of Berlin's two main waxworks during the years of *Waxworks*' production were probably inflation and the aging collections.[24] However, their demise was frequently attributed to a different culprit. As Karlernst Knatz exclaimed in February 1922, "This art is dying of cinema-itis! Waxen puppetry has been on the decline ever since the most uncanny aspects of life have become a reality on the movie screen."[25] On the occasion of one wax museum's closing two weeks later, the *Frankfurter Zeitung* would ask the rhetorical question, "Who killed Castan['s Panopticum]?" Only to answer, "Film, of course."[26] *Waxworks* mobilizes this widespread rhetoric of the death of waxworks and incorporates many of its conventions regarding the exhibition of lifelike figures.

What initially attracted the filmmakers to the topic, which had been popular in early cinema and gained currency with the closing of Berlin's wax museums, remains unknown. The completed film, which today exists only as a fragment, reveals competing traces of Leni's Baroque, orientalist, varieté aesthetic and screenwriter Henrik Galeen's gothic, romanticist, film art ambitions. Leni's original vision for the film, evident in an atmospheric landscape sketch for "The Six Nights of Harun al-Rashid" from May 1920, conflated the Arabic tradition of *1001 Nights* with then-popular stagings of India.[27] By 1921, initial advertisements for what was to be the first production of Paul-Leni-Film GmbH showed three additional pre-modern figures with their exoticized weapons of choice: Harun's scimitar, Ivan's whip, Rinaldo's dagger, and Jack's bare hands. A crucial turning point for the stagnating production came on August 5, 1922, when Leni lost a lawsuit forbidding Galeen from selling two manuscripts, one entitled "Panoptikum" and the other "Wachsfigurenkabinett." As security, Leni acquired the world filming rights to Gustav Meyrink's novella *Das Wachsfigurenkabinett* (1908), but eventually retained little more than the title and returned to one of Galeen's scripts in July 1923 during initial filming at the May-Film-Atelier in Berlin-Weissensee.

With the production of *Waxworks* stagnating in late 1922, Leni's collaboration on an experimental "designer cabaret" called "The Gondola" ("Die Gondel") came to quicker fruition.[28] Drawing on both his earlier stage work and his monumental sets for Joe May, Leni's experimental cabaret designs tended toward colorful, fanciful, ornamental constructions. Herwarth Walden reviewed one of the most memorable numbers: "The public, which loves to live in the foreground, is painted into the background. As a result, there's nothing left for the three dancing girls [. . .] than to dance facing the background."[29] During this particular cabaret routine, the dancers would act out the "Tiller Girls" in slow motion, thereby making the "dance-like aspects of these typical movements intensely visible again."[30] While Leni's delight in rhythm, movement, and visual puzzles foreshadows his more avant-garde Rebus films of the mid-1920s,[31] his cabaret was also a training ground for the film in progress.[32] Ultimately, the gondola motif suggested an imaginary voyage, or, in Hans Reimann's words, an "outing into the land of dreams."[33] It was particularly evident in a planned establishing sequence for *Waxworks*, documented in publicity material and Galeen's script, where the poet gets knocked unconscious from a fairground gondola ride, marking his passage from the real world to the fantasy world.

Speaking to Leni's project of re-enchanting urban modernity, Galeen's script was situated more directly within the German tradition of writings about dolls, automata, and waxworks.[34] In German Romanticism, the wax effigy had been a central figure of the uncanny in Jean Paul's *The Invisible Lodge* (*Die unsichtbare Loge*, 1791–3), *Hesperus* (1792–5), and *Titan* (1797–1803); Bonaventura's *The Night Watches* (*Nachtwachen*, 1804); and Friedrich Laun's *The Wax Figure* (*Die Wachsfigur*, 1818), among many others.[35] While some of these narratives updated the Pygmalion tradition where a woman is the object of an artist's devotion, most of the wax effigies in German Romanticism, like those in *Waxworks*, were created in the likeness of male figures—an expression of each period's crisis of masculinity and national identity.[36] Paradigmatically, one of the characters in E. T. A. Hoffmann's "The Automata" ("Die Automate," 1814), preparing for a visit to the renowned "Mechanical Turk"—perhaps embodied in *Waxworks* by the chess-playing Vizier (Paul Biensfeldt)—relates a "horrible, eerie, shuddery feeling," and expresses contempt for its "mechanical imitation of human motions."[37] As a double of the male author, protagonist, or narrator, wax figures in German Romanticism tended to critique the processes of mechanization, commercialization, and industrialization, which were making the global market into the main criterion for national artistic success.

If the wax figure around 1800 frequently presented a double of either the contemporary male protagonist or the object of his desire, wax figures a century later usually represented historical figures, reflecting both the difficulty of identification with the dying tradition and changing conditions of mass production. Around 1900, waxworks once again became a popular subject of anti-Naturalist literature, from Oskar Panizza's 1890 story "Wachsfigurenkabinett" to Meyrink's *Wachsfigurenkabinett*. In early German fantasy films, neo-Romantic stories related to *Waxworks* can be found in Richard Oswald's *Tales of Hoffmann* (*Hoffmanns Erzählungen*, 1916) and *Uncanny Stories* (*Unheimliche Geschichten*, 1919); Ernst Lubitsch's *The Doll* (*Die Puppe*, 1919); and Karlheinz Martin's now-lost film *The House on the Moon* (*Das Haus zum Mond*, 1921), in which Fritz Kortner played "a waxworks maker à la E. T. A. Hoffmann."[38] However, one of the most relevant intertexts for *Waxworks* might actually be Bertolt Brecht and Erich Engel's *Mysteries of a Barbershop* (*Mysterien eines Frisiersalons*, 1923), a short film set partly at a Panopticum and featuring direct visual citations of two famous waxworks exhibits known as "The Curios" and "Buried Alive."[39] In my analysis, Leni's team aligned themselves with these related films through their use of a frame story and embedded narratives, but sought to distinguish their work through innovative studio set constructions, exemplified by the framing narrative's self-reflexive setting at a fairground waxworks.

In the narrative frame, the word "Panopticum" features prominently at the start of *Waxworks*, when the writer enters a fairground booth supplied with this label, and again at the end, when the word is superimposed over images of his fairground hallucination. Though located in a modern amusement park—presumably, the Berlin Lunapark—the film's main setting is an artisanal waxworks that is struggling to compete with the park's industrial attractions. Their bright lights, fast-moving rides, and other sensory stimuli are described vividly in Galeen's script: "Fairground. Mysterious lights, rotating lamps. Curves of light. A little car whooshes down the track. Gondolas swing on thin, glowing constructions. A carousel turns in the light behind fantastical silhouettes of the dark-black show booths."[40] In Leni et al.'s realization of this setting, Galeen's successive (diachronic) images are translated into a (synchronic) composite image, reminiscent of the carousel in Man Ray's avant-garde short *The Return to Reason* (*Le Retour à la Raison*, 1923). As Katrina Russell argues, this opening sequence announces *Waxworks*' main themes: modernity's attempt to create artificial realities and immersive environments to substitute leisure time for the brutalities of labor under capitalism. In particular, the setting at Berlin's Lunapark evokes the contradictions of (American) capitalist culture through the juxtaposition of moving crowds and whirling rides with the immobilized and disoriented (German) job-seeker.[41] Nevertheless, I would add that the world inside the tent equally recalls the Panoptica located in Berlin's Arcades, which can be read not only as a bourgeois space of conspicuous consumption, but also, in Siegfried Kracauer's words, as a "dark passageway" indicating modernity's own status as a transitional period situated precariously between the old and the new.[42]

After the opening sequence of *Waxworks* establishes the exterior setting in a modern amusement park, the remainder of the film moves into an interior environment more evocative of the pre-modern fairground tradition, and the main theme shifts somewhat abruptly from leisure to labor with the encounter between the young job-seeker and the aging waxworks proprietor. In the extant English-language version of the film, the intertitle containing the job ad flatly states, "WANTED—An imaginative writer for publicity work in a waxworks exhibition," the next intertitle specifies, "Apply, Booth 10, Luna Park," and the proprietor elliptically requests, "Can you write startling tales about these wax figures?" However, these intertitles fail to convey the punchline for the entire frame narrative, evident in a German phrase used so prominently in the film's promotional materials that it functioned like a tagline: "WANTED—A *poet* for an hourly wage" ("*Dichter* / gegen Stundenlohn gesucht").[43] Whereas Scheherazade told one story after the next to prolong her own life, the aspiring bard here hires himself out to the waxworks proprietor for an hourly rate. To truly take over the function of the elderly showman, who no longer appears capable of breathing life into the wax display with his own stories, the poet needs to elevate the intellectual labor of poetic composition into an acceptable form of manual labor. In the framing narrative, their generational struggle for control over the production of images is symbolized by each of their imposing working desks; and, in each episode, it takes the form of an arduous romantic quest that hinges on the validity of the young man's profession as a prerequisite for courting the owner's daughter (Olga Belajeff).

The twofold challenge for the poet in *Waxworks* consists in needing to please these two very different figures—the owner, with his stories, and his daughter, in them—a reflection of *Waxworks*' own attempt to reach both an older Wilhelmine audience and younger Weimar spectators. Over the course of the three episodes in their standard order, the storyteller becomes increasingly more confident at the job, not only proving his worth as a man but also fulfilling a fantasy of social mobility tied to romantic conquest.[44] In each episode, however, the powerful father-figure asserts himself sexually on the powerless daughter-figure, and attempts to capture, confine, and kill the hero, thereby threatening to destroy the fledgling courtship.[45] Despite some comedic moments, the male fantasy remains predicated on structural violence, and the symbolic images only slightly defer the force of otherwise abusive acts. For some viewers, Galeen's scripted sequence of violent deaths by beheading (Harun), torture (Ivan), gunshots (Rinaldo), and stabbing (Jack), may acquire a comedic tone through Leni's touch, thereby evoking the horrific/comedic *Urszene* of the wax museum.[46]

Despite these structural continuities and thematic progressions, which are far more evident in Galeen's script than in the extant version of the film, each episode in *Waxworks* also provides an enclosed narrative unit with its own unique design, characters, and atmosphere. While the fairground Panopticum would have been a small stage, Leni's innovative creation of additional cinematic space through atmospheric architecture makes the film appear to contain multiple worlds, more like the rooms in a wax museum. Just as the waxworks tradition provided lessons in deriving deeper aspects of character and narration from surface features like clothing and physiognomy, *Waxworks* presents an exercise in perceiving aesthetic differences within a seemingly unified whole: the decorative Naturalism of the Baghdad episode, the expressive light and shadow of the Kremlin episode, and the Caligariesque Expressionism of the fairground setting. Hardly arbitrary, the choice of characters for these settings thematizes Enlightenment reason and its "others" in the form of lust (Harun), madness (Ivan), and irrationality (Jack). Furthermore, each figure in the waxworks exhibits symptoms of automation, mechanization, and involuntary reflexes, which are underscored in the enigmatic miniature waxworks mechanism at the center of their wax tableau. At the end of its climactic sequence, when the poet feels stabbed by his creation but it turns out only to have been his pen, *Waxworks* ultimately presents "an evident if excessive moral," to borrow Thomas Elsaesser's brilliant characterization of another Weimar film, "about the process of alienated labor in which the product of one's own work confronts one in monstrous form."[47]

In retrospect, the maliciousness of objects in each of the previous episodes becomes immediately apparent: Harun's magic ring, Ivan's hourglass, Jack's knife, and the poet's pen all seek to undermine their bearers' desires. On a technical level, each object also facilitates lighting tricks and special effects on account of its capacity to reflect or refract light. In fact, *Waxworks* differed from its Expressionist predecessors mainly in its advanced simulations of cinematic space due to new lighting techniques. In contrast to the dramatic light and shadow of *Caligari*, where the famous chiaroscuro needed to be painted directly into the *mise-en-scène*, the lighting in *Waxworks* is far more dynamic. Thanks to technological advances like stronger spotlights and concentrated lighting systems, Leni's team was able to capture the eerie atmosphere of a waxworks at night, when flickering candlelight makes the objects seem to have a life of their own. In a wax museum, too, "the goal was to make mannequins appear as lifelike as possible, to seem as if they *might* return one's look, but not so alive as to threaten the viewer's command of the scene," as film historian Mark Sandberg put it.[48] Ultimately, the modern wax tableau, like the one in *Waxworks*, needed to seem almost within reach, though not close enough to reach back and touch the bourgeois observer, who was supposed to remain in command of the scene.

In the end, waxworks, as the consummate attraction for marrying the thrill of deathly specters with the security of the living gaze, may seem like one of the most unlikely places for a series of romantic encounters like those at the heart of *Waxworks*. However, even in the most terrifying chamber of horrors, there are still living bodies, there are still beating hearts. Correspondingly, Ernst Bloch's little-known essay "Body and Wax Figure" ("Leib und Wachsfigur," 1929) recounts a couple's visit to a waxworks in the Berlin Arcades, which makes them remember an early film featuring an "amorous couple locked in a Panopticum," probably not a reference to *Waxworks* but to one of the many popular wax shorts from the early cinema period.[49] Having overcome their initial trepidation, the couple finally enters the chamber of horrors, but the objects on display, like those in *Waxworks*, no longer terrify them, and the space instead seems like an anatomical museum where "even the puppets and vitrines had stopped gaping at the living world."[50] In anticipation of Bloch's notion of concrete utopia, the wax museum is described as the *locus classicus* for Enlightenment humanism's lost promises, unfulfilled potential, and utopian aspirations. Its obsolescence refers not only to the literal Arcades but also to the historicism and universalism of nineteenth-century humanism.

As an artistic statement about wax, work, and waxworks, Leni et al.'s film suggests a similar revision of common assumptions about obsolescence, in general, and the death of waxworks with the rise of cinema, in particular. Absorbing visual techniques from the waxworks tradition, *Waxworks* offers far more than a nostalgic farewell to a dying tradition, speaking to the multiple afterlives of presumably "dead media" after their own metempsychosis. The historical anthology film presents a collection not only of stories but also of styles, thereby exploring the conceptual duality of the Panopticum captured in Walter Benjamin's assertion that "not only does one see everything, but one sees it in all ways." Training modern urban vision, *Waxworks* encourages visual pleasure and provides several concrete lessons in picking out visual meaning from apparent chaos, which would have been crucial for negotiating the sensory overload of modern entertainment culture. Like the cinema, the modernity of the wax museum consisted in a double movement between scenic coherence and visual variety, between a dazzling whir of sensations and a desire for concentrated immersion in one distant scene. While visitors to a wax museum may tend to get absorbed in one convincing environment, after experiencing several scenes in succession, they will quickly start to experience visual fatigue, cumulative disorientation, and a lack of grounding. Ultimately, a visit to a naturalistic, almost hyper-real waxworks can turn into an uncanny, almost surreal experience, captured in the narrative frame of *Waxworks* and in Leni's anti-realist assertion that "the camera does not capture reality, but rather the reality of our experience," which is "so much deeper, more potent, more gripping than what we look at every day with our eyes."[51]

ACKNOWLEDGMENTS

I am grateful to Reanna Esmail, Carl Gelderloos, and Matthew Stoltz for reading a draft of this essay at a crucial stage, to the editors for seeing it through to completion, and to Angelika Friederici, Tara Hottman, and Katrina Russell for correspondence on the topic.

NOTES

1. Walter Benjamin, *The Arcades Project*, trans. Howard Eiland and Kevin McLaughlin (Cambridge, MA: Harvard University Press, 2002), 531.
2. Since there is not currently a German version of *Waxworks* in circulation, the basis for my analysis is the reconstructed English-language edition on the Kino International DVD.
3. Ludwig Greve, Heidi Westhoff, and Margot Pehle (eds.), *Hätte ich das Kino!: Die Schriftsteller und der Stummfilm* (Munich: Kösel Verlag, 1976), 324. The invitation is also available at <https://www.filmportal.de/node/9515/material/678551/>. Unless noted below, all translations are my own.
4. For popular wax museum guidebooks from Late Imperial Germany, see Angelika Friederici (ed.), *Castans Panopticum: Ein Medium wird besichtigt*, vol. 6 (Berlin: Verlag Carl-Robert Schütze, 2009), B4-1–B4-24.
5. In recent years, waxworks have undergone a revival, which has cast doubt on their presumed status as a "dead medium." For scholarship revising the notion that cinema

made waxworks obsolete, see Michelle E. Bloom, *Waxworks: A Cultural Obsession* (Minneapolis: University of Minnesota Press, 2003); Mark B. Sandberg, *Living Pictures, Missing Persons: Mannequins, Museums, and Modernity* (Princeton, NJ: Princeton University Press, 2003); and Uta Kornmeier, "Taken from Life: Madame Tussaud und die Geschichte des Wachsfigurenkabinetts vom 17. bis frühen 20. Jahrhundert" (PhD dissertation, Humboldt-Universität zu Berlin, 2002).

6. On *Waxworks*' production history, see Henrik Galeen, *Wachsfigurenkabinett: Drehbuch von Henrik Galeen zu Paul Lenis Film von 1923*, ed. Hans-Michael Bock (Munich: Text + Kritik, 1994), 115–38; and Hans-Michael Bock (ed.), *Paul Leni: Grafik, Theater, Film* (Frankfurt am Main: Deutsches Filmmuseum, 1986), 10–40; compare with Jürgen Kasten, "Episodic Patchwork: The Bric-à-Brac Principle in Paul Leni's *Waxworks*," in *Expressionist Film: New Perspectives*, ed. Dietrich Scheunemann (Rochester, NY: Camden House, 2003), 173–86.

7. Herbert Ihering, review of *Waxworks*, *Berliner Börsen-Courier*, November 14, 1924, reprinted in Bock, *Paul Leni*, 286. On the technical term *Stilfilm*, see Kristina Köhler, "Nicht der Stilfilm, sondern der Filmstil ist wichtig! Zu einer Debatte im Weimarer Kino," in *Filmstil: Perspektivierungen eines Begriffs*, ed. Julian Blunk, Dietmar Kammerer, Tina Kaiser, and Chris Wahl (Munich: Text + Kritik, 2016), 91–117.

8. For comparisons between *Caligari* and *Waxworks*, see, for instance, the reviews by Walter Gottfried Lohmeyer, Herbert Ihering, and Ernst Ulitzsch, reprinted in Bock, *Paul Leni*, 285–7; and excerpts from the anonymous reviews in *Die Filmwoche* (1924), *Der Kinematograph* (1924), and *Der Bildwart* (1925), reprinted in "Paul Leni, Dokumentation: Das Wachsfigurenkabinett im Kritik-Spiegel seiner Zeit," *Filmkundliche Mitteilungen* (March 1970), 4–5.

9. See, for instance, the reviews by "G-tz" in *Vossische Zeitung*, November 18, 1924; and Pinthus in *Das Tage-Buch* (1924).

10. On the discourse of living images, see Charles Musser, "A Cinema of Contemplation, a Cinema of Discernment: Spectatorship, Intertextuality and Attractions in the 1890s," in *The Cinema of Attractions Reloaded*, ed. Wanda Strauven (Amsterdam: Amsterdam University Press, 2006), 164–6; on the miniature in film architecture, see Herbert Richter-Lückian, "Monumentalität und Kleinarbeit," *Filmland: Deutsche Monatsschrift* 6 (April 1925): 45–50.

11. "Das Wachsfiguren-Kabinett," *Illustrierter Film-Kurier* 6, no. 39 (1924): 1–8.

12. While Leni's artistic pedigree was generally a boon to *Waxworks*, it also created some unwarranted expectations, as evident in Fränze Dyck-Schnitzer's dismissal of the film as the "long obsolete work of a gifted painter. A clever artisan. Not a film at all according to the laws of the moving image. Much more a sketch for the actors with ornate set designs [. . .] Scenes for the cabaret." See Fränze Dyck-Schnitzer, "Spaziergänge durch die Berliner Filmpremieren," *Berliner Volks-Zeitung*, November 18, 1924.

13. Walter Gottfried Lohmeyer, review of *Waxworks*, reprinted in Bock, *Paul Leni*, 286.

14. For revisionist interpretations of *Waxworks*, see Joel Westerdale's chapter in this volume; Jeffrey S. Timon, "This Divided Regime, Naive and Crafty . . .," *Qui Parle* 11, no. 1 (1997): 21–56; and Kasten, "Episodic Patchwork."

15. See Hannes König and Erich Ortenau, *Panoptikum: Vom Zauberbild zum Gaukelspiel der Wachsfiguren* (Munich: Isartal, 1962), 114–16. At the end of the decade, comedian Karl Valentin even created a short-lived Panopticum featuring many humorous objects.

16. See Kornmeier, "Taken from Life," 31–2; compare Pinthus's review: "One is left wondering: Why do both Tsar Ivan and Harun al-Rashid and their subjects all live together in this labyrinthine expressionist hell?" See Pinthus, *Das Tage-Buch*, 1672.

17. Francesco Pitassio, "Wachsfiguren? Zur Beziehung von Figur, Akteur und bildlicher Darstellung in *Das Wachsfigurenkabinett* von Paul Leni (D 1924)," *montage/av* (2007): 63–83; Westerdale's chapter in this volume; Ciro Inácio Marcondes, "Paul Leni's *Waxworks*: Writing Images from Silence, through Media and Philosophy," *Acta Universitatis Sapientiae, Film and Media Studies* 13, no. 1 (2017): 55–72.
18. Surprisingly, few scholars have considered the importance of waxworks for *Waxworks*. See, *en passant*, Bernhard Siegert, "Die Leiche in der Wachsfigur: Exzesse der Mimesis in Kunst, Wissenschaft und Medien," in *UnTot: Existenzen zwischen Leben und Leblosigkeit: Zwischen Leben und Leblosigkeit*, ed. Peter Geimer (Berlin: Kadmos, 2008), 134–5. The major exception is a draft manuscript: Katrina Russell, "Vivified Myths, Mortified Spectators: Simulacra, Sensation, and the Mise-en-Abîme in Paul Leni's *Das Wachsfigurenkabinett* (1924)."
19. See König and Ortenau, *Panoptikum*, 95; Stephan Oettermann, "Alles-Schau: Wachsfigurenkabinette und Panoptiken," in *Viel Vergnügen: Öffentliche Lustbarkeiten im Ruhrgebiet der Jahrhundertwende*, ed. Lisa Kosok and Mathilde Jamin (Essen: Ruhrland Museum, 1992), 45–9; and Sandberg, *Living Pictures*, 280, n. 25.
20. Sandberg, *Living Pictures*, 95–9.
21. See Kornmeier, "Taken from Life," 249–50.
22. See Friederici, *Castans Panopticum*, D9-21.
23. See Kornmeier, "Taken from Life," 252–4; and Friederici, *Castans Panopticum*, B4-1.
24. See Kornmeier, "Taken from Life," 252–4, 289; and Friederici, *Castans Panopticum*, D9-22–D9-23, F1-1–F1-15.
25. Karlernst Knatz, "Das sterbende Panoptikum," *Deutsche Allgemeine Zeitung*, February 5, 1922, reprinted in Friederici, *Castans Panopticum*, F1-7.
26. Arthur Eloesser, "Castans Ende," *Frankfurter Zeitung*, February 26, 1922, reprinted in Friederici, *Castans Panopticum*, F1-2.
27. On the basis of Leni's sketch, which closely resembled the stereotyped Rajah of Hagenbeck's India rather than the historical Abbasid Caliph, designer Otto Arpke produced a full-color illustration for *Lichtbildbühne*, reprinted in Galeen, *Wachsfigurenkabinett*, 115.
28. See Alan Lareau, "Designer Cabaret in 1920s Berlin: The Blue Bird and The Gondola," *Theatre History Studies* 14 (1994): 115–39.
29. Herwarth Walden, "Die Gondel von Berlin," *Der Sturm* 15 (June 1924): 114.
30. Walden, "Die Gondel," 114.
31. See Erica Tortolani's chapter in this volume.
32. The finances for Leni's cabaret came from the same group of Russian émigrés who owned *Waxworks*' production company Neptun-Film; executive direction of the cabaret was attributed to Henrik Galeen's brother-in-law, John Gottowt, who also starred in the film; and set designs were created by Leni, Ernst Stern, and César Klein, who also provided constructions for *Waxworks*.
33. Hans Reimann, "Exzentrisches Theater," *Die Weltbühne*, June 14, 1923, quoted and translated in Lareau, "Designer Cabaret," 127.
34. On the artificial figures of automata, wax effigies, and living puppets in German Romanticism, see the Afterword in Rudolf Drux, *Die lebendige Puppe: Erzählungen aus der Zeit der Romantik* (Frankfurt am Main: Fischer Taschenbuch Verlag, 1986).
35. See Marianne Vogel, "'Einfach Puppe!' Die Wachspuppe in der Wirklichkeit und in der Imagination in Romantik und Moderne," in *Textmaschinenkörper: Genderorientierte Lektüren des Androiden*, ed. Eva Kormann, Anke Gilleir, and Angelika Schlimmer (Amsterdam: Rodopi, 2006), 107–11.

36. See Thomas Elsaesser, "Weimar Cinema, Mobile Selves, and Anxious Males: Kracauer and Eisner Revisited," in Scheunemann, *Expressionist Film*, 50, 60.
37. E. T. A. Hoffmann, "Automata," in *The Best Tales of Hoffmann*, ed. and trans. E. F. Bleiler (New York: Dover, 1967), 81.
38. See Rudolf Kurtz, *Expressionism and Film*, ed. Christian Kiening and Ulrich Johannes Beil, trans. Brenda Benthien (New Barnet: John Libbey Publishing, 2016), 76.
39. See W. Stuart McDowell, "A Brecht-Valentin Production: *Mysteries of a Barbershop*," *Performing Arts Journal* 1, no. 3 (Winter 1977): 2–14. While *Waxworks* clearly cited the generic waxworks "torture chamber" (e.g. in promotional materials showing Ivan the Terrible wielding an axe above the bound poet), I have been unable to identify any visual citations of specific waxworks tableaux in the film, though this would be a very fruitful avenue for future scholarship on many silent films.
40. Galeen, *Wachsfigurenkabinett*, 17.
41. See Russell, "Vivified Myths."
42. Siegfried Kracauer, "Farewell to the Linden Arcade," in *The Mass Ornament: Weimar Essays*, ed. and trans. Thomas Y. Levin (Cambridge, MA: Harvard University Press, 1995), 337.
43. "Das Wachsfiguren-Kabinett"; Robert Huber, "Das Wachsfigurenkabinett," *Zappelnde Leinwand: Eine Wochenschrift fürs Kinopublikum* 5, no. 11 (1924); Galeen, *Wachsfigurenkabinett*, 17.
44. In Galeen's script, the poet's increasing aptitude is evident in the striking change from prose to verse. Galeen's alternate ending makes the topos of social mobility even more apparent in a scene where the protagonist shows up at a high society ball and his beloved fails to recognize him. See Galeen, *Wachsfigurenkabinett*, 25, 56, 74, 112.
45. Galeen's script makes the story unmistakable. In the first episode, the two lovers are courting; in the second, they are engaged; in the third, they are pregnant; and in the fourth, the quintessential *Frauenmörder* intrudes on their honeymoon.
46. See Sylvia Schimm and Peter Bexte, "Panische Optiken," in *Periphere Museen in Berlin*, ed. Michael Glasmeier (Berlin: Merve, 1992), 145–53.
47. Thomas Elsaesser, *Weimar Cinema and After: Germany's Historical Imaginary* (London: Routledge, 2000), 84.
48. Sandberg, *Living Pictures*, 95.
49. Ernst Bloch, "Leib und Wachsfigur," December 19, 1929, reprinted in *Der unbemerkte Augenblick: Feuilletons für die* Frankfurter Zeitung *1916–1934*, ed. Ralf Becker (Frankfurt am Main: Suhrkamp, 2007), 168.
50. Bloch, "Leib und Wachsfigur," 171.
51. Leni, "Baukunst im Film," 500.

CHAPTER 5

The Proto-Horror-Comedy: *Waxworks*

Joel Westerdale

Before Paul Leni's seminal horror-comedy *The Cat and the Canary* (1927) came *Waxworks* (*Das Wachsfigurenkabinett*, 1924), a film billed today by Kino International as "Paul Leni's Carnival Nightmare."¹ A brief synopsis would certainly suggest that *Waxworks* lives up to the label: a young writer (Wilhelm Dieterle) is hired by the proprietor of a fairground panopticon to compose "startling tales" about three of his wax figures. This provides the frame for the three episodes to follow, featuring Emil Jannings as Harun al-Rashid, Conrad Veidt as Ivan the Terrible, and Werner Krauss as Jack the Ripper. Each of these villains in turn threatens the happiness of a young couple (played in each episode by Dieterle and Olga Belajeff). With its elaborate sets, stark lighting, and diabolical characters, Leni's film fits well into the dark canon of films that emerged out of Germany in the early years of the Weimar Republic—films like Robert Wiene's *The Cabinet of Dr. Caligari* (*Das Cabinet des Dr. Caligari*, 1920), Fritz Lang's *Destiny* (*Der müde Tod*, 1921), F. W. Murnau's *Nosferatu* (1922), and Arthur Robison's *Warning Shadows* (*Schatten – Eine nächtliche Halluzination*, 1923). Indeed, *Waxworks* often anchors such lists of films, which frequently function as metonymic shorthand for early Weimar cinema as a whole. What a brief synopsis inevitably fails to mention, however, and what the inclusion of *Waxworks* in this sinister company would seem to suppress, is the film's substantial comedic aspect. Though the episodes with Ivan the Terrible and Jack the Ripper are predictably grim, the film's longest sequence presents a Baghdad burlesque in which Jannings's lecherous caliph is more clown than villain. Such an episode sits uneasily in the "historical imaginary" (to borrow Thomas Elsaesser's term) that continues to dominate discussions of early Weimar film.

In his watershed study, *From Caligari to Hitler: A Psychological History of the German Film* (1947), Siegfried Kracauer distorts the image of *Waxworks* when he effectively elides its comedic content. He grants Leni's Ivan the Terrible iconic status, closing his book with an allusion to Nazi leaders as "self-appointed Caligaris," "raving Mabuses," and "mad Ivans," but he summarily dismisses the Baghdad episode as an "insignificant prelude."[2] Beyond simply stretching the meaning of "prelude" past plausibility (the sequence, combined with the brief opening frame, constitutes roughly forty-four of the film's eighty-four minutes in the Kino International release), Kracauer's disparaging remark expurgates that large portion of the film that aims not to arouse fear, but to elicit laughter. The Baghdad episode qualifies as comedy, not merely because it has a happy ending featuring the union of a young couple, but because comedy is its dominant modality.[3] Whereas its Expressionist set design might elsewhere intimate psychosis, and Harun al-Rashid's advances might convey sexual menace, modality markers—such as irreverent intertitles and a slapstick chase scene—defuse such threats by distancing the action from both reality and seriousness.

The humor of the film was not lost on early critics: "hilarious, hilarious!" ("köstlich, köstlich!") ran one review.[4] *Die Filmwoche* described "the delicately humorous story of the fat enamored halfwit, the caliph Harun al-Rashid" as a kind of farcical *1001 Nights*.[5] Even the intellectually and culturally ambitious film journal *Der Bildwart*, which berated Jannings's caliph as a "libidinous, foolish fatso and idiot," acknowledged the episode's plot as "inherently funny."[6] The film's resultant generic hybridity led one early reviewer to read it as the product of "a kind of bric-à-brac-feeling."[7] Whereas Ivan the Terrible and Jack the Ripper incite fear, Harun al-Rashid provokes laughter—laughter that has largely been stifled by the historiography of early Weimar cinema.

Comedies, along with adventure films, detective serials, melodramas, and romances, were a staple of Weimar cinema,[8] yet such films still occupy only a marginal place in the era's historical profile. While Elsaesser and others have sought to remedy this situation,[9] the caliginous canon of early Weimar film has proven remarkably resilient.[10] For Kracauer and Lotte Eisner, national temperament or artistic genius ultimately lie behind this sinister cinema, while more recent analyses ascribe it to war trauma or gender anxieties.[11] But regardless of the cause, such accounts take the privileged status of a limited and largely homogenous subset of proto-horror films as their point of departure. The general consensus that *Waxworks* numbers among the proto-horror films that dominate the historiography of the Weimar era reflects a bias that colors early Weimar cinema as a whole. In actuality, *Waxworks* offers a test case for the construction of early Weimar cinema's historical imaginary, for while it shares a great deal with its shadowy brethren—which helps to explain its place in the established canon—it clearly deviates from them. In so doing, it points to filmic possibilities suppressed by the prevailing canon. *Waxworks* provides a glimpse into Weimar film culture both by participating in the dark, mysterious filmmaking considered characteristic of early Weimar cinema, and by going beyond it, pointing to the rich generic diversity of this era's films that is now beginning to receive sustained scholarly attention.

A WEIMAR EXEMPLAR

There is a tension between the written word and filmic image that suffuses the canon of early Weimar films. This tension, which was central to the *Kino-Debatte* of the decade prior to the release of *Waxworks*, speaks to the burgeoning cultural legitimacy of cinema in the Weimar Republic.[12] The objective of high-culture acknowledgment would not be met by making film a new "literary" institution; only by distinguishing itself *from* literature could film establish itself *against* literature. This effort manifests itself repeatedly in the canonical films of the early Weimar Republic: Dr. Caligari's reading-induced madness is etched across the celluloid, "Du musst Caligari werden!" ("You must become Caligari!"). *Nosferatu* is replete with written texts of questionable reliability, such as the framing chronicle, the ship's log, Hutter's letter, and the book *On Vampyres*. Films like *Warning Shadows* and *The Last Laugh* (*Der letzte Mann*, 1924) pride themselves on their independence from verbal intertitles. *Waxworks* presents a culmination of this trend by tracing precisely the trajectory of film's liberation from literature. This exploration of film's distinctiveness leads to a dialogue not only with literature but with painting as well, unlocking the uncanny potential of the moving image. That Leni's film finds something unsettling in its celebration of the filmic apparatus situates *Waxworks* firmly among the exemplars of early Weimar cinema.

Waxworks begins as a film about writing: the young writer (Dieterle) is presented with images—the wax figures—for which he must generate stories, thus structuring the film around the need for written, linear narrative. At the outset, the writer's commission to provide suitable stories for the wax images suggests the reliance of the image on narrative, but by the end of the film, this relationship dissolves. The casting of Dieterle as both the writer and the male lead of each episode highlights the origin of each framed narrative with the writer. The largely coherent stories of Harun al-Rashid and Ivan the Terrible reflect the writer's sustained control over the creative process, emphasized by opening each sequence with a passage written in the poet's hand. The writer relinquishes that control, however, in the final episode, which presents his own nightmare rather than a product of his conscious intent.

This modification manifests itself formally. Dieterle's character drifts off to sleep and in a dream finds himself pursued by Jack the Ripper through a surreal fairground of multiple-exposures with no clear architectural orientation. This sequence is brief—less than five minutes long, compared with Harun al-Rashid's forty minutes and Ivan the Terrible's thirty—but it is effective. For Lotte Eisner, the episode's "chaos of form [is] completely incoherent," resulting in the film's "most Expressionist episode."[3] Kracauer considered it "among the greatest achievements of film art."[4] The camerawork by Helmar Lerski (not Halmar Junge, as credited in the Kino International version) masterfully undermines any coherent sense of architectural space by positioning the writer and his romantic interest, the daughter of his patron, in an obscure landscape of carnival rides and circus tents, jagged stairs and crooked doorways, that dissolve into one another as the serial killer, himself a high-contrast dissolve, pursues the unlucky couple. A brief respite provides a false sense of relief from the pursuit; the woman dons a fur coat and looks around coquettishly, but she quickly finds herself surrounded by an increasing number of ghostly apparitions, all with the visage of Jack the Ripper. The writer leaps to her aid, only to fall victim to Jack's blade. Startled awake, the writer finds himself pierced not lethally through the heart by the killer's knife but harmlessly by his own pen.

As the writer's mastery over the narrative situation declines, the power of the image grows, and as the threat of Jack the Ripper increases, the demands of narrative abate. There is no longer any need for coherent place, such as the exotic Orient of the Arabian Nights or sixteenth-century tsarist Russia; brief visual allusions to the fairground of the frame provide enough spatial context. And indeed, these cues serve more to disorient the action than to contextualize it. Not only does the fairground with its spinning merry-go-rounds and Ferris wheels provide at best an unstable site of action, but these reference points situate the fantastic action within the film's narrative frame, rendering the structural framework of the film itself unreliable. What was a point of stability becomes the site of anxiety.

Whereas in the first two episodes, the writer weaves intricate narrative webs for the wax figures that include romance, deception, murder, and cases of mistaken identity, the final episode presents only the sparest possible storyline. The sequence distills the basic constellation of all three episodes; the happiness of a young couple is threatened by a third, menacing figure.[15] Leni demonstrates here how a narrative of anxiety can be produced filmically without the need for elaborate narrative devices borrowed from literature or history. This attests to the artistic viability of the filmic apparatus, serving as evidence for Erich Pommer's claim that for film the dramatic storyline is ultimately unimportant: "Not the What, but rather the How is what is decisive here, as it is everywhere."[16] The sequence has no real story; the figures have no personalities, and in this sense, this episode is indeed the film's most Expressionist. But more importantly, the sequence demonstrates the independence of film from the kind of written, literary narratives commissioned from the writer in the frame. The way to bring these inanimate objects to life, Leni's film seems to say in its last harrowing episode, is not by writing stories about them, but through the technology of film and the modes of representation it alone enables.

In this final sequence, Leni returns the spectator to the birthplace of cinematic exhibition, and in doing so, aligns *Waxworks* yet further with the sinister films that dominate the Weimar canon. Locating the frame-story, as well as the site of Jack's transgression, at the fairground harks back to the earliest days of film technology, in which the apparatus was presented in tents as a form of cheap, anti-bourgeois entertainment. At such performances, narrative played only a minor role compared with the astonishment evoked by the technology itself.[17] Jack's vivification echoes the uncanny transformation from still to moving image that was the *raison d'être* of these early film screenings. The mere possibility of such transformation (from still to moving image) and transgression (into and potentially beyond the frame) presents a source of anxiety independent from all but the most rudimentary narrative exposition. The allusion to cinema's uncanny origins is, however, not limited to the fairground setting—it is repeatedly evoked by the painterly quality of *Waxworks*, which, like the discourse on word-versus-film, situates the film felicitously in the received canon of early Weimar cinema.

In his review of *Waxworks* for the illustrated film weekly *Lichtbildbühne*, Georg Victor Mendel was taken less by the film's engagement with literature than with painting, declaring, "that it's the *painter* Leni who places his stamp on this work. The entirety is an *artist's caprice*, a graceful game [Spiel] sparkling with wit in which the *painterly* is by far the main thing."[18] This much was to be expected from Leni, who had already made his mark in the German film world as a set designer, particularly for his work with Joe May and Leopold Jessner. In a 1923 production update, Heinz Michaelis reported of *Waxworks*, "Here a film is in production that is transported into the world of the living image not from the world of words [Wortkunst, or word-art], but derives from a purely optical idea."[19] Such reports were entirely in keeping with Leni's own aesthetic priorities: "Film is image," he would write, "a matter for painters. First and foremost. That film is a *moving* image changes nothing."[20]

This preoccupation with the painterly potential of film was by no means singular to Leni, but was an aesthetic impulse felt throughout early Weimar cinema. Kristin Thompson notes that "a painterly approach to film [. . .] lingered in German cinema for about a decade," beginning before World War I with *The Student of Prague* (*Der Student von Prag*, 1913) and continuing to 1924, the year *Waxworks* appeared.[21] Films like *Caligari* feature painted Expressionist sets, and *Nosferatu* is replete with overt visual allusions to the Romantic paintings of Caspar David Friedrich and Biedermeier interiors. The emphasis is on *mise-en-scène*, neatly framed by a largely static camera. This engagement with painting, however, follows a trajectory similar to that of film's relationship with literature, in that what can at first be seen as an attempt to establish the cultural legitimacy of the younger medium through association with a recognized art form proves in fact a foil against which the new medium can establish its independence.

Despite Leni's claim, the fact that these images move does matter, and his own *Waxworks* exploits the opposition of still and moving image. Kracauer describes Veidt's Ivan the Terrible as a "living icon,"[22] for in one particular shot, Ivan stands unmoving in the doorway of a structure akin to an icon screen, his gaunt but immaculately adorned physique framed by the threshold much as the image of a saint inhabits an icon. Facing the camera directly in a chest-level medium shot, Ivan must lower his head to transgress the portal. With the motions of his body hidden beneath his elaborate robes, he slowly and menacingly advances upon the spectator. As he approaches, the camera must tilt upward in order to keep his head in the frame, but it proves unable to contain this subject, and the shot ends with a low-angle close-up of Ivan's hands and chest. Throughout, Veidt seems to gaze directly into the camera, much as he had as Cesare in *The Cabinet of Dr. Caligari*. Though this shot initially presents Ivan as a painting, its menace is enabled primarily in its capacity to do what a painting cannot do—namely, come to life and just possibly transgress the frame.

Figure 5.1 Ivan the Terrible (Conrad Veidt) as a "living icon."

The scriptwriter for *Waxworks*, Henrik Galeen, revisited the transition from still to moving image repeatedly in his screenplays, which include such notable works as *The Golem* (*Der Golem*; written with Paul Wegener, 1914), *The Golem* (*Der Golem, wie er in die Welt kam*; again with Wegener, 1920), and *Alraune* (which he also directed, 1927). His most famous script, *Nosferatu*, had originally included a living painting in the vampire's gallery of ancestral portraits,[33] but instead, Murnau presents Orlock himself repeatedly as a still image come to life. When the vampire initially appears as such, he stands motionless in the dark; slowly, he comes to occupy the peaked threshold of a doorway, much like Ivan would; only after pausing for a moment, motionless, does he transgress the frame and advance on Hutter. The scene is truly iconic, as is the later shot of Orlock at the window staring out at Ellen, looking directly into the camera, neatly framed and motionless, slowly stirring. With its shots composed like paintings, Murnau's *Nosferatu* celebrates cinema by emphasizing its own difference from earlier media—it may remind us of a painting, but the slightest movement takes us into a discrete realm of expectations.

When Leni's Ivan recapitulates this moment, he firmly situates the film in the canon of early Weimar cinema, which frequently returns to the repressed contradiction inherent in the very notion of the *motion picture*. Such moments re-enact the primordial cinematic moment, marking a return to "the uncanny early experience of cinema" that Tom Gunning argues is the origin of the horror film genre.[24] By framing Ivan (or Orlock or Cesare or the Golem or the student of Prague) as a picture and withholding the illusion of movement, the film lulls our expectations. Movement itself, of course, is not horrific, but when something that is not supposed to move does, it can lead to a momentary breakdown in our sense of reality. And once the image transgresses the law of its medium, what is to say it could not transgress the frame of the image? Nicholas Royle has suggested that "the entire [film] 'industry' might be defined as a palliative working to repress the uncanniness of film,"[25] but such scenes as these do just the opposite: they remind us that film itself is already an uncanny apparatus, if we remember that moment of first contact—that moment when a photographic representation violated its obligation to remain static and began to stir, that moment when we could not even rely on the frame of the proscenium to contain the screen's transgressive figures. In this light, the threat posed by Jack the Ripper in the final episode of *Waxworks* proves effective not only in its independence from any but the most rudimentary narrative construct, but also for the way it realizes the potential threat of film by liberating the killer from the narrative frames that kept Harun al-Rashid and Ivan the Terrible in check. Jack bleeds into the world of the frame, just as early film spectators—at least for a moment—feared the world on the screen would bleed into theirs. With this closing sequence particularly in mind, it is not difficult to imagine how *Waxworks* developed a reputation as the kind of proto-horror film considered typical of early Weimar cinema.

FROM CALIGARI TO COMEDY

Culminating in a surreal nightmare that foregoes narrative development and conjures the original uncanniness of the filmic apparatus, the version of *Waxworks* in circulation today plots a trajectory of increasing threat. But at its premiere on November 13, 1924 at Berlin's U. T. Kurfürstendamm, the film was structured differently. Rather than moving from the whimsical curvaceousness of Jannings's caliph, through the claustrophobic narrowness of Veidt's Ivan, to the disorienting sequence with Krauss's spectral killer, the audience at the premiere first encountered Ivan the Terrible, followed by Jack the Ripper, who provided merely an interlude before Harun al-Rashid took the screen. This premiere version concluded the framed narratives with a comparatively light-hearted happy ending that was then immediately reiterated by the frame's own happy ending.

In contrast, the version of *Waxworks* in circulation today follows the order of Galeen's original script, and within a month of the premiere, Leni had reverted to this original sequence.[26] Financial concerns had led Leni to reconsider the structure of the film, which was initially to include a fourth episode that featured the story of Rinaldo Rinaldini. This Corsican robber chieftain—created by Goethe's brother-in-law, Christian August Vulpius, in his novel, *Rinaldo Rinaldini* (1799)—was to have been played by Dieterle. Unlike the other sequences, the figure rendered in wax does not represent the antagonist but rather the hero of the story: Rinaldo rescues the beautiful Violante from Pergolese's henchmen, who have kidnapped her on the way to her wedding with King Theodoro. The gallant highwayman and the future queen spend one night of passion together before forsaking their love. Nine months later, Rinaldo is prepared for the gibbet (why is left unsaid), but the queen, who has just learned of his pending execution, pardons him at the last minute, declaring he should not die on the day she has given birth to the royal "heir." The likeness of Rinaldo, whose episode was to have fallen between those of Ivan and Jack the Ripper, can still be seen in the film alongside the other three waxworks in the fairground panopticon. The sequence was to have been filmed on location in Italy in summer 1923 but appears to have fallen victim to skyrocketing inflation. Indicative of the economic climate, the November 4, 1923 issue of *Der Film* that announced that "*Waxworks* is nearing completion" went for a cover price of 10,000,000,000 marks.[27]

It may be tempting to read Leni's return to the script's original order as evidence of the film's dark intent, but inclusion of the Rinaldo episode would have disrupted the trajectory from comedy to horror. While the comedic element is actually difficult to discern in the original script for the Baghdad episode (Leni's intertitles, for instance, do not coincide with Galeen's), it is apparent in the unfilmed Rinaldo scenes. For instance, in scene 26, Rinaldo engages in a gunfight: he fires two pistols and sticks them back into his belt; he pulls two more, fires them, and sticks them away; then a fifth and sixth; and finally, he pulls a seventh out of his boot. Galeen's script actually miscounts the number of pistols in the scene,[28] but that in itself is telling. It is not about accuracy; the scene is an over-the-top caricature of a gunfight. And the tendency toward comedy is not limited to this scene. For instance, laughs are clearly sought shortly thereafter, in scene 30, when Pergolese's messenger leaves the palace with Violante's ransom; according to the script, "They part as good friends—everyone—even the King waves goodbye."[29] Such a scene would not be out of place in a Lubitsch comedy.

Had Leni been able to include the story of Rinaldo, it would have cast the other episodes in a different light. The trajectory of *Waxworks* would not be of increasing horror, but of the writer's increasing valorization of himself in the stories he tells: in the first episode, Dieterle plays the timid baker; in the second, he is promoted to tortured bridegroom; in the third, he would have risen to heroic robber chieftain; and in the fourth, he plays himself. Furthermore, it would significantly alter the impression of the film as a whole. With the inclusion of Rinaldo, the panopticon would no longer present a rogues' gallery. The presence of a sympathetic hero would mitigate Harun al-Rashid's guilt by association and open up a space for his comic turn. More recent accounts have begun at least to acknowledge the possibility of a comedic impulse in the film. Jürgen Kasten, who has written a rare article dedicated solely to *Waxworks*, examines the film's generic diversity—what he dubs the "bric-à-brac" principle, borrowing the term from Walter Gottfried Lohmeyer's early review in the daily *Film-Kurier*. He points out that the film has no "continuity of style" but includes elements of "gothic-Romantic horror" as well as, in the episode with Harun al-Rashid, "burlesque or comedy."[30] Had the director been able to film the entire script, one can imagine that the film would have been even more generically diverse, and the caliph would seem all the more a clown and less a villain.

Galeen's original script for the Baghdad episode itself harbors few laughs, but Leni's film teases out and expands upon what comedic element is there. Both script and film begin the Harun al-Rashid episode with a rather arbitrary and comic narrative set-up; one of the arms belonging to the wax figure lies on the writer's table, ready for repair. The writer takes this severed limb as inspiration for the story he will invent (and thereby hopefully woo his patron's daughter): how the caliph lost his arm. Leni extends this farcical impulse into the frame story, preparing the spectator for Jannings's exaggerated rotundity with a humorously irreverent intertitle: "The caliph kept his brain from becoming as fat as his stomach by a daily game of Chess with his Grand Vizier." Losing the game, the caliph blames the smoke from a nearby chimney and orders the vizier (Paul Biensfeldt) to "dispatch the smoke-maker," who turns out to be the local baker, Assad (a match-dissolve clearly identifies him with the writer). When the vizier returns empty-handed, the caliph asks where the baker's head is, and the vizier amusingly responds that he must have mislaid it, and then, following the logic of Freud's borrowed kettle, explains that he was distracted by the beauty of the baker's wife, Maimune (or Zarah, as she is named in at least one print) (Belajeff). Here, again, a match-dissolve makes her identification with the writer's love interest unmistakable. Thus begins the action of the episode, which features the corpulent caliph's attempts to seduce the baker's beautiful wife, while the hapless baker himself breaks into the royal palace to steal the caliph's magical wishing ring so that he might fulfill all his wife's desires.

The episode's narrative caprice is amplified by its exaggerated set design, costumes, and performances. Though Expressionist in their eccentricities, these are not the harrowing sets reflective of an anxious mind we know from *Caligari* or Karlheinz Martin's *From Morn to Midnight* (*Von morgens bis mitternachts*, 1921). Rather, the excessively oblate minarets and improbably outsized turbans suggest a world of carnal caricature. The orientalist setting invites comparison with Lubitsch's *Sumurun* (1920), but the set design is actually closer to his farcical *Wildcat* (*Die Bergkatze*, 1921). This is matched by the comically exaggerated acting style. The accentuated eyebrows of Biensfeldt's flirtatious Grand Vizier complement the overly timid jealous gaze of Dieterle's baker, and when the caliph emerges at the end from the baker's sooty oven where he has hidden himself, he snorts and flaps his hands so animatedly as to dissolve any threat the ruler may have presented.

Any sexual menace conceivably posed by the concupiscent caliph is itself never presented as a serious threat. His lechery is treated tongue-in-cheek, both verbally and visually. An early intertitle describes the motivation behind his secret forays among the people as "seeking out the needy, and comforting—the—the lovely," adding a moment of deliberate hesitation that can only be read ironically. In response to Maimune's self-consciousness, the would-be womanizer tells her, "Your lack of clothes doesn't disturb me in the least," and we believe him. Such textual interventions highlight the caliph's libidinous character, but Jannings's performance renders their ironic intent unmistakable. His behavior is playful, as when he throws one of his many seemingly endless necklaces around Maimune's neck without removing it from his own; under other circumstances such a gesture could signal peril, but the flimsiness of the necklace and the caliph's ridiculous comportment never allow the scene to take that turn. In executing the caliph's advances, Jannings extrudes his lips to such an absurd degree as to dissipate any sense of anxiety his kisses might produce. Though portrayed as a lecher, his power is actually over the other male figure. But this, too, is treated frivolously; at the close of the episode, when all have been absolved, the caliph holds the baker and his wife in the folds of his robe. He

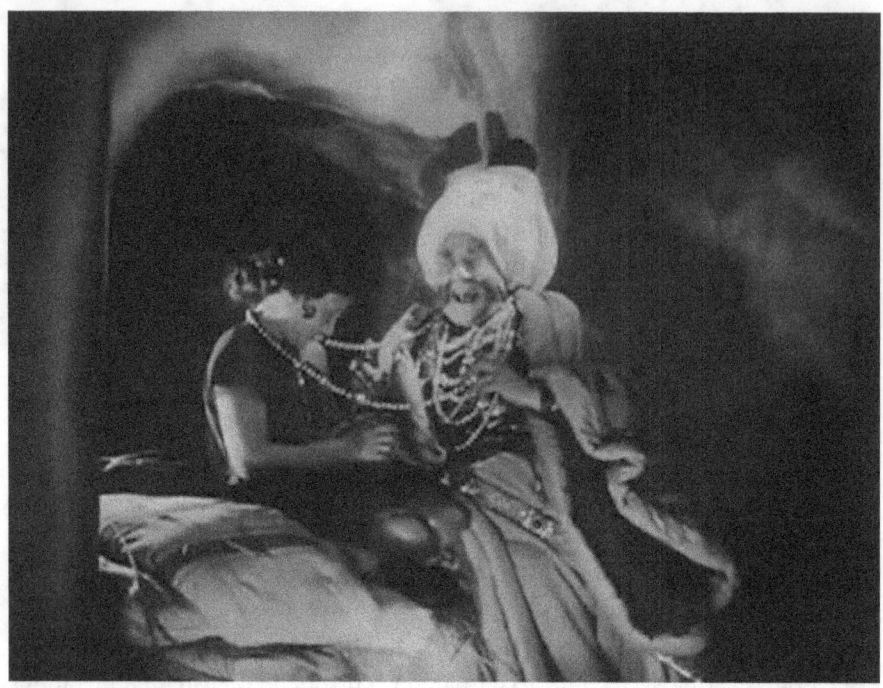

Figure 5.2 The flirtatious caliph (Emil Jannings).

looks down on the baker kindly and winks, but when the baker smiles and winks back, the caliph responds with a chastising glare that puts the baker back in his place. Dieterle's submissive response provides the segment's last laugh, reinforcing the prevailing power dynamic and reintroducing a touch of tyranny into even this burlesque. While this last nod to the caliph's power may fit Kracauer's narrative well, it is also entirely in keeping with the episode's comedic mode.

Eisner describes the Baghdad episode in particular as a parody of Expressionist filmmaking,[31] and although she does not elaborate, one can imagine how she could arrive at such an assessment. While many of the key films from the early Weimar Republic conjure up the original uncanniness of film by re-enacting the transition from still to moving image, the Baghdad episode can be seen to spoof this development; it does not portray a wax figure coming to life, as one might expect, but rather it tells the tale of the wax figure itself. The writer composes a story not about how Harun al-Rashid lost his arm, but about how the waxwork lost its arm—the figure from the frame is presumably the dummy that the caliph kept in his bed to disguise his nocturnal excursions, and which Assad maims in his quest for the wishing ring. In this configuration, the wax figure may transgress from the internal episode into the realm of the frame, but only on account of the ridiculous narrative set-up, not due to some supernatural power on the part of the image. Indeed, even within the confines of the inner narrative, no fantastic events actually occur; the episode pokes fun at this notion when Maimune uses the fake wishing ring to make the caliph "magically" appear from the oven where he has been hiding. The moment is decidedly non-fantastic, and the gag relies precisely on this fact.

The Baghdad episode's ironic treatment of themes favored by Expressionist cinema, compounded by its use of Expressionist sets and acting to comic ends, could appear to lampoon its cinematic predecessors. To call this "parody," however, seems overly deprecatory. The laughter it provokes is not derived from comparison with more serious Expressionist works. Indeed, coming at the beginning of the film, as parody it would only undermine the sequences to come. *Waxworks* may come at the end of the golden age of German Expressionist cinema, but it still revels in its tropes and techniques throughout. Rather than parody, what the Baghdad episode offers is an exploration of the possibilities for German film art left largely untouched by the other episodes that make up *Waxworks*—and by the films that comprise the canon of early Weimar cinema as a whole. It may address the same issues that occupy the Ivan and Jack the Ripper episodes (as well as *Caligari*, *Nosferatu*, etc.), but it spins them differently. Its humorous spin, however, would find little resonance in German film historiography.

Regarding the suppression of comedy in German film historiography, Jan-Christopher Horak writes (with admitted hyperbole), "that film history can be seen as the revenge of intellectuals and the cultural elite, who have always felt themselves to be white knights, protecting the grail of our collective cultural heritage."[32] A glance at the diverging contemporary reviews of *Waxworks* in the *Reichsfilmblatt* (a journal for cinema theater owners) and the culturally ambitious *Bildwart* testifies to the accuracy of this assessment: the former describes the Baghdad sequence as "hilarious" ("köstlich"), the latter as "trite jokes and comedic antics."[33] Marketing concerns and promotional strategies may also have colored the film's reception. Erich Pommer—who sat on the executive committee of Universum-Film AG (Ufa), Germany's largest film production company and the company responsible for the distribution of *Waxworks*—was a vehement advocate of the artistically ambitious *Stilfilm*, or stylized film. By 1924, Pommer had already produced such legendary films as *The Cabinet of Dr. Caligari*, *Dr. Mabuse the Gambler* (*Dr. Mabuse, der Spieler*), and *Destiny*, and though he would later produce such light popular fare as *The Three from the Filling Station* (*Die Drei von der Tankstelle*, 1930) and *The Congress Dances* (*Der Kongress tanzt*, 1931), at the time he maintained that the stylized film could help establish the cultural legitimacy of cinema without sacrificing profitability. In 1922, he noted that the success of films like *Caligari* and *Destiny* proved that "not the worst business is to be made with artistic films."[34] In fact, the way he saw it, "The German film industry made 'stylised films' to make money."[35]

Unlike Ernst Lubitsch, who claimed to make "Lubitsch-films" as opposed to "German" films,[36] Pommer promoted what he considered to be a distinctly German style as a means to overcome the country's cultural and economic isolation after World War I. It is easy to imagine how the darkly Expressionist aspects of *Waxworks* might suit this strategy, while its more comical elements recede in the cultural imaginary. If Pommer's strategy was to carve out a place for German film in the international film market, then it would be little served by promoting comedies abroad due to the already immense popularity of such films from the United States and from France. Yet even as a stylistic film, *Waxworks* would prove a "latecomer" and "transitional film," according to Herbert Ihering's review of the film's 1924 premiere. German film could only overcome the dominance of American movies, he contends, "when it [. . .] doesn't commit itself to creations that have long since been overcome (as happens in *Waxworks*)."[37] His review focuses on the more conventionally "Expressionist" aspects of Leni's film and utterly ignores its comedic elements.

As early as 1934, in an article on "Expressionist Film," Rudolf Arnheim noted that films like *The Cabinet of Dr. Caligari*, *From Morn to Midnight*, and *Waxworks* can seem "inadvertently funny now."[38] But, of course, parts of Leni's film are not inadvertently funny—they are intentionally so. Certainly, the result is somewhat bric-à-brac—Leni had not yet mastered the smooth integration of comedy and horror that makes *The Cat and the Canary* so successful. But then again, that bric-à-brac quality renders *Waxworks* more reflective of early Weimar film culture than the other films that are usually held up as representative. Though the film was conceived already in 1920, it was not shot until 1923 and languished for a year before its actual release in November 1924. By the time of its premiere, the heyday of German Expressionist film was over. On October 11, 1925, *Kinematograph* would report that the only negative of *Waxworks* had been destroyed by fire in the Paris customs office. Less than a year after the film's premiere, the article would describe it as a film "belonging to the epoch-making creations of the German film industry."[39] As scholarly interest in the great diversity of films created in Germany during the early years of the Weimar Republic intensifies, we begin to develop an even greater appreciation of this untimely film that itself was epoch-making not only in what historians choose to remember, but also in what the film itself refuses to let us forget.

NOTES

1. Research for this study, which is part of a larger investigation into Expressionist film and the myth of the "dark German soul," was enabled by the generous support of the Alexander von Humboldt Foundation. This book chapter is adapted from Joel Westerdale, "The Lighter Side of Early Weimar Cinema's Dark Canon: Paul Leni's *Das Wachsfigurenkabinett* (1924)," *German Quarterly* 85, no. 1 (2012): 1–18.

2. Siegfried Kracauer, *From Caligari to Hitler: A Psychological History of the German Film* (Princeton, NJ: Princeton University Press, 1947), 272, 85.
3. See Geoff King, *Film Comedy* (London: Wallflower Press, 2002), 8.
4. Ernst Ulitzsch, review of *Waxworks*, November 17, 1924, reprinted in Henrik Galeen, *Das Wachsfigurenkabinett: Das Drehbuch von Henrik Galeen zu Paul Lenis Film von 1923*, ed. Hans-Michael Bock (Munich: Text + Kritik, 1994), 143. Except for the intertitles of *Waxworks*, all translations from the German are the author's.
5. *Die Filmwoche* 48, November 26, 1924, 1124.
6. Review of *Das Wachsfigurenkabinett*, *Der Bildwart* 12 (1925): 933–5.
7. Walter Gottfried Lohmeyer, "Das Wachsfiguren-Kabinett (U.T. Kurfürstendamm)," *Film-Kurier* 270, November 14, 1924.
8. Hans-Michael Bock and Michael Töteberg (eds.), *Das Ufa-Buch: Kunst und Krise, Stars und Regisseure, Wirtschaft und Politik* (Frankfurt: Zweitausendeins, 1992), 35.
9. See, for instance, Elsaesser on Schünzel's *Hallo Caesar!* in Thomas Elsaesser, *Weimar Cinema and After: Germany's Historical Imaginary* (London: Routledge, 2000), 295–310; Christian Rogowski, "Movies, Money, and Mystique: Joe May's Early Weimar Blockbuster, *The Indian Tomb* (1921)," in *Weimar Cinema: An Essential Guide to Classic Films of the Era*, ed. Noah Isenberg (New York: Columbia University Press, 2009), 55–77; Christian Rogowski, "From Ernst Lubitsch to Joe May: Challenging Kracauer's Demonology with Weimar Popular Film," in *Light Motives: German Popular Film in Perspective*, ed. Randall Halle and Margaret McCarthy (Detroit: Wayne State University Press, 2003), 1–23; and Rogowski's 2010 edited volume, *The Many Faces of Weimar Cinema*; Kristin Thompson, *Herr Lubitsch Goes to Hollywood: German and American Film after World War I* (Amsterdam: Amsterdam University Press, 2005); and the journal *Filmblatt*, published by CineGraph Babelsberg, which focuses on hitherto neglected aspects and genres of German film.
10. Isenberg's *Weimar Cinema*, for instance, adheres closely to the conventional canon, with the single exception of Rogowski's contribution.
11. See Steve Choe, *Afterlives: Allegories of Film and Mortality in Early Weimar Germany* (New York: Bloomsbury, 2014); Anton Kaes, *Shell Shock Cinema: Weimar Culture and the Wounds of War* (Princeton, NJ: Princeton University Press, 2009); Anjeana Hans, *Gender and the Uncanny in the Films of the Weimar Republic* (Detroit: Wayne State University Press, 2014); and Richard McCormick, *Gender and Sexuality in Weimar Modernity: Film, Literature, and "New Objectivity"* (New York: Palgrave, 2001).
12. See Anton Kaes, "The Debate about Cinema: Charting a Controversy (1909–1929)," *New German Critique* 40 (1987): 9, 20.
13. Lotte H. Eisner, *The Haunted Screen: Expressionism in the German Cinema and the Influence of Max Reinhardt*, trans. Roger Greaves (Berkeley: University of California Press, 1969), 122.
14. Kracauer, *From Caligari to Hitler*, 87.
15. See Elsaesser, *Weimar Cinema*, 85.
16. Erich Pommer, "Internationale Film-Verständigung," July 15, 1922, reprinted in *Werkstatt Film*, ed. Rolf Aurich and Wolfgang Jacobsen (Munich: Text + Kritik, 1998).
17. Tom Gunning, "An Aesthetic of Astonishment: Early Film and the (In)Credulous Spectator," in *Film Theory and Criticism: Introductory Readings*, ed. Leo Braudy and Marshall Cohen (New York: Oxford University Press, 1999).
18. Georg Victor Mendel, review of *Waxworks*, *Lichtbildbühne*, November 15, 1924.
19. Heinz Michaelis, Production report on *Das Wachsfigurenkabinett*, *Film-Kurier*, August 29, 1923.
20. Paul Leni, "Das Bild als Handlung. Der Maler als Regisseur," reprinted in *Paul Leni: Grafik, Theater, Film*, ed. Hans-Michael Bock (Frankfurt am Main: Deutsches Filmmuseum, 1986), 109.

21. Thompson, *Herr Lubitsch Goes to Hollywood*, 140.
22. Kracauer, *From Caligari to Hitler*, 86.
23. Scene 41; Eisner, *Haunted Screen*, 243.
24. Gunning, "Aesthetic of Astonishment," 58.
25. Nicholas Royle, *The Uncanny* (New York: Routledge, 2003), 75.
26. Hans-Michael Bock, "Licht/Schatten. Eine Karriere. Eine Recherche," in Bock, *Paul Leni*, 27.
27. Bock, "Licht/Schatten," 26.
28. Galeen, *Wachsfigurenkabinett*, 85.
29. Galeen, *Wachsfigurenkabinett*, 88.
30. Jürgen Kasten, "Episodic Patchwork: The Bric-à-Brac Principle in Paul Leni's *Waxworks*," in *Expressionist Film: New Perspectives*, ed. Dietrich Scheunemann (Rochester, NY: Camden House, 2003), 176; Lohmeyer, "Das Wachsfiguren-Kabinett."
31. Lotte H. Eisner, "Schattenschweres Dekor," in *Offizieller Festspiel-Almanach*, XIV (Berlin: Internationale Film-Festspiele, 1964), 68.
32. Jan-Christopher Horak, "Laughing Until It Hurts: German Film Comedy and Karl Valentin," in *Prima di Caligari: Cinema tedesco, 1895–1920/Before Caligari: German Cinema, 1895–1920*, ed. Paolo Cherchi Usai and Lorenzo Codelli (Pordenone: Edizione Biblioteca dell'Immagine, 1990), 202.
33. *Reichsfilmblatt* 46, 1924, 31; review of *Das Wachsfigurenkabinett*, *Der Bildwart*, 935.
34. Erich Pommer, "Geschäftsfilm und künstlerischer Film," *Der Film*, December 10, 1922, 22.
35. Pommer quoted in Elsaesser, *Weimar Cinema*, 26.
36. Ernst Lubitsch, "Film-Internationalität," in Aurich and Jacobsen, *Werkstatt Film*, 153.
37. Herbert Ihering, "Die Filmsituation," *Berliner Börsen-Courier*, November 14, 1924.
38. Rudolf Arnheim, "Expressionist Film (1934)," in *Film Essays and Criticism*, ed. Brenda Benthien (Madison: University of Wisconsin Press, 1997), 85.
39. Hans-Michael Bock, "Barock und Orient," in Galeen, *Wachsfigurenkabinett*, 135.

CHAPTER 6

Intersectional Avant-Garde: Paul Leni's *Rebus-Film* Series and the Confluence of Experimental Visual Styles

Erica Tortolani

Throughout Paul Leni's careers in Germany and the United States, his films were often credited for their cinematic experimentation and versatility. Moving seamlessly across different genres and laying the groundwork for new and emerging film styles, Leni adapted a diverse range of visual techniques to his own unique perspective as film director, set designer, and illustrator. While the bulk of the literature on Leni focuses on his contributions to German Expressionism and the rise of the horror genre in Hollywood, it has paid little attention to one of his most ambitious projects: the eight-part *Rebus-Film* series. A collaborative effort between Leni, writer Hans Brennert, and cinematographer Guido Seeber, the *Rebus* films premiered for German audiences in December 1925 and are considered the first crossword puzzle films.[1] Two interesting points of analysis emerge when considering the *Rebus* "Kreutzwort-Rätselfilm" enterprise. On one hand, the interactive nature of the series offers insight into early experiments in audience engagement and the larger history of alternative media spectatorship.[2] On the other, the *Rebus* films—incorporating various types of animation, live-action footage, and innovative editing techniques—bear a striking resemblance to many experimental, modernist art movements that emerged prior to or alongside the debut of each installment. It is on this latter point—the experimental nature of Leni's *Rebus* films—that my analysis will take place. In particular, this essay will explore the series' connections to various artistic movements and cinematic styles developed at the beginning of the twentieth century. The few surviving contemporaneous reviews and critiques of the films will serve as a primary point of entry in examining the connections between the *Rebus* series and experimental art movements. The second half of this analysis will present a larger discussion of the historical timeline of such trends in relation to the first *Rebus* installment, giving an overview of important artists, key concepts, and connections to Leni's cinematic work.

REBUS-FILM: ORIGINS AND RECEPTION

Though the *Rebus-Film* series was distributed for international audiences between 1925 and 1927, very little contemporaneous information exists on the films and an even smaller proportion of current-day scholarship is dedicated to analyzing, let alone historicizing, the series. The scarcity of *Rebus* resources is related to the fact that, as of this writing, only one of the series' eight installments, *Rebus-Film Nr. 1*, has been preserved in full and is readily accessible on DVD silent cinema compilations and streaming platforms such as YouTube.[3] Michael Cowan, the leading authority on the *Rebus* films, has noted that the series was eventually and successfully screened outside of Germany during the 1920s after Leni and Seeber had overcome practical and cultural challenges while modifying the films for non-German audiences. These problems were primarily concerned with translation—i.e. adapting the wording of the puzzle clues for English-speaking viewers—but were also related to the transformation of German pop culture references that would otherwise "have little appeal for US audiences," in Cowan's words.[4] Despite the ease with which the *Rebus* crossword puzzles could be solved, the translational and cultural barriers ultimately hindered their popularity overseas. International audiences' lukewarm reception of the films likely accounts for two intertwined outcomes: the minimal scholarly assessments of the films, and the relative lack of attention paid to their preservation compared with other films from that era.

Nevertheless, the surviving information on *Rebus-Film Nr. 1* creates a workable base for analysis. As mentioned above, several publications authored by Cowan have offered keen insight into the *Rebus* series, situating the films within the larger landscape of cultural and educational films, non-narrative cinematic games, and participatory media.[5] Furthermore, a number of German and Austrian film trade journals during the 1920s referenced the *Rebus* films to some degree, providing a valuable historical context lacking in silent-film scholarship. As an example, the December 26, 1925 issue of the Vienna-based trade magazine *Das Kino-Journal* offered contextual clues about the production of *Rebus-Film Nr. 1* in its "Notes" section. Enthusiastically titled "The First Crossword Puzzle Film Finished!," this brief article describes Leni and Seeber's technological and stylistic achievements as they wrapped up production of *Nr. 1*:

> The production of the first crossword puzzle film—which uses some completely new techniques—the "Rebus-Film" distributed by Nemo-Film-Verleih G.m.b.H., has just concluded. Paul Leni and

Guido Seeber . . . have been anxious to find completely new ways to record and edit the crossword puzzle and already their collaboration is likely to attract professional and public circles.[6]

As implied in the article, film industry professionals saw the *Rebus* films as simultaneously a commercial enterprise, an interactive game, and, most importantly, an artistic feat to be appreciated by critics and the public. *Nr. 1* set the tone for the subsequent installments' treatment as both art and commodity, with the former being observed largely in local intellectual circles. This point is best exemplified by a detailed review of the first *Rebus* installment in the December 12, 1925 issue of *Lichtbildbühne*, which lauds Leni's creative vision and, in particular, Seeber's camerawork and animation. Using the metaphor of "black art" ("schwarzen Kunst") to describe the frenzied editing style and stop-motion techniques, the review underscores the series' ability to breathe new life into the static, flat crossword puzzle and "not only captivate the viewer for minutes, but also give him impressions that correspond to reality." Concluding with praise for the sheer amount of technical skill that the collaborators shared in the making of the *Rebus* films—"So we see difficulties upon difficulties that the layman does not even notice"—the review invites readers to observe the films with the same level of critical detail as they would a work of art, thereby, at least implicitly, characterizing it as such.[7] Other publications, such as *Tagblatt*, a newspaper published in Linz, Austria, also help to fill in some of the gaps of the *Rebus* series' history, giving context on when and for whom the films were screened. The September 25, 1926 issue of *Tagblatt*, for example, describes a *Rebus* installment that was part of a larger program supplementing the 1926 feature film comedy *Ein Wiener in Berlin* (also known as *Der Provinzonkel*) that included an Ufa newsreel and short variety show.[8] While brief, this article helps illustrate *Rebus*'s reach outside of Germany and into neighboring European theaters.

The most useful resources on the *Rebus* series are, of course, the existing prints of *Rebus-Film Nr. 1* themselves, the majority of which are based on the English-language version distributed in the US in 1927.[9] Re-released in 2007 as a part of a larger collection of early experimental films on Kino International's *Avant-Garde 2* DVD compilation, the full fifteen-minute version is the most comprehensive source on Leni's larger *Rebus* project and is an appropriate and valuable starting point for assessing the visual look and feel of the series.

Opening on an image of a two-by-two square grid, *Nr. 1* immediately establishes its abstract tone and frenetic pace by cutting to multiple, seemingly random shots of rumbling ocean currents, with each frame flipping and rotating so as to change its perspective for the viewer. The sequence then cuts to a longer shot of ships sailing across the ocean, panning diagonally up and to the right, which then cuts on action to a panning shot of the exterior of a train station. With the camera positioned as if it were attached to the front of the train—speedily moving backwards into a tunnel and then zooming outward to expose train tracks—the sequence then cuts to images of the busy streets of Berlin; multiple people walk by hurriedly with their dogs (both real, and as stuffed toys), cars quickly drive along, and frenetic shots of theater marquees fill the frame.[10] Cutting rapidly between sweeping panning of the city square—complete with large statues, trees lining the streets, and close-ups of strangers' legs swiftly walking by—*Nr. 1* then takes an even more experimental turn. That is, the documentary-like, live-action footage that opens the film is abruptly punctuated by an animated sequence of blank crossword puzzles, each overlapping with one another and multiplying so as to obscure their intricate grid patterns into disorderly masses of black and white. What then follows is one of many shots that uses a technique best described as a type of cinematic collage; autonomous shots, such as a man's hands using a typewriter, a woman fastening a buckle on her high-heeled shoe, and a beverage being poured into a porcelain tea cup, are superimposed in the same frame on top of a black background. Rotating film reels fill the screen, and an animated black cat, inspired perhaps by the famed Pat Sullivan–Otto Messmer cartoon character Felix the Cat, emerges from the spokes and waves politely to the audience.

The games then commence with the entrance of the animated Mr. Rebus, or Herr Rebus as he is referred to in German prints. A simple, two-dimensional figure consisting of a comically exaggerated trapezoid abdomen and stubby, rectangular appendages, Mr. Rebus greets the audience with a tip of his hat and a friendly smile, prompting the audience to get their crossword puzzles out and ready to play. The opening collage of hands typing, writing, and putting on clothes is repeated, this time overlapping to such an extent that objects become obscured and the once visible black background is completely hidden from view. Mr. Rebus, with a large pointer in hand, then displays the crossword puzzle for the audience; in the US version, the puzzle consists of a grid with six words, with half consisting of vertical or "down" words, and the other consisting of horizontal or "across" words.[11] The pattern for showing the clues to each response is as follows: Mr. Rebus counts the number of squares with his pointer, which illuminates and fills them with question marks. A short montage-like sequence follows each grid, substituting linguistic clues common to traditional crossword puzzles with illustrated, stop-motion, and live-action visual hints that allude, literally or thematically, to each word. The first clue, for example, features shots of a young African American girl dancing on a stage and a band playing instruments enthusiastically in a club; together, these create the answer of "jazzband." This pattern is followed with all of the remaining clues. "India," "ice," "arena," "Paris," and "nine" round out the puzzle, with Mr. Rebus intermittently addressing the audience through playful intertitles such as "That was easy, wasn't it?" and "Haven't you gotten it yet?" The visual clues are then repeated with increasing speed, intercutting quickly between identical footage shown earlier in the film, manipulated footage (either sped up, reversed, or rotated) previously introduced to the audience in its first half, or new visuals that offer additional clues for the audience. As a transition between clues and answers, the animated cat from the film's opening quickly runs into a hand-drawn movie theater, followed by a logo of sorts placing the words "Rebus-Film" into a similar, crossword-like grid. Shots of visual clues are shown with an increasingly faster, dizzying pace—as the cat grabs its head in pain, or perhaps madness—while Mr. Rebus reveals the correct answers to the puzzle. Once the crossword is complete, Mr. Rebus explodes into a mass of smaller, geometric pieces, tipping his hat to the audience one final time before his head splinters and disappears.

The *Rebus-Film* series in general, and *Nr. 1* specifically, can be situated within a much larger tradition of experiments in cinematic engagement in early film. In this trend (or fad, perhaps), audience members were encouraged to play along with puzzles and games in popular film magazines, as members of movie fan clubs, and, significantly, in the theaters themselves, before and during feature film screenings. Interactive movie theater games became so popular in the European context, in fact, that films were often produced with the ultimate goal of including, or even structuring their narratives around, a game or contest. Prior to World War I, for example, German director Joe May, who often collaborated with Leni early in the latter's career, created a series of

Figure 6.1 Mr. Rebus ("Herr Rebus") greeting the audience.

so-called *Preisrätselfilme*, or prize-puzzle films, that invited audience members to solve mysteries along with fictional protagonists on-screen.[12] Moreover, as Cowan has noted, the trend of interactive games can be traced to the earliest days of cinema, when optical toys, mind games, and instructional shorts were carefully woven into screenings in order to attract increased viewership.[13] The participatory nature of the *Rebus* series—taking on a gimmicky tone in its elementary-level puzzles and frequent interjections from Mr. Rebus—mirrors many of the short films developed by exhibitors and filmmakers alike during the pre- and postwar era. This characteristic allows the film to serve as a valuable early example of mass media engagement.

Additionally, scholars and contemporaneous critics have observed that Guido Seeber's work in advertising—namely, his animated *Kipho* short made with film producer Julius Pinschewer—had an immediate stylistic impact on the *Rebus* series. An author for *Lichtbildbühne*, for instance, explicitly noted that *Rebus* is an exact continuation of *Kipho*. Seeber, the author wrote, "does not want to advertise with his *Rebus-Films*, but he wants to give the crossword puzzles cinematic life."[14] Aesthetically, *Kipho* and the *Rebus* series share the same types of avant-garde imagery, "ultimately blending abstraction and figuration" through their mixed-media approaches; the films also share a fast-paced, almost rhythmic pacing, and non-narrative structure.[15] Thematically, the shorts are highly self-referential, drawing attention to the very mechanisms for cinematic image production.[16] Overall, however, *Kipho*'s influence on the *Rebus* series points to the intersections between the commercial and artistic in animated advertisements in the 1920s, where visual artists were recruited by companies as "visual experts" to better understand how audiences responded to the ads that they saw in print and on-screen.[17] This tradition of combining art, entertainment, and psychology is reflected in Leni's *Rebus* series, in which audiences are motivated to make cognitive associations between abstract images, and it is at this point where clearer connections between the series and popular art movements can be made.

It is important to note that Leni was active in the Berlin cultural scene, having studied at the Academy of Fine Arts as a teenager and progressively honing his skills as an illustrator and theatrical set designer.[18] By the mid-1920s, Leni had established himself as a skilled film director and graphic designer. His expertise in these areas led his friend, essayist and screenwriter Rudolf Kurtz, to commission him to design the cover art for his seminal 1926 book *Expressionism and Film* (*Expressionismus und Film*).[19] Leni's intricate design is wholly reflective of his experiments in illustration throughout his early career, exhibiting the same types of clean lines, eye-catching colors, and stylized typefaces as some of his past poster work. It is also a valuable case in point for the ways in which Leni utilized the representational strategies of various experimental art movements. Indeed, the formation of the bulk of the modernist movements awakening in the background of Leni's career—Cubism, Futurism, Dada, and the early years of Surrealism are most important for this analysis—were all preoccupied with the central concern of subverting expectations and playing with objective reality. Leni's cover design similarly shows a clear movement away from realism, combining abstract illustrations of human faces and appendages with cut-outs of photographs from German newspapers, movie stills, and other unidentifiable black-and-white images, presumably also from manipulated film stills or other illustrations. These images are structured as diagonal fragments surrounding a large, circular object, which takes on the appearance of a rotating film reel; each of the juxtaposed images is therefore meant to project outward from the reel, in the same way that motion pictures were thrown from a projector onto a movie screen. Not only is this intricate cover design a clever take on the content of Kurtz's book about Weimar cinema and German Expressionism, but it also offers important insight into the ways in which Leni borrowed the visual vocabulary of contemporaneous experimental art movements. From the combination of word and image, illustration and photography, common to Dada; to the suggestion of rapid movement characteristic of Futurism; to the play with shape, texture, and form in Cubism; and the whimsical combination of seemingly unlike images to create meaning apparent in Surrealism, Leni interpreted the representational strategies of the modernist "-isms" with his own unique artistic voice. This and other experimental graphic designs ultimately propelled Leni's experimental film style in the *Rebus* series.

Prior to the publication of Kurtz's *Expressionism and Film*, Leni was recognized across the Berlin cultural scene as a talented up-and-coming artist in his own right and a frequent patron of the arts. As early as 1921, for instance, Leni exhibited some of his set designs at Berlin's annual "Great Art Exhibition" ("Grosse Berliner Kunstausstellung") in which visual artists presented their work in a festival or *biennale*-style event.[20] Leni later described his participation at the 1924 Kunstausstellung in an editorial piece published in *Der Kinematograph* called "Architecture in Film" ("Baukunst im Film"). In this essay, he noted that the exhibition "may be deemed a success," in that it confirmed—in his mind, for the first time—that those working in cinematic set design were considered "independent creative artist[s]," capable of their own individual, artistic contributions to the look and feel of a film.[21] Based on Leni's frequent participation at visual arts events throughout Berlin and his friendship with contemporaries in the German experimental scene, a very strong case can be made for the following claim. Given Leni's personal and professional relationships with other artists and filmmakers, it is highly likely that he attended an "Absolute Film" exhibition event organized by a radical artists' collective known as the *Novembergruppe* ("November Group"). This event was held as a matinee on May 4, 1925 at Berlin's Ufa-Theater Kurfürstendamm—coincidentally, the same theater where

Leni's *Waxworks* premiered in November 1924—and repeated a week later due to popular demand. It showcased a number of key avant-garde film productions, including Hans Richter's *Rhythmus 21* (1921), René Clair and Francis Picabia's *Entr'acte* (1924), Viking Eggeling's *Symphonie Diagonale* (1924), Fernand Léger's *Ballet Mécanique* (1924), and several short pieces by Walter Ruttmann, who in 1927 went on to direct *Berlin: Symphony of a Big City* (*Berlin: Die Sinfonie der Großstadt*), one of the most famous films in the "City Symphony" genre.[22] It is highly likely that Leni, deeply immersed in Berlin's experimental art "scene," took inspiration from these films while laying out his plans for the *Rebus* series.

Indeed, Leni may have been loosely associated with the *Novembergruppe*, the exhibition's sponsor. Evidence suggests that he may have worked alongside it, though it is doubtful that he shared the group's radical political leanings. A rather mysterious account of the origins of the *Novembergruppe* lists Leni as on the group's periphery, with painter Heinrich Richter-Berlin remarking:

> When the revolution was a few days old, many people gathered at noon on Potsdamer Platz to hear new things. When crossing the square I met Max Pechstein. He had a plan. He believed that one should start afresh. I should get my people together and he would bring the bridge. He already had a name: *Novembergruppe* ... The sculptor [Georg] Leschnitzer and the graphic designer Leni had stood ten meters away from us. When I looked around, they disappeared into the subway. Max Pechstein thought it better to do the same. I totally agreed. This is how the *Novembergruppe* was born.[23]

While rather cryptic, this account is valuable in that it places Leni within the larger orbit of the *Novembergruppe*. Moreover, Leni appears to have been a respected figure in the arts throughout the 1910s and 20s, which could have motivated his experimentation in the graphic and cinematic arts, leading to the creation of the *Rebus-Film* series.

An expression of that respect came from Hans Richter, a highly prominent figure in the modernist art movements. In addition to his work as an artist, Richter edited *G: Material zur Elementaren Gestaltung*, a short-lived avant-garde arts journal published from 1923 to 1926. He devoted the final issue of *G*—a double issue, published in April 1926—to film and included a tip of the hat to the *Rebus* series. It consists of a still image from *Nr. 1*—a collage of hands filmed at varying distances from the camera as anonymous people gather pieces of paper and writing instruments, signifying the start of the puzzle-solving process—and a caption that reads: "New means of expression in film are being exploited industrially for the first time. – Crossword-puzzle-film."[24] Richter's short untitled piece does not mention the *Rebus* series by name but explicitly credits Leni for the "concept" and Seeber as "operator." Though a modest little tribute, it signifies what Richter regarded as an important cinematic milestone: the absorption of avant-garde techniques into films designed for general audiences. In addition, the piece is enhanced by the journal issue's rich material that surrounds it: frame blow-ups from the films *Rhythmus 1925*, *Entr'acte*, *Ballet Mécanique*, and *Symphonie Diagonale*; essays by such important figures as Viking Eggeling, Marcel L'Herbier, René Clair, Fernand Léger, Germaine Dulac, and Rudolf Kurtz; and photo-collages by Man Ray. In the pages of this journal and beyond, Leni and his *Rebus* enterprise were keeping company with the world's top avant-garde films and filmmakers.[25]

Overall, Leni's trajectory within and alongside experimental arts circles in Berlin shows a more complicated web of connections in his own films and across the art movements in Europe during this period. As the following analysis will show, the *Rebus* series encapsulates the dialogic nature of the varying experimental arts scenes across Europe, pointing to their intricate commonalities rather than dividing them geographically, ideologically, or stylistically, as is often the case in some art historical records. The *Rebus* films, and *Nr. 1* in particular, demonstrate Leni's careful attention to all aspects of experimental art flourishing at the beginning of the twentieth century.

MR. REBUS GOES TO THE *SALON*: CUBISM, FUTURISM, DADA, AND SURREALISM

While Cubism rose to popularity some twenty years before the debut of *Nr. 1*, it is safe to say that the movement's visual and technical vocabularies, including the fragmentation and layering of disparate textures and images, were still exerting influence on Leni's generation.[26] It is not surprising, then, that Leni's *Rebus* series borrows from the same Cubistic tendencies to play with shape, texture, and perspective. The frequent use of filmic collage in *Nr. 1*, particularly during the aforementioned opening sequence and in the clue for ice—in which spinning ice cream desserts are positioned on an angle and layered on top of one another—is one distinct parallel between the *Rebus* films and Cubism. For Cubists such as Juan Gris (and, later, Futurists like Carlo Carrà), the use of collage transformed classical perspectives; by combining seemingly unrelated fragments of images in order to "reveal new interpretations and send new messages," in the words of art historians Guillaume Apollinaire and Dorothea Eimert, the artists revealed multiple perspectives simultaneously, thereby opening up new modes of seeing for the spectator.[27] So, too, did Leni use the method of collage in *Nr. 1*; the overlapping of otherwise random images in the film's opening, like disembodied hands typing and reaching for pens in their pockets, helps to signal to the audience that the game is about to begin, and much like the anonymous figures on the screen, they should also get ready to play. He repeats this device when giving the clue for ice, in which sequences of layered, rotating ice cream molds and champagne bottles in chilled buckets come together literally (in the same frame) and figuratively (they are each indexical images of the word "ice") for the viewers and help them solve that portion of the rebus. Throughout *Nr. 1*, Leni assembled images from everyday life in a Cubist-style collage and assigned new meanings to them in the context of the crossword puzzle; in so doing, the film mirrored similar types of human perception that modernist artists wanted to display and experiment within their works.

Cubism's visual impact can be seen in the figure of Mr. Rebus, who, reflecting one of the most common visual techniques in the Cubist era, is constructed from exaggerated, geometric shapes. The top-hatted, illustrated character resembles the subjects of a variety of different Cubist paintings like *Man with a Guitar* (Georges Braque, 1911) and *Man with a Pipe* (*L'Homme à la Pipe*, Juan Gris, 1911) that feature a modern male character, composed from a series of two-dimensional blocks and harsh black lines. While one could argue that Mr. Rebus's geometric appearance harks back to the square-like grid of the crossword puzzle, this observation could be taken one step further to include Cubist experiments with (or, rather, in opposition to) conventional portrayals of reality. Cubists, in response to Renaissance and Impressionist art, were inspired by recent shifts in the sciences to move beyond the objective and explore different planes of space, place, and time.[28] The response to this call for subjectivity was the use of geometry, creating images by placing squares on different planes and presenting multiple different spatial views so as to change the ways in which spectators see and interact with the world around them. The geometric appearance of Mr. Rebus—as well as the motif of squares and grids that recall the rebus puzzle—can be understood in the same way. That is, by portraying a character with harsh, jagged angles and comically disproportionate body parts, the *Rebus* series offers new insights into the ways that visual media (in this case, animated film) can present new forms of reality to the viewer. This idea is then carried over into the ways that the montages, filmic collages, and animated insertions are strung together throughout *Nr. 1*, in which multiple perspectives on abstract concepts come together to create concrete answers to the audiences' puzzles. This scientific, almost mathematical approach to image construction is the ultimate Cubist influence on *Nr. 1*, imparting a unique visual style that has implications for subjectivity and representing reality.

Futurism is another important aesthetic influence on Leni's experimental series. According to Martin F. Norden, the Futurists in painting (and, as the 1920s approached, cinema), by and large, took on a "keen interest in the excitement and turbulence of modern urban life and the dynamics of machinery," evident in the frequent use of subject matter such as city streets, infrastructure, and moving automobiles.[29] Although there is little to suggest that Leni was deliberately positioning himself as a Futurist, the *Rebus* series mirrors what many Futurists attempted with their art—to experiment with rapid, frenetic movement characteristic of urban modernity. Panning, tilting, zooming, rotating, and shaking the camera, Leni and Seeber established the motif of movement from the beginning to the very end of *Nr. 1*, their film reflecting the hectic nature of Berlin's city streets and reproducing an apt portrayal of modernity easily recognizable to audiences both in and outside of the original German context. Early in *Nr. 1*, for example, Leni and Seeber included a shot of a leashed dachshund rapidly walking with its owner along a Berlin sidewalk. This image bears a striking resemblance to Giacomo Balla's 1912 Futurist painting *Dynamism of a Dog on a Leash* (*Dinamismo di un cane al guinzaglio*), which also depicts a speedy dachshund, its hyper-movement suggested by Balla's painterly blurring and multiplication of its legs. Leni and Seeber captured movement within the frame throughout *Nr. 1*; clues for the crossword answer "nine," for instance, include stop-motion animated matryoshka dolls, playing cards, and pick-up sticks appearing and disappearing onscreen. Even when there are static or slow-moving objects in each of the clue segments, Leni and Seeber added motion to them by employing in-camera tricks such as reversing or speeding up the footage. These strategies further strengthen *Nr. 1*'s connections to Futurism.

Besides the explicit use of motion, Leni also drew several other connections between *Nr. 1* and Futurism, namely in his use of *mise-en-scène*. The Paris clue sequence, which reveals the Eiffel Tower framed by a triangular iris, is framed in a way that makes an interesting visual parallel to *Tour Eiffel*, painted by French Futurist Robert Delaunay in 1911 and portraying the titular Parisian landmark as a series of exposed, rusted metal beams accompanied by dense clouds. *Nr. 1* can also trace part of its iconography to Umberto Boccioni's *The Laugh* (*La Risata*, 1911); the jazzband sequence, which features the rowdy and chaotic interiors of music clubs, makes a direct visual connection to the painting, which shows a colorful, equally chaotic scene of patrons in a crowded dancehall.[30] Leni's frequent shots of automobiles and busy city streets in *Nr. 1* also draw interesting parallels to some Futurist artworks and their fascination with mechanized motion and speed. Pieces including Carrà's *Jolts of a Taxicab* (*Sobbalzi di carrozza*, 1911), Christopher Richard Wynne Nevinson's *The Arrival* (1912), and Raymond Duchamp-Villon's abstract sculpture *The Large Horse* (*Le Grand Cheval*, 1914) become aesthetic counterparts to Leni's *Nr. 1* through their exploration of movements of ships, cars, and other vehicles. The argument can easily be made, therefore, that Leni's work echoes the goals of the Futurist movement and extends them for a modern 1920s audience.

One of the more compelling connections that can be made between the *Rebus* series and experimental art lies in its use of spontaneity, wordplay, and interaction, traits most common in the so-called "anti-art" movement

Figure 6.2 One visual clue for "Paris."

of postwar Europe, Dada. Leni's *Rebus-Film* series solicits the same types of interactivity and cognitive problem-solving as its Dada counterparts minus the latter's political trappings. *Nr. 1*'s opening and the clues sections for each of the crossword answers follow the same tendency toward randomness that Dada artists subscribed to in their artworks. Leni's films involved, according to Cowan, "the rapid identification of simultaneous phenomena in movement," presenting seconds-long clips of image clues that, when taken as a whole, have one-to-one correspondences with the answers in the rebus puzzle.[31] For example, the clue for "nine" features images of an animated calendar, a moving abacus, a pair of dice, playing cards, toys, and candle sticks. Individually, each shot has no meaning aside from its surface image; the depicted objects have no relation to one another and are incongruous to the remainder of the film, which for the most part uses live-action footage. However, when audience members mentally stitch these images together and note their formal characteristics—each image features the number nine, or comes in a set of nine—they can conclude that the answer to the puzzle is "nine." It can be assumed, then, that much like Dada artists, Leni adopted the technique of free association, stringing seemingly abstract and random images together in order to create new meanings for the viewers.

Furthermore, *Nr. 1* shares important connections to Dada experiments with cinema during the larger part of the 1920s, specifically through the manipulation of scenes of modernity through camera and editing techniques. It is worth underscoring the point that *Nr. 1* and the *Rebus* series as a whole were not nearly as politically charged as, say, René Clair and Francis Picabia's influential Dada short *Entr'acte*, which historian Malcolm Turvey has described as making a targeted aggression toward the viewer and, subsequently, the "materialistic self-interest of the bourgeoisie."[32] Instead, Leni adopted similar devices *sans* politics, including superimpositions, rotated and mirrored images, and rapid editing techniques in order to disorient the viewer. Moreover, *Nr. 1* parallels Dadaistic films like Marcel Duchamp's *Anemic Cinema* (1926) and Léger's *Ballet Mécanique* in its use of on-screen language and wordplay; in addition, Leni's frequent use of abstract shapes, patterns, and overall image distortion is shared in many of Man Ray's filmic experiments, particularly in his 1923 short, *Return to Reason* (*Le Retour à la Raison*). Mr. Rebus, too, holds striking visual similarities to Dada/Cubist/Futurist film experiments; most notably, he bears a conceptual resemblance to the animated and fragmented figure of Charles Chaplin ("Charlot") who introduces *Ballet Mécanique* and later implodes into smaller shapes near the end of the film. Above all, *Nr. 1* engages with Dada film experiments through its intrinsically goal-oriented structure (in that it motivates the audience to solve a word puzzle) that is deliberately broken up by disruptive editing patterns. Extending the aims of Dada in the plastic arts, filmic Dada often oscillates between continuity and discontinuity, featuring objects whose initial, causal relationships are fractured and later haphazardly reassembled as the narrative progresses.[33] Viewers are therefore invited to find these causal links in the seemingly random assemblage of images on-screen, coming to some sort of resolution during the film's conclusion. The clues and answers sequences in *Nr. 1* reflect a similar type of structuring, in which various interrelated clips for each clue are shown and later interrupted by Mr. Rebus's verbal interjections (in the US print) or the comic performance of the animated cat. Much like Dada films, the significance of each shot to the puzzle is eventually revealed, but not without some mental acuity on the part of the audience.

The Dada movement is an important tool for dissecting the playful, seemingly spontaneous visual components of Leni's *Rebus* series; another adjacent movement, Surrealism, helps to further understand the seemingly arbitrary combination and succession of images in *Nr. 1*. It is important to consider, borrowing from scholar Sarane Alexandrian, that the defining line separating Surrealism and Dada involves a move beyond objective reality into the so-called "purely interior model" of image creation that was not only deeply rooted in the subconscious but also wholly non-random, taking on an intricate structure that could be best understood through careful analysis.[34] The filmic medium proved to be an apt instrument for displaying and better understanding the internalized, unconscious motives of the artists, allowing for a more innovative platform for experimentation, as J. H. Matthews has offered.[35] It would come as no surprise, then, if Leni—who lived and worked at the same time as Surrealist artist-filmmakers of the era—took inspiration from this movement while developing the *Rebus* series. Structurally, the flow of images in *Nr. 1* can be likened to the same, psychological types of free association and image construction as endorsed by Surrealist artists. Ray's *Retour* and later works like *Emak-Bakia* (1926) and *L'Étoile de mer* (1928) immediately come to mind, pairing disjointed narratives accompanied by text and shots of rotating objects and starfish (in *Emak-Bakia* and *L'Étoile*, respectively); Leni, too, intercut blurry, disjointed images of Berlin city streets with seemingly random objects, giving a similar dream-like quality to the film. Likewise, the use of superimpositions and other editing techniques adds to *Nr. 1*'s resemblance to a dream. Much like Brazilian artist Alberto Cavalcanti's Paris-centered City Symphony film *Rien que les heures* (1926) and its memorable shot of overlapping, blinking eyes, *Nr. 1* superimposes disembodied hands and feet in his film, so as to collapse real space and time and transport the viewers into the world of the unconscious.

NR. 1 AND EXPERIMENTAL FILM STYLES

Leni's emulation of experimental film styles was not strictly limited to these visual art movements; the *Rebus* films have clear connections to the simultaneously emerging style of montage made popular by Soviet theorists and filmmakers such as Sergei Eisenstein, Lev Kuleshov, and Dziga Vertov. Two defining features of Soviet montage stand out during this foundational period: "associative montage," or the use of free association through visual repetition to generate meaning; and "rhythmic montage," or the alternation of different durations of shots in a sequence, that both manipulate cinematic space and work against hegemonic modes of representation in modern society.[36] Leni's *Rebus-Film* series extends the adjacent project of Soviet montage filmmakers through the adoption of both of these editing techniques. As mentioned previously, *Nr. 1* distinctly uses the method of free association to help audiences find answers to each of the clues in the crossword puzzle. Throughout the film, images that resemble each other, or have the same type of indexical value, are edited together in sequence; in order for audiences to understand their value, they have to combine these visual clues with their own frames of reference and lived experiences. Clues for Paris, for example, feature the juxtaposition of landmarks like the Eiffel Tower, Notre Dame, and the Arc de Triomphe with shots of busy Parisian streets. Taken individually, these images would be essentially meaningless but, when assembled together through the rapid editing style of montage, they are presented as one unit, and the audience is able to arrive at the answer of Paris from these visual clues.

Furthermore, the pacing of the film parallels that of rhythmic montage; each of the clues is shown in similarly timed intervals, giving the audience enough time to view and evaluate them on-screen. Once the answers portion of *Nr. 1* begins, the pacing of each shot increases in speed, to test the audience's skill in rapidly identifying image clues and, from the perspective of montage filmmakers, collapse the boundaries of space and time constructed within traditional modes of filmic representation. The characteristic speed of Soviet montage is replicated in *Nr. 1*, offering a new perspective on the shifting urban landscape in Berlin and abroad.

Cinematic experiments in representing urban life were of course not unique to Soviet montage filmmakers. The City Symphony film, which geographically was much closer to Leni (having been popularized in Germany by experimental documentarist Walter Ruttmann), reflected a larger tendency in protodocumentary filmmaking akin to Futurism in painting: fascination with the rapid pace of everyday life. These so-called "avant-docs"—a term coined by scholar Scott MacDonald in "Avant-Doc: Eight Intersections"—became microcosms of the very cities that they represented, exploring the joys, and oftentimes dangers, of living in the city. Following in the tradition of early travelogues and ethnographic films, City Symphonies featured real-life footage of the places they depicted.[37] From its opening sequence, *Nr. 1* establishes itself within the realm of avant-doc filmmaking and, consequently, the City Symphony genre. Featuring Seeber's skillful, mobile camerawork and editing that moves between Berlin, Paris, Spain, and India, *Nr. 1* captures the hustle and bustle of everyday life, oftentimes using pans, wipes, and dissolves to mimic the very speed in which automobiles and passersby move.[38] Additionally, in a visual link to films like *Manhatta* (1921), a mini-City Symphony created by painter Charles Sheeler and photographer Paul Strand, *Nr. 1* offers sweeping shots of urban landscapes, emphasizing building façades in addition to their interior, structural components. The Paris clue sequence is one key example of this, as the camera pans upward and films through the steel beams of the Eiffel Tower. The speed with which people rush by in the Berlin sequence, sometimes running into or swerving past the camera, offer further connections to the City Symphony films. Berlin is a large, hectic city, but it is nevertheless a shining example of European modernity. Clues for India—which display towering landmarks, dancers, and townspeople riding elephants—also hark back to the travelogue roots of the City Symphony films, inadvertently establishing an interpersonal distance between "home" and "away," "us" and "other."[39] All in all, *Nr. 1* adopts the same type of visual and rhythmic language as its contemporary City Symphony films, taking on an interesting position in the trajectory of avant-doc filmmaking.

CONCLUSION

In the years leading up to and following the *Rebus-Film* series, Leni considered himself amongst the growing number of visual experts amplifying the artistic value of cinema across Germany. As Leni wrote,

> The way the film is shot, the directions of motion, the movements: all of these factors are as vital to the architect's decision-making process as the way lighting is placed, the camera's position, the angle of view, and the choice of what is placed in the frame. It takes real talent to bring an artistic vision to completion when one faces such extensive limitations.[40]

While Leni was specifically discussing the role of the set designer or "architect," the same types of unique skill can be applied to the much larger task of directing films, of which he maintained success despite the ever-evolving technological and aesthetic demands of the medium. Leni's expertise as a cinematic artist, too, was routinely recognized across European and American arts groups even after his turn to commercial cinema in the mid-1920s, having been featured in the October 1925 matinee of Britain's elite Film Society, amongst fellow film artists like Ruttmann, Richter, and Eisenstein.[41] Moreover, Leni's *Rebus* films were regarded amongst other colleagues in the so-called "independent cinema" circle such as Cavalcanti, Ray, and Dulac in the October 1929 issue of the cinema magazine, *Close Up*, as part of a "happy blend of films that have already become classics and those that are the work of the advance guard" across several Belgian cinema clubs.[42] The *Rebus-Film* series, rather than adopting a position as a mere gimmick in the larger history of film exhibition, therefore serves as a larger experiment with multiple avant-garde styles in the visual/plastic arts as well as the evolving medium of film. Marking a period of transition in Leni's professional life—from the end of his German career to the beginning of his short-lived American career—the *Rebus-Film* series gives insight into Leni's sheer creative capacity, offering a unique lens for exploring his specific artistic process. The series points to the larger talent Leni possessed in adopting new artistic styles and adapting them to his unique perspective, creating a style all of his own.

NOTES

1. Michael Cowan, "Moving Picture Puzzles: Training Urban Perception in the Weimar 'Rebus Films,'" *Screen* 51, no. 3 (September 2010): 211. The crossword puzzle *per se* is considered the brainchild of *New York World* editor Arthur Wynne, a Liverpool native who published his first crossword construction in the *World* in 1913. See Deb Amlen, "How the Crossword Became an American Pastime," *Smithsonian Magazine*, December 2019, available at <https://www.smithsonianmag.com/arts-culture/crossword-became-american-pastime-180973558/>.

2. See Cowan, "Moving Picture Puzzles."
3. The only other installment in the series known to exist as of this writing is *Rebus-Film Nr. 3*, which can only be viewed at the Filmarchiv/Bundesarchiv in Berlin. See Cowan, "Moving Picture Puzzles," 199.
4. Cowan, "Moving Picture Puzzles," 200.
5. See Michael Cowan, "Learning to Love the Movies: Puzzles, Participation, and Cinephilia in Interwar European Film Magazines," *Film History: An International Journal* 27, no. 4 (2015): 1–45.
6. "Der Erste Kreutzwort-Rätselfilm Fertig!" *Das Kino-Journal*, December 26, 1925, reprinted in *Paul Leni: Grafik, Theater, Film*, ed. Hans-Michael Bock (Frankfurt am Main: Deutsches Filmmuseum, 1986), 184–5.
7. Review of *Rebus Nr. 1*, *Lichtbildbühne*, December 12, 1925, reprinted in Bock, *Paul Leni*, 184–5.
8. "Kolosseum Kino, 'Ein Wiener in Berlin,'" *Tagblatt* (Linz, Austria), September 5, 1926.
9. Each installment of the *Rebus-Film* series was screened before the start of a feature film; the clues to the puzzle were shown one week, and their solutions were subsequently revealed at a later screening. Available copies of *Nr. 1* combine clues and solutions into a single film, rather than separating them into two distinct films.
10. The film includes a swish pan of the Palast-am-Zoo, Berlin's largest movie theater. Although partially illegible due to the deliberately shaky camerawork, the Palast's marquee reads, "Emil Jannings in Varieté." This may be an intentional wink-and-nod to Leni's own involvement with the exhibition of E. A. Dupont's film at that theater; Leni had designed the live prologue for *Varieté*, which opened at the Palast less than a month before the debut of *Rebus Nr. 1*. See Martin F. Norden's chapter in this volume.
11. According to Cowan, the US print of *Nr. 1* was modified to remove German-specific answers to help it resonate with and attract American audiences. The number of words in each grid changed from eight (in the German version) to six (in the US version), and the answers themselves were adapted from German pop culture and geographic references to American ones (e.g., switching "Jannings" to "jazzband"). See Cowan, "Moving Picture Puzzles," 199–200.
12. Leni later returned to the *Preisrätselfilme* for his final film, *The Last Warning*. Midway through, exhibitors would stop the film and allow spectators to submit their guesses for "whodunit," and then resume it to reveal the correct answer. See Shawn Shimpach's chapter in this volume.
13. Cowan, "Learning to Love," 19.
14. Reprinted in Bock, *Paul Leni*, 184.
15. Michael Cowan, "Absolute Advertising: Walter Ruttmann and the Weimar Advertising Film," *Cinema Journal* 52, no. 4 (Summer 2013): 51.
16. In *Nr. 1*, this self-referentiality is demonstrated in a variety of different ways, including shots of film marquees, collages of film reels, and the transition between clues and answers featuring the animated cat entering a movie theater. In *Kipho*, Seeber mostly draws attention to the cinematic apparatus, featuring gears, film reels, and the projection instrument itself. See Michael Cowan, "Advertising, Rhythm, and the Filmic Avant-Garde: Guido Seeber and Julius Pinschewer's Kipho Film," *October* 131 (Winter 2010): 23–50.
17. Cowan, "Absolute Advertising," 60
18. See Kerstin Rech, "The Director Paul Leni: The Man with the Gifted Look" ("Der Regisseur Paul Leni: Der Mann mit dem genialen Blick"), *Stuttgarter-Zeitung*, July 8, 2015, available at <https://www.stuttgarter-zeitung.de/inhalt.der-regisseur-paul-leni-der-mann-mit-dem-genialen-blick.75fc77a2-c1b9-45e8-9761-9a9291ee4e53.html>.

19. Kurtz and Leni's friendship and creative partnership began in the 1910s and continued up to Leni's death in 1929. Kurtz, who wrote a lengthy obituary for Leni published in the September 21, 1929 issue of *Lichtbildbühne*, was a noted figure in the Berlin arts scene. He was the editor-in-chief of *Lichtbildbühne* and may have introduced Leni to avant-garde visual and performing artists, catalyzing Leni's experimentation with alternative modes of representation. For more on Kurtz and Leni, see Christian Kiening and Ulrich Johannes Beil, "Afterword," in Rudolf Kurtz, *Expressionism and Film*, ed. Christian Kiening and Ulrich Johannes Beil, trans. Brenda Benthien (New Barnet: John Libbey Publishing, 2016).
20. See "Baukunst und Kunstgewerbe auf der Grossen Berliner Kunstausstellung," *Die Kunst: Monatshefte für Freie und Angewandte Kunst*, July 1921, n.p.
21. Paul Leni, "Baukunst im Film," *Der Kinematograph*, August 4, 1924, reprinted as "Architecture in Film," in *The Promise of Cinema: German Film Theory 1907-1933*, ed. Anton Kaes, Nicholas Baer, and Michael Cowan (Oakland: University of California Press, 2016), 499.
22. For details on the "Absolute Film" matinee, see Walter Schobert, "'Painting in Time' and 'Visual Music': On German Avant-Garde Films of the 1920s," in *Expressionist Film: New Perspectives*, ed. Dietrich Scheunemann (Rochester, NY: Camden House, 2003), 241–3. Schobert's chapter includes a facsimile of the one-page "Der Absolute Film" program, which lists *Ballet Mécanique* as *Images mobiles* and *Rhythmus 21* as *Film ist Rhythmus*. For contemporaneous discussions of the exhibition, see "Film-Schau," *Vossische Zeitung*, May 5, 1925; and Rudolf Arnheim, "Der absolute Film," *Das Stachelschwein*, August 1925, 56–8, reprinted as "The Absolute Film" in Kaes et al., *Promise of Cinema*, 460–1.
23. Heinrich Richter-Berlin quoted in Uwe Stiehler, "Müllgrubenkunst Attackiert die Stützen der Gesellschaft" ("Garbage-Pit Art Attacks the Pillars of Society"), *Märkische Oderzeitung Strausberg*, December 28, 2018. A slightly different translation from the one offered here may be found in Joan Weinstein, *The End of Expressionism: Art and the November Revolution in Germany, 1918-1919* (Chicago: University of Chicago Press, 1990), 27.
24. By "exploited industrially," Richter was referring to the work of commercial filmmakers. He clarified his stance a few years later in a piece titled "Neue Mittel der Film-Gestaltung" ("New Means of Film Design"), in which he observed the convergence of avant-garde and commercial filmmaking practices. He wrote: "In our nonunified society, industry (economically oriented) and 'avant-garde' (artistically oriented) are still at odds with each other. The dissolution of this opposition is less a question of artistic development and far more one of societal development. The amalgamation of feature film and art film into 'FILM' is taking place slowly, but it is occurring nonetheless." See Hans Richter, "Neue Mittel der Film-Gestaltung," *Die Form: Zeitschrift für gestaltende Arbeit* 4, no. 3 (February 1, 1929): 56, reprinted as "New Means of Filmmaking," in Kaes et al., *Promise of Cinema*, 474.
25. In addition, an announcement heralding the publication of Rudolf Kurtz's *Expressionism and Film*, which mentions Leni by name as the book's cover designer, adorns the back covers of this issue and the previous one (no. 4, published in March 1926). Both issues, including their front and back covers, are reproduced in their entirety in *G: An Avant-Garde Journal of Art, Architecture, Design, and Film 1923-1926*, ed. Detlef Mertins and Michael W. Jennings, trans. Steven Lindberg and Margareta Ingrid Christian (Los Angeles: Getty Research Institute, 2010), 203–40. The brief acknowledgment of the *Rebus* films noted in the text is on p. 221.
26. Guillaume Apollinaire and Dorothea Eimert, *Cubism* (New York: Parkstone International, 2012), 13; Jack Flam, "Menu du Jour: Word and Image in Cubist Painting," in *Cubism: The Leonard A. Lauder Collection*, ed. Emily Braun and Rebecca Rabinow (New York: Metropolitan Museum of Art, 2014), 136.

27. Apollinaire and Eimert, *Cubism*, 41; see also Elizabeth Cowling, "Juan Gris: Four Collages," in Braun and Rabinow, *Cubism*, 120.
28. Apollinaire and Eimert, *Cubism*, 1.
29. Futurists were, by and large, preoccupied with three key ideas: the humanization of machines, the mechanization of humans, and the fast pace of modern urban life. All three help distinguish the Futurists' work from that of the Cubists, whose art, while still emphasizing modernity, tended to analyze and synthesize stationary subjects—portraits, still-life arrangements, landscapes—from multiple perspectives. Interestingly, the characteristics of Futurism and, to a lesser extent, Cubism were shared by Soviet montage theorists and filmmakers during the 1920s, pointing to the greater interconnectedness of European modernist art movements. For more on this general topic, see Martin F. Norden, "The Avant-Garde Cinema of the 1920s: Connections to Futurism, Precisionism, and Suprematism," *Leonardo: Journal of the International Society for the Arts, Sciences, and Technology* 17, no. 2 (April 1984): 108–12.
30. Didier Ottinger (ed.), *Futurism* (Paris: Éditions du Centre Pompidou, 2009), 130.
31. Cowan, "Moving Picture Puzzles," 217.
32. Malcolm Turvey, *The Filming of Modern Life: European Avant-Garde Film of the 1920s* (Cambridge, MA: MIT Press, 2011), 79.
33. Turvey, *Filming of Modern Life*, 84.
34. Sarane Alexandrian, *Surrealist Art*, trans. Gordon Clough (New York: Thames and Hudson, 1985), 60.
35. J. H. Matthews, *Surrealism and Film* (Ann Arbor: University of Michigan Press, 1971), 79.
36. Alexander Graf, "Paris-Berlin-Moscow: On the Montage Aesthetic in the City Symphony Films of the 1920s," in *Avant-Garde Film*, ed. Alexander Graf and Dietrich Scheunemann (Amsterdam: Rodopi, 2007), 82; Anna Lawton, "Rhythmic Montage in the Films of Dziga Vertov: A Poetic Use of the Language of Cinema," *Pacific Coast Philology* 13 (October 1978): 46–7.
37. Scott MacDonald, "Avant-Doc: Eight Intersections," *Film Quarterly* 64, no. 2 (Winter 2010): 50–7; Erica Stein, "Abstract Space, Microcosmic Narrative, and the Disavowal of Modernity in *Berlin: Symphony of a Great City*," *Journal of Film and Video* 65, no. 4 (2013): 4–6.
38. Seeber apparently traveled across the globe to get footage of the exotic locales for each clue. See Cowan, "Moving Picture Puzzles," 198. For Seeber's thoughts on the importance of highly mobile camerawork, see Guido Seeber, "Die taumelnde Kamera," *Die Filmtechnik* 5 (1925), 92–3, reprinted as "The Delirious Camera," in Kaes et al., *Promise of Cinema*, 503–5.
39. Stein, "Abstract Space," 6.
40. Leni, "Baukunst im Film," 500.
41. See Malte Hagener, *Moving Forward, Looking Back: The European Avant-Garde and the Invention of Film Culture, 1919–1939* (Amsterdam: Amsterdam University Press, 2007), 92; BFI National Library, "The Film Society 1925–1929: A Guide to Collections," available at <https://www.bfi.org.uk/sites/bfi.org.uk/files/downloads/bfi-the-film-society-1925-1939-a-guide-to-collections.pdf>.
42. Carl Vincent, "The Independent Cinema in Belgium," *Close Up*, October 1929, 270–1.

CHAPTER 7

Bravura Beginnings: Paul Leni and the Art of the Prologue

Martin F. Norden

A hush settled over the opening-night crowd at Manhattan's Colony Theater as the heavy curtains parted halfway to reveal a shocking sight at center stage: a manacled convict strapped to an electric chair. It was an actor in the hot seat, of course, but his appearance was startling nonetheless. His face lit with a greenish-blue spotlight aimed up from the footlights, he stared bleakly out at the audience as an off-stage voice boomed, "You have been outside the law!" Suddenly, the stage went pitch-black, the immediate darkness signaling the criminal's demise. After a moment, the curtains opened all the way to reveal a new scene: a police sergeant and a newspaper reporter seated at a table in the foreground, starkly lit by a single hanging spotlight. "That's what happens to all of 'em in the end," said the sergeant gruffly. He then leaned into the journalist: "Lemme tell you a story."[1]

So began the aptly named "The Police Sergeant's Story," a live introduction to *Outside the Law*, a 1920 Universal movie that opened in revival at the Colony on May 9, 1926. Known in the film business as a prologue, the brief theatrical performance featured a half dozen actors, the Kam Tai Chinese juggling troupe, Chinatown images projected onto a scrim, and striking lighting effects. The audience members watched transfixed as multiple storylines began unfolding: the tale of the convicted man and the young woman he murdered, the framing story of the cop and the reporter, and, a few moments later, *Outside the Law* itself, a Tod Browning underworld thriller starring Lon Chaney and set partially in San Francisco's Chinatown district. Unbeknownst to the audience, a fourth story was underway as well. A kind of overarching narrative, it centered on a forty-year-old German expatriate intently watching the live proceedings from the wings: Paul Leni, then presenting his first American-based creative work.

Figure 7.1 Opening night for Tod Browning's *Outside the Law* and Paul Leni's accompanying prologue, "The Police Sergeant's Story."

This fourth tale—the story of Leni's work as a prologue producer—forms the focus of this chapter. Film historians have long known that Universal Pictures president Carl Laemmle recruited Leni to come to Hollywood in 1926. Leni had co-directed the internationally acclaimed *Waxworks* (*Das Wachsfigurenkabinett*) in Germany two years before, and his work on this film might seem a suitable credential for employment as a Hollywood director. However, numerous newspaper and trade-journal articles of the time suggest that Laemmle initially had different plans for his new employee; he wanted Leni to design movie sets and head up a newly created prologue department at Universal City. It was not until after the success of his American prologues that Leni made the transition to Hollywood director. In other words, his reputation and impressive work in Germany as a visual artist, set and costume designer, prologue producer, and film director had caught Laemmle's attention, but it was his work as a Manhattan-based prologue producer that demonstrated to "Uncle Carl" that he had a thorough understanding of American tastes and expectations and could rise to the challenge of directing films in the US.

Relying heavily on contemporaneous newspaper and trade-journal accounts, this chapter examines Leni's film-related work immediately before and after his arrival in New York City in the spring of 1926. In particular, it traces the prologues he staged in Ufa's mammoth Palast-am-Zoo theater in Berlin for such films as E. A. Dupont's *Varieté* (1925), Ernst Lubitsch's *Forbidden Paradise* (1924), and Herbert Brenon's *Peter Pan* (1924), and two he created for Universal films exhibited in New York's Colony Theater: the aforementioned "The Police Sergeant's Story" and "Tremendous Trifles," performed ahead of William Seiter's comedy *Rolling Home* (1926). This chapter argues that Leni's months-long work on these live productions formed a critical bridge between the German and American phases of his multifaceted filmmaking career. They served as a series of directorial "auditions," in a sense, and paved the way for Leni's brief but impactful career as a Hollywood director.

RISE OF THE PROLOGUE

"The Police Sergeant's Story" is an example of a live event that movie theater owners in urban areas would often stage in an effort to fill their large houses on a daily and nightly basis during the late silent-film era. A typical prologue might consist of a one-act play specifically written as a lead-in to the film with which it was paired and often featured characters modeled after ones in that film. It might also include a dance routine, songs, an orchestral performance, or some combination thereof. The key consideration is that the main ingredients of the stage performance would be thematically related to the movie that followed it in the hope that they would put the audience in the proper mood to receive the film. Atmosphere was everything.

The idea of live, on-stage introductions to films had been around for years. However, the emergence of long-form films and the construction of large-capacity film theaters—developments that occurred nearly simultaneously during the first half of the 1910s—made it clear to American film exhibitors that simple, spoken introductions from the stage were not going to work anymore. They needed to fill their thousands of seats on a regular basis, and, for them, lavish prologues were the answer.

By 1917, prologues had become so popular that they were taken into account during the design and construction of American motion picture theaters. Consider, for example, the following commentary in a 1917 issue of *Motography* concerning the construction of the Rialto, a 3,000-seat theater in Newark, New Jersey:

Space for an orchestra of large proportions promises music of unusual excellence, while lighting and stage effects are being planned which will make possible the presenting of big pictures on a scale never attempted before, including as it does the staging of elaborate prologues to the screen dramas, in keeping with the subjects treated and especially written and rehearsed to surround the audience with the atmosphere of the picture before it appears upon the screen.[2]

By the 1920s, prologues had become an essential part of film exhibition in American big-city theaters. An exemplary house that depended heavily on prologues for its success was Brooklyn's 3,000-seat Mark Strand Theater. In a 1926 essay, Edward Hyman, the Strand's managing director, wrote that his team had started working with prologues shortly after the theater opened in 1919 and since "that time we have developed the prologue until it stands forth as one of the most important incidents of the program." He then went on to discuss the do's and don'ts of prologues:

The prologue which attempts to lift a scene or sequence from the story would defeat its own purpose because it would destroy the continuity. On the other hand, an atmospheric prologue which is built upon the basic principles of entertainment and art, without endeavoring to give information concerning the feature film, is very likely to win 100% approval from the audience.[3]

He suggested that it was quite appropriate to copy a setting from the film but not use it to duplicate a narrative development in the film:

Into this setting you may put your artists, but have them do nothing which would take parts out of the picture itself. It is possible to build original incidents through means of vocal solos, dance interpretations, instrumental numbers and pantomime. With an act so constructed we have found that this is just what the people want. They are given entertainment for the eye and for the ear, while at the same time they are being put in the mood associated with the feature itself. It is very important that the public be in the proper mood when the picture begins.[4]

Hyman's description perfectly captures the sense of American prologues, which had become the envy of German theater owners. Prologues in Germany during the postwar years tended to be rather simple,[5] and these exhibitors were intrigued by the large-scale performances that had become commonplace in urban American movie theaters. They were about to find out if such prologues could work in their own houses.

AMERICAN-STYLE PROLOGUES COME TO BERLIN

Berlin's largest film theater was the Palast-am-Zoo ("Palace by the Zoo"), so named due to its proximity to the city's zoological gardens. This theater, which could hold thousands of patrons, was one of hundreds in Germany controlled by the Universum-Film Aktiengesellschaft, a film company far better known by its acronym, Ufa. In the summer of 1925, the Palast-am-Zoo underwent major renovations under the supervision of a new management team led by Sam Rachmann. An American who wore multiple business administrative hats,[6] Rachmann and his colleagues modeled the rebuilt theater after a famous Broadway venue: the 4,000-seat Capitol Theater. With its deep-red/nut-brown color scheme, gold brocade curtain, and colored spotlights, the Palast's new interior bore an unmistakable resemblance to that of the Capitol, site of many elaborate prologues.[7]

Rachmann was interested in more than just physical renovations; he also wanted to revamp the theater's exhibition practices. To that end, he brought in two experts who had extensive experience with prologues in the United States: Ernö Rapée and Alexander Oumansky. It was hardly a coincidence that Rapée and Oumansky, in their respective capacities as musical director and ballet master, had worked for the Capitol and other large film theaters in the US. In short, the American-style prologue was about to be transplanted into Berlin's largest theater.

Rapée and Oumansky quickly set to work in their new artistic home and produced their first collaboration in late September 1925. An advertisement in the September 25, 1925 issue of Berlin's *Vossische Zeitung* announced the reopening of the Palast-am-Zoo that evening with the American film comedy *Charley's Aunt* (playing in Germany under the title *Charleys Tante*), starring Syd Chaplin. The evening's pre-film entertainment consisted of a jazzy musical introduction performed by the seventy-five-piece Ufa symphony orchestra under Rapée's baton and a song-and-dance prologue titled "German Student Life in a Foreign Land" ("Deutsches Studentenleben in der Fremde"), set in an English college. According to a report in *Exhibitors Herald*, it was the first time that a combination of live orchestral music, a dance performance, and a film had been offered in Germany.[8]

Though their previous work had been widely praised in America, Rapée and Oumansky discovered that German audiences and critics did not respond especially well to their style of prologues. For example, a critic for the *Berliner Tageblatt und Handels-Zeitung* praised Rapée's orchestra but came down hard on the "German Student Life" performance that led into *Charley's Aunt*. Calling it a "terribly strange" production that left the audience dazed and exhausted, the reviewer condemned the raucous prologue as "something that does not belong in a modern movie theater."[9]

Figure 7.2 Berlin's Palast-am-Zoo Theater, site of many a Leni prologue.

This reaction was a sign of difficulties to come for the Palast's management team over the next two months. Though the films drew significant crowds, a backlash began building against the prologues. According to German filmmaker Georg Victor Mendel, the concept of a prologue "has been experimented with a lot, and in particular the Ufa Palast-am-Zoo has spent a lot of money and effort on it. Nevertheless, the result was not very pleasing." Mendel, who witnessed many performances at the Palast first-hand, suggested that the Rapée–Oumansky prologues did not always relate to the films that followed them. Audiences who had come to the Palast mainly to see the films were therefore confused as to the prologues' purpose and found them by turns irritating or boring. As Mendel noted, "The public began to protest against the prologues."[10]

All this changed, however, after Rachmann searched for, and found, a visual designer who had a thorough understanding of German audiences, a flair for big, splashy production numbers, and a solid background in cinema: Paul Leni, a graphic artist with strong connections to the worlds of set design, costume design, and lighting in theater and film. Already famed for his many movie set designs and burgeoning career as a film director, Leni had recently returned to his theater environs; he provided set designs for live performances at "The

Gondola" ("Die Gondel"), a Berlin cabaret that he co-founded in 1923, and an elaborate theatrical revue curiously titled *Look Out! Wave 505!* (*Achtung! Welle 505!*) in early fall 1925. Staged at the Theater im Admiralspalast on the other side of Berlin's zoological gardens, *Look Out! Wave 505!* was an unqualified hit. In a review datelined September 5, 1925, *Variety*'s longtime Berlin-based correspondent C. Hooper Trask noted that this live production, a potent mixture of music, bawdy comedy, and dance, was "by far the best" of several revues performed in that theater and that "the scenery by Paul Leni is also of international quality," in his words.[11] Learning of Leni's reputation, Rachmann had likely taken in performances at The Gondola or the Theater im Admiralspalast, or both, and came away highly impressed with Leni's work. This was the person he needed.

Despite an extremely busy schedule that included work in theater, film, and graphic arts, Leni welcomed the opportunity to join the Palast creative team. He was especially pleased that his first assignment was to develop a prologue for a major film directed by his colleague E. A. Dupont: *Varieté* (1925), a sordid tale of trapeze-artist passions starring Emil Jannings and Lya de Putti. Having designed the sets for five Dupont films in the early 1920s, Leni knew precisely what would enhance the *Varieté* experience for Palast audiences. According to filmmaker Georg Victor Mendel, the addition of Leni to the Palast team made all the difference:

> The situation suddenly changed. The memorable evening was the premiere of the Ufa film *Varieté*. The prologue to *Varieté* was by Paul Leni, Germany's most ingenious film architect. This prologue met with great applause, and the idea was well received by the critical public. With an enchanting idea, *Varieté*'s sense was compressed into three minutes, a colorful, spirited dream, a miniature revue scurried past, preparing the audience for the spirit of the film that appeared on the screen. It was a complete success.[12]

Ushered in by Leni's prologue, *Varieté* debuted at the Palast-am-Zoo on November 16, 1925. According to *Variety*'s Hooper Trask, *Varieté* was the first film shown at the Palast to receive the full-fledged American prologue treatment. The prologue's main action played out against a setting consisting of sharply angled Cubist-like shards painted in shades of gray. Though Trask found Leni's color scheme a bit wanting, he found much to praise:

> The prolog to the film was excellent. It consisted of a series of fast-moving vaudeville acts hurried across the stage in a grotesque fashion. Each number only played about half a minute. The climax was an exaggerated [African American] dance, well executed by Oumansky and Peggy White. The idea and the scenery are credited to Paul Leni, the

film director and scene designer. The idea was good, but the scenery a depressing gray, quite unsuited to the action.[13]

Trask was hardly alone in his appreciation for Leni's work. Indeed, the prologue created quite a stir among Berlin's community of critics. "For the first time since the opening of the Ufa Palast-am-Zoo, one can speak of a completely successful stage show," raved Fränze Dyck-Schnitzer of the *Berliner Volks-Zeitung*.[14] Fritz Olimsky of the *Berliner Börsen-Zeitung* lauded it as well:

> The prelude on stage is magnificent; in just a few minutes—as, for example, a gifted painter might do with a few striking strokes—a motif is sketched. The variety scene is characterized in an unusually impressive manner, by parodying, perhaps quite grotesquely, an entire variety program with its particular rhythm. This stage show is by far the best we have ever seen of its kind.[15]

Another critic wrote:

> The film's premiere took place last night at a sold-out house amid the thunderous applause of the captivated audience. A film prologue, designed after an idea by Paul Leni, depicts a parodic vaudeville performance that, briefly crowded together and blended by individual images, leads to the tragic play.[16]

Figure 7.3 Leni's design concept for the *Varieté* prologue.

Herbert Ihering, one of Germany's premier film and theater critics during the Weimar years, offered an unequivocally positive assessment of Leni's work. His review, which appeared in the *Berliner Börsen-Courier*, included these glowing comments:

> The Ufa Palast has broken with the boring opera and dance preludes and (according to an idea by Paul Leni) has chosen a prologue that splendidly leads into the film. A *Varieté* parody, brilliantly enhanced, sharply worked out in the tempo, then blurring, disappearing; without a break, the film begins. The prologue was designed along the same lines as those of the film, as it should be.[17]

Leni followed his *Varieté* triumph with a prologue that supported the work of another close colleague: Ernst Lubitsch, who directed three films for which Leni had designed the settings in the late 1910s. Again working in collaboration with Rapée and Oumansky, Leni created a production that led into Lubitsch's 1924 Hollywood film *Forbidden Paradise*, a costume drama that had its German premiere at the Palast on December 4, 1925 under the title *Das verbotene Paradies*. The film, set in late 1700s Russia and starring Pola Negri as Catherine the Great, had as its prologue "In the Doll Shop" ("Im Puppenladen"), which allowed Leni a chance to riff playfully on the film's rather gaudy and overwrought costuming. One of the musical themes was a motif inspired by Victor Herbert's 1903 operetta *Babes in Toyland*. Costumed as toy figures, Oumansky and Peggy White danced in front of ten enormous toy soldiers that had been painted onto a backdrop. As a part of the routine, other dancers joined the performance after stepping out of a row of tall, thin gift boxes that eerily resembled the titular enclosure of *The Cabinet of Dr. Caligari* (*Das Cabinet des Dr. Caligari*, 1920).[18]

Leni's designs also included views of Russia's iconic onion-domed buildings. A nighttime scene showed a handful of women meeting in a room at the base of a multi-turreted structure loosely modeled after St. Basil's Cathedral, while other figures—including women dressed in babushkas and resembling squat matryoshka dolls—entered the harshly lit room. In a daytime scene, women prostrated themselves in front of the building as female Cossacks danced on an elevated platform near a giant portrait of Pola Negri in character as Catherine the Great.[19]

Variety's Trask summed up the prologue and its lead-in to the film that evening:

> The Russian prolog to the feature was again danced before scenery by Paul Leni. This time he had the good idea of building it up in three levels, allowing very interesting dance formations. However, the picture was not

simple enough—a little cluttered. Rapée staged it well and Oumansky's choreography was superior. Several characteristic Russian dancers stood out, and Oumansky and Peggy White did a very amusing tin soldier and doll dance to Herbert's *Babes in Toyland*. The audience was enthusiastic and applauded right through the opening titles of the feature.[20]

Forbidden Paradise and its multi-part prologue played at the Palast through December 17, 1925. The Palast management team decided that the next film to be exhibited at that theater—*A Waltz Dream* (*Ein Walzertraum*), directed by Ludwig Berger—did not require a prologue because of its length; at nearly 105 minutes, it was considered a relatively long film for the time.[21] Not wishing to deprive themselves of Leni's formidable talents while waiting for the Berger film to run its course at the Palast, Sam Rachmann and his colleagues assigned Leni to develop a prologue for a different film scheduled to open at Ufa's nearby Mozartsaal Theater: Herbert Brenon's 1924 Hollywood film *Peter Pan*, starring Betty Bronson as the title sprite and Ernest Torrence as Captain Hook.

Peter Pan opened at the Mozartsaal on December 17, 1925 and once again Leni was at the peak of his form. Playing on the movie's travel-to-another-world theme, his prologue included a scene depicting multiple modes of transportation: a train chugging through the hilly countryside, an ocean liner cruising in the distance, and, floating overhead, two hot air balloons. In a sly reference to Leni's Gondola cabaret and its ability to whisk patrons off to imaginary lands, the only human figures visible in his elaborate design ride in the balloons' gondolas. Intriguingly, the more prominent of the gondola-toting balloons sails above three rounded, crescent-topped buildings and a minaret; audiences familiar with Leni's design work would have little difficulty connecting these structures to his settings for the Gondola production of *1001 Nights* and, of course, the Harun al-Rashid sequence in *Waxworks*.[22]

The prologue's only negative element was something beyond Leni's control. The Mozartsaal management attempted to enhance the fairytale dimensions of *Peter Pan* and its depiction of childhood by including what critic Fritz Olimsky identified as the first Ufa synchronous sound film: *The Little Match Girl* (*Das Mädchen mit den Schwefelhölzern*), an adaptation of Hans Christian Andersen's bittersweet 1845 tale. Directed by Guido Bagier, written by Hans Kyser, and starring Else von Möllendorff and Wilhelm Diegelmann, this brief 1925 film unfortunately ran into major technical problems at the Mozartsaal because of its tinny soundtrack. As Olimsky noted of this attempt at synchronous sound:

> the invention is still too much in its infancy for an artistic effect to be created. For the time being, we are reminded of the beginnings of the gramophone; many, not to say most, of the sounds are reproduced in a distorted timbre, and all of it is far from satisfying.[23]

Peter Pan and its Leni-designed prologue played at the Mozartsaal through December 29, barely giving Leni enough time to develop a prologue for another American film looming on the Palast horizon for the new year: Buster Keaton's *The Navigator* (1924). Under the title *Buster Keaton, der Matrose*, this film opened at the Palast on January 4, 1926 and played about two weeks. Leni's prologue had some similarities to the one he designed for *Varieté*, particularly its high-energy dance parody. "After the spirited second rhapsody of Liszt and the Ufa weekly newsreel, the first highlight of the evening was a jazz carnival on stage," wrote Olimsky. "Rapée parodied a pure unadulterated jazz band, in-between dance performances barely a minute long each, all in a great whirlwind."[24] Unfortunately, some reviewers did not give Leni proper credit for his work; fellow filmmaker Georg Victor Mendel bitterly observed in the trade journal *Lichtbildbühne* that "an overzealous journalist recently insisted that Rapée be credited with the oversight" of *The Navigator*'s prologue when in fact the credit should have gone to Leni.[25]

The Ufa powers-that-were determined that *The Navigator*'s immediate follow-up at the Palast—the Ufa production *The Poacher* (*Der Wilderer*)—did not require a prologue. *The Poacher* opened on January 21 and continued through February 4, giving Leni time to develop a prologue for the next American film to hit the Palast screen: *The Lost World* (1925), a dinosaur fantasy adventure based on Arthur Conan Doyle's 1912 novel and featuring the stop-motion animation work of Willis O'Brien.

On February 5, 1926, *The Lost World* opened at the Palast under the title *Die verlorenen Welt*. To help promote the film, Leni published an article in the February 7, 1926 issue of *Der Film* in which he employed imagistic and highly fragmented prose to describe his rather surreal vision for *The Lost World*'s prologue. "Dark stage. Shrieking voices. Moaning and groaning, and slowly fading in: a jungle," he wrote. As the set brightens and its colors intensify, the sounds of the jungle animals fade and the "large spooky moving shadows of the animal world" disappear. An ape high up in a palm tree watches as a golden canoe bearing a jazz band glides into view. The musicians perform on oversized saxophones while young women appear on stage and dance to the band's music. The musicians and the dancers then move offstage, and the scene returns to its original gray murkiness. An explorer then enters the scene. After chasing away a lingering saxophone, he eagerly investigates his surroundings but is not quite sure what he has discovered. "Is it the bone of an Ichthyosaurus or the jaw of a Diplodocus??? Eternal Change . . . Lost World," Leni wrote.[26]

In addition to incorporating Ernö Rapée's jazz ensemble work, Leni's prologue featured a nature-themed *pas de deux* danced by Alexander Oumansky and Valentina Belova. A reviewer for the *Berliner Börsen-Zeitung* appreciated the collaborative effort that went into the prologue, though, once again, Leni's work went unacknowledged. The reviewer, perhaps the same one whom Georg Victor Mendel had chastised for neglecting to attribute *The Navigator*'s prologue to Leni, wrote that the combination of *The Lost World* and its prologue "was an undisputed triumph." The reviewer continued:

> The current program, whose artistic and musical direction is in the hands of Ernö Rapée, may be considered extremely successful. In particular, he has understood how to playfully illustrate the play of the forces of nature in *The Lost World*. The stage show, which presents "Dance of the Hours" from the opera *La Gioconda* by Ponchielli, also deserves recognition. The main role, "The Night," is presented in a choreographic and artistic manner by Alexander Oumansky; he is assisted by Valentina Belova in the role of "The Day." The idea of the whole ballet is expressed in the final dance, which is intended to embody the harmony of the whole of life.[27]

In all likelihood, Leni's final prologue in Germany was for the Ufa film *Manon Lescaut*, the Arthur Robison–Hans Kyser adaptation of the famed novel by Antoine François Prévost. It premiered at the Palast on February 16, 1926 and played through February 25. Since Leni had also served as the film's set and costume designer, he had the unique opportunity to develop a prologue that complemented his own film work. A writer for *Motion Picture News* noted that Leni had occasionally designed both a film's settings and its prologue,[28] and *Manon* was likely one of those instances—perhaps the only one.

The *Manon* critical commentary focused almost exclusively on the film itself and offered scant information on the prologue's specifics; the Ufa symphony orchestra performed Ernö Rapée's score for it, and one *Manon* reviewer alluded to Leni's elegant rococo settings "behind the gold curtain of the Palast-am-Zoo."[29] Nevertheless, the period costumes and settings he had created for the film, which would have been similar to the ones for the prologue, received considerable attention. For instance, a *Berliner Börsen-Zeitung* critic applauded his work, writing that "Paul Leni gave the film a captivating, often very atmospheric frame with his buildings."[30] Hans Lustig of the *Vossische Zeitung* called the film "a success," suggesting that it "saves the honor of the costume film yet again" and praising Leni for creating sets and décor that dispelled romanticized notions of what Parisian parlors, streets, and marketplaces would have looked like in the early eighteenth century.[31] Leni doubtless took enormous satisfaction from his months-long prologue work and the reviews that followed, but he could not help but ponder the major life changes that were coming as a result of his successes; an important film executive *von Amerika* had been in touch with a compelling offer.

ENTER UNCLE CARL

Universal Pictures president Carl Laemmle had spent the summer and early fall of 1925 in Europe overseeing his company's continental interests, and he devoted a significant part of his time to learning more about Ufa, its films, and its filmmakers. As a native son of Germany, the gregarious and affable Laemmle was quite well-known among Ufa executives; indeed, they had modeled their new production facility at Neubabelsberg after Laemmle's Universal City studio complex and delightedly gave him an extended tour of it during his stay.[32]

Laemmle's visit was related to his ongoing plans to internationalize Universal. That summer, he reached a tentative agreement with Ufa to finance some of its films in exchange for the right to exhibit Universal films in Ufa-controlled theaters across Germany. In addition, he began approaching European actors and directors about working for him in Hollywood. His early "conquests" included E. A. Dupont, an Ufa director then at work on *Varieté*, and André Mattoni, a Czech actor under contract to Ufa and known as the "blond Valentino." Leni's visibility as a filmmaker had increased significantly since the Berlin premiere of *Waxworks* on November 13, 1924, and it is entirely possible that Laemmle met with him that summer as well. Laemmle noted in a 1927 advertisement that Leni's "work attracted my attention when I was abroad,"[33] and perhaps the two of them chatted on the set of *Manon Lescaut* at Ufa's Neubabelsberg studios.

Laemmle returned to the US in October 1925 but came back to Berlin later that year to consummate the Ufa deal for which he had laid the groundwork months before.[34] He departed New York on December 5, arrived in Berlin on December 14, and almost immediately commenced a series of negotiating sessions with Ufa executives that stretched over the next few weeks. The negotiations did not go as planned (Paramount and Metro executives had heard of the proposed deal and outmaneuvered Laemmle at the bargaining table), leaving him with fewer options for internationalizing Universal.

After the Ufa negotiations, Laemmle decided to remain in Berlin for a few days in mid-January to rest, celebrate his birthday (he turned 59 on January 17), and perhaps view a few films and meet with German filmmakers.[35] The endlessly curious Laemmle would have had difficulty keeping himself away from Berlin's Ufa theaters (he was intrigued by all aspects of the movie business, having broken into it as an exhibitor twenty years before), and it is extremely likely that he took in one or more screenings that featured Leni's prologues: *Peter Pan* at the Mozartsaal, *The Navigator* at the Palast, perhaps even one of the Palast's final screenings of *Forbidden Paradise* at the beginning of his visit. Laemmle would have been impressed by the American-style prologues he saw in Berlin, and he learned much more about Leni, who like Laemmle hailed from the German state of Württemberg. Laemmle departed Berlin near the end of the third week in January, arriving in New York City on February 3. Though the Ufa negotiations had not gone the way he wanted, Laemmle had made significant progress along another track toward his goal of internationalizing Universal Pictures.[36]

LENI ARRIVES IN AMERICA

The exact date of Laemmle's signing of Leni is unclear, but we do know that the German government issued visas on March 19, 1926 to Leni and his wife, Leonore "Lore" Sello.[37] It is therefore reasonable to assume that Laemmle had extended an invitation to Leni to come to Universal well in advance of that date, perhaps during one of his trips to Berlin in 1925–6. By coincidence, *Waxworks* premiered in New York City only one day before the issuance of the Leni–Sello visas. Clearly, Laemmle's decision to hire Leni did not hinge on the success of *Waxworks* in America, though Laemmle probably had an inkling that the film would attract a huge amount of attention.

Leni and Sello departed Hamburg on board the appropriately named liner *Hamburg* on April 9, 1926 and arrived in New York City eleven days later. They did not immediately leave New York for the west coast, however; instead, they remained in Manhattan while Leni began working on his first American assignment: "The Police Sergeant's Story," the Colony Theater prologue noted at the beginning of this chapter. Working in close collaboration with four new colleagues—Colony technical director Jerry DeRosa, Universal presentation artist Jack Savage, Colony musical director Edward Kilenyi, and publicist Raymond Cavanagh—Leni developed the elaborate prologue in time for *Outside the Law*'s Broadway re-release on May 9.

By all accounts, "The Police Sergeant's Story" was an unqualified success. *Moving Picture World* columnist Van Buren Powell was moved to write a letter to Universal lauding the prologue. A self-described "hard-boiled" trade journalist, Powell wrote that *Outside the Law* was the first film he had seen in months in which he lost himself in the film's story, adding "largely, I am certain, this effect was produced by the really marvelous atmosphere created by the prologue." He continued:

> At no other picture introduction within my recollection have I been so completely spellbound by simple, sincere, direct and masterly creation of atmosphere—and that others in the audience around me remarked "clever" and "isn't that a wonderful way to get you in the spirit of the picture" and "ah"—merely corroborates my respectfully offered congratulations for your way of putting over this really fine re-release.[38]

J. H. Hodgkinson of the Jacobsen-Hodgkinson publishing house offered a similar perspective. In a letter to Universal, Hodgkinson wrote that *Outside the Law*

> is made more enjoyable by the carefully constructed and ably presented prologue. This, to my mind, serves to create an atmosphere that thoroughly enhances the picture. Great credit is due whoever conceived this method of causing a large audience to get in the proper thought channel for such an exceptional picture as *Outside the Law*.[39]

Outside the Law concluded its Colony run on June 5, and Leni followed up the outstanding if rather grim "The Police Sergeant's Story" with something decidedly different: "Tremendous Trifles," a lively and humorous prologue that served as a lead-in to *Rolling Home*, a 1926 Universal comedy starring Reginald Denny as a down-on-his-luck fellow who masquerades as a millionaire. This prologue–film tandem opened at the Colony on June 6, 1926, and a reviewer for the *Exhibitors Herald* reported on Leni's work and the audience's reaction to it:

> Assisted by Jerry DeRosa and Raymond Cavanagh, Paul Leni offered his second presentation for Universal, "Tremendous Trifles." It was conceived by Leni and DeRosa staged it. Cavanagh offered the script. It was well worked out and the audience found it pleasing, giving it a good hand.[40]

The *Exhibitors Herald* reviewer then described the prologue's details and the way they evoked the spirit of the late Frank Winfield Woolworth, who had made millions selling hairpins and other five-and-dime items:

> The curtains drew to show a man on the center of the stage asking if anyone in the audience had ever seen a million dollars. Then a stage setting showing a pile of money sacks was shown. Two men in green livery were hoarding the gold. Questions were flashed on the screen in the background. This was followed with flashes of information like "The hairpin made fifteen million," following which a liveried man came on the stage with a huge hairpin, then the Woolworth building, followed by a man with a floor truck full of ten cent articles; and so on. Then a few bars of music and the announcement about "Yes, We Have No Bananas." The liveried men went into a dance and then sang the song. They were joined by six pretty misses and as they left the stage another flasher [i.e., flashed title] announced that Reginald Denny also had an idea for making a million; the picture followed. The odd way of

presenting people on the stage and the flashes on the drops went over well with the audience and Ray Cavanagh competently snapped out his questions and other matter. He kept them interested.[41]

Bill Reilly of *Moving Picture World* was also impressed. He wrote:

> The prologue that serves as an atmospheric introduction to the spirit of the picture and at the same time in the very essence of its conception is of the motion picture, in the vein of the motion picture, is that conceived by Paul Leni and executed with the assistance of Jerry DeRosa as an introduction to Denny's *Rolling Home* at New York's Colony. It isn't a series of illustrated titles; it is the substitution of titles on the scrim in place of speeches by the characters who bring out in action the theme that it's the little things, backed by clever ideas of turning them to account, that makes the millionaire—and that is the fundamental of *Rolling Home*.[42]

"Tremendous Trifles" was not uniformly well received. Reilly had suggested that the new type of prologue as represented by Leni's work was "told in snappy, novel titles and entertaining action,"[43] but *Variety* reviewer Robert Sisk evidently saw this trend as a weakness, noting that Universal has rented the Colony "to show its own product, and apparently the order has gone out to cut down on the prologs." He went on:

> Paul Leni, billed as a "noted European director," is credited with the ideas for them. If the current "prolog" is an idea he conceived to be picture house entertainment, it is plainly a case of being unfamiliar and out of tune with the Broadway picture house standards.[44]

Sisk's nationalistic bias aside, Leni's artistic accomplishments at the Colony demonstrated an important point: whether rooted in melodrama or comedy, his work strongly appealed to American audiences.

ANALYSIS

Carl Laemmle's interest in bringing Leni into the Universal fold is certainly understandable; the younger man's wide range of professional experiences in graphic design, theater, and film made him an attractive prospect. Intriguingly, though, the initial trade-press coverage of the Laemmle–Leni agreement did not mention directing; instead, the reports indicated that Laemmle hired Leni to design sets, lighting, and prologues for others' films and head up a new prologue department at the studio.[45] Adding to the fogginess surrounding the signing, Leni had listed his occupation on the *Hamburg* passenger manifest as "stage manager," not film director.[46]

There was no question that Leni had the technical expertise to be a Hollywood director, but perhaps Laemmle saw a few things that gave him pause. One concern may have been the uncertainty surrounding Leni's role in the production of *Waxworks*, which premiered in the US about a month before his arrival in New York. Though Leni is often regarded as the film's sole director, he actually shared directorial responsibilities with Leo Birinski, a Ukrainian playwright whom Leni knew from their work together on several Joe May films the year before. In the original version of *Waxworks*, Leni is credited with the *Regie* (direction) but Birinski is listed as in charge of *Spielleitung*, a term that literally translates as "play management" and is generally understood to mean actor supervision. In defining the term, Weimar cinema scholar Christian Rogowski noted "the practice of bringing in a theater person to film shoots who would specifically work with the actors, while the main 'Regisseur' would handle all other aspects of the film."[47] This may have been the case with *Waxworks*, but the division of directorial duties remained unclear. A *Filmland: Deutsche Monatschrift* reviewer, who wrote under the pseudonym "Cinemax," called the film's distinction between *Regie* and *Spielleitung* a "prize mystery." On the day *Waxworks* opened at Berlin's Ufa-Theater Kurfürstendamm, Cinemax asked several pointed questions: "What is play management, what is direction? On the program for the *Waxworks* premiere at U. T. Kurfürstendamm today is this: Direction Paul Leni, Play Management Leo Birinski. So who had the production?" Laemmle may have been just as baffled as Cinemax as to who was actually in charge of the film and why Birinski's participation was necessary.[48]

In addition to this possible concern, Laemmle wanted assurance that Leni thoroughly understood American tastes and was up to the challenge of working in Hollywood's high-pressure environment. Paul Gulick, head of Universal publicity, noted that Leni's signing was somewhat of a risk for Laemmle. In a piece written after Leni had started working on his first American film, *The Cat and the Canary*, but months before *Cat* reached the screen, Gulick wrote that Laemmle

> has a remarkable faith in hunches. One of these hunches is Paul Leni. None of this artistic and accomplished gentleman's past performances is a positive guarantee that he will be a big success as a moving picture director. His reputation in Berlin is rather that of an impressionistic painter, and therein lay such reputation as he had acquired in America. As a general thing, artists who have been most successful either as painters, as writers or theatrical producers, have been indifferent successes when they lend their names to motion picture productions. The fact was that they had centered their attention so much on the art nearest

their hearts that it lacked the fluidity and adaptability which is required for moving picture technique. But this did not deter Mr. Laemmle. Paul Leni had other abilities which qualified him just as well as his knowledge of composition and color for the task of directing. In addition to that, Leni had embraced heart and soul the American view-point, a thing which so few Europeans are willing or able to do.[49]

Leni's work on "The Police Sergeant's Story" and "Tremendous Trifles" was the turning point. It demonstrated to Laemmle and other Universal executives that he was adept at mounting productions with flair and flamboyance, that he was comfortable working within very different genres, and that he was not a provincial filmmaker familiar only with German tastes. He proved that he understood the American market and had adapted to it quite well.

The timing could not have been better for Leni. Universal acquired the film rights to John Willard's creepy stage comedy *The Cat and the Canary* in early June 1926, right around the time that *Outside the Law* and "The Police Sergeant's Story" were concluding their highly successful run at the Colony.[50] Laemmle knew the *Cat* property would benefit from evocative set designs and deft handling of lighting, and he realized that Leni's light-and-shadows wizardry in "The Police Sergeant's Story," to say nothing of his kindred work on German films and prologues, showed he had the expertise to tackle such a project. Laemmle no doubt read and agreed with *Moving Picture World*'s assessment of Leni's *Outside the Law* prologue:

> The production is not unusual in the presentation of a new idea of stage craft, but the mounting of an old idea which has almost been lost to the present generation of theatregoers. It belongs to the days of the "black art" which modern stagecraftsmen are resurrecting to more practically demonstrate the value of lights, shadows, black spaces and shaft lighting.[51]

In addition, Leni's prologue included several spooky moments in which a deceased young woman, played by an actress wearing a flowing white gown and illuminated by blue side lighting, appeared as a ghostly vision to the man who had murdered her.[52] These supernatural touches, coupled with Leni's comedic turn in "Tremendous Trifles," boded well for his ability to handle *Cat*'s famed shudder-giggle qualities.

AFTERMATH

Convinced that he had hired the right person, Laemmle duly summoned Leni to Universal City in early June to hand over *Cat*'s directorial reins. Leni and his wife departed New York for Los Angeles on June 10, only a few days after two key occurrences: the opening of the *Rolling Home*–"Tremendous Trifles" pairing, and Universal's acquisition of the filming rights to *The Cat and the Canary* as reported in the press.[53] Leni had never seen a staging of *Cat*, so Universal arranged for him to view a summer-stock production of it in Jamestown, New York, on the couple's way to California.[54] They arrived in Los Angeles on June 17—a mere two days before the *Rolling Home*–"Tremendous Trifles" combo concluded its two-week run at the Colony—whereupon Leni immediately began working on the *Cat* adaptation.

Leni had actually left the prologue business at a fortuitous time. Exhibitors were becoming increasingly resistant to the idea of staging elaborate prologues, citing their huge expense and complexity. In late April 1926, Georg Victor Mendel reported that the American-style prologue had already been abandoned in Berlin. As he wrote in *Lichtbildbühne* in an article titled "The Prologue's Obituary" ("Nekrolog auf den Prolog"), "The stage show in the form of a 'prologue' relating to the content of the film has run its course much faster than even the pessimists had suspected. Today, even the leading Ufa-Palast-am-Zoo does not do it anymore."[55] With the movie industry on the threshold of the synchronous-sound era, exhibitors were discovering they no longer needed prologues to pull in audiences; the novelty of recorded dialogue, however technically flawed at first, was enough to ensure high attendance.

Though prologues were rapidly winding down in the late 1920s, Leni's experiences as a prologue producer taught him the importance of using introductory material to get audiences into the proper mood for the main narratives to follow. He started emphasizing introductions woven into the films themselves: in-film prologues, we might call them. Though the idea was not at all new—such scenes had been incorporated into films for years prior to Leni's Hollywood ascendancy, such as *The Cabinet of Dr. Caligari* and *Waxworks*—he made sure to include them in his films for Universal.

The Cat and the Canary has such a built-in prologue. The film begins with a gloved hand wiping away dust and cobwebs to reveal the film's opening titles. The titles are followed by a sequence that has no counterpart in the play: a shot of Cyrus West's castle-like mansion—a forbidding, multi-spired structure that would have served as a suitable setting for a German Expressionist film—dissolving into a collection of giant medicine bottles with an ill West among them. They dwarf him, as do three large, hissing, black cats that are separately superimposed. A title-card reads: "Medicine could do nothing more for Cyrus West, whose greedy relatives, like cats around a canary, had brought him to the verge of madness." Several inheritance-related documents, including one held by a claw-like hand coated in fur, are superimposed over views of the bottles/mansion, followed by a forward-tracking shot suggesting the point of view of West's ghost as the camera travels down a mansion hallway. This highly imaginative sequence works well as a means of immediately putting the audience into the proper mood for the macabre narrative to follow. After a trade-show viewing of the film in May 1927, Oscar Cooper of *Motion Picture News* opined that the film's highlight was "the remarkably fine atmosphere," calling it "the picture's outstanding achievement."[56] Exhibitors discovered that they did not need to add a mood-setting prologue; it was already included.

Ever the astute businessperson, Carl Laemmle seized on this point. In one of his "Straight from the Shoulder" trade advertisements, he tried to appeal to balky exhibitors by pitching *The Cat and the Canary* as a film that did not require a live prologue: "Many people have said that elaborate 'presentations' calling for the squandering of huge sums of money are not wanted in moving picture palaces. Many people have said it, but *The Cat and the Canary* is proving it!" He added that the film

> needs no fluff. It needs nothing but good projection, plus whatever you are in the habit of adding in the form of music. *The Cat and the Canary* is the kind of a picture which can be projected ice-cold in a projection room before the hardest-boiled kind of critical audience, without suffering.[57]

Leni could not help but be amused; the very productions that helped land him a job as a Hollywood film director—his prologues, especially "The Police Sergeant's Story"—were now being written off by his boss as "fluff."

Mindful of Laemmle's newly expressed repudiation of live prologues, Leni continued to incorporate brief, prologue-like opening narratives into his films. *The Chinese Parrot* (1927) had a five-minute introductory scene that featured Anna May Wong as an exotic dancer; in fact, a *Variety* reviewer specifically called the scene a prologue.[58] *The Man Who Laughs* (1928) begins with a five-minute sequence centering on the captured Lord Clancharlie's final encounter with James II; it is a powerful, tone-setting sequence that has no direct equivalent in Victor Hugo's novel.[59] *The Last Warning* (1928) opens with a montage of multiple superimposed images, many filmed by a mobile camera, that depict the brightly lit marquees of such Manhattan venues as Madison Square Garden and the Strand, Rivoli, Capitol, and Central theaters.[60] Representing Broadway's vibrant nightlife and featuring much fragmented, kaleidoscopic dance imagery, this introductory sequence is conceptually quite similar to Leni's high-energy prologues for *Varieté* and *The Navigator*. The sequence also includes a rapidly spinning title-card that eventually pauses to read "BROADWAY, ELECTRIC HIGHWAY OF HAPPINESS—STREET OF NIGHT CLUBS, THEATRES, LAUGHTER." One of many snappy titles peppered throughout the film, it is akin to the "flashes" Leni created for his *Rolling Home* prologue.

There is little question that the resonant built-in prologues of *The Last Warning* and Leni's three other Universal films reflected his abiding belief in the importance of arresting, mood-inducing introductions. Though live prologues were rapidly declining in the age of sync-sound movies, Leni understood their value and adapted them to meet the needs of the changing film exhibition scene. In so doing, this multi-talented filmmaker showed that he had learned his "beginning" lessons well.

ACKNOWLEDGMENTS

The author presented a shortened version of this essay at a joint conference of the European Network for Cinema and Media Studies (NECS) and the History of Moviegoing, Exhibition, and Reception (HoMER) Network, held in Amsterdam in June 2018. Most Berlin film exhibition dates in this chapter were taken from the daily "Film-Spielplan" listings in the *Deutsche Allgemeine Zeitung*.

NOTES

1. For a highly detailed description of "The Police Sergeant's Story," including its dialogue, lighting and musical cues, costuming suggestions, and set-design illustrations, see "Universal Presentations," *Universal Weekly*, May 29, 1926.
2. "Theater Takes Valuable Church Property," *Motography*, May 19, 1917. For more information about prologues, see Epes Winthrop Sargent, "Adding to the Pictures," *Moving Picture World*, June 8, 1918; and "This Woman Exhibitor Tells You How," *Motion Picture News*, July 6, 1918.
3. Edward L. Hyman, "Prologues Are Paramount," *Exhibitors Trade Review*, January 9, 1926.
4. Hyman, "Prologues Are Paramount."
5. For example, Gustav Fröhlich, star of Fritz Lang's *Metropolis*, remembered a time when, as a teenager, he earned fifteen marks a night by merely reciting a prologue for the 1918 Otto Rippert film *The Path that Leads to Damnation* (*Der Weg, der zur Verdammnis führt*). See Gustav Fröhlich, "Gustav Fröhlich," in *Filmkünstler: Wir Über Uns Selbst*, ed. Hermann Treuner (Berlin: Sibyllen-Verlag, 1928), n.p.
6. In addition to serving as the Palast-am-Zoo's new manager, Rachmann was Famous Players' Berlin representative and the head of Ufa's distribution. See "Important Changes Follow Ufa Deal with Americans," *Variety*, January 20, 1926.
7. For a discussion of the renovated theater and its strong similarity to the Capitol, see Harry Knopf, "Berlin Picture Theatres Described," *Motion Picture News*, September 11, 1926.
8. "American Methods Rule in Rebuilt Berlin Theatre," *Exhibitors Herald*, October 10, 1925.
9. "Filmstart am Zoo," *Berliner Tageblatt und Handels-Zeitung*, September 26, 1925. A photograph of this prologue in rehearsal may be found in *Motion Picture News*, June 19, 1926.
10. Georg Victor Mendel, "Der Kampf um den 'Prolog,'" *Lichtbildbühne*, February 2, 1926, reprinted in *Paul Leni: Grafik, Theater, Film*, ed. Hans-Michael Bock (Frankfurt am Main: Deutsches Filmmuseum, 1986), 200.

11. C. Hooper Trask, "Berlin Plays," *Variety*, September 16, 1925.
12. Mendel, "Der Kampf." Leni expressed his continuing interest in *Varieté* years later by dressing up as Boss Huller, the character played by Emil Jannings, for a circus-themed party held by Carl Laemmle. See Grace Kingsley, "At Papa Laemmle's Hollywood Circus," *Screenland*, December 1928, 94.
13. C. Hooper Trask, "House Reviews," *Variety*, January 20, 1926. For a reproduction of Leni's design, see Bock, *Paul Leni*, 198.
14. Fränze Dyck-Schnitzer, "*Variété*," *Berliner Volks-Zeitung*, November 17, 1925.
15. Fritz Olimsky, "Neue Filme," *Berliner Börsen-Zeitung*, November 17, 1925.
16. "Ein Grosses Deutsches Filmwert," *Vossische Zeitung*, November 17, 1925. Leni was so proud of his *Varieté* prologue that he worked in a sly and somewhat subliminal reference to it in his first *Rebus* film, a series discussed at length in Erica Tortolani's chapter in this volume. Less than thirty seconds into the film, a swish pan rakes the front of the Palast-am-Zoo; eagle-eyed viewers will discover *Varieté*'s title highlighted on the theater's marquee.
17. Herbert Ihering, review of *Varieté*, *Berliner Börsen-Courier*, November 17, 1925, reprinted in Bock, *Paul Leni*, 198.
18. See Bock, *Paul Leni*, 199.
19. See Bock, *Paul Leni*, 197.
20. Trask, "House Reviews." Trask noted other elements, some Russian-themed, that led up to Leni's prologue. They included a performance of Tchaikovsky's *1812 Overture* and Boris Kroyt's rendition of Henryk Wieniawski's *Souvenir de Moscou*.
21. Trask, "House Reviews."
22. See Bock, *Paul Leni*, 203. The hot air balloons may have also been an acknowledgment of *The Wonderful Wizard of Oz* and its late author, L. Frank Baum.
23. Fritz Olimsky, "Peter Pan," *Berliner Börsen-Zeitung*, December 20, 1925.
24. Fritz Olimsky, "Neue Filme," *Berliner Börsen-Zeitung*, January 6, 1926. Rapée's use of a jazz band during *The Navigator*'s prologue is also noted in "International Jazz Band Is Big Hit in Berlin," *Variety*, February 3, 1926.
25. Mendel, "Der Kampf."
26. Paul Leni, "Wie ich mir den Prolog zur *Verlorenen Welt* dachte," *Der Film*, February 7, 1926, reprinted in Bock, *Paul Leni*, 199.
27. "Neue Filme," *Berliner Börsen-Zeitung*, February 7, 1926.
28. "A Creative Director," *Motion Picture News*, May 29, 1926.
29. Harry Knopf, "Germans Favor Original Film Music," *Motion Picture News*, September 25, 1926; "*Manon Lescaut*," *Deutsche Allgemeine Zeitung*, February 17, 1926.
30. "Neue Filme," *Berliner Börsen-Zeitung*, February 17, 1926.
31. Hans G. Lustig, "Manon Lescaut," *Vossische Zeitung*, February 17, 1926.
32. "Laemmle Is Due From Europe," *Motion Picture News*, October 10, 1925.
33. Carl Laemmle, "Watch This Column," *Photoplay*, March 1927, 15. A retrospective article in *Universal Weekly* stated that "shortly after the exhibition of [*Waxworks*] he accepted the offer of Carl Laemmle to join his company and make pictures at the Universal studios." However, the timeline implied in this statement could not be verified by other sources. See James Hood MacFarland, "Leni Likens Film Game to Spirited Tennis Tilt," *Universal Weekly*, January 26, 1929.
34. "Universal Confirms $4,000,000 Deal With Ufa; Laemmle Off for Berlin," *Moving Picture World*, December 5, 1925.
35. "Universal Gets Big Release Advantages in Ufa Compromise," *Exhibitors Herald*, January 16, 1926.

36. Laemmle's internationalization plans are briefly discussed in "Policy Outlined," *Film Daily*, September 9, 1926. See also "Laemmle Sails to Close $3,800,000 Deal with Ufa," *Exhibitors Herald*, December 19, 1925.
37. The date of the issuance of Leni's visa is indicated in a document dated April 20, 1926 and titled "List or Manifest of Alien Passengers for the United States Immigration Officer at Port of Arrival." This document is a detailed list of all non-immigrant passengers on board the SS *Hamburg*, which sailed from Hamburg, Germany, on April 9, 1926 and arrived at New York City on April 20. See "Passenger and Crew Lists of Vessels Arriving at New York, New York, 1897–1957," NARA microfilm publication T715, film no. 3832, image no. 00685 (Washington, DC: National Archives and Records Administration, n.d.).
38. Powell quoted in "Trade Paper Man Praises Prologue at Colony Theatre," *Universal Weekly*, June 5, 1926.
39. Hodgkinson quoted in "Colony Prologue Puts Audience in Right Mood," *Universal Weekly*, May 29, 1926.
40. "New York Colony," *Exhibitors Herald*, June 19, 1926.
41. "New York Colony."
42. Bill Reilly, "What's New?" *Moving Picture World*, June 19, 1926.
43. Reilly, "What's New?"
44. Robert Sisk, "Colony," *Variety*, June 9, 1926.
45. For examples of the press coverage, see "Dr. Gates Home After 40 Years' Work in Turkey," *New York Herald Tribune*, April 19, 1926; "Prologue Dept for 'U,'" *Film Daily*, April 25, 1926; and Arthur W. Eddy, "How B'Way Does It," *Film Daily*, May 16, 1926. The new Universal unit was actually called a "mechanical presentations department," and the idea was that Leni would oversee sound film recordings of musical stage acts, similar to Lee de Forest's "Phonofilms," that could be shown in smaller theaters unable to mount elaborate live prologues.
46. "Passenger and Crew Lists," n.p.
47. Christian Rogowski, email message to author, July 16, 2018.
48. Cinemax, "Das Endlose Celluloidband," *Filmland: Deutsche Monatschrift*, December 1924. However, an eight-page issue of *Illustrierter Film-Kurier*, devoted entirely to *Waxworks* and published at the time of its release, listed Leni as sole director and made no mention of Birinski in any production capacity. See "Das Wachsfiguren-Kabinett," *Illustrierter Film-Kurier* 39, no. 6 (1924): 2. Confusion of a different sort occurred in the fall of 1926, when a *New York Sun* review of *Manon Lescaut* indicated that the film's "settings and costumes were designed by Paul Leni, who did a similar service for *The Three Wax Works*." This review did not mention Leni's directorial work on the latter film, making it sound as if his contributions were strictly related to settings and costuming. See "In Filmdom," *New York Sun*, November 24, 1926.
49. Paul Gulick, "Shadows as a Movie Motif," *Amateur Movie Makers*, March 1927.
50. "*Cat and Canary* Rights Purchased by Universal," *Exhibitors Weekly*, June 19, 1926. The article is datelined June 8.
51. "The Prologue," *Moving Picture World*, June 5, 1926.
52. "Universal Presentations."
53. "Leni Leaves for Coast," *Film Daily*, June 6, 1926.
54. Chester Bahn, "Chester B. Bahn's Stage and Film Chat," *Syracuse Herald*, June 15, 1926. *Cat* was performed by the Century Players at Shea's Theater in Jamestown that summer. A sample listing of the show may be found in "Evening Events," *Jamestown Journal*, June 12, 1926.
55. Georg Victor Mendel, "Nekrolog auf den Prolog," *Lichtbildbühne*, April 27, 1926, reprinted in Bock, *Paul Leni*, 201.

56. Oscar Cooper, "The Cat and the Canary," *Motion Picture News*, May 20, 1927.
57. Carl Laemmle, "When a Picture Needs No Fluff," *Universal Weekly*, October 15, 1927. Ironically, a live prologue had been developed for *Cat*'s trade-show exhibition in London in May 1927. Billy Stewart, manager of London's Rialto Theatre, had created a simple stage set made up of two large cages, each occupied by a singer: Jack Wright, dressed as a cat, and Sylvia Tress, as a bird. They sang a specially written song, during which the cat escaped from his cage and tried to reach the bird through her cage's bars. For a brief discussion and photo, see "Effective Presentation Designed for 'Cat and Canary' Showing," *Universal Weekly*, June 4, 1927.
58. "*The Chinese Parrot*," *Variety*, January 11, 2918.
59. Hugo's novel does include two prologue-like "Preliminary Chapters," but the first is about Ursus and Homo the wolf dog, and the second is about the *comprachicos*.
60. Just as Leni's first *Rebus* film includes a shot of the Palast marquee promoting *Varieté*, *The Last Warning* contains a reference to his immediately preceding film, *The Man Who Laughs*. Broadway's Central Theatre had exhibited *Man* in the spring of 1928, and its marquee promoting the film is among this opening sequence's overlapping images of theater signage.

CHAPTER 8

Paul Leni's *The Cat and the Canary*: Adaptation into Genre

Rebecca M. Gordon

Paul Leni's first directorial job at Universal Studios was an adaptation of the stage melodrama *The Cat and the Canary*. Like John Willard's 1921 play on which it was based, Leni's film was very popular. Film critics and reviewers, however, were puzzled by the film's combination of the familiar and the shockingly innovative, especially Leni's visual techniques and optical effects. Some reviewers thought the plot fairly mechanical and similar to predecessors such as Harold Lloyd's comedy short *Haunted Spooks* (1920) and D. W. Griffith's long-winded *One Exciting Night* (1922). Nonetheless, a *Film Daily* critic found that the familiar plot twists and old jokes were "so cleverly executed that under Leni's direction they become new." A *Photoplay* critic was skeptical about the "artiness" of the film, noting that "Leni uses trick angles galore," but also thought that the artfulness of the film "helps the atmosphere of mystery and murder," resulting in "corking melodrama." The *New York Times*, more uniformly positive, hailed the film as "the first time that a mystery melodrama has been lifted into the realms of art."[1]

Contemporary critics had not yet invented a label for what Leni's stylistic innovations had done to a familiar narrative, but those innovations were quickly copied and utilized in later "spooky house" films, such as *Seven Footprints to Satan* (1929), *The Bat Whispers* (1930), and *The Old Dark House* (1932), with varying degrees of success. Reviews of these films often note the German or European influence on their visual style and the effect of that style on viewers. By the time Paramount studios remade *The Cat and the Canary* as a talkie in 1939, however, the stylistic innovations that Leni had introduced, and that had infused horror and dread into Willard's familiar plot, were themselves so recognizable, especially when used as a backdrop for fast-talking comedy, that they were no longer confusing. Instead, they could be identified as part of a pattern—or indeed, a separate genre. *Motion Picture Daily* proclaimed that the 1939 *Cat and the Canary* accomplished "a wedding of laugh and thrill so neatly contrived as to equal, virtually, a new film formula." *Hollywood Reporter* named that formula, calling the film "a comedy-thriller par excellence."[2] Though few reviews mention that the film was specifically a remake of Paul Leni's 1927 work, the visual set pieces in the 1939 adaptation were clearly borrowed from Leni's film. More to the point, the 1939 version recreates a tempo that Leni invented; thus the formula of the 1939 *The Cat and the Canary* was not new so much as a thoroughly recognizable, yet pleasingly updated, exemplar of the genre.

Leni's *The Cat and the Canary* presents a visual and aural iconography still essential to film and televisual "old spooky house" narratives and creates a rhythm that remains the hallmark of horror-comedy: namely, a pattern of growing tension followed by release. This chapter argues that Leni's film and the films it influenced—including its own remakes—lent formal and affective shape to what trade magazines of the 1920s and 30s called the thriller-chiller-comedy, inaugurating horror-comedy as a genre.

It is important to note that the copies of Leni's *The Cat and the Canary* most readily available to audiences today are not identical to what American audiences saw in 1927, for no original 35mm American release print of the film is known to exist. Film preservationist Christopher Bird, who worked on Photoplay Productions' 2004 restoration of the film, explained that the Photoplay version was a necessary admixture of scenes drawn from a 1930s 35mm nitrate print of the American release and a pristine European release print that sometimes shows significant editing and compositional differences from the American print. These differences do not change the film's plot but shift our sense of Leni's artistry—or, rather, make us aware that American audiences saw the best illustration of that artistry. Though prints of the film survive in 16mm, copies that have been transferred to video from 16mm inevitably show signs of age, scratching, and loss of tinting, all of which are a shame, since, as Bird wrote, the real stars of the film are its subtle lighting and photography.[3]

Bird's descriptions of the differences between the European and American releases of Leni's film, even down to specific takes, confirm an important point: that the film Americans saw in 1927 was, if anything, even more dynamic than versions available to us today. The editing was smoother, the tempo sharper, the acting crisper, the lighting and cinematography even more evocative. In addition to the 2004 Photoplay DVD and a 2005 restoration created by Film Preservation Associates, which I use as resources, a 16mm print of Leni's *The Cat and the Canary* is housed at the University of Wisconsin's Center for Film and Theater Research, where I first viewed and took notes on the film. Though the fuzziness of that print makes it difficult at times to identify all the objects on the screen, Leni's stylistic flourishes remain distinctive and help explain why critics found the film so astounding and why it has had such a lasting influence.

PAUL LENI AT CARL LAEMMLE'S UNIVERSAL STUDIOS

In the 1910s, Universal had been a successful producer of quickly made one- and two-reel films, but studio founder and president Carl Laemmle was slow to shift his company into a feature-making operation. Two 1923 films produced by a very young Irving Thalberg, *The Hunchback of Notre Dame* and *Merry-Go-Round*, convinced Laemmle that American audiences wanted "bigger pictures,"[4] and he quickly reorganized his production operation to that end. Positive responses to Lon Chaney's performances as Quasimodo and as the Phantom in *The Phantom of the Opera* (1925) further convinced Laemmle that Americans were eager for more "macabre" films. Laemmle frequently returned to his native Germany to seek directors, cinematographers, and actors who could bring their craft to Universal. By the mid-1920s, with Germany's economy collapsing in the aftermath of World War I, Laemmle was able to cherry-pick the best. Paul Leni was one of these talents.

The film that brought Leni to Carl Laemmle's attention was unquestionably *Waxworks* (*Das Wachsfigurenkabinett*, 1924), a three-part anthology on which Leni also served as production designer. Certainly Leni's thrift in creating the film's effects must have appealed to Laemmle, whose studio was known for its low-budget films. As Museum of Modern Art film curator Iris Barry noted, the set design of the Jack the Ripper segment in *Waxworks* "was a triumph of craft and economy, since its unforgettably macabre effect was contrived entirely with some sheets of painted paper, ingenious lighting, and camerawork."[5] The segment's ghoulishness may also have attracted Laemmle, for Universal had already secured a niche in the horror genre. Laemmle offered Leni a contract, and Leni arrived in Hollywood in 1926, joining other German émigrés such as E. A. Dupont, Ernst Lubitsch, and F. W. Murnau.

Leni's work as a set designer and director of *Waxworks* indicated that he, like many of his compatriots, was adept at using the tools of cinema to create a haunting, horrific mood. This is precisely what Laemmle wanted for Universal, and he gambled that Leni could bring to Hollywood the skills that he and other German directors had developed for exploiting the audience's emotional rhythms. Laemmle assigned the direction of *The Cat and the Canary* to Leni, and his gamble soon paid off.

LENI AND *THE CAT AND THE CANARY*

Leni's manner of combining *The Cat and the Canary*'s familiar melodramatic plot with innovative visual techniques seemed, to some American eyes, almost experimental. Jason Joy, head of Studio Relations for the Motion Picture Producers & Directors Association, wrote to Will Hays:

I think *The Cat and the Canary* is too much a mixture of Hollywood and Berlin. If [Leni] had stuck to his German training, he would have turned out a much better picture. However, it's a good job and held my interest all the way through, in spite of the fact that I had seen the stage play two or three times.[6]

Other critics more explicitly identified the "German training" Joy mentioned. A reviewer for *Film Daily*, for example, was intrigued by "the introduction of shadows, flickering lights, and, above all, the array of new and interesting camera angles" in the film.[7] The formal elements to which this reviewer alluded—lighting, visual design, framing, camera height, and camera mobility—indicate Leni's facility with German Expressionist cinematic techniques, which he modified to suit Hollywood purposes. However, those modifications involved not only visual style but also narrative tempo; indeed, as I will show, Leni's innovations with tempo may have been the factors that had the greatest impact on the development of "old dark house" comedy-horror.

Leni's German style is notable from the start of the film, which opens with a shot of a blank white card. A leather-gloved hand reaches up to sweep away dust and cobwebs, revealing the title of the film, the cast, and the identity of the director; simultaneously, the dust and cobwebs indicate decrepitude. The first shot of Cyrus West's mansion—actually a small model set against a matte painting—is effectively grotesque, partly because of the mansion's impossibly tall, pointed spires, and partly because of the eerie, green-tinted light that seems to emanate from behind the mansion.[8] The spires dissolve into images of giant, empty bottles, while the lower right corner of the screen brightens, as if with a spotlight, to reveal the huddled figure of Cyrus West. A title-card informs us that West is convinced that his greedy relatives have been trying to drive him crazy, and that he has long felt like a canary surrounded by cats. On cue, superimposed images of enormous cats appear among the bottles that encircle West, cowering on his easy chair. The old man springs to his feet in defiance against the imaginary cats, then slumps into torpor. The film self-consciously alludes to this composition later in the narrative, after Annabelle West is named heiress to the West fortune. As she sits at a corner of the dining table, high-backed chairs throw shadows across her and the walls, resembling bars. The family lawyer, Roger Crosby, notices this and warns her that having inherited the family fortune, "You are just like your uncle—in a cage, surrounded by cats."

Light and shadow are played for strong effect throughout the film.[9] Though Expressionist lighting is typically used to imply character motivations and story causality, and to impart to objects or people a special luminosity and quality of "ineffability," all part of what Thomas Elsaesser identified as the "surplus value of lighting style,"[10] Leni also wielded light to effect both chills and comedy. He did so primarily via the narrative's easily frightened comic characters, Cousin Cecily and Aunt Susan. Arriving during a storm, they blow through the mansion's front door and are met by Mammy Pleasant, the dour housekeeper. Clutching Cecily in the deeply shadowed foyer, Susan whispers, "Gosh, what a spooky house!" The camera cuts to large, grotesque shadows wavering on a wall. The shadows seem unmotivated, until Cecily and Susan walk through the main hallway and the shadows shrink to nothing. As they move away from the foyer, the jittery ladies stare at another big, creepy shadow on the wall, which dwindles once Mammy Pleasant enters the frame from the right, dragging the ladies' copious luggage behind her. The shadows are eerie in and of themselves, but the film's deliberate delay in letting audiences know their source is both imaginative and disarming.

Later that evening, frightened by news that a maniac is on the loose, Cecily and Susan decide to share Cecily's room for the night, unaware that their equally skittish cousin (and erstwhile hero) Paul Jones—who has just spotted the film's villain—is hiding under Cecily's bed. While Cecily undresses, titillating Paul and audiences alike, Susan insists that Cecily check under the bed before blowing out the lamps. When Cecily checks, lamp in hand, light reflects off the lenses of Paul's glasses. Those glowing ovals of light, combined with Paul's impassive expression, are chilling; the film plays Susan's histrionic response for comedy, and Paul seems (mostly) harmless, but Leni's use of light renders the scene effectively unnerving, corroborating the views of contemporary critics who praised Leni for his ability to shift the villainy from character to character and keep the audience guessing.

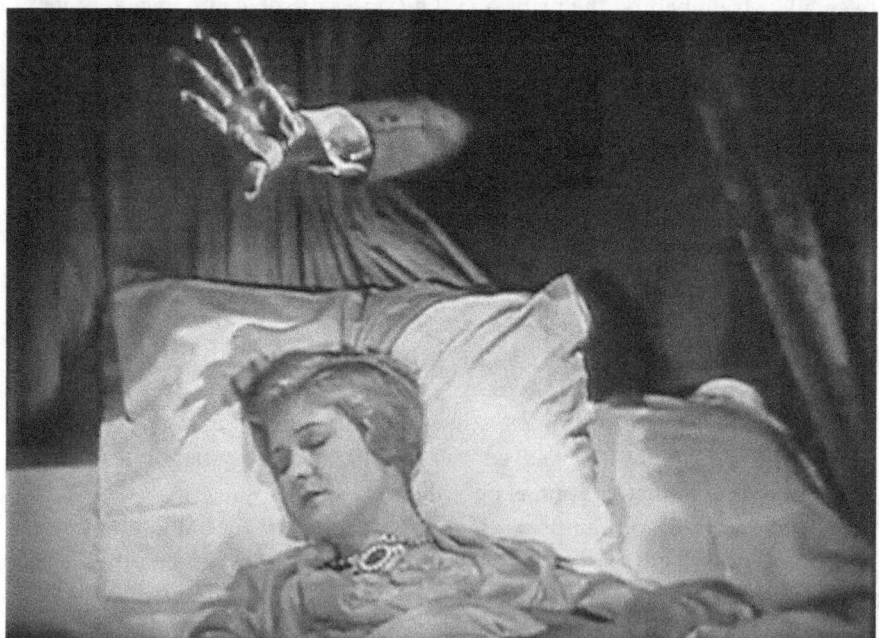

Figure 8.1 Laura La Plante as harassed heiress Annabelle West in the 1927 *The Cat and the Canary*.

Mobile framing is perhaps the subtlest of Leni's "new" techniques. Near the beginning of the film, a title-card states that since Cyrus West's death his ghost has wandered unhappily through the mansion. In the following shot, the camera slowly tracks through a long corridor, while richly draped curtains billow in the hall as the camera passes. The camera lingers over the curtains, pans right, and floats along the corridor—a subjective expression of Cyrus West's ghost that effectively suggests that the house is haunted. Film historian Lotte Eisner remarked specifically on the "inexpressible feeling of horror" Leni provoked through this image, one that has since become iconographic.[11] More generally, as Jan-Christopher Horak has pointed out, Leni's fluid camera in this film

> not only simulates movement around the relatively static figures of the characters, it also plays formally with perceptual positions, e.g. when [Leni] moves the camera slowly away from a character as the actor walks away from the camera, creating a strange sense of movement without movement.[12]

That critics did not mention this technique by name suggests that the use of mobile framing and dolly shots for deliberate effect was new to American eyes and could only be described in terms of camera angles.

We can be reasonably certain that Eisner saw the American release of this film, for the American and European versions of the hallway scene are quite different. In the European version, this particular shot is not only off-center with the camera further to the right, such that the billowing curtains seem only to be gently blowing near the windows rather than across the hallway, but the camera also seems to move straight ahead; this is in contrast to its gentle weaving from right to left as it travels up the hallway in the American release. The result is the difference between an expression of ghostliness and a less-charged expression of searching.[13]

Leni's production had an almost immediate impact on other films. As Graham Petrie put it, *The Cat and the Canary* "laid down the ground rules that the comedy-mystery and the 'Old Dark House' films were to follow for many years to come," not unlike what *Stagecoach* would do for westerns twelve years later.[14] These ground rules were not just a matter of a new look crafted through a so-called German technique, however; instead, Leni effectively reshaped the audience's affective responses to and expectations of a genre, leading audiences to experience—literally to feel—something new. A critical component of that "something new" was his command of rhythm and tempo.

SHAPING RHYTHM AND RESPONSE IN *THE CAT AND THE CANARY*

In both horror and comedy, and certainly in any admixture of the two, what matters is where the "beat" falls after a given build-up. Thus, how an audience has been prepared to experience that beat via the film's rhythm also matters, not only for the clarity of the narrative but also for understanding the genre. Rhythm, like affect, is an element of what Anna Gibbs has called "mimetic communication," which she defined as "the corporeally based forms of imitation, both voluntary and involuntary, on which literary representation ultimately depends."[15] According to Gibbs, these forms of imitation at their most primitive involve "the visceral level of affect contagion," a phenomenon described by Elaine Hatfield and her colleagues as a synchrony of "facial expressions, vocalizations, postures, and movements with those of another person" that produces a tendency for those persons to "converge emotionally."[16] Affect contagion, which lies at the heart of mimesis, is the bioneurological means by which particular affects are transmitted from body to body.

Though there is no generalizable theory of affect, Gibbs pointed to the system of innate affects elucidated by American psychologist Silvan Tomkins as particularly rich for understanding, and explaining, affect contagion and mimetic communication. Tomkins has considered the ways in which the affect system is involved with our response to the stimuli of the world, and how we form theories about how the world works. In Tomkins's system, affects are not personal, internal responses to external events but responses to stimuli of all sorts that show themselves physically in facial and postural reactions. Such reactions communicate outwardly, publicly, as both responses to and relays for further affect contagion without necessarily ever becoming conscious acts. Actors startled in the course of being recorded on film, say, can transmit that action to an audience that collectively reacts in kind. Furthermore, Tomkins's system considers the question of how something is remembered and combined with other memories to make meaningful predictions. In Tomkins's system, what we learn through affects becomes programmed as "scripts" that govern our behavior; new affect combinations can be experienced and, having been experienced, learned at an autonomic level and copied or deployed later. This consideration of how a new affectively charged experience can be folded into prior experience is particularly useful for thinking about how audiences respond to, and then become accustomed to, innovations on established forms.

From an aesthetics perspective, film theorists from Béla Balázs to Charles Affron to Noa Steimatsky have argued that affect contagion from screen to and through the audience is central to how cinema works—certainly silent cinema. We may see two advantages of considering the effects of Leni's innovations on his 1927 audiences and on later films via affect theory, at least of the Tomkins stripe (in addition to film history and aesthetics). Such an approach affords a way to account for Leni's effective "shaping" of audience emotions that felt new even though the plot of *The Cat and the Canary* was old hat, and it allows for a way of thinking about film sequences as sequences of feeling that can be experienced, remembered, learned, and re-experienced. It is a process crucial to a viewer's recognition of a given genre, and certainly to the successful recreation of such rhythms by other filmmakers, which is a key part of the process by which genres emerge.

One way Leni established a rhythm for his actors—a rhythm ultimately conveyed to spectators—was by beating a drum during rehearsals and takes; he was "a firm believer in the proper cadence," according to *Universal Weekly*.[17] Leni's drumbeats gave actors a sense of how quickly or slowly to move, emote, gesticulate, or react, or, conversely, how long to remain still.[18] Beyond shot-by-shot timing, however, whole sequences from *The Cat and the Canary* demonstrate Leni's capacity for shaping affective rhythms and particular talent for generating distress, the low-level sensation of discomfort and dread that often leads to chills or thrills when the distressing build-up stops.

By definition, a spooky old house movie provides thrills and chills, and usually, some comedy. Thrills are the result, typically, of something that comes as a surprise to the audience (often through a surprise to a character) and, if effectively executed, make viewers jump in their seats. Chills are different; they are not a matter of fear, at least not of real fear, because the film viewer is never in a position of needing to preserve his or her own life. Rather, chills result from terror provoked through the deliberate creation of ongoing discomfort or concern, otherwise defined as distress. Distress is a physical response to too much of just about any stimulus: hunger, cold, noise, heat, loud speech, bright lights, intense or enduring emotions. Any of these, should they go on too long (which is, of course, subjective), can cause distress. For the film viewer, the experience of watching something happen whose outcome the viewer can predict but the character-in-peril cannot may well cause distress because the viewer can do nothing. Also, if we experience affects we have never felt before and cannot name, we can experience distress from the situation of not knowing exactly how to identify what we are experiencing. As we shall see, whole sequences from Leni's *The Cat and the Canary* operate via distress. In this film, I argue, Leni's hallmark—beyond his undeniable visual innovations—is a particular rhythm of a slow build-up of chills, marked by sudden thrills and occasional moments of comic relief that are nonetheless narratively dependent upon distress.

For instance, though the sequence during which Cyrus West's relatives gather to hear West's will is partially played for humor, overall it demonstrates Leni's skill at developing slow-building distress. The will must be read at midnight. Annabelle West is the last to arrive at the West mansion. Aunt Susan glances at the clock, noting the time—a few minutes past midnight—and chastises Annabelle for her tardiness. Roger Crosby, the lawyer, remarks that the clock has not struck since Cyrus West died twenty years ago. Suddenly, a close-up of the clock face dissolves to reveal the clock's gears; though dusty and cobwebbed, the gears begin to move and strike the hour, startling Annabelle and

Cousin Cecily. Gradually, superimposed over the image of the clockworks, the relatives gather around the table to watch Roger open envelopes holding Cyrus West's will. Tensions rise as the relatives listen to West's last wishes; the film cuts from relative to relative on a steady beat, each relative's gestures—Susan's nervous hands, Harry Blythe's studied impassivity, Paul Jones's wistful doodling of "Paul Jones—Millionaire!"—indicating their respective intensity of greed.

After much suspense, the only descendant with the surname "West"—Annabelle—is named the heir. Her inheritance, however, is conditional; Cyrus West knew his relatives thought him insane, so a psychiatrist must establish his heir's sanity. At this, Susan punches the dining table and declares, "Now I *know* he was crazy!" Suddenly, the portrait of Cyrus overlooking the room falls to the floor as if in response. The family, viewed from overhead, jumps up, and Susan is shocked into hysterics. Although Susan's reaction is played for laughs, the comic relief of her shock does not entirely alleviate the distress the audience experiences while waiting to know the contents of West's will, nor does the surprise triggered by West's falling portrait entirely ease that distress, because the aerial view of the family that follows seems motivated by West's ghostly presence.

Perhaps more distressing for the audience, whose sympathy is sutured to Annabelle, is Roger's disappearance into the library walls and Annabelle's frustrated cries for help. While attempting to tell Annabelle who Cyrus West chose as his second heir should Annabelle be proven mad, Roger is grabbed by a menacing clawed hand from behind a secret panel in the library. Annabelle is oblivious—her gaze is directed elsewhere—until she notices his absence. The thrill of watching a hairy clawed hand grab Roger morphs, for the audience, into empathetic frustration when Annabelle tries to convince her relatives that Roger has disappeared. Flanked by her vaguely threatening cousins Harry and Charlie in a medium shot, Annabelle seems indeed like a canary surrounded by cats, her distress heightened by her relatives' skepticism. Meanwhile, the audience is helpless to help *her*.

About halfway through the film, Annabelle discovers a diamond necklace secreted in her room, also part of her inheritance. She puts it on and goes to bed. A few moments later, shadows cross over her. The camera cuts to the curtained wall just above Annabelle's head. Gradually, the curtains around her bed part, and a clawed hand with long, tapering fingers emerges, circling slowly over Annabelle as if searching for something. At one moment the clawed hand stops, approaches Annabelle's neck slowly, then pulls back—fingers clenched upward as if in alarm. The clawed hand relaxes, gropes about Annabelle's neck and chest, and rips the necklace from her throat. She sits up instantly, screaming. The audience, whether familiar with Willard's original play or with the conventions of mystery melodrama, thus expects to be thrilled, but Leni, dollying the camera close to Annabelle's face, made her scream particularly memorable: a series of intertitles with the word "Help!" issues from Annabelle's wide-open mouth toward the audience. The typography is tiny at first—HELP!—then grows to enormous proportions to approximate volume: HELP!

Annabelle's relatives come running in response to her screams but are dismissive. Susan, on the verge of panic, whispers to Cecily, "She's gone stark raving mad!" Through careful editing and blocking, the scene aligns the audience with Annabelle, forcing viewers to endure further distress. Frustrated by her relatives' lack of imagination and fearful for her own sanity, Annabelle breaks loose from her cousins and pounds the wall next to the bed, finding a loose board. A cut reveals a mechanism hidden in the wall beginning to creak, and a pulley beginning to move. Another cut shows a panel shifting away to reveal Roger's corpse, standing upright in a closet. The shot is held for a long moment, creating a chilling effect following the distressing build-up. Finally, in a series of quick cuts Roger's body pitches face-first to the floor. Moments later, Annabelle faints, relieving the tension both she and the audience were made to experience. In these scenes and throughout the film, Leni effectively submitted both characters and audience to distress, reshaping what had often been predictable "beats" of comedy and thrill in previous mystery melodramas.

Long before *The Cat and the Canary*, audiences could expect secret panels, ghostly apparitions, spooky shadows, and assorted implications of sociopathic behavior (incest, fratricide, patricide, matricide, and so on) from the mystery melodrama. But Leni's techniques—especially composition, lighting, and new narrative tempos—gave greater weight to the gloomy atmosphere than had been typical in previous iterations of the genre and, as William K. Everson put it, added "gusto" to the film's comic moments, such as Paul hiding under Cecily's bed.[19] Later films, copying Leni's visual techniques, pacing, and affective rhythms, quickly turned *The Cat and the Canary* into a repository of stylistic and narrative maneuvers that could be redeployed to re-create particular feelings. Leni's *The Cat and the Canary* acts, in a broad sense, as a collection of scenarios and affective patterns that later films in the comedy-horror subgenre were compelled to use in order to be recognized as part of that genre. Repeated use of these techniques made them conventions, and in making them conventions made Paul Leni a prime creator of horror-comedy.

THE CAT AND THE CANARY (1939)

The Cat and the Canary has been remade multiple times; in 1930 alone, Universal released both an English version, *The Cat Creeps*, and a Spanish version, *La voluntad del muerto*.[20] In 1939, Paramount Pictures remade *The Cat and the Canary* again, starring Bob Hope and Paulette Goddard. Directed by Elliott Nugent, the film inherits Paul Leni's visual style; lighting choices, camera movement, and narrative set pieces clearly echo the 1927 release. The will-reading scene, the library scene in which the lawyer disappears, and the discovery of his corpse stuffed into a wall replicate Leni's work almost exactly. However, the affective rhythm of this remake has shifted. Reviews of Paramount's 1939 *The Cat and the Canary* use the label "thriller-chiller-comedy" for the first time (that I have discovered), which indicates not only the kind of film it is but the sensations the viewer will feel, and in what order. Indeed, the phrase "thriller-chiller-comedy" demonstrates how the film uses comedy, rather than chills or thrills, to create the biggest punch or beat, and suggests that a specific generic *feeling shape* for comedy-horror has been achieved. But this is paradoxical. The 1939 *The Cat and the Canary*—a remake of a film that was an originator of a genre—alters the affective pattern that the 1927 version had made the hallmark of the genre itself.

The remake's lasting popularity has a lot to do with the success of its star, Bob Hope, in the role of Wally Campbell (a variation on the Paul Jones character played in 1927 by Creighton Hale). Wally, a radio actor, cracks wise throughout the movie about events that remind him of the plots of murder melodramas, irritating his relatives but amusing the film's audience, who are presumed to be "in the know." In addition to refashioning the story's milquetoast hero and adopting a different emotional rhythm from Leni's 1927 film, the Paramount version revises multiple details from Willard's original play that Leni left intact. Instead of meeting twenty years after the death of the patriarch (now "Cyrus Norman"), the relatives meet ten years later. The location of the family home shifts from a mansion on the Hudson River to a decrepit plantation house in the bayous of Louisiana. Instead of Annabelle West, the heroine is a modern young woman named Joyce Norman. These and other elements recall Thomas Leitch's description of a particular type of remake, the update. Remakes, Leitch wrote, "seek to mediate between the contradictory claims of being just like their originals only better in several different ways."[21] Updates, specifically,

> are characterized by their overtly revisionary stance toward an original text they treat as classic, even though they transform it in some obvious way, usually by transposing it to a new setting, inverting its system of values, or adopting standards of realism that implicitly criticize the original as dated, outmoded, or irrelevant . . . Updates in general are not content to occupy a subordinate position to the . . . classics they adapt but compete directly with those classics by accommodating them to what are assumed to be the audience's changed desires.[22]

The film's reflexivity on its genre status suggests that Paramount anticipated a sophisticated audience with a sense of Hollywood film history. Above all, the 1939 version allows its viewers, through the film's self-consciousness and retooled affective rhythms, to be pleasantly scared and yet defend themselves from the distress, dread, and horror that Leni and other German directors had specialized in and made palpable in Hollywood films.

Bob Hope's fast-talking persona brings a snappy quality to the film that, in addition to altering the film's affective patterns, updates the speed of the narrative as well. Contemporary reviews bear out this perception. The *Hollywood Reporter*, for example, described the film as "a superbly staged remake, briskly paced, perfectly cast and lusciously photographed." *Variety* noted that, while "retaining the basic spooky atmosphere and chiller situations of Willard's original play, Paramount injects plenty of legitimate comedy," foreseeing that the film "will hit a consistent stride down the line in the subsequents." *Motion Picture Herald*, meanwhile, applauded Paramount for having "solved neatly for itself, exhibitors and customers the heretofore perplexing problem of what to do with Bob Hope."[23] What the film "does with" Bob Hope is cast him as a sort of surrogate for the audience; Wally Campbell's knowledge of the way melodrama plots work provides a degree of assurance or safety for the viewer *and* for the heroine, Joyce Norman, played by Paulette Goddard. Wally bears witness to her, and the audience's, experience.

For example, the heroine in Paramount's 1939 version is molested in her sleep by a hairy clawed hand that emerges from the paneling above her bed, just as Annabelle is in Leni's 1927 film. The thrilling moments of the clawed hand grabbing at her neck and her scream in response are, as in Leni's film, drawn out to create empathetic distress for Joyce, especially when her relatives doubt her sanity. In Leni's film, the distress the audience feels for Annabelle builds as she attempts to prove that there *are* secret panels behind her bed; that distress relaxes when she discovers the lawyer's corpse. The camera lingers on his body as if to force her relatives to admit that Annabelle was right all along. Then, Annabelle faints. In the 1939 version, Joyce is awakened by the clawed hand groping around her neck; she screams for help, but *then* faints, changing the emotional rhythm of the sequence. Her relatives run and bring her to. When they suggest that her report of a clawed hand coming out from behind the wall is crazy, Joyce becomes not only frustrated but obdurate, growing angry rather than distressed. It is Wally, however, not Joyce, who finds the secret panel behind Joyce's bed and somehow opens the passage into which the attorney's body has been stuffed. Earlier, Wally had helped Joyce find the family diamond necklace (a task Annabelle completed alone) and saw her with it before she went to bed, so he knows she is not lying about *that*.

Wally even accuses the relatives of having it in for Joyce: "You'd all like to prove that Joyce is crazy, wouldn't you, because that would give you another chance at old Norman's dough!"

Wally's accusation not only confirms the plot of this film, which an audience familiar with *The Cat and the Canary* would know, but also, as a stage actor, Wally brings his knowledge of such plots to bear on the immediate circumstances. When the relatives chastise Wally for believing Joyce's story about a clawed hand coming out of the wall, Wally replies, "Haven't you clucks ever heard of secret passageways and panels?" Wally's outburst on Joyce's behalf spurs audience relief, rather than dread or distress. Even at chilling moments in which he is in serious danger, Wally blurts out parallels from musty old plays. Strangely, though, Wally does not seem to know how the plot he is currently in will end, thus the film still provokes distress when Wally finds a secret passageway in the house and gets stuck there, and when Wally and Joyce find themselves in a shed behind the main house, confronting the villain. Rather than lingering chills, however, this film's affective rhythms unfailingly shift the audience's anticipation from the next thrill or chill to the next humorous bit.

Wally's reflexive jokes about the genre fulfill a further purpose; they eliminate the need for the film to insist on a ghostly presence, thus evacuating it of a central element of Leni's version: the psychological angle. In Leni's 1927 film, chills and psychological terror—the "creepy" feelings associated with German Expressionist style—were conveyed in part through a tonal ambiguity about the sanity or insanity, guilt or innocence of Annabelle's relatives, in part through the ease with which it seemed Annabelle might indeed be declared medically insane even though she is not, and in part through the way the film retained a certain plausibility about the possibility of Cyrus West's ghostly presence.[24] In the 1939 version, the supernatural elements of the 1927 film have been sanitized, scientized, and evacuated of psychological terror; the extent of the danger our heroine is in never rises above the worldly.

While Joyce Norman half-listens to Roger Crosby's warnings that she beware her relatives (before he disappears behind a bookcase), she reads from a volume titled *The Psychology of Fear*. A close-up of her page reads:

> What happens when a cat is allowed to come close to a canary in a cage? The bird, seeing the terrible eyes of its enemy so close, is often frightened to death. Numerous experiments conducted by leading psychologists both in this country and abroad have proven this to be true in the majority of cases. The size or sex of either the animal or the bird, in no way changed the result.

The passage is ridiculous, but its tone of certainty "cleanses" fear of any obscure taints—like the unconscious or the irrational, or indeed the possibility of the supernatural. A modern heroine, Joyce is fearless, and apparently devoid of uncanny sensibilities.

In Willard's original play, Annabelle West must be examined by a psychiatrist who will determine her sanity. As characterized by Willard, the psychiatrist, Dr. Patterson, is a tall man in black clothes with a black hat, who glides noiselessly into the room, and before whom Annabelle shrinks in terror.[25] In Leni's 1927 adaptation, the examining doctor bears a striking resemblance to Dr. Caligari, iconically recalling "German" concerns with ambiguity, the uncanny, and interior states of mind, as well as the threat of maniacal authority figures. In the 1939 adaptation, however, though the conditions of the patriarch's will remain the same, no doctor comes to examine Joyce Norman to determine her sanity. Instead, the original play's concern for mental hygiene is displaced onto the rational science of behavioral psychology. Authority over Joyce's sanity falls not to a doctor, but to Joyce herself and to Wally Campbell, who supports Joyce and confirms her unattested experiences through his knowledge of the formula of murder mysteries, including things like the likely placement of secret panels and passageways. Wally's genre acuity doubles as a kind of knowledge of the house's unconscious.

The 1939 version's genre playfulness and its detachment from interiority make evident the extent to which the art brought to Hollywood by German émigrés in the 1920s had, by 1939, been naturalized as "Hollywood" style. Reviews of the remade *The Cat and the Canary* reflect this evolution, for they neglect to mention either "German film style" as an influence or Leni's film, at least directly. The 1939 film's lack of a serious psychological angle, along with the film's pursuit of comedy over thrills, also suggest the context of the time: the outbreak of World War II. The US was not yet militarily engaged in the war, but Germany was clearly a threat, and the American public was still in the grip of the Depression. Psychological thrills and chills were not what Hollywood wished to foist on a worried domestic market, and certainly not on even more worried foreign markets. Furthermore, in popular culture psychoanalysis remained a German—more specifically, a Jewish—field of knowledge production, suspect for its racial provenance as well as its fundamental claim of the existence of the unconscious, and hence of a self divided against itself.[26] The 1939 *The Cat and the Canary* reflects an Americanized version of psychology that had been absorbed into mainstream discourse purged of its "European" (i.e. occultish, irrational, even uncanny) elements. In this film, the threat to heroine Joyce Norman is never interior (her mind working against itself) but always exterior.

In "Twice-Told Tales: Disavowal and the Rhetoric of the Remake," Thomas Leitch wrote that a remake's intertextual stance, the "general attitude

Figure 8.2 Paulette Goddard as updated heroine Joyce Norman in the 1939 remake of *The Cat and the Canary*.

it adopts toward its original, helps define the way the audience makes sense of their experience of the film as a whole." He argued further that the term "disavowal" is apt in

> specific ways to the remake's model of intertextuality, since remakes by definition establish their value by invoking earlier texts whose potency they simultaneously valorize and deny through a series of rhetorical maneuvers designed at once to reflect their intimacy with these earlier texts and to distance themselves from their flaws.[27]

Paramount's 1939 *The Cat and the Canary* disavows two of the original's powerful claims: the existence of psychological unknowns, and the probable mental weakness and greed of the American moneyed class. This disavowal only works, however, by arousing remarkable self-consciousness about genre considerations. In the 1939 remake, the joke is not on Leni's film but on the subgenre of the thriller-chiller-comedy itself; the film arouses the audience's consciousness of the feelings it is expected to feel, in what order, and through what mechanisms.

CONCLUSION

Iris Barry opined in the 1940s that Leni's cinematic style and capacity for evoking horror suggested that his talents could have been put to far richer artistic and intellectual uses than genre films. By many counts, including his own, however, Leni was comfortable with his Hollywood role. Jan-Christopher Horak writes that Hollywood studio executives "had few ideas about what to do with the [German] talent they had acquired except to force them into the same tired genres that Hollywood produced on an assembly line." Leni, however, "successfully negotiated the American studio system on his first attempt."[28] Not only did *The Cat and the Canary* receive rave reviews and command a huge box office success, his film created a template for an entire subgenre.

Paul Leni's *The Cat and the Canary* created a visual and aural iconography still essential to film and televisual "old spooky house" narratives. But Leni also created the tempo or rhythm that remains the hallmark of horror-comedy. Arguably, genre is a matter of feeling rather than form, for audiences refuse to categorize films under particular generic rubrics when the feeling the film conveys "isn't right." Indeed, some genres may be defined as a feeling shape. The thriller-chiller-comedy is certainly such a subgenre. Genres of any kind are shaped by affective structures as much as they help shape them. What is interesting about the thriller-chiller-comedy is that its process of becoming a genre has largely been a process of remaking Paul Leni's *The Cat and the Canary*.

NOTES

1. Review of *The Cat and the Canary*, *Film Daily*, May 27, 1927; "The Shadow Stage," *Photoplay*, July 1927, 55; Mordaunt Hall, "The Screen," *New York Times*, September 10, 1927.
2. Roscoe Williams, "Hollywood Reviews," *Motion Picture Daily*, October 30, 1939; review of *The Cat and the Canary*, *Hollywood Reporter*, October 25, 1939.
3. Christopher Bird, "'Europe Ain't Gonna See This Scene!': Working with Variant Versions in Photoplay Productions' Restoration of *The Cat and the Canary*," *The Moving Image: The Journal of the Association of Moving Image Archivists* 9, no. 2 (Fall 2009): 150.
4. Richard Koszarski, *An Evening's Entertainment: The Age of the Silent Feature Picture, 1915–1928* (New York: Charles Scribner's Sons, 1990), 89.
5. Iris Barry, "Film Notes. Part 1: The Silent Film," *Bulletin of the Museum of Modern Art* 16, no. 2/3 (1949): 60.
6. PCA Collection, Margaret Herrick Library, Academy of Motion Picture Arts & Sciences, Beverly Hills, CA.
7. Review of *The Cat and the Canary*, *Film Daily*.
8. Both the American and European 1927 releases of the film were similarly tinted, an element restored in the 2005 and 2004 DVDs of the film.

9. Lighting is used to especially powerful effect to characterize Mammy Pleasant and convey her relationship to the Wests and the house. The character is probably a reference to Mary Ellen Pleasant (1814–1904), who was born into slavery and later became an entrepreneur, a key supporter of the Underground Railroad, and a central figure in a popular San Francisco ghost story. The light on Mammy Pleasant indicates (better than the actress's makeup) that she is a person of mixed race, thereby raising the stereotypical assumption that she is in close communication with whatever spirits inhabit the house. The racial shorthand employed in Willard's play and Leni's film is not very self-evident, but Mammy Pleasant's racial difference is strongly marked in the 1939 Paramount remake and made even more obvious by the remake's setting: an old plantation house in a Louisiana bayou.
10. Thomas Elsaesser, *Weimar Cinema and After: Germany's Historical Imaginary* (New York: Routledge, 2002), 44.
11. Lotte H. Eisner, *The Haunted Screen: Expressionism in the German Cinema and the Influence of Max Reinhardt*, trans. Roger Greaves (Berkeley: University of California Press, 1969), 125–7.
12. Jan-Christopher Horak, "Sauerkraut & Sausages with a Little Goulash: Germans in Hollywood, 1927," *Film History* 17, no. 2/3 (2005): 241.
13. While many silent-era films produced for domestic and foreign markets were shot using a two-camera set-up with cameras adjacent to one another, such a procedure would have been cumbersome on the set of *The Cat and the Canary*, which used many tracking shots. Instead, it seems that Leni filmed some takes almost as "rehearsals" for the desired take, and the better takes were used in the American release. See Bird, "'Europe Ain't Gonna See,'" 154–5.
14. Graham Petrie, *Hollywood Destinies: European Directors in America, 1922–1931*, rev. edn. (Detroit: Wayne State University Press, 2002), 215.
15. Anna Gibbs, "After Affect: Sympathy, Synchrony, and Mimetic Communication," in *The Affect Theory Reader*, ed. Melissa Gregg and Gregory J. Seigworth (Durham, NC: Duke University Press, 2010), 186–7.
16. Gibbs, "After Affect," 186; Elaine Hatfield, John T. Cacioppo, and Richard L. Rapson, *Emotional Contagion* (Cambridge: Cambridge University Press, 1994), 5.
17. "Paul Leni is Drum Major of Directorial Tempo," *Universal Weekly*, September 22, 1928.
18. According to Christopher Bird, the Universal editing team supervised by Lloyd Nosler took the best of Leni's takes to create "a flowing, smooth experience" in the American release print, marked by careful action cuts and efficient matches on action in line with Leni's rhythmic cues. In the European version, by contrast, certain long shots are held "just a few frames too long," and at least one close-up shot "starts two seconds . . . too early," leading to a far different experience and much less carefully timed film. See Bird, "'Europe Ain't Gonna See,'" 157–8.
19. William K. Everson, *American Silent Film* (New York: Da Capo Press, 1978), 332.
20. Both of these are considered lost films.
21. Thomas Leitch, "Twice-Told Tales: Disavowal and the Rhetoric of the Remake," in *Dead Ringers: The Remake in Theory and Practice*, ed. Jennifer Forrest and Leonard R. Koos (Albany: State University of New York Press, 2002), 45.
22. Leitch, "Twice-Told Tales," 47.
23. Review of *The Cat and the Canary*, *Hollywood Reporter*; review of *The Cat and the Canary*, *Variety*, November 1, 1939; review of *The Cat and the Canary*, *Motion Picture Herald*, October 28, 1939.
24. See Simone Natale's chapter in this volume.

25. John Willard, *The Cat and the Canary: A Melodrama in Three Acts* (New York: Samuel French, 1927), 85.
26. For a discussion of the backlash against German and Hungarian émigré directors and their impact on Hollywood cinema, see Horak, "Sauerkraut & Sausages."
27. Leitch, "Twice-Told Tales," 44, 53.
28. Horak, "Sauerkraut & Sausages," 258, 241.

CHAPTER 9

Specters of the Mind: Ghosts, Illusion, and Exposure in Paul Leni's *The Cat and the Canary*

Simone Natale

INTRODUCTION

One of the main characteristics of ghosts is that they are able to invite a great variety of interpretations, meanings, and uses. In Shakespeare's dramas and in ancient religious rituals, in gothic novels and in spiritualist séances, in horror movies and in the New Age spiritual movement, specters have been responsible for popular amusements, irrational fears, experimental inquiries, and acts of devotion. This multiform character also shaped the way ghosts have been represented throughout film history on the cinematic screen. Cinematic specters have appropriated different narrative, symbolic, and metaphorical roles—so many that it is perhaps more precise to describe ghost movies as a plurality of genres with a common theme, rather than as an individual genre.

This essay focuses on Paul Leni's 1927 *The Cat and the Canary*, arguing that this film remediated a long tradition of spectacular entertainments based on the rejection of supernaturalism, and how such rejection has important consequences in the narrative frame and in the nature of the gratification invited in their audience. From this point of view, Leni's movie can be grouped within a particular class of ghost movies: those where the existence of the true "protagonist" of these movies, the ghost, is ultimately refused and relegated to the realm of human imagination and trickery. The defining characteristics of these movies is that they tell a ghost story without believing in ghosts; or, to put it in other words, that they propose to the audience an interpretation of the story that denies the status of reality to the world of ghosts and specters. Most haunted house comedies from the 1930s to the 1960s—such as *The Old Dark House* (1932), *The Ghost Breakers* (1940), and *Scared Stiff* (1953)—follow this basic structure; however, this type of film also includes movies that play more ambiguously with the borders between hallucination and reality, such as Jack Clayton's *The Innocents*.[1] After providing a brief summary of the plot and the production history of *The Cat and the Canary*, the essay addresses this movie by referring to aspects from the cultural history of ghosts. Particular emphasis is given to how the film can be framed within the tradition of spiritualist exposés, to the characterization of ghosts as creations of our mind, to the use of superimposition effects, and to the question of sound, which paradoxically plays a quite relevant role despite its being a silent movie. Finally, in the conclusion, I interrogate how works of fiction such as *The Cat and the Canary*, by relying on the allure of the supernatural but at the same time refusing to accept its claims, point to the apparently contradictory power of our fascination with the occult.

DISSECTING THE GHOST OF *THE CAT AND THE CANARY*

Directed by German expatriate Paul Leni in 1927, *The Cat and the Canary* was produced by Universal Pictures in the United States. The film adapted John Willard's 1921 stage melodrama, which had premiered in New York the following year. The plot focuses on the inheritance of millionaire Cyrus West, whose relatives aim at his fortune with greed, like cats around a canary. Before dying, West demands that his will be read only twenty years after his death. As twenty years have passed and the day arrives, all the potential heirs meet in West's old mansion, which has acquired the reputation of being haunted by the ghost of its deceased owner. The will nominates the niece Annabelle West (Laura La Plante) as heiress, but with a condition: at the end of the night, she needs to be judged mentally sane by a psychiatrist. If she fails, the heritance will pass to the second person nominated in the will. During the night her mental sanity is strained by seemingly supernatural events, such as a mysterious hand coming out of the mansion's walls and the sudden disappearance of the lawyer who read the will—just before he could mention the name of the second person nominated in it. The "ghost," however, is finally revealed to be none other than one of West's nephews, Charles Wilder (Forrest Stanley), the second heir nominated in the will. His plans are finally exposed, and the ghostly apparitions debunked as the result of trickery, the gloomy atmosphere of the old mansion, and the overexcited imagination of Annabelle and the other relatives.

The film proved to be a critical and popular success, justifying the employment of Paul Leni, who had accepted Carl Laemmle's invitation to move from Germany to Hollywood and become a director of prologues at Universal Studios.[2] Like other German filmmakers who moved to the other side of the Atlantic in that period, Leni contributed a range of visual and stylistic ideas to the burgeoning American film industry. In *The Cat and the Canary*, he used some stylistic devices typical of German Expressionism, adapting them to a plot that had already stood the test of the popular theatrical circuit. Particularly noteworthy was his insertion of the Expressionist-style chiaroscuro lighting in an American film, an aspect that would characterize several Universal horror and film noir productions throughout the 1930s and 40s.[3] Rebecca M. Gordon notes that while Expressionist lighting is typically used to imply character motivations and to bestow upon people and objects a certain ineffable character, Leni uses light and shadow effects to create both dramatic and comic effects.[4] The film, in fact, is considered one of the first examples, if not the first, of a film genre that functions through the ambiguity between emotional thrill and humor: the thriller-chiller-comedy.

While Leni's *The Cat and the Canary* certainly helped secure the ghost as a relevant trope of cinematic fiction, it is only by looking beyond the temporal and contextual boundaries of film history per se that one might comprehend how the theme and the figures of the ghost acquire and convey meaning on the cinematic screen. Film history and criticism demand what Lynda Nead calls "an integrated approach to visual media," a perspective that focuses on the connections and spaces *across* different media and practices.[5] Tackled from a similar perspective, movies that challenge the existence of ghosts—such as *The Cat and the Canary*—relate to a larger tradition that goes beyond the boundaries of film history to embrace literary and theatrical works, but also popular scientific lectures and magic shows that attempted to expose the deceitfulness of ghostly apparitions.

FROM SPIRITUALIST EXPOSÉS TO CINEMATIC GHOSTS

In an essay on the intermedial character of early cinema, André Gaudreault suggests that film historians should adopt "a retrospective, rather than a progressive, point of view," addressing cinema in reference to earlier media and practices, rather than to its later evolutions.[6] A similar approach is fruitful not only for the study of early cinema but in the analysis of other aspects of film history as well. In the specific case of *The Cat and the Canary*, it is by looking at the cultural history of spiritualism and belief in ghosts throughout the nineteenth and early twentieth centuries that one may gain insights for the interpretation of the film.

Emerging as a popular belief and a religious movement in the mid-nineteenth century, spiritualism was based on the belief that certain persons, called mediums, could establish a channel of communication with the spirits of the dead. This communication was usually performed in meetings or events called séances, where one or two mediums were joined by other sitters in contacting the spirits.[7] The rise of belief in spiritualism was counteracted by the emergence of rationalizing attempts that aimed at exposing spiritualist séances as the result of trickery, hallucination, or sensory deception.[8] These were called *spiritualist exposés* and took the form of pamphlets and popular scientific lectures denouncing the falsehood of spirit phenomena. Scientists of the caliber of Dmitri Mendeleev, William Benjamin Carpenter, Michael Faraday, and Hugo Münsterberg participated in the tradition of spiritualist exposé, challenging the reliability of spiritualist claims through the appeal to fields such as physics and psychology.[9]

The debate on spiritualism, however, went far beyond the realm of experimental science to include a broader range of practices, by which this rationalizing discourse was converted into an established form of live entertainment. Throughout the nineteenth century, popular scientific lecturers discussed the claims of spiritualism and supernatural phenomena, often carrying out their scientific endeavors with a popular and spectacular approach.[10] Starting in institutions devoted to the popularization of science such as the London Polytechnic,[11] this tradition of spiritualist exposés began to involve a growing number of stage magicians in Europe and North America. Some of the most famous magicians of the nineteenth and early twentieth centuries, including the American Harry Houdini, delivered magic shows that aimed to expose the tricks practiced by spiritualist mediums during their séances.[12] The audience expected to find in these shows phenomena similar to those observed at a spiritualist séance, but within a different interpretative framework; in contrast to mediums, in fact, magicians openly admitted that their feats were the result of illusion and trickery, rather than of supernatural phenomena.[13] The anti-spiritualist shows of stage magicians, or spiritualist exposés, became one of the most successful forms of stage conjuring and helped account for the success of magic spectacles as popular entertainment in the nineteenth century.[14] This genre became more and more important as stage magic reached its zenith, between the 1870s and the 1900s.[15]

Spiritualist exposés have sometimes been linked to early and silent cinema. Matthew Solomon describes film as "an anti-spiritualist medium," observing that the tradition of exposés of the trickery of spiritualism was "one of stage magic's earliest and most important contributions to the history of cinema."[16] Indeed, several of the magicians involved in pioneering early cinema had carried out some form of anti-spiritualist show in their careers.[17] For instance, David Devant, who bought the first Robert W. Paul projector and entered into film production, previously performed spiritualist exposés in London at the Egyptian Hall.[18] Likewise, Nevil Maskelyne, son of magician and anti-spiritualist author John Nevil Maskelyne and a stage magician himself, patented a film projector, the Mutagraph, featuring continuous instead of intermittent motion.[19] At least two of the earliest developers of the trick film genre, Georges Méliès and George Albert Smith, were inspired by the tradition of spiritualist exposés, at which they hinted in their cinematic productions.[20]

The contribution of spiritualist exposés to the new cinematic technology also concerns the characterization of the figure and the theme of the ghost as represented on the screen. Performing spiritualist exposés, end-of-the-century magicians such as John Nevil Maskelyne, Harry Kellar, and Harry Houdini understood better than anyone else the spectacular and theatrical potential of spiritualism and of belief in the supernatural.[21] The tradition to which they contributed provided a significant precedent in which the exposure of the inauthenticity of ghosts was turned into a spectacular practice that—like cinema itself—implicitly hinted at the deceitful and hallucinatory nature of spectatorship.[22] It is within this tradition that, retrospectively, one might include films that represent the ghost as the fruit of hallucination and delusion. In fact, by equating ghostly apparitions to perceptual delusion and depicting the haunted house as a space of deception and trickery, these films take up several elements from the rationalizing discourse of spiritualist exposé.

In *The Cat and the Canary*, belief in the supernatural is evoked constantly. At the beginning of the film, for example, the caretaker of the old mansion, Mammy Pleasant (Martha Mattox) states she does not feel lonely in the empty house since she does not need "the living ones." At the same time, however, the film challenges her belief as superstition or the fruit of madness and delusion. As in the case of spiritualist exposé practiced on-stage by professional magicians, the rationalizing discourse of anti-spiritualism is converted into an entertaining and spectacular element. The ghost plays thereby a double role. On the narrative level, it provides the film with a supernatural and occult aura that has the potential to fascinate the audience;[23] on a metaphorical level, it embodies broader cultural concerns regarding the deceitful nature of sensory perception and, more widely, of the human mind.

THE SPECTRALIZATION OF THE MIND

In *The Female Thermometer* (1995), literary scholar Terry Castle explores how during the nineteenth century, the word "phantasmagoria" changed its meaning from referring to something external and public, a spectacle conjured through optical tricks and a magic lantern, to describing something internal and subjective: human imagination. She links the emergence of gothic literature in the late eighteenth and early nineteenth centuries with a new consideration of the mind as a space inhabited by "ghosts," that is, by fantasies and imaginations. Castle called this process "spectralization of the mind," a dynamic by which the specters were reframed in the realm of the human mind as hallucinations and illusions rather than as supernatural phenomena. Castle argues that throughout the twentieth century up to the present day, this process continued to shape the representation of the ghost with its metaphoric connections to mental states. As Castle notes, in fact, we are used to the metaphor of the haunted consciousness; we speak of being haunted by memories and pursued by images inside our heads.[24]

By treating ghostly apparitions as products of all-too-human fears, expectations, and delusions, *The Cat and the Canary* plays a legitimate part in the "spectralization of the mind" described by Castle. The rationalizing discourse that dismisses belief in ghosts as pure superstition mitigates the fear that ghosts arouse in the public, creating the condition for the movie's combination of hilarious and mysterious themes. The comical effect relies ultimately on the identification of the character's and the spectator's position; as the guests in West's old mansion, we feel chilled and tense despite the rationalist assurance that ghosts exist only in our imagination. The characters in the movie refuse the existence of the supernatural and yet, like us, become the victims of the fear and fascination that the supernatural evokes. The paradox becomes particularly evident with the arrival of the psychiatrist, a Caligari-like figure who needs to assess if Annabelle is mad; he fixes his mesmerist gaze on both Annabelle and the audience, and his inquiry becomes an investigation of the specters not just in the heroine's mind, but in everybody's. "What makes you so nervous tonight?" asks the psychiatrist, to which Annabelle responds only after a long pause—just the time for us to reflect on an answer, too.

THE MEANING OF SUPERIMPOSITION

Among the different kinds of spiritualist exposés performed on-stage or illustrated in popular publications by stage magicians, the exposure of spirit photography—a spiritualist practice based on the belief that it is possible to capture the image of a ghost on the photographic plate—plays a particularly significant role.[25] As skeptics have often underlined, these images can be explained as the product of photographic tricks, such as multiple exposure and other superimposition techniques, which were commonly used in photographic practice well before spirit photography emerged. Struggling to demonstrate the inauthenticity of spiritualism, and eager to find all possible visual and spectacular means to do so, stage magicians like Jacoby in Germany and Maskelyne in Great Britain produced images similar to spirit photographs but openly acknowledged as photographic tricks. In so doing, they helped establish superimposition as a visual technique that wavered between fictional and religious contexts, allowing for its association with the worlds of belief and entertainment at the same time.

In *The Cat and the Canary*, superimposition is one of the most effective visual effects employed. This technique is used relatively sparingly but with meaningful results throughout the film. In early and silent cinema, superimposition effects were used for three main aims: to represent ghosts and other supernatural apparitions, to represent hallucinations and thoughts produced by a character's mind, and to depict the events and atmospheres of dreams.[26] In *The Cat and the Canary*, the use of superimposition also displays a range of characterizations and meanings. Yet throughout the movie, ghosts are never visually represented as superimposed images. Ghosts are in fact not represented visually at all, but rather embedded in visual or aural events that can be explained rationally or exchanged for supernatural phenomena. The film, as a consequence, leaves open the possibility to interpret the nature of these events. The spectators, as well as the film's fictional characters, can decide if what they "see" or "hear" is a ghost, or they can give another interpretation to what they see, hear, and feel.

Rather than representing ghosts as something external, *The Cat and the Canary* posits ghosts as a matter of interpretation, a choice that is taken at the level of our mind. It thus follows the trajectory of the spectralization of the mind. While superimposition is not used to represent "real" ghosts, it is employed to represent the specters of the mind. At the beginning of the movie, for instance, superimposed images of cats hint at Cyrus West's obsessions; the vision symbolizes the greed of his relatives, among whom Cyrus feels like a defenseless canary circled by cats.[27] The character's thoughts are depicted as faint, transparent images—a well-established iconography to represent ghosts in media and popular entertainments such as photography, drawing, phantasmagorias, and stage magic shows.[28] To be haunted by specters, in this sense, also becomes in visual terms "to find oneself obsessed by spectral images," as Castle puts it.[29]

GHOSTS AND THE PROBLEM OF NOISE

Interestingly, the silent movie *The Cat and the Canary* employs superimposition to render not only mental thoughts but also sounds and aural events. Superimposition effects are employed to depict visually the noise of the knocking at the door and, in another scene, the stroke of a clock.[30] The trick helps to visualize in a striking manner those sounds that were to provoke the chills of the impressionable characters (and spectators). But the necessity to substitute sound with visual effects in a silent film does not explain alone why the movie employed superimposition, an aesthetic that, as mentioned above, is inextricably linked with the iconographic tradition of representations of ghosts in Western culture. My contention is that this use of superimposition to represent sounds has to do with the status the film gives to ghosts as irrational interpretations of sensorial events.

In 1927, Leni's film came near the end of the era of the silent film. Though *The Cat and the Canary* was produced as a silent movie, sound plays a peculiarly relevant role in it. As Robert Spadoni points out, "this film, had it been a sound film [. . .] would had been a feast of noise implemented, like the host of visual techniques Leni deployed, to make viewers jumpy." The richness of sensorial chills that also somehow have an (in)audible nature is underlined by the reactions of the film's characters to aural events, and Spadoni reports that the *Motion Picture News* predicted that the film would "score best when presented mostly with mechanical sounds effects rather than customary musical accompaniment."[31]

Intangible by definition, invisible in many cases, ghosts have always entertained a particular relationship with the realm of sound. The first manifestations of spirit agency in spiritualism were rappings, and spiritualist phenomena frequently consisted of noises and sounds. The darkness or semi-darkness of séance rooms forced spirits and mediums to rely on non-visual experiences. As Steven Connor points out, "the members of the séance would see much less than they would touch, taste, smell and, most importantly, *hear*."[32] In the frame of a spiritualist séance, each sensation and event could be explained and understood as a spirit message. Spirit communications supposedly delivered from the beyond were often barely understandable phenomena, relying on the interpretation of spiritual mediums to become of some meaning to the sitters. Phenomena as different as movements of objects, a sudden current of air, a barely inaudible rap, and the feeling of being touched were interpreted as spirit messages.

The status of sensorial perception in this context can be aptly described by referring to the concept of noise in communication theory. According to Claude Shannon's mathematical model of communication, the fundamental aim of communication is to reproduce exactly or approximately a selected message at another point. In order to do so, one needs to distinguish meaningful information from the distortions, labeled *noise*, which may intervene in the process.[33] With Shannon's communication theory in mind, the history of the spiritualist movement in the nineteenth century can be regarded as an effort to transform noise into information or, in other words, to understand every sensorial event as significant information. In spiritualism the idea of noise was almost completely banned, and every event could be regarded as a spirit message, rather than as interference or distortion. The conventionality of this interpretation was acknowledged even by committed spiritualists. As one commentator recognized, for instance, in the case of table rappings,

> the interpretation of sound—its investment with sense—is purely conventional. We may build up a system of laws to enable us to give a proper and uniform expression to it, but we make sound to signify just what is most convenient for us.[34]

A spiritualist writing in 1853 listed among audible spirit phenomena knockings, rappings, jarrings, creakings, and tickings. These "peculiar noises, indicative of more or less intelligence" could be very loud, distinct, and forcible, or less distinct and more gentle, but were all "audible realities."[35] What counted was not the nature of the sounds, but the interpretation that was given to them as evidence of ghostly agency.

If spiritualists conceived aural phenomena within a context banning noise as non-relevant information, critics of spiritualism had a very different approach to the problem; they considered the knockings and rappings heard by spiritualists at séances as noise, rather than as meaningful information (i.e. the spirit message). Critics hinted at the problem of sensorial perception, whereby noises of ordinary origins could be exchanged for a sign of the presence of ghosts.[36] They stressed that the hearing of anomalous sounds implies the possibility of madness or hallucination—that is to say, the existence of the "specters" of the mind.

In *The Cat and the Canary*, the dialectic between ghosts and rationalizing discourses is resolved in the film's dismissal of the possibility that ghosts do exist, in its refusal of the interpretation of noises as signs of spirit presence. The film evokes such spectralization of sound by inserting noises as moments of shock that underline the characters' propensity to believe in the supernatural, being scared and excited by sensorial events. The arrival of Paul Jones (Creighton Hale) in the house just before the reading of the will, for instance, is introduced by a hectic scene in which he reports hearing a loud noise, possibly a shot—an event that left him shaken and scared. His inability to understand the origin of noises signals the characterization of Jones throughout the entire film; easily influenced by the atmosphere of the house and the strange events that happen during the night, he more than any other character embodies the film's comical representation of people's sensitivity to supernatural claims and sensorial delusions. Those who believe in ghosts, the film implies, are the ones who more than any other are receptive to the chilling effect of noises.

Superimposition, in this regard, functions within a context where not only visual hallucinations but also aural chills are activated as specters of the mind. As David Toop notes, "the interpretation of sound as an unstable or provisional event, ambiguously situated somewhere between psychological delusion, verifiable scientific phenomenon, and a visitation of spectral forces, is a frequent trope of supernatural fiction."[37] Spiritualism's interpretation of sounds as ghostly events is regarded as a sign of madness and deception; the specter, in this case too, is located in our imagination, rather than in the external world.

CONCLUSION: THE FASCINATION WITH THE SUPERNATURAL

As Vivian Sobchack suggests, special effects "point behind and beyond the film's story to the grounding technology that allows these special imaged instances to exist at all."[38] Superimposition effects, however, recall not a single technology but rather a set of practices, technologies, and icons that evoke—in contexts as different as spiritualism, magic lanterns, stage magic, and photographic amusements—the intervention of the supernatural. In the application of this technique in *The Cat and the Canary*, we find a strategy that characterizes the film's wider appeal to its spectator. Like in the spiritualist exposés performed by stage magicians, the refusal of ghosts comes together with a self-aware usage of the fascination that supernatural claims inspire in the public. The ghost is denied, domesticated, but also employed as a powerful means to attract the audience toward the show. It is used as a chilling, uncanny element and at the same time as a comic expedient to amuse the viewer, who is encouraged to laugh at the naivety of the characters. In such an apparently contradictory use of the supernatural trope, Leni's film reminds us that ghosts are often produced by our own mind; at the same time, however, it implies that the occult is scary and entertaining enough to make it a feasible subject for a successful movie. Like other fictional works and spectacular shows that represent ghosts only to deny them, it points to the contradictory power of our relationship with the occult; we are irresistibly attracted by the supernatural, even if we refuse to believe in it. The enlightening and rationalizing endeavors of debunking ghosts, in this sense, is an inherent part of such an inescapable fascination with the occult. It is due to this fascination that spiritualist exposés appealed to large masses of people throughout the nineteenth and twentieth centuries. It is due to this persisting fascination, too, that ghost movies denying the existence of ghosts, such as *The Cat and the Canary*, count among successful instances of supernatural fiction in the history of film.

By adopting a retrospective approach and by employing elements that are external to the cinematic screen, this chapter has addressed Paul Leni's *The Cat and the Canary* as pertaining to a wider tradition of spectacular shows that focus on ghosts and yet openly refuse them, relegating the specter to the realm of human imagination. This approach is consistent with media archaeological studies that address cinema and other media as elements of a broad media culture, rather than in isolation from each other.[39] Moreover, by referring to elements from the history of belief in ghosts, the chapter aims to call for the necessity to integrate contexts that are usually separated from each other, such as the history of film and the history of religious belief. Literature addressing the cultural history of ghosts is often divided into two separate traditions that address respectively fictional and "real" ghosts. While many attempts have been made to question how the belief in spirits has influenced the work of writers, filmmakers, and TV producers,[40] less attention has been given to the possibility of comparing the experience of those who believe in spirits with those who consume products of fiction on ghosts. Film scholars often do not take into account how ghost movies and horror films, and the belief in ghosts and spiritualist practices, depend on a fascination—felt by those who believe in ghosts as well as by those who firmly deny their existence—with the occult and the supernatural. The popularity of ghost movies such as *The Cat and the Canary* is built upon this fascination with the occult, upon the emotions evoked by the conception of ghosts—whether we believe in them or not.

ACKNOWLEDGMENTS

A first draft of this essay was presented at a screening of *The Cat and the Canary* organized for the presentation of the Exhibition "Diversamente vivi: Zombie, fantasmi, mummie, vampiri," National Museum of Cinema, Turin, Italy, in October 2010. I would like to thank Sarah Pesenti Campagnoni and the Mario Gromo Library of the National Museum of Cinema for contributing to the organization of this event, as well as the curators of the Exhibition, Giulia Carluccio and Peppino Ortoleva. A follow-up draft was published in *Cinematic Ghosts: Haunting and Spectrality from Silent Cinema to the Digital Era*, ed. Murray Leeder (New York: Bloomsbury Academic, 2015) and adapted for this book.

NOTES

1. Following Tzvetan Todorov's categorization of the fantastic, the uncanny, and the marvelous, these movies would pertain to the genre of the uncanny, that is, to those works of fiction in which the hesitation between a natural and a supernatural explanation is finally resolved in a decision for the former. See Tzvetan Todorov, *The Fantastic: A Structural Approach to a Literary Genre* (Ithaca, NY: Cornell University Press, 1975).
2. Kevin Brownlow, "Annus Mirabilis: The Film in 1927," *Film History: An International Journal* 17, no. 2 (2005): 168–78.
3. Jan-Christopher Horak, "Sauerkraut & Sausages with a Little Goulash: Germans in Hollywood, 1927," *Film History: An International Journal* 17, no. 2 (2005): 241–60.
4. Rebecca M. Gordon, "Between Thought and Feeling: Affect, Audience, and Critical Film History" (PhD dissertation, Indiana University, 2007).
5. Lynda Nead, *The Haunted Gallery: Painting, Photography, Film c. 1900* (New Haven, CT: Yale University Press, 2007), 2.
6. André Gaudreault, "The Diversity of Cinematographic Connections in the Intermedial Context of the Turn of the 20th Century," in *Visual Delights: Essays on the Popular and Projected Image in the 19th Century*, ed. Simon Popple and Vanessa Toulmin (Trowbridge: Flicks Books, 2000), 10.
7. On the emergence of spiritualism in the nineteenth century, see John Warne Monroe, *Laboratories of Faith: Mesmerism, Spiritism, and Occultism in Modern France* (Ithaca, NY: Cornell University Press, 2008); Robert S. Cox, *Body and Soul: A Sympathetic History of American Spiritualism* (Charlottesville: University of Virginia Press, 2003); Ann Braude, *Radical Spirits: Spiritualism and Women's Rights in Nineteenth-Century America* (Boston: Beacon Press, 1989); and Janet Oppenheim, *The Other World: Spiritualism and Psychical Research in England, 1850–1914* (Cambridge: Cambridge University Press, 1985).

8. David Walker, "The Humbug in American Religion: Ritual Theories of Nineteenth-Century Spiritualism," *Religion and American Culture: A Journal of Interpretation* 23, no. 1 (Winter 2013): 30–74; Erhard Schüttpelz, "Mediumismus und moderne Medien. Die Prüfung des europäischen Medienbegriffs," *Deutsche Vierteljahrsschrift für Literaturwissenschaft und Geistesgeschichte* 86, no. 1 (March 2012): 121–44; Simone Natale, "Spiritualism Exposed: Scepticism, Credulity and Spectatorship in End-of-the-Century America," *European Journal of American Culture* 29, no. 2 (2010): 131–44.
9. Sofie Lachapelle, *Investigating the Supernatural: From Spiritism and Occultism to Psychical Research and Metapsychics in France, 1853–1931* (Baltimore: Johns Hopkins University Press, 2011); Michael Pettit, *The Science of Deception: Psychology and Commerce in America* (Chicago: University of Chicago Press, 2013).
10. Aileen Fyfe and Bernard V. Lightman (eds.), *Science in the Marketplace: Nineteenth-Century Sites and Experiences* (Chicago: University of Chicago Press, 2007); Bernard V. Lightman, *Victorian Popularizers of Science: Designing Nature for New Audiences* (Chicago: University of Chicago Press, 2009); Iwan Rhys Morus, "Worlds of Wonder: Sensation and the Victorian Scientific Performance," *Isis* 101, no. 4 (2010).
11. Jeremy Brooker, "The Polytechnic Ghost: Pepper's Ghost, Metempsychosis and the Magic Lantern at the Royal Polytechnic Institution," *Early Popular Visual Culture* 5, no. 2 (2007).
12. Matthew Solomon, *Disappearing Tricks: Silent Film, Houdini, and the New Magic of the Twentieth Century* (Urbana: University of Illinois Press, 2010).
13. Peter Lamont, "Magician as Conjuror: A Frame Analysis of Victorian Mediums," *Early Popular Visual Culture* 4, no. 1 (May 2006): 21–33.
14. Simon During, *Modern Enchantments: The Cultural Power of Secular Magic* (Cambridge, MA: Harvard University Press, 2002).
15. Lionel A. Weatherly, *The Supernatural?* (Bristol: Arrowsmith, 1891); John Nevil Maskelyne, *Modern Spiritualism: A Short Account of Its Rise and Progress, with Some Exposures of So-Called Spirit Media* (London: F. Warne, 1876).
16. Solomon, *Disappearing Tricks*, 27.
17. Erik Barnouw, *The Magician and the Cinema* (New York: Oxford University Press, 1981).
18. Edwin A. Dawes, "The Magic Scene in Britain in 1905: An Illustrated Overview," *Early Popular Visual Culture* 5, no. 2 (2007).
19. Dan North, "Magic and Illusion in Early Cinema," *Studies in French Cinema* 1, no. 2 (2001): 70–9.
20. See Simone Natale, "A Short History of Superimposition: From Spirit Photography to Early Cinema," *Early Popular Visual Culture* 10, no. 2 (May 2012): 139–42. Méliès possibly attended John Nevil Maskelyne's spiritual exposés at the Egyptian Hall in 1884, when he traveled to London for deepening his knowledge in the magician's secrets. Elizabeth Ezra, *Georges Méliès: The Birth of the Auteur* (Manchester: Manchester University Press, 2000), 8. The long-standing tradition of spiritualist exposés reverberates in some of his movies, such as *L'armoire des frères Davenport* (*The Cabinet Trick of the Davenport Brothers*, 1902) and *Le portrait spirite* (*A Spiritualist Photographer*, 1903).
21. As I have shown elsewhere, spiritualist séances often had a spectacular character, being performed by mediums on a theatrical stage and offered to a paying audience as a form of entertainment. See Simone Natale, *Supernatural Entertainments: Victorian Spiritualism and the Rise of Modern Media Culture* (University Park: Pennsylvania State University Press, 2016).
22. On how cinema invited spectators to reflect on the deceptive nature of their perception, see Simone Natale, "The Cinema of Exposure: Spiritualist Exposés, Technology, and the Dispositif of Early Cinema," *Recherches sémiotiques/Semiotic Inquiry* 31, no. 1–2–3 (2011): 113–29. See also, on spiritualism and early cinema, Murray Leeder, *The Modern Supernatural and the Beginnings of Cinema* (London: Palgrave Macmillan, 2017).

23. As Simon During notes, after all, stage magicians who performed spiritualist exposés also had profited from their audience's fascination with the world of the occult. See During, *Modern Enchantments*, 71.
24. Terry Castle, *The Female Thermometer: Eighteenth-Century Culture and the Invention of the Uncanny* (New York: Oxford University Press, 1995).
25. Natale, "Short History."
26. André Bazin, "The Life and Death of Superimposition (1946)," *Film-Philosophy* 6, no. 1 (2002).
27. The use of superimposition in this scene functions at the same time as an allegorical summary of the plot and as a visualization of Cyrus West's thoughts, with the latter interpretation reinforced by the fact that the image of the cats is superimposed on that of the old man, hinting at the existence of a mental, subjective reality.
28. See Brooker, "Polytechnic Ghost"; and Tom Gunning, "To Scan a Ghost: The Ontology of Mediated Vision," *Grey Room*, no. 26 (Winter 2007): 94–127.
29. Castle, *Female Thermometer*, 123.
30. A similar strategy was employed in other films of the time, including Sergei Eisenstein's *Strike* (1925). See Sergei Eisenstein, *The Film Sense* (New York: Harcourt Brace Jovanovich, 1975), 80.
31. Robert Spadoni, *Uncanny Bodies: The Coming of Sound Film and the Origins of the Horror Genre* (Berkeley: University of California Press, 2007), 55.
32. Steven Connor, "The Machine in the Ghost: Spiritualism, Technology and the 'Direct Voice,'" in *Ghosts: Deconstruction, Psychoanalysis, History*, ed. Peter Buse and Andrew Stott (New York: St. Martin's Press, 1999), 208. On spiritualism and sound technologies, see also Anthony Enns, "Voices of the Dead: Transmission/Translation/Transgression," *Culture, Theory and Critique* 46, no. 1 (2005): 11–27.
33. Claude E. Shannon, "The Mathematical Theory of Communication," in *The Mathematical Theory of Communication*, ed. Claude E. Shannon and Warren Weaver (Urbana: University of Illinois Press, 1949), 29–125. See also Juan A. Suarez, "Structural Film: Noise," in *Stillmoving: Between Cinema and Photography*, ed. Karen Beckman and Jean Ma (Durham, NC: Duke University Press, 2008), 62–89.
34. Napoleon Bonaparte Wolfe, *Startling Facts in Modern Spiritualism* (Chicago: Religio-Philosophical Publishing House, 1875), 24.
35. Adin Ballou, *An Exposition of Views Respecting the Principal Facts, Causes and Peculiarities Involved in Spirit Manifestations* (Boston: Bela Marsh, 1853), 1.
36. Joseph Jastrow, "The Psychology of Deception," *Popular Science Monthly* 34, no. 10 (December 1888): 145–57; George M. Beard, "The Psychology of Spiritism," *North American Review* 129, no. 272 (July 1879): 65–80.
37. David Toop, "'Chair Creaks, Though No One Sits There': Decomposition and Liquidity," *New Formations* 66 (Spring 2009): 134–44.
38. Vivian Sobchack, "Science Fiction Film and the Technological Imagination," in *Technological Visions: The Hopes and Fears That Shape New Technologies*, ed. Marita Sturken, Douglas Thomas, and Sandra J. Ball-Rokeach (Philadelphia: Temple University Press, 2004), 146.
39. William Uricchio, "Film, Cinema, Television . . . Media?" *New Review of Film and Television Studies*, 2014; Siegfried Zielinski, *Deep Time of the Media: Toward an Archaeology of Hearing and Seeing by Technical Means* (Cambridge, MA: MIT Press, 2006); Thomas Elsaesser, "The New Film History as Media Archaeology," *Cinémas* 14, no. 2–3 (2004).

40. See, for instance, Pamela Thurschwell, *Literature, Technology and Magical Thinking, 1880–1920* (Cambridge: Cambridge University Press, 2001); Castle, *Female Thermometer*; Carrol L. Fry, *Cinema of the Occult: New Age, Satanism, Wicca, and Spiritualism in Film* (Bethlehem, PA: Lehigh University Press, 2008); and Emily D. Edwards, *Metaphysical Media: The Occult Experience in Popular Culture* (Carbondale: Southern Illinois University Press, 2005).

CHAPTER 10

Misfitting in America: Paul Leni, Conrad Veidt, and *The Man Who Laughs*

Gábor Gergely

Gwynplaine (Conrad Veidt), the "laughing mountebank," the lost heir to the Clancharlie estates, has been seized by the Queen's men. His beatific fiancée, the blind actress Dea (Mary Philbin), is the only cast member of the traveling sideshow unaware of his capture. When the hour of the performance is upon them, the playwright (in truth, freak-show entrepreneur) Ursus (Cesare Gravina) urges the troupe he had assembled around his two marketable wards to pretend nothing is wrong. Suddenly, the film's soundtrack erupts with calls of "Gwynplaine." Crowd sounds have been heard before, but these are recognizable human voices matched, albeit imperfectly, with individuals making the sound. The troupe's intention is to convey the sense of an impatient mob in the stalls, but their dismay at Gwynplaine's arrest is palpable, and the effect is of a handful of individuals mournfully calling out for a lost companion. The tearful Dea, visibly disturbed, perhaps aware that something is amiss, goes through the motions of the show, playing her part in the pretense of normality.

Post-synchronized sound here permits multiple meanings to emerge. There is a remarkable, complex engagement with the illusion of presence. We watch as the blind actor cannot see behind the aural illusion to the pretense of a presence, which masks a silence. This silence is, in truth, Gwynplaine's absence. This *mise-en-scène* of the unequal relationship between those who see and the one who cannot see conveys simultaneously the sense of a presence and also the absence it is designed to mask. The figure of the person who cannot see in the context of a silent film is a possible figure of identification for the viewer of a silent film with added sound at the dawn of sound cinema. That is to say, the selective use of sound (some sounds are heard but others are not) places the audience in a position that can be likened to Dea's, in that information perceived via one of the senses is partially complemented and at times contradicted by limited information available via another sense. The blurring of silent cinema, where presence is not the product of a mutual referral between a body and a space,[1] with aspects of sound cinema, which provided such eagerly seized opportunities to explore sonority, most notably in the Universal horror-cycle of 1930–5, creates a moment of rich complexity. The production of the sounds of mirth typically provoked by Gwynplaine's presence is intended to indicate his presence to one who cannot see that he is not in truth there. At the same time, however, the laughter sounds unconvincing to Dea, who has grown up listening to people laugh at Gwynplaine. Thus the sounds generated to create the illusion of Gwynplaine's presence in effect refute the illusion they are intended to conjure up.

This essay digs deeper into this complex dynamic of absence and presence to argue that the film engages with the trauma of displacement, the only solution for which is a final displacement into a zone beyond community and ordered space, unlinked from the film's present, the "here" and "now." Indeed, Gwynplaine and Dea are reunited in ecstatic bliss on a ship sailing off into the painted horizon. The film's play-within-a-film structure and its keen focus on the actor's position in the community as a body onto which meanings are projected, a figure of identification and rejection, make this a meta-text that can provide an interpretive framework for the films of exile and émigré actors in Hollywood.

CONTEXT

The Man Who Laughs (1928) was the fifth collaboration between Paul Leni as director and Conrad Veidt as star. They had worked together previously on the much better-known *Waxworks* (*Das Wachsfigurenkabinett*, 1924), in which Veidt played Ivan the Terrible.[2] *The Man Who Laughs* was perhaps Leni's biggest film to date, but it has not endured in popular memory. After many decades of relative obscurity, the film has recently attracted scholarly attention, most notably in Ian Conrich's essay in Stephen Prince's horror reader and Matthew Solomon's chapter in Murray Pomerance's anthology on laughter in the cinema, and it is now frequently mentioned in works on Hollywood's appropriation of German Expressionist aesthetics and personnel.[3] This essay, then, continues the recent effort to unpack this remarkably rich text, situated so tantalizingly at the intersection of silent film and early sound cinema.

Carl Laemmle began preparations for *The Man Who Laughs* before audiences heard Al Jolson utter his world-famous line, "You ain't heard nothing yet," in *The Jazz Singer* (1927). *The Man Who Laughs* was earmarked as Universal's third "Super-Jewel" production in 1925, when Laemmle acquired filming rights.⁴ It was intended to repeat the box office success of the Lon Chaney Super-Jewels *The Hunchback of Notre Dame* (1923) and *The Phantom of the Opera* (1925) and thereby to cement Universal's reputation as a studio that matched artistic aspiration with commercial ambition. The film's $1,000,000 budget was 7 percent of Universal's total annual production costs for the season.⁵

Veidt's breakout performance was in the role of the somnambulist Cesare in *The Cabinet of Dr. Caligari* (*Das Cabinet des Dr. Caligari*, 1920), and his reputation for artistry was cemented in the roles of Ivan in F. W. Murnau's *Desire* (*Sehnsucht*, 1921) and the titular pianist in *The Hands of Orlac* (*Orlacs Hände*, 1924), among others. Leni's reputation derived from *Waxworks* and *The Cat and the Canary* (1927), his first film for Universal. *The Man Who Laughs* was based on an 1869 Victor Hugo novel and made use of the themes of disfigurement, dangerous desire, and excess emotion that had been central to the Lon Chaney hits. Universal proclaimed *The Man Who Laughs* an outstanding box office hit in its first, silent run.⁶ Its box office was affected by the advent of sound. Sound technology's novelty appeal and rapid adoption across the industry prompted Universal to add sound effects, crowd noises, a full orchestral score, and an original song over the closing credits to make *The Man Who Laughs* with its epic sweep, frenetic action sequences, crowd scenes, and spectacular visuals an exemplar of the argument that sound film is not merely silent cinema with added sound.⁷

The film tells the story of Gwynplaine, whose face was disfigured in childhood by a *comprachico* surgeon on the orders of the vindictive James II (Sam De Grasse) as punishment for his father's rebellion against the English Crown. When freak shows featuring surgically disfigured children are banished from the country, Gwynplaine is abandoned. Stumbling through snow-covered Cornish sand dunes, he finds a blind orphan, Dea. The two unfortunate children are taken in and raised by Ursus, an itinerant playwright and producer. Gwynplaine, now an adult, becomes a sensation as a clown and attracts the notice of the malevolent Barkilphedro (Brandon Hurst), formerly court jester to James, now *eminence grise* to Queen Anne (Josephine Crowell). The two cook up a malicious plan to force the libertine Duchess Josiana (Olga Baclanova) to marry Gwynplaine so she can retain the Clancharlie estates, which she had been gifted by the Crown. Gwynplaine is ennobled but defies the Queen's order to marry Josiana. He escapes London and is reunited with Dea and Ursus as they row out to embark on their exile.

This essay focuses on Conrad Veidt's performance, makeup, and costuming to argue that Gwynplaine can be productively read as an exilic body. I propose this term as a way of understanding the uses and usefulness of European émigré stars for Hollywood. Gwynplaine's fixed grin marks him permanently and indelibly as different. This corporeal inscription of his and his father's not belonging marks Gwynplaine's soul and underpins his understanding of himself and of his liminal position on the edges of society. The essay draws on Hamid Naficy's work on exilic and "accented" cinema to suggest that Leni's work can be understood to reflect on displacement and exile. It further draws on disability studies, particularly the work of Rosemarie Garland-Thomson and her notion of the misfit, to argue that the foreign body, or more specifically the body of the foreign star, is marked in various ways as failing or unable to fit into the host environment.

It is important to note at this juncture that Veidt himself was not an exile at this stage in the sense that he had not yet made a permanent move away from Germany.[8] His first foray to Hollywood was a temporary one, driven by his towering reputation as one of Europe's most important film artists. I therefore do not suggest that Veidt's role and performance in *The Man Who Laughs* is exemplary of the exilic bodies I discuss in *Foreign Devils* and elsewhere.[9] Rather, in this essay I argue that Gwynplaine is prototypic of the exilic bodies that populated the Universal horror-cycle, "B" movies of the 1930s and 40s, and the general output of Hollywood's "Poverty Row" studios.

Veidt's stardom was built on intensely physical performances in which his tall, thin, sinewy body and languid gait and gestures combined with a remarkable expressivity of mimicry, making full use of delicate eyebrows and a forehead that seemed to have no end, enormous eyes, and a thin upper lip set above a full lower lip. Veidt was both a great beauty and revered as a great actor. The decision to distort his face into a lurid grin seems all the more remarkable. Publicity material focused on Veidt's unique ability to isolate his facial muscles, attributing it to his earlier medical studies in Germany.[10] While it seems to obey a certain logic that an actor noted for the expressivity of his face should be set the challenge of having to convey sorrow with lips drawn into a hideous grin, it is also an extraordinary denial of the logic of Veidt's stardom. The marketing spin suggests Veidt's suitability for his role was dictated by obscure knowledge acquired elsewhere. This was fantasy cooked up by the marketing team: in truth, Veidt joined the theater in the face of paternal opposition after completing secondary education, and never undertook any medical studies.[11] This tension between the expressivity for which he was noted and the rigidity of the expression fixed on his face by script and Jack Pierce's makeup makes the film and its central performance particularly noteworthy, and a prototype of the narratives of exile and displacement that characterize the films of émigré actors who moved to Hollywood, following what Phillips and Vincendeau called "journeys of desire."[12]

Figure 10.1 Conrad Veidt, in Jack Pierce's make-up, as Gwynplaine on stage.

AN ACCENTED FILM

In his groundbreaking work on the films of diasporic and exilic filmmakers, Hamid Naficy argues that the filmmakers' personal experiences of displacement inform, inflect, and disturb the narratives and aesthetics of their films. For Naficy, the filmmakers' accent is a marker of foreign birth and can be apprehended in the formal characteristics of the films that they make. The accent, Naficy suggests, penetrates and permeates the "deep structures" of the exilic directors' films.[13] While the accent of some exilic directors, particularly those working in experimental forms and artisanal modes of production, is very strong, the accent of those working in the mainstream is harder to trace. While I take issue with the term and argue it needs to be problematized as part of an exclusionary discourse that dislocates the "foreign born" and assumes the universality of the point of view of the native, I contend that the foreign accent, and therefore articulations of exile and issues of displacement, is ubiquitous in Hollywood cinema.

 The Man Who Laughs is a good example. Indeed, many of the cast and crew were at various stages of migration, including the director, star, and makeup artist as well as producer Laemmle, production manager Paul Kohner, his assistant Lew Landers, and story supervisor Béla Sekely. It is not my argument that this level of "foreign" involvement is unusual for Hollywood, nor that the director's personal story of migration is primarily to account for the exilic inflection of Hollywood films. What I am arguing is that there is nothing extraordinary about this, and that Hollywood films often do address in some ways, however obliquely, the experience of displacement. *The Man Who Laughs* does this quite strikingly by telling the story of someone forever marked as standing apart, a figure held up for rejection as the other against whom "our" bodies can be held up as belonging to, and representative of, the norm. The intense emotions prompted in Josiana by the sight of Gwynplaine, which turn to grief when she is ordered by the Queen to marry him, can be explained by her shared position with Gwynplaine as an outsider who does not fit into the environment in which she finds herself. In order to explore this observation more fully, I turn to disability studies scholar Rosemarie Garland-Thomson's notion of the misfit.

Garland-Thomson proposed the term "misfit" to theorize "the lived identity and experience of disability as it is situated in place and time."[4] This permits a turn away from "the linguistic-semiotic-interpretive" framework of Butlerian performativity toward the material and ways of understanding difference as "an incongruent relationship between two things."[5] The problem, Garland-Thomson has suggested, "inheres not in either of the two things but rather in their juxtaposition."[6] Disability, then, is not the failure of a body compared with an ideal (that does not in truth exist), but a mismatch between a body and the way in which space has been organized. Disability is a matter of ideology as applied to space: namely, architecture and design. As Garland-Thomson noted, "When the spatial and temporal context shifts, so does the fit, and with it meanings and consequences."[7] In other words, displacement can serve to highlight inequities of spatial arrangements. And indeed, films that tell stories of displacement are also often stories of bodies that do not fit. *The Face Behind the Mask* (1941), in which Peter Lorre's immigrant watchmaker Johnny Szabó turns to crime after suffering life-changing burns in a hotel fire, is an exemplary film that makes this link between displacement and misfitting explicit.

I argue that the notion of the misfit can help us make sense of Veidt's role and performance as Gwynplaine in *The Man Who Laughs*. Shifting away from—albeit not rejecting—the Butlerian approach that foregrounds the discursive-performative aspects of bodies and bodily identities that I employed in my 2012 book *Foreign Devils*, I propose here a spatiotemporal understanding of the foreign misfit to argue that the corporeal impairment deliberately inflicted on Gwynplaine disables him by making him incongruent in his context. His appearance provokes stares, laughter, and, in some, pity: expressions of "wonderment," a need to "recognize what seems illegible, order what seems unruly, know what seems strange."[8] He is called a jester and a clown, but his only joke is his hope that he may be accepted for who he is; that his "smile" may be overlooked. He sticks out and fails to fit in, and thereby serves as a reminder of the robustness of the spatial arrangements with which he is a misfit. I consider this incongruence in key scenes of the film: the highly Expressionistic Cornish sand dunes sequence, the freak-show performance attended by Josiana, and Gwynplaine's escape from the House of Lords.

It is important to note here that the film provides a narrative logic for the disfigurement of its star; while Lon Chaney's Phantom is inherently diseased (a matter of heredity), Veidt's Gwynplaine *becomes* disfigured. Disfigurement is a process in which an inscription takes place to mark the body as a reminder to self and others of the body's misfit. Gwynplaine is an embodiment of misfitting a community as a result of a traumatic marking that inscribes his corporeal difference. It takes place off-camera, before the start of the film. We hear of it alongside Lord Clancharlie (also played by Veidt, but with stubble and without the grin), who has surrendered to trade his own life for his son's. The disfigurement is the inscription of his father's exile and rebellion, which performs the son's exclusion from the community. As a result, Gwynplaine is marked as not fit to participate in the ordinary. However, precisely because the marking takes place off-screen and before the start of the film, the inscription of the father's "sin" onto the child invites links with the biblical notion of the punishment to the fourth generation of those who hate God,[19] and, via this circuitous route, with the logic of heredity, inherent difference, and race. The misfit occurs in multiple layers, then. He misfits by virtue of the surgical enlargement of an orifice, which conjures up notions of vulnerability to penetration, and the targeted paralysis of a muscle group, which fixes him in the outward signs of an affective state unlinked from any bodily process of amusement or laughter. Gwynplaine's is a body, then, that is both vulnerable and limited in affective potential, at least as far as the play of affects on the face is concerned. He misfits his own body, moving beyond a mismatch between outward appearance and inward emotion. It suggests an organic split, a bodily failure, a difference to self. In this, Gwynplaine is a close relative of the mad scientist (e.g. Peter Lorre in *Mad Love*, 1935), the bloodsucking foreigner (Bela Lugosi in *Dracula*, 1931), and the man who impersonates his evil twin (Veidt in *Nazi Agent*, 1942).[20]

The significance of the mark requires comment, too; the trade in children for the *comprachico*'s knife relies on the utter moral corruption and total destitution of parents who sell their children. The mark, then, relegates the highborn Gwynplaine to the bottom of the social hierarchy. He may have been born into an aristocratic family, but the mark on his face displaces him from his heritage and culture, relocating him into a wholly different sphere. It flips the world as he knows it, and therefore it transforms his own sense of self. The fixed grin is both cause and symptom of this displacement from the category of the fit into that of the misfit.

The surgical distortion of Gwynplaine's face makes him an object in the sense that he has one specific use as a result: to be a clown. Displacement has shifted the body and its relationship with space and community, so that its fit (usefulness) is to misfit (not be of use). The logic that a man with a fixed grin has a single specific use—namely, that he should be a clown—is so strong that the film never pauses to query it. Ursus, "the Philosopher," becomes a freak-show entrepreneur, so utterly irresistible is the power of the disfigurement. The thing that makes Gwynplaine a body uniquely fit for the purposes to which Ursus puts him, is the thing that makes him unfit/misfit for anything else. The power of the transformative mark is so strong that it displaces those around him; it makes Ursus an other, too. And indeed, Ursus's fate is to be exiled alongside Gwynplaine.

THE FIGURAL: THE ZONE OF INDISCERNIBILITY

We meet the child Gwynplaine as the "Gypsy" *comprachico* surgeon Dr. Hardquanonne (George Siegmann) hastily flees England. Gwynplaine is living proof of the illegal trade in surgically disfigured children and abandoned on the shore. As the ship casts off, Gwynplaine stands, buffeted by winds and peppered by snowflakes, on a highly stylized beach set. A fade-in to footprints in the snow opens a remarkable set of images. He stumbles off a sand dune onto a dead woman cradling a mewling babe as carrion crows fling themselves at the huddle of rags, corpse, and newborn and then flap away, as if thrown by invisible hands (perhaps those of the animal handlers). Gwynplaine gathers up the babe and wanders off. The sequence, which has coupled Expressionistic sets, dark backdrops, and plenty of fake snow, then moves to a sequence of three shots, which I would like to consider in some detail.

The three shots are successively longer and darker. Objects and figures in the frame become harder to discern as we move from limited legibility to abstraction. The first is a four-second long shot in which Gwynplaine, in the bottom left of the frame, moves painfully slowly forward and slightly to the left. The dimly lit, predominantly charcoal-gray image is divided by a dim horizontal line (ramshackle fencing, perhaps). A faint pool of light picks out Gwynplaine and is echoed in the top right quadrant of the image. The second shot lasts six seconds. Gwynplaine, situated in the same bottom left quadrant but now wobbling toward the camera, seems to make no progress despite his immense and clearly painful efforts. The image is darker than the preceding shot, rendered barely legible by the black zigzag of the fencing running across it diagonally from top left to bottom right with a dim pool of light picking out Gwynplaine. The final shot is remarkable: a thin horizontal shaft of bright light bisecting a pitch-black image. A faint backlight picks out Gwynplaine's form, although without the preceding shots, the viewer would be unable to tell if the faint movement in the center of the frame were human, animal, or an object moved by imperceptible forces. In the context of the previous shots, the image is read as a distant long shot, but its illegibility renders it abstract. Isolated from the sequence, this third image is impenetrable. The three shots can be read as a movement beyond something and toward disorientation. They add up to the spatiotemporal displacement of a body marked as carrying the father's transgression against a community that rejected him, and which he sought to reconfigure.

The notion of the figural, as proposed by Gilles Deleuze, may be helpful here to think through this remarkable movement from legibility to impenetrability. For Deleuze, the figural, in painting, is the isolation of the figure "to avoid the *figurative*, *illustrative*, and *narrative* character the Figure would necessarily have if it were not isolated."[21] While figures in the cinema may be isolated in the frame, their position in a sequence of frames and shots creates a relationality that produces a narrative. "The figurative (representation) implies the relationship of an image to an object that it is supposed to illustrate; but it also implies the relationship of an image to other images in a composite whole,"[22] Deleuze noted. This is certainly applicable to the sequence discussed above, but, as scholars have pointed out,[23] cinema's narrative logic does not rule out the potential to embrace the figural. In the instance of the three shots discussed here, I argue that the abstraction of the images and the simultaneous isolation of the figure coupled with its indiscernibility from the space that is around it, but also behind, above, and alongside it, produce the figural. The three shots share with Francis Bacon's paintings a disorganization of the human form, which produces a *zone of indiscernibility* or *undecidability*,[24] where the boundaries between the human form and the space in which it figures are blurred. The filmic narrative is here disrupted with the effect that displacement from the human and from spatiotemporal logic is foregrounded. By virtue of the sequence's position in the narrative—which it puts on hold—this movement from the figurative to the figural is significant in the context of a film that deals with the horrors, pleasures, and uses of the freak show, and the bodies that populate it.

CARNIVAL: A PLACE OF SUBVERSION (BUT NOT FOR GWYNPLAINE)

The film's treatment of displacement is not confined to oblique articulations via highly abstract visual cues. The first full performance of "The Man Who Laughs" stage show, Ursus's "comedy in two acts" about evil overcome by beauty, invites a Bakhtinian reading. The show closely follows the logic of the carnival, as elaborated by Mikhail Bakhtin and applied to the cinema by Robert Stam.[25] Indeed, each time we enter the Southwark Fair, it is introduced to the audience with a virtuoso sequence in which the gleeful subversion of order and the flattening out of hierarchies is coupled with a playful suspension of conventional camera placements, resulting in a riotous burst of movement. In the first scene at Southwark, the camera rises vertiginously above the fair, mounted on one of the cars of the fair's Ferris wheel, shown in the immediately preceding shot, then swoops back down. In the second Southwark sequence, Leni's camera picks out the tousled, laughing Josiana, groped by four drunks as she takes a seat on a merry-go-round. She is dressed as a maid, but her clothing is disordered, threatening to slip off and reveal her bare breasts. As she spins out of, then into shot, her skirt flaps up to reveal, fleetingly, her undergarments. The horizontal movement of the merry-go-round echoes the camera's earlier extraordinary movement on a vertical plane. The camera movements and the movement of the figures in the frame enhance the sense of the transgression of boundaries and temporary breaking down of strict hierarchies that, for Bakhtin and Stam, characterize the carnival space.

Ursus's comedy is somewhat incongruous with the seventeenth-century setting. "The Man Who Laughs" is more medieval morality play than Restoration theater. The fleeting moments we see show the masked Gwynplaine fighting against monstrous beasts. Dea appears center stage and her radiant beauty stills the fight. Gwynplaine lowers his weapon as the beasts cower. The curtain closes behind Gwynplaine, who is unmasked by Ursus and one of the stagehands. The crowd erupt in laughter as the joke is revealed: the "hero" was no hero but a disfigured clown. Josiana, seated above the stalls on a single armchair in the circle, leans forward, her eyes bulging with desire through the delicate jeweled mask she holds before her face. Her mouth is half open, showing fine teeth that occasionally bite into sensuous lips. Her chest heaves with passion, and her eyes close under heavy lids in an extraordinary performance of erotic yearning. Unused to this response to his grin, Gwynplaine can barely keep his eyes off her. He performs to the crowd but keeps his eyes on the duchess. As Gwynplaine provokes gales of laughter in the crowd with his appearance that places him outside of the human community into what Judith Butler has called an uninhabitable zone beyond,[26] Josiana, herself a transgressor and thus an outsider, can barely contain her desire for a body that, like hers, is misfit. As Garland-Thomson notes, the "encounter between a starer and a staree sets in motion an interpersonal relationship [. . .] a dynamic struggle [that] can tickle or alienate, persist or evolve."[27] The film foregrounds this dynamic, intimate encounter of wonderment between two misfits.

Figure 10.2 Olga Baclanova as Josiana drinking in Gwynplaine's performance.

In perhaps the most remarkable image in this sequence, Gwynplaine steps behind the curtain and closes it around his own neck, isolating his face and head. His disembodied head is like a trophy on the wall. His face is framed not only by the curtain but also by his mop of wiry hair, swept back from his forehead to leave no aspect of the fixed grin covered. His face has been covered in thick white makeup, giving it a doughy texture, with laugh lines from the nose to the corners of the mouth drawn in black pencil. The combined effect of the makeup and the separation of the head from the body via the curtain is that of a body prepared for surgery. It is as if the audience were invited to adopt the medical gaze of the surgeon contemplating the area bared for incision. The dynamic relationship between staree and starers takes place in this sequence along multiple vectors: the audience laugh, hoot, and holler; Dea turns the empty stare of her unseeing eyes at Gwynplaine, her wonderment frustrated, destined never to be satisfied; Ursus looks at his prize performer with the pride of a producer already counting the night's takings; and Josiana stares with unconcealed, ecstatic desire. The carnival space is, then, fragmented and multiple. It is a space that can accommodate multiple fits between bodies, which, in other contexts, misfit each other and their environment.

As Stam notes, Umberto Eco's reading of the carnival as a space that in truth serves power only is problematic: elitist, Eurocentric, simplistic.[28] It ignores the many ways in which the activity, mobility, and variety of carnival provide opportunities for more than the mindless pleasures of the mob, distracted by bread and circus. Indeed, Southwark Fair's potential as a great, if temporary, class leveler is the chief focus of the sequence that introduces Josiana to the audience. The fair's potential for a range of transformative encounters is also noted: Ursus hopes to make a fortune during the run of "The Man Who Laughs," as does the less fortunate (but monstrous) Hardquanonne, tortured to death off-screen by Barkilphedro's goons. The crowd that flocks there engages in a celebration of the grotesque, excessive body, which helps in the "social overturning and the counterhegemonic subversion of established power via the 'world upside down,'" in Stam's words.[29] As Garland-Thomson's work helps us note, the visual encounters that take place are varied and multidirectional, not simply directed at the misfit, but returned by the misfit.[30] Moreover, different starers stare differently, each producing an encounter that cannot be easily mapped against Eco's simplified reading of the carnival space. Gwynplaine plays a crucial part in the spectacle and is the site of intersection of the stares discussed, and for this reason he is stuck in perpetual carnival. For Gwynplaine, the carnival is not a transitory space of temporary subversion; it is permanent. The carnival's definition is the place where Gwynplaine is.

When Gwynplaine is taken to the palace, the carnival ends. Just as the grin makes him an objectified entity (with a single use: to be a clown), so too the permanence of the carnival makes it a place of oppression for him. It is a carceral space (a space where he is ceaselessly subjected to inquisitive stares) from which he hopes to be freed. This desire to be free (or at least to be afforded temporary relief) is illustrated in the scene in which Gwynplaine receives a note of invitation from the duchess after the staging of "The Man Who Laughs." In a wonderfully natural performance of the actor at rest, Gwynplaine has a scarf over one shoulder, which he is using to wipe the makeup from his brow. A member of the troupe stands next to him. He, too, is in the process of wiping off his makeup. The painted clown's face comes off to reveal an ordinary human face underneath. Gwynplaine looks at him with longing. The man quips with unthinking callousness, "What a lucky clown you are—you don't have to rub off *your* laugh." Gwynplaine's face creases into a grimace that screams: are you serious? The grin cannot be wiped off his face any more than he can ever leave the carnival. The zone of uninhabitability, the transitory space of the temporary relief from a rigid hierarchy, is precisely the zone he inhabits.

(MISFITTING) CLOTHES MAKE THE MAN (MISFIT)

Gwynplaine's misfit within the community is articulated in the film's centerpiece scene in the House of Lords. Following Barkilphedro's cruel machinations (motivated in part by Josiana's recognition of his desire for her, which she pretends to invite, only to spurn the more hurtfully), Gwynplaine is restored to his title of Lord Clancharlie and is invested as a peer of the realm. We see him escorted from a carriage to the chamber where the Lords sit. He steps from the carriage gingerly while holding a delicate silk handkerchief up to his mouth. The clothes are ill-suited to the man, and Veidt conveys the sense of a man ill-suited to the clothes. However, the costume is disrupted by more than Gwynplaine's discomfort in clothes to which he is unused. The frilly lace, shimmering silks, and abundant curls of his ample wig misfit the fixed grin. While the formality of the rococo costume speaks of an attempt to control, contain, and cover the body to impose order on unruly nature, the grin reminds us of the permeability of the body, the imperfection of the barrier between inside and outside, and puts to the lie that which the clothes are intended to convey. Indeed, the peers are outraged by the presence amongst them of a man who laughs. They read his fixed grin as laughter at the institution of the House of Lords and the Queen. "A King made me a clown!" he reminds the assembled Lords. Gwynplaine's defiance of the Queen's order to marry Josiana is received with further indignation. A Queen made you a Lord, they tell him, to which he ecstatically replies, "A Queen made me a Lord—But first, *God made me a man!*" (italics in original title-card). He attempts to invoke a higher power than the highest in the realm to claim for himself a rightful place in the heteronormative phallocentric order. He misrecognizes himself as one who fits, and fails to understand that his identity and belonging are performed by others and are a product of the responses he prompts.

As suggested by the foregoing descriptions, the concept of misfitting is intimately connected to a major concern of period dramas: the reproduction of settings and costumes. Painstaking attention to detail and the attempt to achieve complete authenticity, which were central to the film's marketing campaign,[31] are key elements of the costume drama genre and have bearing on the way that studio publicity and marketing departments position such films in the marketplace. As Susan Hayward has observed, the financial limitations and material constraints add further complexity and appeal to an enduringly popular genre.[32] However, this aspiration to authenticity has the effect of highlighting anachronisms: the medieval figures of the court jester, the disfigured wandering clown, the carnival itself. We may call these temporal misfits. As Hayward notes, "the costume drama genre speaks to history 'then' and 'now,'"[33] and, indeed, the 1920s were a period when US attitudes to immigration hardened, and exclusionary federal policies such as the 1921 Emergency Quota Act and the 1924 Immigration Act were enacted. That is to say, migration and displaced bodies were in the foreground of popular and political discourse. The attempt to marry the ambition of truthful reproduction with moments of invention also produces spatial misfits. By this I mean misfits who are in the wrong place but not necessarily at the wrong time. A spatial misfit is the presence of one who ought not to be in a given space. This misfitting presence, Gwynplaine the laughing clown's presence in the House of Lords, his presence in the vestments of a peer of the realm, disrupts that space and the meaning of the vestments (and the investiture), and produces the space anew as a space of rupture. The presence of the misfit, the incongruence of body and space, reveals both the body and the space as failing to function properly. Indeed, the outrage of the Lords soon gives way to hilarity. The peers fall about laughing and their ordered rows of lace and curls become a disheveled mass that echoes the raucous crowds of Southwark Fair.

It is worth pausing here to revisit the figural, but this time as Belén Vidal theorizes it in her discussion of period films. Approaching the term from the direction of psychoanalysis and Jean-François Lyotard, she notes that "the figure is at the same time form and its transgression."[34] She goes on to trace "a way of thinking about the fantasy of estrangement and identification posed by the period film through the fragment and the figure."[35] The "distance of historicity," Vidal notes, is in tension with "the immediacy of representation."[36] In the instance of *The Man Who Laughs*, we see this distance accentuated by the film's ambitions of authenticity coupled with the exaggeration of the remoteness of the Restoration period by introducing medieval elements into the mix. This distance is in tension with the immediacy of the figure, enhanced by the textural (costumes) and the sensuous (the erotic body of the duchess and the abject body of the clown), which could also be called the haptic and the affective.

Vidal argues that "the figurative layers that structure representation in narrative [produce] a present-in-the-past that captures the incompleteness of either, and a double movement of displacement and return."[37] The costume drama, with its combination of authenticity, distance, immediacy, and sensuousness, produces a set of tensions that, according to Vidal, are rooted in displacement. These spatiotemporal tensions and transgressions are spelled out and performed by Gwynplaine in his maiden speech to the Lords. He concludes his defiant rejection of the Queen's order to marry Josiana by announcing, "Gwynplaine, the clown, goes back to his people!" This declaration suggests a misreading of his position in society. Living in a permanent carnival, that is to say, as a performer whose presence signals carnival to the communities he enters, he mistakes the paying public for "his people." He escapes from the palace and breaks free from a space in which his misfit is all too plain to see. However, he fails to realize—for the moment—that there is no place for him to return to. He has no place in any community, for he is a performer whose mask cannot be removed, and therefore any community immediately becomes his audience. His place in any community is to invite the stare, to be the body that fails to fit, the body that misfits the community.

The film's final scenes take the realization of Gwynplaine's permanent and universal misfit to its logical conclusion: removal from the community and a final displacement beyond the zone of the norm. He fights his way back to the tavern where Ursus's production of "The Man Who Laughs" had been staged, only to find it shuttered. Without Gwynplaine, there is no show. The show is Gwynplaine. Therefore, there is no space for Gwynplaine that is not a stage for the performance of "The Man Who Laughs." Told that Ursus and Dea were in the process of embarking on exile, he makes his way to the port and rows out after them. Dea and Gwynplaine are united in the film's penultimate tableau of the ecstasy of escape from a space and community with which they are—by virtue of Gwynplaine's disfigurement—misfit. The two bodies are disorganized by a blurring and a bleaching through excess light. They merge into each other and become indiscernible by a shared backlight against a black background. Space falls away, is flattened out as the figural, this step into the zone of indiscernibility and undecidability, concludes Gwynplaine's journey from initial displacement to a final movement beyond.

CONCLUSION

What this essay has tried to show is that *The Man Who Laughs* deploys a complex dynamic of absence and presence and thereby engages with the trauma of displacement, the only solution for which is a final displacement into a zone beyond community and ordered space. Gwynplaine and Dea's final union in ecstatic bliss unmoored from the film's present on a ship sailing off into the painted horizon, their blurred embrace in a zone of indiscernibility against the backdrop of the endless sea, underscores the film's concern with the yearning for relief from a permanent state of misfit. Moreover, the film's play-within-a-film structure and its keen focus on the actor's position in the community as a body onto which meanings are projected make this a meta-text that provides an interpretive framework for the films of exile and émigré actors in Hollywood in the sound era. Garland-Thomson's notion of the misfit, and the dynamics of staring, in conjunction with the Deleuzian concept of the figural, helped to highlight spatiotemporal ruptures that drew attention to the film's complex engagement with the transformative trauma of displacement. Veidt's exilic body, enhanced by his powerful performance, Jack Pierce's groundbreaking makeup, and the costly and virtuosic costuming, helped us read *The Man Who Laughs* and its disfigured protagonist as prototypic of the early sound period's other exilic bodies, such as Bela Lugosi and Peter Lorre. The notion of the exilic body, in turn, helps to theorize the uses of the émigré actor for Hollywood as the site of intersection of stares and gazes, and the complex set of questions of migration, displacement, belonging, exclusion, and misfitting that they set in play.

NOTES

1. I am mindful of Jean-Luc Nancy's definition of sonorous presence and would like to note here that presence in silent cinema can be very helpfully theorized as sonorous. Following Nancy's argument, presence can be understood as the mutual referral between a body and a space. That is to say, presence is the interaction, via sound, of a sensing body and the space in which that sensing body produces and perceives sounds. Although filmmakers' means in this regard were limited in obvious ways in the silent era, they could, nonetheless, conjure up ideas of sounds. In *The Man Who Laughs* Leni does more than that using post-synchronized sound. See Jean-Luc Nancy, *Listening*, trans. Charlotte Mandell (New York: Fordham University Press, 2007); and Gábor Gergely, "Sonority, Difference and the Schwarzenegger Star Body," *Film-Philosophy* 23, no. 2 (June 2019): 137–58.
2. The other three were *The Mystery of Bangalore* (*Das Rätsel von Bangalor*, 1918), *Prince Cuckoo* (*Prinz Kuckuck: Die Höllenfahrt eines Wollüstlings*, 1919), and *Patience* (*Patience: Die Karten des Todes*, 1920).
3. See Ian Conrich, "Before Sound: Universal, Silent Cinema and the Last of the Horror-Spectaculars," in *The Horror Film*, ed. Stephen Prince (New Brunswick, NJ: Rutgers University Press, 2004), 40–57; Matthew Solomon, "Laughing Silently," in *The Last Laugh: Strange Humors of Cinema*, ed. Murray Pomerance (Detroit: Wayne State University Press, 2013), 15–29; Vincent Brook, *Driven to Darkness: Jewish Émigré Directors and the Rise of Film Noir* (New Brunswick, NJ: Rutgers University Press, 2009); Wheeler Winston Dixon, *A History of Horror* (New Brunswick, NJ: Rutgers University Press, 2010); Lucy Fischer (ed.), *American Cinema of the 1920s: Themes and Variations* (New Brunswick, NJ: Rutgers University Press, 2009); and John T. Soister, *Of Gods and Monsters: A Critical Guide to Universal Studios' Science Fiction, Horror and Mystery Films, 1929–1939* (Jefferson, NC: McFarland, 2005).
4. A full-page advertisement in *Motion Picture News* shows a photograph of Carl Laemmle Sr. signing the contract to acquire the rights to film Hugo's novel. Seated next to Laemmle is Jean Maurice Paul Jules de Noailles, 6th Duke of Ayen. The caption reads: "A million dollar contract signed in Paris by Carl Laemmle and Société Générale de Films 36 Avenue Hoche, Paris. The first super-special production to be 'The Man Who Laughs.'" See advertisement, *Motion Picture News*, August 22, 1925, n.p.
5. "Big money development in production is cited by Universal which states that 'Uncle Tom's Cabin,' costing $2,000,000 and 'The Man Who Laughs,' costing $1,000,000 total more than the year's production budget of ten years ago. Then, the budget was considerably under $3,000,000 while the current budget is declared to be over $15,000,000." See Phil M. Daly, "And That's That," *Film Daily*, April 22, 1928, 5.
6. Advertisement, *Film Daily*, June 17, 1928, front cover.
7. Universal announced in late June 1928 that it would "synchronize" the film after a fairly successful first run as a silent film. See advertisement, *Film Daily*, June 26, 1928, 4–5. Soister suggests sound was added in post-production, but trade papers show the film had an initial run as a silent feature from April to June 1928. See Soister, *Of Gods and Monsters*, 11; and advertisement, *Film Daily*, June 17, 1928, front cover.
8. Veidt relocated to the UK in 1933. He was naturalized as a British subject before the outbreak of war, which saved him from repatriation as an enemy national. See Jerry C. Allen, *Conrad Veidt: From Caligari to Casablanca* (Pacific Grove, CA: Boxwood Press, 1987), 259; and Alastair Phillips and Ginette Vincendeau (eds), *Journeys of Desire: European Actors in Hollywood—A Critical Companion* (London: BFI, 2006), 460.

9. See Gábor Gergely, *Foreign Devils: Exile and Host Nation in Hollywood's Golden Age* (New York: Peter Lang, 2012); and Gábor Gergely, "'The Jungle Is My Home': Questions of Belonging, Exile, and the Negotiation of Foreign Spaces in the *Tarzan* Films of Johnny Weissmuller," in *Projecting the World: Representing the Foreign in Classical Hollywood*, ed. Anna Cooper and Russell Meeuf (Detroit: Wayne State University Press, 2017), 69–88.
10. Solomon, "Laughing Silently," 27.
11. For a biography of Veidt, see Allen, *Conrad Veidt*.
12. See Phillips and Vincendeau, *Journeys of Desire*.
13. Hamid Naficy, *An Accented Cinema: Exilic and Diasporic Filmmaking* (Princeton, NJ: Princeton University Press, 2001), 23.
14. Rosemarie Garland-Thomson, "Misfits: A Feminist Materialist Disability Concept," *Hypatia: A Journal of Feminist Philosophy* 26, no. 3 (Summer 2011): 591.
15. Garland-Thomson, "Misfits," 592–3.
16. Garland-Thomson, "Misfits," 593.
17. Garland-Thomson, "Misfits," 593.
18. Rosemarie Garland-Thomson, *Staring: How We Look* (Oxford: Oxford University Press, 2009), 3.
19. See Exodus 20:5, KJV.
20. See Gergely, *Foreign Devils*.
21. Gilles Deleuze, *Francis Bacon: The Logic of Sensation*, trans. Daniel W. Smith (London: Continuum, 2002), 2.
22. Deleuze, *Francis Bacon*, 2–3.
23. Chiefly D. N. Rodowick in his *Gilles Deleuze's Time Machine* (Durham, NC: Duke University Press, 1997) and *Reading the Figural, or, Philosophy after the New Media* (Durham, NC: Duke University Press, 2001).
24. Deleuze, *Francis Bacon*, 21.
25. Robert Stam, *Subversive Pleasures: Bakhtin, Cultural Criticism, and Film* (Baltimore: Johns Hopkins University Press, 1989).
26. Judith Butler, *Bodies That Matter: On the Discursive Limits of "Sex"* (London: Routledge, 1993), 3.
27. Garland-Thomson, *Staring*, 3–4.
28. Stam, *Subversive Pleasures*, 91–2.
29. Stam, *Subversive Pleasures*, 93.
30. Garland-Thomson, *Staring*, 3–4.
31. John T. Soister, "An Introduction," sleeve note essay for *The Man Who Laughs*, DVD (New York: Kino International, 2003).
32. Susan Hayward, *The French Costume Drama of the 1950s: Fashioning Politics in Film* (Bristol: Intellect, 2013), 25–6.
33. Hayward, *French Costume Drama*, 37.
34. Belén Vidal, *Figuring the Past: Period Film and the Mannerist Aesthetic* (Amsterdam: Amsterdam University Press, 2012), 42
35. Vidal, *Figuring the Past*, 43.
36. Vidal, *Figuring the Past*, 43.
37. Vidal, *Figuring the Past*, 43.

CHAPTER II

Masculinity and Facial Disfigurement in *The Man Who Laughs*

Bruce Henderson

It is a truism that virtually any film adaptation of a great work of literature inevitably fails to capture the qualities that made the literary text "great." In particular, the need to cut scenes and streamline complex narrative strands is usually viewed as a loss. In addition, film is usually seen as being far less successful at communicating the interiority of characters that has become so central to the novel's endeavor post-Henry James and his inheritors, such as Joyce, Woolf, and Faulkner. Film can provide the sense of immediacy and visual specificity that a novel cannot, the argument goes—and, for purist readers, that is also film's drawback. No matter how gifted the actor, Vanessa Redgrave is still probably no one's ideal Clarissa Dalloway, nor Milo O'Shea anyone's perfect Leopold Bloom—but who could be, given the differences between reading and seeing, the verbal and the visual?

Paul Leni's *The Man Who Laughs* (1928) may indeed be one of those rare instances in which a film adaptation is, in many respects, an improvement on the original "classic" novel. There are some crucial changes in the adaptation of the novel to the screen that need to be addressed and, no doubt, different readers and viewers will come to different conclusions about the choices made. In addition, the visual nature of film—particularly, silent film, and this film came just as sound was being introduced—allows the "authors" of the film (in this case, director Leni and leading man Conrad Veidt) to achieve effects that may get lost within Hugo's labyrinthine prose. The film manages to "tell" what Seymour Chatman might call the "deep structure" of the film's *sujet* while making large and usually judicious edits to its *discourse* (i.e. the narration and commentary with which Hugo surrounds his story).[1]

The most dramatic change the filmmakers effected—and it would be continued in the comic book adaptation done for the *Classics Illustrated* series a few decades later—is in the tragic conclusion. The novel ends with the death of Dea in Gwynplaine's arms, after she has had one visionary moment, followed by Gwynplaine's subsequent suicide; he walks off the boat into the abyss, the ocean from which he had ironically been saved at the beginning of the novel. The film ends with a reunion aboard the boat; Gwynplaine rejoins his "true" family, Ursus, Homo, and Dea, in a final embrace that speaks to the future marriage of the lovers. The concluding shot is imbued with an almost blinding light, enshrining Dea and Gwynplaine in a kind of angelic glow, an apotheosis in which nature, sometimes cruel and disorderly, for once balances things out.

So, a happy ending seemed *de rigueur*, yes, but other readings are possible for this changed ending, readings that, in interesting ways, may allow the film to be seen as an early argument for the value of the lives of disabled people and the possibility of a positive representation of a man with facial disfigurement. The novel takes Gwynplaine to the docks after his failed attempt to use the platform of the House of Lords to take a stand against the economic injustices of the nobility against "the people." In despair, he resigns his title to Lord Dirry-Moir and leaves town to avoid a duel with him over the honor of Dirry-Moir's mother. The film diverges from the novel in making Gwynplaine's "escape" (as the scene is titled on the DVD version) a scene in which Gwynplaine is saved from losing his grip on a roof by other townspeople. The scene includes acrobatic moves reminiscent of the Douglas Fairbanks swashbucklers of the time, including a swordfight in which Gwynplaine stabs a guard. Such an alteration, in the codes of the time, restores a kind of lost masculinity to Gwynplaine, reminding us, in ways the novel never quite does, that Gwynplaine's body was as "fit" as any other man's. While this may suggest a kind of ableist privileging of "muscular Christianity," it also dramatizes the fact that one kind of disability (facial disfigurement, in this case) need not cancel out other masculine qualities. In the case of Gwynplaine, whom the film feminizes in ways to be discussed below, this athleticism creates a sense of balance within the iconicity of the character. More importantly, perhaps, it does not cancel out those qualities society would label feminine in Gwynplaine—and which it does hold up for affirmation.

What about the decision not to have either Dea or Gwynplaine die, then? In a sense, within the film's algebra, after so much physical exertion, it would seem a waste to follow it with the death of the two lovers. If one thinks closely about their deaths in the novel, it is reasonable to question whether they were absolutely necessary there, too. Perhaps, following Graham Robb's biographical reading of the novel,[2] one might say Hugo felt the need to demonstrate how damaging the "laughter" of the nobles had been in his own life—how his exile was a kind of death, even though he was on the verge of returning from it. It certainly can be seen as strengthening the novel's rhetorical and romantic pathos to end with the demise of its two virtuous characters. If their loss is enough to produce a kind of revolutionary agony within readers, then the novel's ending works. But, as one of the tests of tragedy might be put, can one argue that their deaths are inevitable and necessary? Ursus and his troupe have been banished from England, presumably forever, so there really is no reason that the lovers must die, say, for Gwynplaine to escape a forced marriage to the Duchess Josiana.

Another sense in which the altered ending may be seen as offering a positive vision for disability in general and for disabled masculinity in particular is in the affirmation of the worth of the disabled hero and heroine and in the authenticity of their love for each other. Indeed, earlier in the film, Gwynplaine explains to Ursus that Josiana's attraction to him affirms his own right to marry Dea. "A woman has seen my face and yet may love me!" he says by way of a title-card. "If such a thing is possible, then I have the right to marry Dea." A double-edged psychology complicates this sentiment. On the one hand, it validates Dea's own "right" to have a suitable husband, suggesting that she should be able to have a spouse who would "pass muster" with sighted women and should not have to settle for a disfigured man. At the same time, of course, it also reifies a sightist perspective by suggesting that a seeing woman's response is more valid than Dea's to Gwynplaine's worthiness. In a twisted way, it is as if Gwynplaine is saying he has no right to "trick" Dea into marrying him just because she cannot see how ugly he is. Ursus immediately points out the illogic in Gwynplaine's statement: "Forget such nonsense. Dea loves you—and she'll never see your face," he says. Ursus's position is not only more practical but also elegant in its simplicity. For him, the issue is irrelevant; Dea loves Gwynplaine and it matters little how others see him, period. Nonetheless, the validation of the able-bodied woman's estimation of him (as corrupt as we understand it to be) is a powerful influence on Gwynplaine, offset by the father figure who loves both his adopted children.

Thus, the reunion of the lovers at the end of the film may be seen as conveying a more positive model of disability than the novel's. While it is difficult to ignore the narrative's use of complementary disability, the final frames of the film suggest that Gwynplaine's adventure in the realm of the nobles has taught him a valuable lesson about his own worth and the meaning of genuine love. It is a lesson not so different from the one Dorothy would learn about a decade later in *The Wizard of Oz*, another narrative that celebrates the discovery of an authentic sense of self in what one always has. Indeed, we can easily imagine Gwynplaine uttering the words "There's no place like home" at the conclusion of *The Man Who Laughs*, even though home, for him, finally consists of people rather than a place.

Other changes to Hugo's novel in its adaptation to film include a straightening out of narrative chronology and sequencing, a strategy that eliminates the interminable explanatory flashbacks of the novel that pull the reader away from the principal characters' lives. For example, Dr. Hardquanonne (an invented name, presumably meaning something like "absolutely harder than all others," like "sine qua non"), appears about eight minutes into the film as the "surgeon" who has mutilated the young Gwynplaine; however, his literary counterpart does not show up until the fifth chapter in the novel's second "book." This roguish character reappears in the scenes taking place during Gwynplaine's adulthood; he is now a mountebank who recognizes Gwynplaine and tries to send word of his existence to Josiana in a blackmail attempt, only to have his note intercepted by another character who appears much earlier in the film than in the novel: Barkilphedro, who shares the note with Queen Anne to curry favor with her. In addition, the elder Lord Clancharlie is depicted in the opening of the film as much more heroic in trying to save his son's life than he is in the novel. He thus gives Gwynplaine a legacy of honor to inherit instead of a mere place in a particular bloodline that passes down a title. His father is a man to live up to in deed and thought, and Gwynplaine achieves his patrimony in the film's final act, both in court and in his escape from England.

In addition to these changes in plot, director Leni brought to the film the lessons he learned as an early participant in German Expressionist film, a movement in which Veidt also played an important role. In this style of filmmaking, which owed as much to Freudian theories of the unconscious and the dream-state as it did to any dramatic traditions, light and shadow, but particularly shadow, become characters in their own right; they create spaces of knowing and unknowing, consciousness and unconsciousness, places where lines between reality and illusion are tested and questioned. Thus, the hidden fears that haunt us all, from childhood nightmares to adult anxieties, become manifest yet also remain somehow covered or screened. What and how we see—and are seen—are omnipresent super-themes of such films. While there was not yet an articulated theory of cinematic scopophilia, such as would emerge in feminist film theory with such critics as Laura Mulvey and Linda Williams in the 1970s and onward, many of these films allowed audiences to experience both the pleasures and perils of seeing and being seen. The films often treated seeing as a perverse act, one filled with a phobic loathing of self and others that took viewers and characters into realms of abjection, of refusal of that which audiences saw mirrored back at them.

Although these elements were present in an earlier Universal adaptation of a Hugo novel—the 1923 Lon Chaney vehicle *The Hunchback of Notre Dame*—they become much more substantial in this film thanks to Leni's artful use of the camera and Veidt's almost too-palpable facial performance. In the five years that passed since *Hunchback*, it is clear that the art of the camera had continued to develop and that one can discern the difference between a director with a specific signature and one who simply sets the camera up: what Andrew Sarris and others might call the distinction between an *auteur* and a studio director.[3]

Leni was comfortable with both crowd scenes (revealed by his adept use of pans and long-distance shots) and those requiring more intimacy. In particular, Leni devoted considerable screen time to scenes in which two characters are featured prominently or exclusively. These "two-shot" scenes are typically ones that feature Gwynplaine and a second character, so viewers are constantly being asked to compare and contrast Gwynplaine's face in relation to other, more normative ones, whether other male faces (such as Ursus and Dirry-Moir in particular), female faces (particularly the two poles of blonde femininity, Dea and Josiana), or even the non-human face of Homo the wolf, with whom Gwynplaine is twice contrasted in mirroring profile shots, matching the noses and jaws of both against each other.

The other notable aspect of Leni's *mise-en-scène* is his specific choice in presenting Gwynplaine to the audience. While, of course, we view Gwynplaine's entire body in various scenes, Leni, whenever possible, restricts our focus to Gwynplaine's face and, more often than not, from a three-quarters perspective. Rarely are we asked to see Gwynplaine's face full-on; when we are, it occurs primarily when he is "in performance," either on-stage or in another highly public forum, such as the House of Lords. When he is alone in private, or with members of his stage family, he is typically seen with part of his face shadowed or naturalistically occluded by the angle from which we see him. For instance, when he is in an embrace with Dea in some of the scenes, his face is partially buried; at other times, when in despair, we see him with head lowered, in profile, or with one quarter revealed. It is telling—and remarkable—that the final shot of him and Dea presents both characters in full-face. It is as if they are on-stage, turned out in a presentational stance (such as the position performers in musical plays typically use when delivering a song) rather than in the more representational poses that we have seen throughout the film.

One effect of these partial-perspective shots of Gwynplaine is to increase his own humanity within the visual rhetoric of the film and to encourage non-disfigured viewers of the film to identify more strongly with him. As opposed to Chaney's Quasimodo, who seems to exist more fully in frontal shots, Veidt's Gwynplaine has a privacy and a kind of psychological subjectivity suggested by these angles; he is not simply a monstrous individual "on display." He is capable of performing as one when he chooses, however, such as when he shows his face (almost like a stripper builds suspense in her or his performance) by standing full-front at the end of "Chaos Vanquished," the morality play written by Ursus and performed by Gwynplaine, Dea, and company. Though the nature of his disfigurement more severely limits his ability to change expressions, Veidt's Gwynplaine, due in part to Leni's camera choices, emerges more fully human than Quasimodo on-screen.

Veidt's performance has much to do with the power of Gwynplaine. The film was originally envisioned as yet another in Lon Chaney's series of horror films, but contractual obligations made his participation impossible. While Chaney would have brought his own strengths as a performer to Gwynplaine, Veidt was able to create a character whose inner life was always communicated in ways that felt as if they were somehow cued to descriptive passages in the novel. This is all the more remarkable, given the fact that the prosthetic dentures created for Veidt made it all but impossible for him to speak; therefore, most of his performance had to be created from his eyes and bodily tension.[4] Indeed, this is a performance that might be said to be acted, on the one hand, through the intense modern psychology of what eyes and facial muscles might achieve, and, on the other, through the large, not to say inappropriate, physical gestures and positioning passed down from the elocutionary acting tradition of the nineteenth century. Veidt's stage training made him able to use his body to communicate from afar, so crowd scenes and public scenes, such as his indignant address to the House of Lords, carry with them the forcefulness of any romantic play. Even his specific arms motions, such as the out-turned palm and arm, suggesting recoil, banishment, and rejection, are gestures an actor with Veidt's experience would have long been familiar with; they had been codified by such early teachers, directors, and performers as François Delsarte and Thomas Sheridan and discoverable during this period in the teachings and pedagogy of Rudolf Steiner, mystic and founder of the eurythmic performance style.

As thrilling as Veidt's use of his whole body is in the film, it is his face to which the camera always returns. Before Veidt takes on the role of the adult Gwynplaine, the camera has already been introduced to the smile in an early scene in which the child Gwynplaine brings baby Dea to Ursus. Rather than keeping the entire scene in darkness, as Hugo does, Leni shows us the smile on the child in a scene in which Ursus, harshly chastising Gwynplaine for apparently laughing at the news that Dea is blind, suddenly realizes the nature of the smile. While, on the one hand, this may be seen as destroying the suspense of building up to the entrance of the adult Gwynplaine, it does have the effect of humanizing the disfigurement. The adult Gwynplaine's smile, which is so much larger than the child's, has been implanted in the audience's vision, thereby minimizing the shocked reactions the audience might otherwise have and allowing it to focus more on the effects of the smile on Gwynplaine and his onlookers within the film.

Veidt's first appearance is heralded by the calls of excited children that "The Laughing Man is coming!" suggesting not fear on their part, but anticipation and a sense of a performance that may well be familiar to them. The film then cuts to the image of Gwynplaine in front of a mirror, preparing for his performance in one of his most customary poses in the film. The image suggests a complex narcissism informed by psychological and sociological concerns. The face is depicted in a close-up shot, completed by the mirror, and already there is an apparent tension in the facial muscles, not simply where the disfigurement has been performed, but more actively in the forehead and the eyelids; if this is the face of a clown, it is also the face of a man desperately trapped by the mask he has been given to wear. The setting is the Southwark Fair, which a title-card describes as "a rattle for the masses to make them laugh and forget," a succinct summary of Hugo's own sociopolitical critique of the England of Queen Anne.

In the first domestic scene, Gwynplaine interacts with Dea, played by Mary Philbin, who three years earlier played Christine Daaé to Chaney's Erik in *The Phantom of the Opera* and who received top billing in this film. There is a shyness to Gwynplaine's physical response to Dea, an almost feminine reticence or modesty, in which he looks at her primarily through sidelong glances or with head slightly lowered. He plays with her hair, even to the point of putting strands of it in his mouth. It is an odd gesture that suggests both an inability to express his love and desire directly to her and a kind of childish oral fetishism of the beloved's body, but only through an innocent consumption of it.

The scene shifts and the film introduces the villains of the piece: Barkilphedro, Josiana, Lord Dirry-Moir, and Queen Anne. They continue the visual theme of the smile, each one, excepting Queen Anne, introduced and defined by a smile or set of smiles. Barkilphedro (Brandon Hurst), identified as Josiana's jester, has a smile as painful as Gwynplaine's but malevolent in its mixture of feigned obeisance to the nobles whose bidding he pretends to do (while carrying out his own plans) and its bitter, almost anaesthetized quality. Josiana's smile has both a lasciviousness—a sign of her own unbridled self-pleasure—and a cruel and insolent quality, as she mocks all around her, whether the peasants at Southwark, Lord Dirry-Moir, or even her half-sister Queen Anne.[5] Josiana is played by former Moscow Art Theatre actor Olga Baclanova, who will, a few years later, play the arch-villain of all disability-as-horror films, the duplicitous Cleopatra in Tod Browning's *Freaks* (1932). Lord Dirry-Moir (Stuart Holmes) is first introduced to the viewer in a cameo painting of him, which has him wearing a facial look that, in the terms of the day, reads as somewhat imbecilic and a moustache that almost makes him look as if he has a cleft palate. When he actually appears, it is clear that the moustache is simply an adornment and his face is "normally" constructed; however, there is nonetheless a sense of a clown about him that mirrors Gwynplaine—though, in Kristeva's terms, Gwynplaine would seem to be the "clean and proper" clown, whereas Lord Dirry-Moir is the travesty, produced by a too-decadent life.[6] Anne (Josephine Crowell) appears as a dour, unsmiling tyrant, dressed in women's clothes but looking like a man in drag or an embodiment of one of Sir John Tenniel's drawings for the *Alice* books. She is a kind of less-loving Victoria; she smiles only when she has the opportunity to threaten or exert authority. All of these smiles are, finally, even more perverse than the one imposed on Gwynplaine.

The scene in which Gwynplaine and Josiana first see each other is built on a number of "mirror" shots. It begins with Gwynplaine once again in front of his makeup mirror; this time he is shown applying the whiteface of the clown (and it is this scene of him that provides the most convincing argument for his inspiration of the Joker in the *Batman* series). The camera then cuts to Josiana fidgeting in her "box," using a jeweled mask-lorgnette to peer at the audience. The performance proceeds, with Gwynplaine saving Dea from the beast-like characters who represent aspects of Chaos. He has done this with his mouth still covered by a scarf; there is a cut to Josiana, whose own face is difficult to read—are the emotions anger, indignation, curiosity? Then, as Gwynplaine reveals his face to the crowd, there is a series of superimpositions in which we see him laughing with the crowd, the crowd laughing with (or at?) him, and Josiana, her face growing more and more intense as she apparently experiences a potent combination of curiosity, revulsion, and desire; indeed, her heaving chest suggests that she is on the verge of hyperventilating in response to the pleasure and pain of this sight.

After the performance, Ursus asks Gwynplaine if he had seen the "lady," to which Gwynplaine replies yes. A close-up of his eyes with welling tears suggests his own complex longing and the terrible experience of being seen through eyes not simply conditioned to respond with laughter; Josiana, who has thus far been defined through her own decadent laughter, had not laughed once while viewing Gwynplaine for the first time. Another performer, the one who has taken the traditional garb of the clown (whiteface and tricorn hat), says to Gwynplaine, "What a lucky clown you are—you don't have to rub off *your* laugh." Yes, but he *cannot* rub off his laugh; that is the Faustian bargain someone else made for him long ago. Gwynplaine receives Josiana's note, which in the film is rendered thusly: "I am she who did not laugh. Was it pity or was it love? My page will meet you at midnight." With this note, Josiana raises a set of polar opposites different from the ones in the note in the novel. In the book, she is certain of her love; here, she allows a space for what might still be viewed as its opposite: a pity that would preclude any genuine sense of potential adult romantic or sexual desire for Gwynplaine.

Gwynplaine goes to see Josiana in her chambers. On his way, and even when he is in her room and watching her while she sleeps, he wears a black scarf around his face, covering his mouth like a kind of screen. This is not, of course, the first time Gwynplaine has covered his mouth with a scarf (he even did so in his first appearance as a child). In fact, it becomes a striking repeated visual motif throughout the film, operating on a number of different potential levels of meaning. On the one hand, it serves a dramatic purpose, allowing Gwynplaine to pass through the streets of London unrecognized by others, as his mouth is the only remarkable feature he possesses. But it also becomes a kind of odd, Expressionistic kind of prophylactic, a bandage for a psychic as well as aesthetic wound. The scarf seems to operate as a barrier between Gwynplaine's mouth— his uncontrollable central physically defining feature—and his fulfillment of desire (recall that his intimate relationship with Dea was first established by his inserting strands of her hair into his mouth).

Although it is by no means what Leni and Veidt probably intended, there is a sense in which the covering of the mouth has the effect of drawing attention to Gwynplaine's "queerness." That which he must cover, out of shame, is not his phallus, but perhaps the opposite of the phallus, an enlarged opening over which he has no command, except to hide it from society. If one can posit the phallic woman, perhaps Gwynplaine may operate on some symbolic level as the vaginal man (or whatever the equivalent to phallic would be in this case). Obviously, there is no reason to think that Gwynplaine is literally impotent, but he has been reduced to the role of that which is seen, that which, in Elkins's sense, is penetrated visually by others.[7] If not the vaginal man, then this opening—and the shame about it that he feels when not displaying it as a way of earning a living—may put Gwynplaine in the realm of the anal, with the language of desire the abjected "material" that is emitted from the mouth, like the fluids Kristeva imagines as originating in fantasies of the maternal.[8]

In this sense, it may be possible to expand the significance of Gwynplaine's covered mouth to a larger sense of the disabled masculine. Whereas it has been noted that sexist discourse of Western civilization, going all the way back to Aristotle, has figured the feminine as "always already disabled," it is possible to say that, in some way, the disabled man is "always already demasculinized," either feminized or neutered (sometimes both, as the two terms can be viewed in phallocentric discourse as synonymous). Gwynplaine's mouth, whose very shame-filled covering must simultaneously draw attention to its non-normative difference, is not unlike other forms of hiding/stripping that mark many disabled men's bodies as desiring masculinity but rejecting their own non-normativity. Think of the man with a spinal cord injury, whose wheelchair may come to symbolize a lack of phallic functionality, or a visually impaired man, whose blindness (and cane, not an apt substitute for phallic power) may lead to the need to engage in interdependence, which has traditionally been viewed as the realm of the feminine, and so forth. Even in the sexual economy of homosexuality, such men are probably viewed as "bottoms," assumed to take the pleasuring of other men through their inevitable receptivity as their "rightful" role.

Josiana gradually removes the scarf from Gwynplaine's mouth; this is the one scene in which Veidt did not wear the prosthetic dentures, thus making his mouth seem more "natural" and accessible. She approaches the mouth as a fetish, the adoration of which is as important as the actual accomplishment of a sex act. As if to dramatize the very question of dominance that the covering and uncovering of the mouth suggest, the two tumble on top of the bed, now Gwynplaine on top, now Josiana, as if they are struggling, clumsily, to see who gets to be the master. A bell rings, signaling a message for Josiana, and the coitus is interrupted before any more clothing can be removed. In an interestingly instinctive gesture,

Gwynplaine immediately covers his mouth again, as if afraid he will be discovered "undressed" by an intruder. The message is from Anne, informing Josiana that Gwynplaine has been discovered to be the real Lord Clancharlie and that Josiana is to marry him. Josiana, not telling Gwynplaine, gazes into the distance, as if utterly unable to sort out the difference between her desire for the non-normative man and her resistance to the discipline of the Crown. Gwynplaine, who has been gazing at her with love, quickly recognizes, without a word passing between them, the horror of his desire for her, presumably because it is in conflict with what he recognizes as a purer love for Dea. In the most elocutionary moment in the film, he gestures with his arm across his mouth (a gesture that can be found in nineteenth-century handbooks for performers), recoils from her, and leaves. Josiana, alone, weeps and is comforted only by her pet monkey.

Gwynplaine returns to the caravan, is shown in profile again with Homo, and discovers Dea asleep on the steps of the caravan. This shot reiterates one of our earliest visual memories of Gwynplaine—when he as a child has come upon the infant Dea in her dead mother's arms—except here Dea is not dead but waiting faithfully for the return of her love. Dea holds Josiana's note, though of course she could not have read it; Gwynplaine carefully takes it away and tears it up, a sign that he wishes to erase the previous scene and pledge himself to Dea only. As he bends down, dipping out of frame for a moment, to lie on Dea's lap, she awakens, and a sung interlude "When Loves Comes Stealing" follows on the soundtrack. During the music, she feels his face, moving her fingers on his mouth, and says, "God closed my eyes so I could see only the real Gwynplaine." While, on the one hand, this is a kind of repetition of the sentimental notion suggested throughout the novel that inner sight is of a higher dimension than the physically visual, the juxtaposition of this with her actual "reading" of his mouth suggests a multiplicity of ways of "seeing" that do not preclude the sensory. She does not go so far as to insert her fingers into his mouth, but her lingering play of them there suggests an increasingly erotic potentiality between the characters, with the mouth the object of knowledge, the object of desire. In his turn, Gwynplaine carries Dea into the caravan, as if a groom carrying his bride over the threshold on the wedding night. Ursus awakens and welcomes them back into the chaotic order of this assembled family unit. This is a "family we choose," to use the title of a popular book about queerness and kinship, as opposed to a deterministically biological one.

Following the novel, there is next the scene in which Gwynplaine is "arrested," taken to the prison, and identified by Hardquanonne as the legitimate Lord Clancharlie. Ursus waits outside the prison, but a passerby tells him, "Those who go in there never come out—don't wait." He sees guards transporting a coffin out of the prison and, assuming Gwynplaine has been killed, returns to the caravan. Standing next to the space where the performances have been given, Ursus notices Gwynplaine's name painted as an advertisement, and he weeps; for him, only the inscribed trace of the real, corporeal Gwynplaine remains. However, an immediately following scene between Anne and Barkilphedro informs the audience that Gwynplaine is not dead but will in fact be made a peer in the House of Lords the next day.

In the next scene, the film painfully dramatizes the attempts by Ursus and the other players to convince Dea that Gwynplaine has returned. They do so by mimicking crowd noises calling for him and fabricating Gwynplaine's presence. There is something of Erving Goffman's notion of theatricality in everyday life in this scene, as the performative dimension is most importantly in the social and interpersonal dimensions of the "play."[9] There is no paying audience or leading man, but these troupers, guided by the age-old dictum that "the show must go on," use the trappings of performance to restore order—even if it is an illogical and only temporary and feigned one—to their world. Barkilphedro interrupts this performance and in turn engages in a performative statement when he declares that "Gwynplaine, the laughing mountebank, is dead." Like the efforts of Ursus and the company, there is a falseness to this statement, though, ironically, Ursus's speech act of using performance to insist that Gwynplaine is still alive will prove to be true.

The presentation of Gwynplaine as Lord Clancharlie to the House of Lords is next and it very deftly and powerfully compresses what took Hugo several chapters to narrate to an economical encounter between the hero and the nobility. Now attired in the wigs and costumes of the peerage, Gwynplaine rides in a carriage with Barkilphedro. The carriage gets caught in a traffic jam with Ursus's caravan, headed to the docks (as Ursus and his company have been ordered to leave England by that evening), and Gwynplaine and Barkilphedro walk through the street to get to the House. Once again, Gwynplaine covers his mouth, suggesting that, like Macbeth, these "strange garments cleave not to [his] mold." Meanwhile, Homo has recognized Gwynplaine, perhaps by scent, and leads Dea to the House. As Gwynplaine enters, other peers pass around the handbills that were distributed during the Southwark Fair, underscoring the point that they view Gwynplaine's presence among them to be as much of a grotesque masquerade as his performance in the play (though perhaps missing out on the latter's moral dimensions). One goes so far as to enunciate this, making reference to "a clown in the House of Peers." Queen Anne enters, which allows the filmmakers to build up this scene even more; the Body Politic is present for Gwynplaine's rhetorical breakthrough to self. Indeed, the film shows Gwynplaine performing his own sense of liminal identity. As he bows to Anne, he alternates between covering and uncovering his mouth, as if undecided how to act within this place, where he, by birth but not by cultivation, belongs. In the meantime, Dea arrives and Dirry-Moir, recognizing her, tries to get her into the chamber so she will know Gwynplaine is alive.

In the actual moment of Gwynplaine's presentation to the peers, he is still covering his mouth with his hand and the look on his face suggests nothing so much as someone trapped, under the surveillance of those who will not understand the nature of his performance. There is something of the actor's nightmare here, in which the actor dreams of going on-stage not knowing his or her lines. When he does reveal his face, his carved smile is immediately misinterpreted, with cries of "He laughs at the Queen's command!" and "He laughs at the House of Lords!" exclaimed by various peers. Dirry-Moir says to Dea, "Can't you tell he's in there? Listen to them laugh!," suggesting that she can know Gwynplaine by the way others respond rather than by his own speech.

As Gwynplaine stands there with his eternal laugh on his face, in a sense stripped publicly and forced to undergo the symptomatic, even surgical "gaze" accompanying the laughter thrown at him—a laughter he can distinguish from the laughter he received as a performer—Leni moves in with a close-up of Gwynplaine's eyes weeping copiously. As if aware of the nakedness of his eyes, he uses his handkerchief to cover them, leaving his mouth exposed, as if unable to decide which is more shameful: the unmanly, though genuine, tears their laughter has induced or the smile that their system of government has engraved on him.

And then Gwynplaine finds himself, finds his true identity. He pulls down the handkerchief, exposing both the weeping, wounded eyes, and the gaping, always open, always vulnerable mouth. He finds himself through speech, through the use of this disfigured mouth to speak with power and force. Leni and Walter Anthony, the film's titles-writer, reduce Hugo's many pages of oration to a few succinct sentences that capture the anti-aristocratic politics of the novel and of Gwynplaine's position as a man of the people. Responding to the news that he is to be forced to marry Josiana for his resistance to the addition to the consort's bank accounts, he says, "I protest!" adding, "I shall not be forced into this hateful marriage—not even on the Queen's command!" Cries asking him how he dare refuse such a command follow, to which he responds in a succession of title-cards: "A King made me a clown!" and "A Queen made me a Lord—" and, most powerfully, "But first, *God made me a man!*" (italics in original title-card). Through the agency of the organ that as a physical feature earned him a living but now allows him to be an orator, he becomes a participant in his own self-governance. As he leaves the room, Dirry-Moir says admiringly, "Make way for a Peer of England." On his way out, Gwynplaine says to Barkilphedro, "Gwynplaine, the Clown, goes back to his people! You go to the Queen for your reward!" This moment between the two "clowns" (recall that Barkilphedro has been identified as Josiana's jester) is yet another of these mirroring moments, but it is a decisive, definitive one in which Gwynplaine's smile is forever disengaged from the moral duplicity of Barkilphedro's. Gwynplaine covers his mouth once more and leaps through a window to escape, almost as if he has superhuman powers.

As he runs through the crowded streets to return to his family, he finds himself back at the inn yard where the performances were given and sees his name and the name of the company and play painted through, putting them out of existence. As Barkilphedro sends his men to capture Gwynplaine, the various fight scenes described near the beginning of this analysis take place. When Gwynplaine gets to the dock, he discovers the boat carrying Ursus and Dea has just set sail, and he calls out her name, the volume of which is suggested in its capitalization on a title-card: "DEA!" As Barkilphedro tries to stop him, Homo the wolf leaps into the water and, in a moment of dramatic irony, attacks the man, biting his face and holding on tenaciously; no doubt Barkilphedro will be the next "man who laughs." Gwynplaine rejoins his family and he and Dea are framed together, as described before, faces adhering to each other, both gazing in their own way into the bright light of the horizon that represents their future together.

This film is a complex meditation on masculinity and disability, in some respects more powerful in this regard than the novel. Veidt's embodiment of Gwynplaine permits director and viewer to consider the myriad ways in which this laughing man means and can be read at the same time. Veidt's performance is an extraordinarily emotional one. While the stoic codes of masculinity that were embodied by such actors as John Wayne, Gary Cooper, and Humphrey Bogart were yet to come, the 1920s were a time when masculinity, particularly as it related to film actors, was beginning to be seen in crisis. It was the period in which homosexuality began to be more visible, not only in such enclaves as Greenwich Village, but through readings of some of the major male film stars of the time. Indeed, editorials were written about Rudolph Valentino, suggesting his European version of maleness owed much to the "powder puff pansy." Some believe that Valentino's death was precipitated by a fight in which he was trying to "prove" his masculinity and died as a result of internal injuries. While the attribution of cause of death remains apocryphal, the boxing match was a reality, an attempt to perform a kind of masculinity made popular by such writers as Hemingway.

Veidt's Gwynplaine is not quite the "powder puff," but he is also less determinedly masculine than even Lon Chaney's monstrous outsiders. His willingness and ability to be expressive almost to an extreme degree (underscored by Leni's *mise-en-scène*) adds complexity to this image of the disfigured man. Despite the fact that half of his face has been made permanently inexpressive (or singularly expressive), Gwynplaine ironically becomes one of the most memorable and emotionally complex male characters of the silent film era, with Veidt's performance in its own way looking forward to Charles Laughton's complicated and resonant Quasimodo in William Dieterle's 1939 remake of *The Hunchback of Notre Dame*. As Veidt so eloquently demonstrated in *The Man Who Laughs*, to be disfigured is not to be robbed of emotional and masculine power; it simply requires the audience to see and experience that power in new and richly rewarding ways.

ACKNOWLEDGMENT

This chapter was adapted from the author's dissertation, "Cain's Brothers: Facial Disfigurement and Masculinity in 19th and 20th Century Narratives" (PhD dissertation, University of Illinois at Chicago, 2006).

NOTES

1. Seymour Chatman, *Coming to Terms: The Rhetoric of Narrative in Fiction and Film* (Ithaca, NY: Cornell University Press, 1990), 29.
2. Graham Robb, *Victor Hugo: A Biography* (New York: Norton, 1997), 428–9.
3. See Andrew Sarris, *The American Cinema: Directors and Directions, 1929–1968* (New York: Dutton, 1968).
4. Though synchronous-sound filmmaking was already underway in Hollywood at the time of the film's production, Universal decided to produce *The Man Who Laughs* as a traditional silent film but added a musical soundtrack, sound effects, and occasional non-synchronized vocalizations from background characters. The dentures that Veidt was forced to wear and his relative unease with English at this stage of his career were contributory factors to this decision, no doubt.
5. The film is vaguer than the novel about Josiana's virginity; if a virgin, she nonetheless does not seem a stranger to sexual pleasure.
6. Julia Kristeva, *Powers of Horror: An Essay on Abjection*, trans. Leon S. Roudiez (New York: Columbia University Press, 1982), 101–3.
7. See James Elkins, *The Object Stares Back: On the Nature of Seeing* (New York: Harcourt, 1996).
8. Kristeva, *Powers of Horror*.
9. See Erving Goffman, *Stigma: Notes on the Management of Spoiled Identity* (Englewood Cliffs, NJ: Prentice-Hall, 1963).

CHAPTER 12

Cinematic Space and Set Design in Paul Leni's *The Last Warning*

Bastian Heinsohn

By the time *The Last Warning* premiered at the Colony Theater in New York City on January 6, 1929, director Paul Leni had established a reputation as an "artist of lights and shadows" among Hollywood directors.[1] Leni's three films since his arrival in Hollywood two years earlier, *The Cat and the Canary* (1927), *The Chinese Parrot* (1927, now lost), and *The Man Who Laughs* (1928), can be considered the culmination of his expertise as a set designer and director after developing and honing his skills in Berlin.[2] It was his 1924 German masterpiece *Waxworks* (*Das Wachsfigurenkabinett*) in particular, that attracted the attention of Universal Studios boss Carl Laemmle, who saw in Leni a master of his craft from Europe equal to the likes of émigré directors F. W. Murnau at Fox, Mauritz Stiller at MGM, Michael Curtiz at Warner, and Ernst Lubitsch at Paramount.[3] Leni's untimely death coincided with a dramatic transitional phase not only at Universal Studios but all over Hollywood. The success of Warner Bros.' 1927 milestone *The Jazz Singer*, which pioneered the use of synchronized dialogue, initiated the shift to sound film that saw its completion around 1930. Furthermore, the emergence of Hollywood as a powerful film industry with its own stars and a glamorous global appeal led to a significant fatigue of imports from Europe, ranging from movies to actors (whose accents often made it impossible for them to find work in the new sound era) to even directors. Sound became the much-watched "baby" in Hollywood, as Leni put it in a 1929 interview published in the studio newspaper *Universal Weekly*,[4] while the era of silent films and their strong emphasis on showing—for example, through magnificent and extravagant set designs, rather than telling by way of intertitles—came to an end.

Leni's *The Last Warning* from 1929 fell, as Tim Bergfelder and his colleagues put it, "into a moment in film history in which set design was given more prominence and attention than perhaps during any other period."⁵ Set design is one of the central elements of *mise-en-scène*, yet the crew members responsible for creating the "world" within which a film's plot unfolds have traditionally been much less recognized than the director, the actors, and perhaps the cinematographer. The director usually takes most of the credit for creating the cinematic worlds in the studio or on location. The positions as set designer and art director emerged fully in their own right only in the early 1930s, when Hollywood studios developed unique signatures and styles that distinguished themselves from each other. The extravagant set of *The Last Warning* on Universal's studio lot, a replica of the Paris opera house's interior with numerous additional behind-the-stage rooms, sealed doors, and secret passages, was as breathtaking as it was already outdated. Universal reused the studio's Stage 28, initially built in 1924 for *The Phantom of the Opera* (1925), the successful adaptation of the 1910 novel *Le Fantôme de l'Opéra* by Gaston Leroux. Universal reutilized this sound stage multiple times in subsequent years.⁶ *The Last Warning*, Leni's final film, serves as a key example of a new beginning for Universal Studios at the brink of a new decade and the ascendency of sound film. "When the décor of a specific film merits publicity," stated Charles Affron and Mirella Jona Affron in their book on the meaning of set designs in film history, "it is only for high costs and size."⁷ This certainly holds true for the set of *The Last Warning* and for Leni's previous Hollywood films. In fact, Leni was criticized for the high costs of his films' lavish sets; for example, the *Film Spectator* exclaimed in 1928 in a critical assessment on the production costs of *The Man Who Laughs* that "Paul Leni is first of all a master of investiture, and then a story-teller, thus reversing the qualities that a director should possess."⁸ This analysis investigates the meaning and role of the set design in *The Last Warning* beyond its magnificence and uniqueness and also beyond its possible interpretation of a spatial representation of inner turmoil, so often attached to Expressionist or post-Expressionist sets surrounding haunted house stories and narratives of entrapment and *angst*. *The Last Warning* is a development in a kind of Hollywood cinema greatly indebted to German Expressionism.⁹

The origin of the film *The Last Warning* goes back into the 1910s as it was adapted from a play based on Wadsworth Camp's 1916 novel *The House of Fear*. The novel was adapted for the stage by Thomas Fallon as a play in three acts and served as the source text for the script of *The Last Warning*. Fallon's play was staged on Broadway at the Klaw Theatre (demolished in 1954) and ran from October 1922 to May 1923 for reportedly 238 performances.¹⁰ Fallon's adaptation was performed at least until 1927, when it was staged at the Athenaeum Theatre in Melbourne. In cinema, however, times had changed dramatically towards the end of the 1920s, not only in regards to technical advances with the coming sound era, but also, and most importantly, in regards to a transformed audience appetite for movies and for the movie experience in the beginning of the 1930s. A growing separation from foreign imports, especially from Germany, emerged and made work for foreign directors increasingly difficult. In times of cinema's emerging sense of emancipation within the entertainment industry and its significant technical advances, the fast growing US film industry became the prime example of American big business and ushered in the "Golden Age of Hollywood" marked by cinematic creativity, global appeal and impact, and financial success.

Hollywood studios differed greatly during the 1920s and early 1930s in regards to genres and sets. Metro-Goldwyn-Mayer was known at first for lavish sets and big-budget historical epics such as *Ben-Hur: A Tale of the Christ* (1925). Towards the end of the 1920s, MGM, and to a lesser degree also Paramount and RKO, became the studios that developed a stronger emphasis on modern architecture and sleek Art Deco exteriors and interiors, without giving up any of the grandeur and finesse found in their sets from the decade's early years.[11] At Universal Studios, however, set design differed greatly, and films produced under the guidance and supervision of studio boss Laemmle (the typical Universal film at the time seldom lacked the introductory title-card "Carl Laemmle presents") exhibited a distinctive look. Universal focused its production on the horror genre and, to a lesser degree, on the musical genre, balancing much of its yearly output between mystery-horror films on one hand and films that highlighted showmanship and stage performances on the other, such as Wallace Worsley's *The Hunchback of Notre Dame* (1923), Paul Fejos's *The Last Performance* (1929) and the musical *Broadway* (1929), Universal's first all-sound film, Rupert Julian's adaptation of *The Phantom of the Opera*, and the musical revue *King of Jazz* (1930), filmed in an early two-color Technicolor process.

The increasing importance of Universal's art department in the early 1920s under the guidance of the young British set designer Charles D. Hall and the emergence of set designers and architects as crucial film crew members can perhaps be credited to another émigré, the Austrian director Erich von Stroheim. Universal Studios reportedly promoted the extravagant 1922 production *Foolish Wives* as "The First Million Dollar Picture," its expense related mostly to the extravagant recreation of a Monte Carlo central square on the studio's outdoor lot.[12] Fame and importance were usually ascribed to directors and actors, yet the studio's art departments grew substantially in importance during the 1920s. As Mark Shiel states in his examination of set design in classical Hollywood films, set construction at major studios at the time was "one of the most important expenditures in a film's budget, and usually the most expensive after the screenplay and salaries of directors and stars."[13] Around the mid-1920s, the art directors at Universal were progressively occupied with creating sets that resembled in design and atmosphere those of the Expressionist films produced in Weimar Germany. Universal's Hall was responsible for the building of the opera house set for *The Hunchback of Notre Dame* adaptation in 1923 and also supervised the production of Leni's *The Last Warning* six years later.[14] Leni used his mastery of light and shadows to make the set look as if it were built exclusively to serve him as director, set designer, and storyteller. The pre-existing set allowed Leni one last opportunity to create a stylized, eerie mystery story that could combine his distinct Expressionist cinematic style and his films' predominantly ghostly themes with Universal's emerging flair for producing horror films and using lavish theatrical sets. The resulting film would appeal, he hoped, to the taste of an American audience that expected and appreciated a mix of horror and entertainment, or in other words, thrills with a grain of comedy or slapstick humor.

However, *The Last Warning* was received rather coldly by American audiences and critics at the time. In addition to the inadequacies of the sound quality in the semi-sound version shown at the film's New York premiere, several critics attributed the film's failure to thrill or entertain moviegoers to the fact that it was released in a time when film posters greatly highlighted the "thrills" and the "fun" (and the sound) of upcoming movies.[15] Mordaunt Hall of the *New York Times* wrote that "Leni goes at the idea of this mystery with a rather heavy hand." Hall praised the setting as "especially impressive"; however, he also suggested that "Leni goes a little too strong on the use of cobwebs" and dismissed the story as "things [that] appear to be cast in the mold now quite familiar with spooky yarns."[16] *Photoplay* stated that Leni's film has a "distinguished cast, with massive sets and effective, futuristic photography, but there's no story. The title writer has to explain a thousand irrelevancies in the last reel."[17] *Variety* was equally unimpressed by the overall film but did praise the set, concluding that *The Last Warning* is a

> thrill picture running too long to attain its full effect, and not a good talker in the final analysis. On the other hand, it is a talker, has its thrill moments and an imposingly photographed production behind it, plus a big cast. Figures to do all right minus unusual grosses one way or the other.[18]

The narrative space in Leni's *The Last Warning* is limited to the inside of the opera house, with only two minor shots and sequences of the stylized exterior of the building. An elaborate dynamic montage sequence of Broadway's flashing neon signs serves as the film's introductory sequence, setting the mood and locating the plot in the space of the modern urban metropolis of New York City. All narrative action takes place inside the theater building, recalling the cinematic spaces of Leni's *Kammerspielfilme*, especially *Backstairs* (1921). Leni's first film for Universal, *The Cat and the Canary*, similarly made use of a strict limitation of space and characters to heighten suspense in a haunted house plot. Uncanny ghost stories, disembodied spirits, and mysterious forces beyond characters' control had been a staple in 1920s German cinema. Universal, as "the most European of the American studios," as Ian Conrich has suggested, had successfully transplanted plots, themes, style, and techniques from Germany to Hollywood during the 1920s by way of importing actors, directors, designers, and staff in many areas of the studio's branches.[19] Laemmle had a "penchant for hiring relatives and other German-speaking emigrés," as Richard Koszarski put it.[20] A great number of Hollywood films, especially films produced at Universal, were set in present-day Europe and often in the innocent prewar years in order to appeal to the American audience's fascination with Europe at the time. A large portion of Americans were in fact fairly recent immigrants from Europe, especially in the country's urban centers like New York, Chicago, and Los Angeles. Films set in Europe simultaneously assured Universal the continued export of its film productions to European audiences who were increasingly drawn to the movies by the entertainingly extravagant film productions made in Hollywood. However, towards the end of the 1920s and in the early 1930s, Universal began to move away from horror films set in constrained and distorted interior spaces that transmitted the mood of existential anxieties typical of spaces in German Expressionist arts. Universal's interest in Expressionist imagery remained strong, yet the studio's trajectory shifted increasingly towards more light-hearted horror-comedy films with an emotional and humoristic touch, such as James Whale's *Frankenstein* (1931) and *The Old Dark House* (1932).[21] The shift was perhaps the result of the changing zeitgeist towards the end of the 1920s and in the early 1930s and a stronger desire to enjoy movies as a form of entertainment rather than a highly stylized art form from a traumatized and war-shaken Germany.

Figure 12.1 Hidden corridors and trap doors: publicity still for Paul Leni's *The Last Warning* (1928).

The Last Warning's restricted setting of an opera house interior space is conducive to the "whodunit" character of the film's detective story. After the initial introductory montage sequence setting the scene on New York's Broadway, the audiences—the one in the film and the one watching the film—learn about a mysterious murder case that happens during a live performance of a play called *The Snare*. The lead actor John Woodford (played by D'Arcy Corrigan, who appeared uncredited in *The Man Who Laughs*) suddenly and shockingly dies on-stage and the play ends abruptly. The subsequent bizarre and unexplained disappearance of the body from a room behind the stage creates a veritable scandal. Three of the key suspects, the leading lady Doris Terry (Laura La Plante, who also starred in Leni's *The Cat and the Canary*), the play's director Richard Quayle (John Boles), and its protagonist's understudy Harvey Carleton (Roy D'Arcy) turn out to be involved with Woodford in what was perhaps a love triangle. Yet, they are proven not to be responsible for the body's disappearance. The theater shuts down and is abandoned for years, but the murder remains unsolved and the body has not been found. Arthur McHugh (Montagu Love), a theatrical producer, wants to reopen the theater with plans to stage the same fateful play with as many of the original cast members as possible. When McHugh enters the gloomy, abandoned, cobweb-filled theater, he finds Woodford's former personal assistant roaming around the building and behaving strangely and suspiciously. The original cast and one new actress gather to start rehearsals. Soon, unexplained spirits and threatening letters begin to surround and haunt cast members and producers, creating an eerie atmosphere throughout the back spaces. The warning letters, signed with "John Woodford," are the eponymous last warnings to the crew to refrain from reopening the theater. The investigation of the murder case is complex and, to many film critics reviewing the film at the time of its initial release as well as to observers today, quite confusing with a strong and unnecessary focus on side characters and rather irrelevant and misleading details in inconclusive subplots.

Following the Affrons' influential taxonomy of set designs in cinema, the décor in *The Last Warning* places it into the highest category that they title "Level Five: Set as Narrative."[22] Leni's film matches some of the definitions the Affrons provide for Level Three ("Set as Embellishment") and Level Four ("Set as Artifice"), but the opera house stage and Leni's decision to make this film in the tradition of his earlier *Kammerspielfilme* shift the focus and the attention to the set. The Affrons state that "décor becomes the narrative's organizing image, a figure that stands for the narrative itself."[23] While the camera takes the spectator through various rooms and hidden spaces behind the opera house stage, we are constantly reminded of the interconnectedness of these spaces and thus understand them to be contiguous. In contrast to vast spatial possibilities and freedom of movement in sets, spatial limitations require a high degree of exploitation of available space and thus limit the production designer's and the film director's ingenuity and ability to use the space creatively. Leni negotiated between the spatial constraints and the freedom of movement through the use of a free-floating and constantly roving camera in order to expand the constrained behind-the-stage spaces. Furthermore, the camera expanded space by capturing new corridors, secret staircases, and half-open doors leading to, or at least indicating, additional rooms hidden behind walls and hallways where the immediate action takes place.

In order to understand more fully the ways that Leni used the space of the set that Charles D. Hall had created for a previous film, it is important to examine how camerawork and lighting supported the effective exploitation of space for narrative purposes. When analyzing the function of set design for the narrative and the set's impact on the viewer, it is impossible to separate set design from the overall cinematographic approach that includes lighting and camerawork. The elaborate Broadway montage sequence with its circular movements, moving shapes, flickering neon signs, and illuminated entrance of Woodford Theatre creates a crucial element of exterior space that will, for most of *The Last Warning*, remain off-screen once we enter the building from the street early in the film. The montage sequence focuses on fast-paced circular movements and references the turbulent and dynamic movements in the fairground scenes that introduced films such as *The Cabinet of Dr. Caligari* and *Waxworks*. The montage suggests a vast exterior space in the center of a metropolis, thereby greatly underscoring its opposite space: namely, the confines of a soon-to-be haunted Woodford Theatre. This scene showing the camera approaching the theater's main entrance from the street outside and then cutting to its interior spaces indicates a trespassing of borders between the outside world and the inside world of the theater filled with mystery, murder, ghosts, and an overall strangeness dominating the atmosphere. The scene is thereby reminiscent of scenes that transition from the real to the strange, perhaps most prominently in Murnau's 1922 film *Nosferatu*, when the film's protagonist, the real estate agent Thomas Hutter, crosses a bridge in the Carpathian Mountains and enters the strange lands surrounding Count Orlock's castle. *The Last Warning* cuts from a scene that frames the theater entrance in a static shot to a moving camera floating through the auditorium while leaving behind the outside world of Broadway's neon-lit streets. It subsequently stays inside the theater's gloomy interiors except for a brief sequence depicting the arrival of the coroner to examine the body, and another that shows the theater and neighboring buildings slowly covered by a collage of newspaper headlines related to Woodford's death. The theater's façade aptly resembles a sleeping face, and, after the headlines melt away and the audience learns that the building has been closed for years, the sleeping face portentously reawakens as the shades over its two eye-like windows are rolled up.

Figure 12.2 Character placements in confined spaces: witnesses and suspects in a mysterious murder case in *The Last Warning*.

Several intertitles in *The Last Warning* address aspects of space inside the theater building.[24] "At the end of a secret passage" states an intertitle, suggesting that something might be lurking in the dim corners of a mysterious hallway. Another intertitle exclaims "A sealed door," behind which Woodford's corpse or perhaps his ghost may roam and that begs to be opened. "It's like rifling a tomb—," says Arthur McHugh, "—but I have to do it." Doors, either open, half-open, or closed, are constantly visible in the film and thereby subtly allude to a second off-screen space in addition to the world on the urban streets outside the theater. The rooms behind the stage are shot in such a way that the viewer can see only a fraction of the room, with corners and parts of the room barred from view. Most rooms are cramped and have low ceilings, leaving little to no space for the characters inside. Groups of sometimes up to a dozen characters fill the tight frame in several scenes. Consider, for example, the scene soon after the police arrive at the theater and begin investigations. A medium shot in this scene places potential suspects, witnesses, and police investigators, altogether thirteen people, within the frame. In subsequent shots, the distance between characters and the framing of characters together in two-shots or individually allow, eventually misleading, clues towards characters' relationships and possible motives for the murder. The film continues to take place in mostly tiny rooms, located on at least three different floors in the theater. The theater consists of five or more floors beginning with a level under the stage. Above this ground-level basement floor, the auditorium and the stage constitute the most expansive space. At least three balconies are visible in *The Last Warning*, but, as Heisner states, the sound stage consisted of five balconies and an auditorium that could hold up to 3,000 extras.[25] Behind the theater stage, staircases indicate at least one upper story with perhaps an additional floor on top of that. The film's sequences take place in several individual rooms all over the theater, making the space coherent. However, space expansions are shown step by step, opening up new corridors, stairs, and doors leading to new rooms that may reveal new plot information or carry secrets regarding the mysterious murder case.

The mobile camera functions to smooth transitions between floors and to make the cinematic space—the theater in its entirety—coherent, vast, and imposing despite its numerous individual and mostly confined rooms. In several sequences, the camera floats through space in vertical and horizontal ways in addition to tilting and panning to capture the narrative action. The "nervous mobile camerawork," as Léon Barsacq describes the cinematography in *The Last Warning*, results in the camera taking on a life of its own by constantly drawing attention to itself in effective and self-conscious ways.[26] The camera is placed on a dolly, on a moving trap door on-stage moving downwards into the basement level, on a crane allowing the camera to fly through space, and on a swing above the stage imitating acrobatic movements of a ghostly character on the run. However, this particular sequence captures the swinging character in the frame, thereby giving the camera its own character, as if in the middle of the pursuit through the space above the stage. In a later scene, the camera takes on the point of view of a falling stage prop, simulating the crashing fall onto the stage and barely missing the actors rehearsing the play. Here, the camera is separate from the point of view of any character and gives life to an inanimate object, thereby increasing the overall uncanny atmosphere in what one character calls "the nasty old haunted house." The free-floating camera, while not revolutionary, is still highly remarkable for filmmaking in 1928, when the technical apparatus was still massive in size and weight and usually navigated by one or two groups of crewmembers located immediately next to or near the camera.

In addition to the highly fluid camera movements that make use of confined spaces as much as possible only to highlight the constraints, a good number of camera shots are crucial in emphasizing space. Close-ups, extreme close-ups, and rapid camera movements towards significant objects simulating a technical camera zoom leave little space beyond the captured object. For example, we see extreme close-ups of handwritten notes and other potential, and eventually misleading, clues towards the solution of Woodford's mysterious death and the disappearance of his body. Sudden camera movements towards objects are frequent in *The Last Warning*: for example, a quick movement towards the "Doris Terry" sign on Terry's dressing-room door and a camera's fast leap towards Terry's face as she screams frantically in response to the news that Woodford's body has disappeared. Regular close-ups are used in rather conventional ways typical of early classical filmmaking to show characters' facial reactions, most often expressing astonishment, surprise, and fear, to turns in the plot and new revelations in the ongoing investigations. Close-ups and extreme close-ups fulfill the double function of drawing the viewer's attention to specific plot elements and props in the frame while narrowing space in the frame and thereby increasing the atmosphere of claustrophobia that dominates the narrative action throughout the film.

The claustrophic atmosphere in *The Last Warning* is further accomplished through lighting. The way a film set is lit plays a crucial role in evoking moods, particularly for Leni, who in his theoretical writings on film in the early 1920s always stressed that lighting was as important to the success of a movie as the film's set, acting, and plot. In his 1921 text "Das Bild als Handlung: Der Maler als Regisseur" ("The Image as Plot, the Painter as Director"), Leni wrote:

> Through light and shadows, through limiting or emphasizing must the décor, the scenery, become an active player. The acting persons and the space must become a composition. The image, the moving image, must emerge and trigger the impressions and the mood, in the viewer, which the plot demands.[27]

Leni stressed the point that the set design must merge with the plot so that it becomes the plot itself.[28] Mindful of the Affrons' taxonomy of set design's importance for films, it is safe to argue that the set goes beyond a mere "punctuation" of the narrative, defined as set design functioning as elaborative support of the plot. As a film that fits in the genre of mystery-thriller, *The Last Warning* utilizes set design to thrill the audience. The opera house plays a major part in the film's impact to unsettle the viewer and to create an atmosphere of anxiety and uncanniness. The set is an essential part of the narrative—the film never leaves the confined spaces for more than few brief moments— and presents itself as a coherent and constant presence despite its many individual rooms, staircases, and floors that serve as spatial background for individual scenes. *The Last Warning* falls into what the Affrons call "Set as Narrative," the highest category in their evaluation of the role of set designs in films. "Décor becomes the narrative's organizing image," they state, "a figure that stands for the narrative itself. [It] takes on for the spectator a relationship to the narrative akin to that which it has for the characters."[29] With only two minor sequences plus two rather space-less and extremely stylized montage sequences suggesting the hustle and bustle of nightlife on Broadway, the film's narrative space is for the most part the theater's interior. Furthermore, the Woodford Theatre imposes on its surroundings in the narrative space and greatly impacts the film's few exterior shots. The first exterior shot focuses on the building's façade during the theater's shut-down (that, in its stylization, also resembles a face suggesting a sleeping animate object). The second exterior shot shows the theater from the outside as a source of alarm and panic with emergency personnel and police rushing into the theater. According to interviews and reports about future projects, Universal and Leni had hoped to move away from films with "sets as narrative" with a planned project entitled *The Bargain in the Kremlin* which, according to an early announcement, would have been a "Russian story in which the principal character is a violinist."[30] This and other projects were not realized, at least with Leni in the director's seat, but the release of *The Last Warning* came at a time when the new trend in the industry was to move out of the studios and increase the number of exterior shots by making use of the increasingly professionalized outdoor studio infrastructure and the natural landscapes of California.

Set design's strong ties to other areas in the filmmaking process often blur its important and unique role within each film. Set design is, as Bergfelder and his colleagues have stated, "fundamentally hybrid and fluid" because it cannot effectively function separately from elements such as props, lighting, acting, makeup, costumes, and, as Leni would add, the plot itself.[31] In 1922, Leni compared the various elements of film production to a recipe's ingredients that are all equally essential, emphasizing acting and plot on one hand, and decoration and lighting as part of set design on the other. He stated that "not one is more important than the other. It is the mixture that counts. And the ingredients need to be good: The acting and the set design."[32] Of all of his writings, Leni's 1924 essay "Architecture in Film" ("Baukunst im Film") is perhaps his most precise and the strongest statement about the effect and the importance of lighting and set design in cinema. He advocated for a non-realistic representation of spaces such as building exteriors and interiors in order to place the viewer within the subjective content of the scene, allowing the audience to feel and experience what the protagonists experience. He wrote:

> In order to produce the desired atmosphere, it is not enough to simply copy beautiful spaces of the kind that one finds in castles and people's homes. A decorative concept must draw instead on the emotional content of the scene, producing a composition that hits the right notes.[33]

Leni was less interested in mirroring the splendor of the theatrical set. Instead, he preferred what Jürgen Kasten has called an "architecture of mood," and the cinematic representation of the Woodford Theatre in *The Last Warning* is a representation of subjective experiences, dominated by an air of menace and outright fear of unknown and ghostly forces roaming around the theater space.[34]

Leni gained his reputation as the wizard of light and shadows from his stylistic approach to his previous films, which he outlined in his "Architecture in Film" article:

> Lighting technology has gradually allowed us to create characteristic cityscapes and snapshots of natural landscapes both in the studio and outside. Were the architect to produce a picture-perfect copy, the resulting image in the film would have no identity, no personality of its own. The opportunity must be there to accentuate and give shape to the most essential and characteristic features of a natural object in such a way that they lend the resulting image a particular style and tone.[35]

Dim lighting creates additional barriers and constraints to the lit space in the center of the frame. The non- or minimally lit spaces around the immediate action in several scenes create dark frames and add to the sense of claustrophobia and mysteriousness. This lighting method is reminiscent of the cinematic technique from the 1910s and the early 1920s when iris shots highlighted important objects or characters in the center within a circular frame and blocked out the edges of the image.

Perhaps due to the film's visual and atmospheric links to early 1920s European cinema and especially to the uncanny mystery films that were the staples of Weimar cinema art films at the beginning of the decade, critics in Germany responded to *The Last Warning* with mixed feelings, largely balancing their praise of the acting and set design with a rather negative assessment of the plot. The film's plot was generally perceived as overloaded, too detailed, and misleading. The *Lichtbildbühne*, for instance, noted on August 28, 1929, a day after the film's German premiere at the Ufa-Theater Kurfürstendamm in Berlin, that the film script suffers from an abundance of plot details ("Stoffülle") and consequently from confusion ("Unübersichtlichkeit"). However, the paper praised Leni's set:

> Leni embellished the plot with all the magic of his artistic decorative skills. Only a painter's eye could capture the run-down theater in such stylish details; only a master of seeing finds so many picturesque moments to show ruin and decay.[36]

The *Berliner Börsen-Courier* responded similarly, stating that "wrong leads and coincidental moments confuse the viewer, who does not know in nor out. We are in a maze or in a magic castle." However, the set design and Leni's work as director received high acclaim as a "masterpiece."[37]

The overall sense of the film's reception, both in the US and abroad, is that *The Last Warning* somehow missed the new trends in Hollywood's emerging boom years. The set design, while impressive and noteworthy, turned into a burden for this film through its retrograde and somewhat foreign feel during a crucial moment of fast-paced technological advancements in Hollywood. Yet, the film's effort to evoke the antiquated feel of the Woodford Theatre in the way Camp described it in *The House of Fear* is laudable. Consider Camp's characterization:

> Woodford's blind exterior appeared to repel the thought of intrusion. It had an air of asking to be left alone in its decay. The anxious northward march of theatrical prosperity had long deserted it. On one side it was flanked by a towering loft building. A motion-picture house nestled impudently close on the other. From such surroundings, although it was no more than sixty years old, the structure projected an atmosphere of antiquity as arresting as that which reaches one from a mediæval castle in some foreign countryside.[38]

In this quote from the 1916 novel, Camp describes the rather old-fashioned architecture of a classical theater built for live stage performances and indicates its sense of displacement in light of a new, emerging entertainment industry: the movies. The theater set used in *The Last Warning* becomes an obstacle and a heavy burden linked to the old world, in terms of both filmmaking and geography. In this respect, the set embodies the past in a film that was released in a time when émigré filmmakers had to adapt and reinvent themselves to address the more light-hearted taste of US audiences and the commercial nature of the Hollywood industry. As Graham Petrie has pointed out, films by émigré filmmakers around this time are meaningful contributions to cinema, yet they usually missed the financial expectations in a time of heightened pressure on studios to produce commercial successes.[39] The common trajectory of directors like Paul Leni, Benjamin Christensen, Paul Fejos, and Mauritz Stiller was to be free to produce their first Hollywood films according to their own creative ambitions and style to often rather mediocre financial success. With increasing financial pressures on the large studios in an increasingly competitive environment towards the beginning of the 1930s, the foreign directors had to either adapt or—what was most often the case—break with the studio.[40]

Leni was aware of the impending changes that were in the air. In its magazine, Universal stressed that Leni's film projects following *The Last Warning* would mean a clear departure in style and theme. *Universal Weekly* quotes Leni stating, "I don't want to be associated with the lights and shadows and spooky corridors. They just happened. My next picture will be different. Whatever it is, the setting will be harmonious, not of major importance."[41] As if to show

how crucial this departure would be for the sake of Leni's career and for the studio's future trajectory going into the 1930s, the article made the following point:

> Leni has evoked warm praise for his direction of mystery films. He prefers other types of pictures. He is associated with the successful creation of atmosphere. He impishly asserts that he would like to direct a picture with no atmosphere and terrible settings.[42]

The Last Warning must be considered a key example of a film whose production and release fall into a crucial transitional era in Hollywood. The era of silent horror ended, but as Gerd Gemünden has pointed out, "the stage had been set for the genre's future growth."[43] One could even go further, as Petrie did, in assessing the particular importance of Leni's unique Hollywood films and argue that his visual style "was to be a major link between the visual richness and daring of the finest works of the late silent era and the film noirs of [Robert] Siodmak and others in the 1940s."[44] Despite the fact that the intricate and labyrinthine set of *The Last Warning* is a crucial tool in developing the suspenseful detective story, the set is also indicative of the transitions from European to American filmmaking styles that were underway in 1929. Leni's last film marks a farewell to a certain way Hollywood films were made and designed, the beginnings of a farewell to German influence in Hollywood, and an unfortunate and untimely farewell to Paul Leni, whose death just three months after the film's German premiere meant that he would neither witness nor directly contribute to shaping Universal's future at the brink of the next level of rapidly developing American filmmaking, the Golden Age of Hollywood.

NOTES

1. "The Laemmle Specials—a New Universal Brand," *Exhibitors Herald and Moving Picture World*, April 28, 1928.
2. *The Man Who Laughs* received mostly mediocre reviews and was a commercial failure for Universal Studios. Yet, Leni was widely celebrated for his mastery of light and shadows and reviewers applauded particularly the film's set design.
3. In an almost uncanny coincidence, three of the five most prominent émigré directors of the silent era—namely, F. W. Murnau, Mauritz Stiller, and Leni—were to pass away prematurely around the time when sound film became the norm.
4. Leni quoted in James Hood MacFarland, "Leni Likens Film Game to Spirited Tennis Tilt," *Universal Weekly*, January 26, 1929.
5. Tim Bergfelder, Sue Harris, and Sarah Street, *Film Architecture and the Transnational Imagination: Set Design in 1930s European Cinema* (Amsterdam: Amsterdam University Press, 2007), 25.

6. Paul Fejos's *The Last Performance* (1929) with Bela Lugosi was partly shot on this set, located on Stage 28 at Universal Studios. The Royal Albert Hall sequence in Tod Browning's *Dracula* (1931), again with Lugosi, was shot here as were parts of James Whale's 1935 film *Bride of Frankenstein*. Elements of the iconic set, also known as the "Phantom Stage," served as a stop on the Universal studio tour until all remaining parts were eventually demolished in 2014.
7. Charles Affron and Mirella Jona Affron, *Sets in Motion: Art Direction and Film Narrative* (New Brunswick, NJ: Rutgers University Press, 1995), 6.
8. "Picture That Eats Up Carl Laemmle's Money," *Film Spectator*, March 31, 1928.
9. *The Last Warning* was released in at least two different versions when it premiered in 1929: a now lost part-talkie version, announced in ads with the remark "50 per cent talk," and a surviving silent version with sound effects, which in 2016 was restored and shown at special screenings in selected cities.
10. Gerald Bordman, *American Theatre: A Chronicle of Comedy and Drama 1914-1930* (Oxford: Oxford University Press, 1995), 190. Fallon's adaptation was reportedly widely praised by critics. For a sample review, see George Jean Nathan, "The Critic as Idiot," *The Judge*, August 26, 1922, 11.
11. For more on the studios' emphasis on modern designs, see Donald Albrecht, *Designing Dreams: Modern Architecture in the Movies* (New York: Harper & Row, 1986), 75-108.
12. Richard Koszarski, *An Evening's Entertainment: The Age of the Silent Feature Picture 1915-1928* (Berkeley: University of California Press, 1994), 236.
13. Mark Shiel, "Classical Hollywood 1928–1946," in *Art Direction and Production Design*, ed. Lucy Fischer (New Brunswick, NJ: Rutgers University Press, 2015), 50.
14. Charles D. Hall oversaw the sets for three of Leni's four films for Universal: *The Cat and the Canary*, *The Man Who Laughs*, and *The Last Warning*. For a detailed history of the role of art departments at Universal, see Beverly Heisner, *Hollywood Art: Art Direction in the Days of the Great Studios* (Jefferson, NC: McFarland, 1990), 25–40.
15. According to the *Variety* film critic, twenty-five minutes of the now lost semi-sound version were spoken dialogue. See "The Last Warning," *Variety*, January 9, 1929.
16. Mordaunt Hall, "The Screen," *New York Times*, January 7, 1929.
17. "The Shadow Stage," *Photoplay*, February 1929, 76.
18. "The Last Warning," *Variety*.
19. Ian Conrich, "Before Sound: Universal, Silent Cinema, and the Last of the Horror-Spectaculars," in *The Horror Film*, ed. Stephen Prince (New Brunswick, NJ: Rutgers University Press, 2004), 44.
20. Koszarski, *Evening's Entertainment*, 236. It is estimated that Carl Laemmle, founder and president of Universal Pictures Corporation, employed around seventy European relatives, for whom he had tirelessly written affidavits. See Bastian Heinsohn, "Carl Laemmle's Protégés: Everyday Life in Exile after Escaping Nazi Germany through Help from Hollywood's Film Mogul," in *Exile and Everyday Life*, ed. Andrea Hammel and Anthony Grenville (Leiden: Brill Rodopi, 2015), 85–106. For more information on how Laemmle accommodated friends and family members at Universal Studios, see Bernard F. Dick, *City of Dreams: The Making and Remaking of Universal Pictures* (Lexington: University of Kentucky Press, 1997), 58–72.
21. Nevertheless, the Expressionistic iconography remained strong in the horror comedies, as can be seen, for instance, in *Dracula*, *Frankenstein*, and *Bride of Frankenstein*. Whereas *The Old Dark House* falls into the category of a horror-comedy, *Frankenstein* may serve as a bridge film between a serious uncanniness in Universal's horror films and the light-hearted horror-comedies that were to follow. As *New York Times* critic Mordaunt Hall wrote after the film's premiere, *Frankenstein* allowed the audience chills mixed with

comedic entertainment; he described the film as "one that aroused so much excitement at the Mayfair yesterday that many in the audience laughed to cover their true feelings." See Mordaunt Hall, "The Screen," *New York Times*, December 5, 1931.
22. Among the Affrons' film examples that fall into this category are *Mr. Smith Goes to Washington* (1939), set in and around a public chamber; *Rebecca* (1940), set in a castle; *Grand Hotel* (1932), set in a Berlin hotel; and *Le jour se lève* (1939), set in a single room.
23. Affron and Affron, *Sets in Motion*, 159.
24. The film still in Figure 12.2 from *The Last Warning* is from the restored version, kindly made available to the author as a personalized DVD screener by NBC Universal in Los Angeles.
25. Heisner, *Hollywood Art*, 280.
26. Léon Barsacq, *Caligari's Cabinet and Other Grand Illusions: A History of Film Design*, rev. and ed. Elliott Stein (Boston: New York Graphic Society, 1976), 222.
27. Paul Leni, "Das Bild als Handlung: Der Maler als Regisseur," reprinted in *Paul Leni: Grafik, Theater, Film*, ed. Hans-Michael Bock (Frankfurt am Main: Deutsches Filmmuseum, 1986), 12–14.
28. Leni, "Das Bild," 12–14.
29. Affron and Affron, *Sets in Motion*, 158.
30. "Leni Leaves for Universal City to Make 'Bargain in the Kremlin,'" *Universal Weekly*, January 26, 1929.
31. Bergfelder et al., *Film Architecture*, 15.
32. Paul Leni, "Ausstattung/Spiel," *Der Kinematograph*, January 29, 1922, reprinted in Bock, *Paul Leni*, 122–3.
33. Paul Leni, "Baukunst im Film," *Der Kinematograph*, August 4, 1924, reprinted as "Architecture in Film," in *The Promise of Cinema: German Film Theory 1907–1933*, ed. Anton Kaes, Nicholas Baer, and Michael Cowan (Oakland: University of California Press, 2016), 500.
34. Jürgen Kasten, "Episodic Patchwork: The Bric-à-Brac Principle in Paul Leni's *Waxworks*," in *Expressionist Film: New Perspectives*, ed. Dietrich Scheunemann (Rochester, NY: Camden House, 2003), 177.
35. Leni, "Baukunst im Film," 500.
36. Review of *Die letzte Warnung* (*The Last Warning*), *Lichtbildbühne*, August 29, 1929, reprinted in Bock, *Paul Leni*, 317.
37. All untitled reviews are reprinted in Bock, *Paul Leni*, 316–19.
38. Wadsworth Camp, *The House of Fear* (New York: Doubleday, Page, 1916), 5.
39. Graham Petrie, *Hollywood Destinies: European Directors in America, 1922–1931*, rev. edn. (Detroit: Wayne State University Press, 2002), 166.
40. Petrie, *Hollywood Destinies*, 166.
41. Gertrude Warburton, "Watch Paul Leni!" *Universal Weekly*, January 12, 1929.
42. Warburton, "Watch Paul Leni!"
43. Gerd Gemünden, "Parallel Modernities: From Haunted Screen to Universal Horror," in *Generic Histories of German Cinema: Genre and Its Deviations*, ed. Jaimey Fisher (Rochester, NY: Camden House, 2013), 31.
44. Petrie, *Hollywood Destinies*, 217.

CHAPTER 13

The Last Warning: Uncertainty, Exploitation, and Horror

Shawn Shimpach

The Last Warning (1929), which would prove to be Paul Leni's final film, stands as a visually bold and entertaining tribute to the encounter between German Expressionism and Hollywood style. Based on Thomas Fallon's 1922 stage play of the same name and Wadsworth Camp's 1916 novel *The House of Fear*,[1] *The Last Warning* is also situated at the intersection of silent and sound cinema; one version of the film was among the last silent films produced by Universal Pictures, while another was one of the studio's first lip-synchronized motion pictures. Its production was supervised by a rising member of the next generation of film producers, the first to grow up with movies: Carl Laemmle, Jr., barely out of his teens.

The Last Warning thus occupies a liminal position in the history of Hollywood. Neither fully representing the end of an era nor quite signaling the start of the next, it may be productively understood to sit between eras, bridging a number of changing Hollywood practices. This bridging is clear from a variety of factors, including Universal's production of silent and synchronized-sound versions of *The Last Warning* and the various exhibition configurations in which the film was shown: sometimes as the evening's feature accompanied by one or several short subjects, sometimes sharing the proscenium with any number of various live acts and other entertainments. It is also clear from the range of already dated yet in some ways prescient "exploitations" employed to entice viewers to the theaters in which it was screening. In other words, this bridging of eras is apparent when considering the strategies informing the film's production and exhibition, which foreshadow the ways Hollywood would deal with and be shaped by extreme uncertainty about its product, future, and especially its audience in the decades to come. As William Paul has observed of a different, and later, radical break with past exhibition practices, "the manner in which films are presented to the audience effectively tells us something about who Hollywood thinks its audience is."[2] The manner in which *The Last Warning* was presented to the audience may indeed tell us something about how Hollywood imagined its audience during this transition from silent to sound and into the classical studio era. In the case of *The Last Warning*, however, it may also demonstrate the confusion Universal was experiencing about who its audiences were at the time and how to reach them.

Stylishly winking and self-aware, *The Last Warning* makes for a superbly apt example of the complexity of overlapping residual and emerging practices in filmmaking and exhibition during this transitional period. It is a film in which a murder occurs on-stage in a Broadway theater before a capacity audience, but despite the horrified, bewildered, and yet intrigued reactions of all those witnesses, the narrative moves quickly to suggest that the real story and all the excitement, romance, mystery, and horror are occurring backstage, just beyond the audience's view. Similarly, despite a mysterious narrative, impressive aesthetic and technical achievements, and a cast of appealing actors, the challenges faced and tricks used to produce and promote *The Last Warning*, behind the scenes as it were, are perhaps even more fascinating and historically telling than the resulting film itself.

SOUND

The Last Warning's production came about during heightened uncertainty resulting from motion picture audiences' eager response to synchronized-sound films. Following the cultural phenomenon and financial success of Warner Bros. Pictures' 1927 film *The Jazz Singer*, which featured a synchronized musical soundtrack and included a couple of dazzling, apparently improvised short sequences of lip-synchronous singing and dialogue, excitement among filmgoers swelled for seemingly any film that featured actors whose speaking could be heard. Demand for sound films was sudden, decisive, and something of a surprise to many (although surely not all) working in the motion picture industry.

Carl Laemmle had been one of the original independents, promoting the role of movie stars, challenging and eventually defeating Thomas Edison's film trust, the Motion Picture Patents Company, and finally founding Universal Pictures from his previous company, the Independent Moving Pictures Company (IMP). By the end of the 1920s, Laemmle had gained a reputation for nepotism that earned him the nickname "Uncle Carl" on the studio lot and culminated in the appointment of his son, Carl Laemmle, Jr. (also known as "Junior Laemmle") to chief of production at age twenty-one in 1928. While establishing this lineage for his legacy, Carl Sr. was apparently skeptical and reluctant to reinvent his business (and invest in the elaborate and expensive equipment needed) to produce synchronized-sound movies. Though audience demand and competing studios soon made the production of sound movies unavoidable, Laemmle was nonetheless defiant. "No Universal picture must depend upon the novelty of sound and dialogue to get by. Each picture must stand on its own feet as excellent entertainment," he declared. "All the music, or sound or talking in the world will not take the place of the four cardinal principles of the motion picture—story—direction—action—photography."[3] Donald Crafton observed that Universal's most reliable exhibitors were rural and small-town theaters, many of which were having difficulty affording the expensive and time-consuming conversion to sound. Laemmle, Crafton noted, "advertised his commitment to silent as a sign of support for the small theater by taking an oath that Universal would never stop making the old kind of films."[4] In a 1929 issue of *Film Daily*, Laemmle wrote: "I am not one of those who believes that talking pictures sound the doom of silent pictures."[5] Universal was therefore somewhat slow, reluctant, and halting in its adoption of what Laemmle and others thought and hoped was merely a fad: synchronized-sound movies.

Charged with directing his first "partial-talkie,"[6] meanwhile, Paul Leni took a more measured, although not entirely embracing, view of synchronized-sound films. Around the time of *The Last Warning*'s release, he remarked to a reporter that synchronous sound was still in its infancy:

> Sound is like a baby now. Everyone is watching it, criticizing it, over-concerned with it. If an old man crossed a crowded street, no one would pay any attention to him. If a baby tried such a crossing, everyone would shout. Sound pictures are like that. They will grow up in time and be healthy adults. They will add dramatic value to certain types of films. They will not be suitable to others. I believe in time that people will take sound for granted.[7]

Awkwardly enacting this measured response, *The Last Warning* was ultimately produced in dual versions, released as both a silent film, complete with occasionally stylized intertitles to convey dialogue, and as a sound film with some lip-synchronized dialogue sections, accompanying music, screams, and appropriately scary sound effects. This approach and the views expressed by Leni were not as hedging as they may appear today. It was not uncommon for silent and sound versions of the same film to be produced and distributed during this time. As Crafton reminded us,

> though it is easy to look back at the heyday of the dual version (roughly 1928 through mid-1930) and see it as a transitional stage, this view is not quite accurate. For a while many in the Hollywood establishment envisioned a permanent state of coexistence in which silent and sound production would reach a state of balanced equilibrium.[8]

The Last Warning was one of a host of films during this brief era—as theaters throughout the country invested in sound playback equipment—to either hedge its bets or strive for equilibrium. It took two simultaneous approaches to reaching its audience during a time of rapid upheaval and extreme uncertainty.

If Leni advocated a balance between silence and sound, this does not seem to have been his approach to the actual production of *The Last Warning*. The film's flamboyant cinematography is the work of Hal Mohr, who, years later, recalled working with Leni, whose director's chair had

> a hand-crank siren screwed on one side of it; in the pocket of it he had a couple of pistols loaded with blank cartridges; he had a police whistle, a thing around his neck, and a, oh, a big bronze Chinese gong-type of thing alongside of the chair . . . It was supposed to be a haunted theater, and he had these wild chases through the thing. It was like a three-ring circus. When he was directing a scene you would hear the siren going, the whistle blowing, beating the hell out of the gong, pistol shots all over the place. That was Leni's way of directing.[9]

Clearly the transition to a mode of production in which sound equipment and the camera would be recording simultaneously would impose new restrictions on some directing habits, yet audience demand for sound could not be disregarded.

The sound version of the film is today apparently no longer extant. All reports indicate that it ran several minutes longer than the silent version, with approximately twenty-five minutes' worth of synchronized dialogue at the start and near the end of the film; thus, it was only a partial "talkie." Most trade-press reviews of the film suggested the lip-synchronous sequences slowed the film's pacing considerably and added little to the narrative or characterizations. Even a journal advocating for recorded sound use, *Sound Waves*, declared *The Last Warning* "a hard one to swallow after seeing some good talking pictures." *Variety* meanwhile declared it "a thrill picture running too long to attain its full effect, and not a good talker in the final analysis." *Variety* wrote that Leni "has way overdone it in footage" and blamed the prolonged running time of eighty-seven minutes on the "footage necessary when the characters speak," concluding that "Leni should learn that dialog must have pace." *Film Daily* summarized the film as rehashing "all the old stuff but Leni's atmospheric direction keeps it interesting," while also noting its "poor sound effects." Newspaper reviews often drew similar conclusions. For instance, the *New York Times* argued "there are too many outbursts of shrieking, merely to prove the effect of the audible screen, to cause any spine-chilling among those watching this production," while the *New York Evening Journal* concluded, "while the cast does good work and Leni's effects are excellent, the development of the story sags, partly because of several inexpertly added talking and sound sequences."[10]

Yet the overwhelming audience interest in synchronized-sound films during this era led exhibitors and fans to be more likely to embrace the sound elements. *Exhibitors Herald and Moving Picture World*, for example, insisted that "sound effects are just naturally adapted to the business of mystery pictures, and as a result, *The Last Warning* is likely to out-thrill Universal's earlier chill-drama *The Cat and the Canary*."[11] *Harrison's Reports*, a publication describing itself as "a motion picture reviewing service by a former exhibitor devoted exclusively to the interests of exhibitors," agreed, noting that

> because of the fact that it has been synchronized with music, has been fitted with sound effects and the characters are made to talk in several of the situations, its value as a mystery melodrama is naturally enhanced; it should appeal to the picture-going public better.[12]

Even *Variety* acknowledged the audience demand for sound films, allowing, despite its criticism of the film as "not a good talker," that "on the other hand, it is a talker." Meanwhile the fan-oriented magazine *Motion Picture* suggested, amid the nation's ongoing Prohibition era, that it was worth seeking out the sound version of *The Last Warning* because "a mystery picture without sound is like ginger ale without gin. It simply hasn't any kick."[13]

Despite such mixed review results for the addition of synchronized sound, ambivalently undertaken in this case, the very fact that a synchronized-sound version was produced along with the silent version attests to the power of audience demand and the ambivalence in addressing audiences during a time of transition.

THEATERS

The advent of synchronized-sound filmmaking was not the only reason for Universal to feel uncertain about its audiences. Although Universal was one of the oldest of the eight major studios of the studio era, it is considered, along with Columbia and United Artists, one of the "little three" for lack of ownership of any theater chains. Realizing this shortcoming too late, Universal had in fact invested in a theater chain in 1925 through a financial reorganization, but the investment proved both too little and too late and by 1927 Universal had begun to sell off this chain.[14] By the time *The Last Warning* was officially released, following a few select preview screenings on Christmas Day 1928, Universal had only a single first-run theater in

New York City, the Colony Theater on Broadway and 53rd Street, which it was leasing from B. S. Moss. *The Last Warning* was booked there in its prestige feature debut on January 6, 1929.

This lack of successful owned-and-operated exhibition outlets combined with rising production costs to limit Universal's profits, making the effective marketing of its films all the more essential. By the end of the 1920s, Universal was known for producing low- to mid-budget genre films and "B" pictures. Carl Laemmle had used Woolworth's as a metaphor to describe Universal's success in the 1920s "through the merchandising of vast quantities of cheap goods."[15] Yet cheap goods were inherently limiting, particularly since the transition to sound required greater investment, distinct audience appeals, nimble adjustments, and, for a while, dual versions of the same film. Adding to the turmoil was the era's still wildly varied exhibition practices, over which Universal had quite limited control and which were in any case disrupted by the transition to sound film. Throughout the silent era, the experience of a single film would differ depending on where and when it was viewed. Theaters, rather than filmmakers, supplied sound to accompany films, utilizing phonographs, pianos, fiddles, squeeze boxes, all the way up to entire orchestras. Some theaters added their own sound effects to accompany action on the screen, even live narrators to explain events and perhaps speak some improvised dialogue. Each theater would provide a different experience of the same movie. Some films were distributed with commissioned scores in an attempt to provide consistency of experience as well as associate particular tunes with the film for promotional purposes. As producers began experimenting with the transition to synchronized sound, the viewing experience remained inconsistent with some films featuring synchronized music and effects and eventually dialogue in some locations, while playing as a silent film in theaters not yet wired for sound or wired for a different sound system.[16] At the same time, many theaters did not restrict their shows to motion pictures exclusively but combined the screenings of full-length and short films with live performances ranging from musicians to contortionists to animal acts. Leni himself had earlier been involved in the production of live prologues for feature film premieres. The context of reception was out of the control of a film's producers and varied dramatically from locale to locale.

In the case of *The Last Warning*, the result was a wide range of potential viewing experiences. In Seattle, for example, the sound version of the film topped a program of otherwise live vaudeville stage performers.[17] In Birmingham, Alabama and Springfield, Massachusetts, it played with filmed comedy shorts and news reels, but no live acts. In Rochester, New York, it screened with a short, a newsreel, and six acts of vaudeville. In Baltimore, Maryland, it screened with an episode of the *Tarzan* serial, a newsreel, and five acts of RKO vaudeville.[18] In Richmond, Virginia, meanwhile, the silent version played, accompanied by an organ, along with a newsreel and two acts.[19] In Chattanooga, Tennessee, the silent version was accompanied by an orchestra and screened along with four live acts. In Portland, Oregon, *The Last Warning* headed a bill that also included five varied vaudeville acts, "with attendance all that could be desired."[20] Finally, in New York City, a *Motion Picture News* headline complained that "stage entertainment weakens appeal of feature and good short" at the Colony Theater, elaborating on a showing of *The Last Warning*:

> The feature runs for an hour and 25 minutes. Then there are 25 minutes given over to Jimmy Carr and his orchestra, nine minutes to one of the Walter Futter *Curiosities* and seven minutes to a Castle short, *Down Hawaii Way*, in color that was most effective.
>
> In addition to the Jimmy Carr orchestra there were the Earle Bros., a team of dancing boys who showed little, and a girl by the name of Maud Linde with a contortionistic offering. The latter was decidedly out of place for a Broadway picture house and smacked decidedly of burlesque.[21]

Viewing contexts varied widely from theater to theater. For a studio like Universal, without its own theaters, the mercy and the whim of exhibitors added to the uncertainty of the audience's response to their filmmaking. This was further exasperated by the methods theaters employed to attract audiences. In an effort to provide some regularity, however, Universal was not yet averse to involving itself in these adventures of movie exploitation.

EXPLOITATION

Throughout the 1920s, studios, producers, and theaters used a variety of forms of advertising, publicity, and showmanship to attract the attention of potential audiences. Most of what is now referred to as marketing might have been labeled exploitation during this era as the term became widely used and applied. *Universal Weekly*, an insider industry newspaper Universal Pictures produced and published for its exhibitors, noted simply that "exploitation enters into every modern business . . . In the motion picture industry, however, it is as important a factor as the product itself." This was from a special issued dedicated explicitly to exploitation that included within its pages "the benefit of concentrated exploitation, such as heralds, complete campaigns and posters."[22]

Figure 13.1 A poster designed by Paul Leni, director of *The Last Warning*.

Indeed, theaters, theater chains, movie producers, studios, and press agents would often undertake spectacular stunts to achieve publicity for their film. As Koszarski summarized:

> Throughout the twenties, pressbooks and trade papers were filled with suggestions for bizarre "exploitation tips." An exhibitor might be urged to rush an ambulance to his theater, which would carry off on a stretcher a "raving maniac," driven crazy from laughing at the comedy featured inside. Ukulele competitions, elaborate parade floats, and mysterious contests and giveaways seem to have been standard local fare. Trade papers were filled with photos and letters from exhibitors across the country proudly displaying some new exploitation stunt.[23]

For most industry trade publications, exploitation was considered central to the film exhibition business. *Motion Picture News*, for example, ran a regular section featuring "exhibitor ad tips" as well as exhibition statistics for films currently in release under the headline "Exploitation Hints on All Films." *Film Daily* ran a regular column featuring "tips which mean dollars for showmen" under the unsubtle heading "Exploit-O-Grams."

Universal Pictures was a willing participant in certain kinds of exploitation for its films. For example, it encouraged exhibitors showing Leni's film *The Man Who Laughs*, still in theaters at the start of 1929, to participate in a studio-sponsored contest seeking the best answer to the question, "Why do alluring women love homely men?" To increase participation and attract crowds at the movie theaters, "$2000 in cash prizes are being offered to the general public by Universal for the best answers to the question." To be certain the point was clear, the studio's trade press ads noted that "it's a knockout exploitation idea for exhibitors."[24] Koszarski concluded simply that "Today it is hard to weigh the value of such exhibitor stunts, but they were highly regarded at the time. It was even considered possible for stunts alone to make a theater competitive."[25]

In November 1928, Universal signed press agent Harry Reichenbach to a brief exclusive contract for work on publicity ideas, "in full harmony with the present publicity, advertising and exploitation departments."[26] Press agents were regularly employed to mastermind many of these stunts and contests to assure maximum exposure and publicity. Reichenbach, however, was perhaps the "most notorious of them all"[27] having already gained fame (or infamy) for his extreme exploitation stunts which reportedly included letting loose a live lion inside New York's Belleclaire Hotel to promote a *Tarzan* movie, encouraging Rudolph Valentino to grow a beard and capitalize on the controversy among fans, and tricking reporters and the New York City police department into dragging the Central Park reservoir for a supposedly lost Turkish virgin to publicize release of Universal's 1920 Tod Browning film *The Virgin of Stamboul*. In the fall of 1928, he began work on *The Last Warning* among other soon-to-be-released pictures.[28]

Before *The Last Warning*'s premiere, Reichenbach had already been engaged in exploitation stunts on behalf of the film. *Exhibitors Herald and Moving Picture World* ran a story about a letter sent to exhibitors involving *The Last Warning* that drew the police to Reichenbach's offices and led to a "boy" being fired from Reichenbach's employ. Reichenbach, described as an "exploiter deluxe," claimed innocence in this stunt, in which a letter, mimeographed but in longhand and signed by the fictitious "Richard Quaile," was mailed to small-town exhibitors and appeared to threaten "not only your theatre, but your very existence," concluding, in part, "this is the last warning I can give you." Reichenbach blamed a "boy in his office" for what he called this poor attempt at publicity. Universal claimed no knowledge of Reichenbach's activities, insisting "he works independently from his department as special Universal exploitation man." In any event, the article about the stunt gave (perhaps dubious) publicity to Reichenbach and the forthcoming *The Last Warning*.[29]

With or without press agents involved, however, Laemmle was not often afraid to have his own name associated with exploitation of a certain kind for the films he was producing, particularly when it involved a hard sell to exhibitors. One ad, appearing at the start of 1929 in trade journals, was part of a series designed to appear as if written quickly by Laemmle himself ("Straight from the Shoulder Talk by Carl Laemmle") and was directed to exhibitors. It implored theater managers not to overlook *The Last Warning*. The lengthy missive was headlined "Warning!" and included the following selling points:

> Whether you get *The Last Warning* in synchronized or silent form, get it—that's the main point, get it! . . . All the psychology of years of showmanship experience has been brought to bear in the making of *The Last Warning*. Every trick of the camera and every new idea of group and stage lighting has been employed with the utmost skill. It is a gem of a story, done in the ultra modern manner—and you can take vast amount of pride in showing it to your public. The first and most important thing is to be dead sure that you get it. The second and next most important thing is to give it an advertising campaign worthy of such a production.[30]

This was a hard-sell ad from a "little three" Hollywood studio, signed by its president, concerned about getting exhibitors on board and noting exploitable aspects of the film. It encouraged further exploitation, assuring ambivalent exhibitors, "Your audience will tell you 'That's the kind of stuff we want. Give us more like that.'"[31]

Additional exploitation took on a number of forms, both local and national, subtle and outrageous. Some simply implied exploitable content and relied on the power of the exclamation point. An ad for the Strand Theater, for example, enticed viewers to *The Last Warning* by declaring, "Beware! Excitement Awaits You! Eerie mystery that will send shivers down your spine!" Universal's full-page ad for the film similarly exclaimed, "Featuring Mystery! Drama! Chills! Excitement! Suspense! Action!" Both repeated the tagline "the picture of a thousand thrills." The *Motion Picture News* column "Live Exploitation Tips from Exhibitors" recommended that theaters "exploit it as the original all talkie crook play."[32] The manager of the Keith-Albee Theater in Boston similarly suggested promoting the film as the "first all-talking mystery of screen."[33] The *Exhibitors Herald-World* reported from Chicago, meanwhile, that "over 2000 people attended the midnight showing of Universal's *Last Warning* at the Chicago theatre on January 12."[34]

More extensive exploitation stunts were constructed around the expansive punning possibilities of the film's title as much as its content. The publicity manager of the State Theater in Toledo recommended his strategy of a teaser campaign, "including billboards shrieking, 'Gamblers, this is the last warning!', and 'Speeders, this is the last warning!', [which worked] to good effect in connection with the newspaper advertising."[35] Similarly, *The Last Warning* was given "unusual exploitation" in New Haven with newspaper ads running for five days prior to the first screening in multiple newspapers in the area. The first read "This is the First Warning," the second read "This is the Second Warning," and then "The Last Warning" was directed to targeted groups—doctors, bootleggers, pedestrians, and "speeders"—until the day before the opening night when ads read "See The Last Warning Ad on page 4." A version of this "teaser" for the film, "a natural for exploitation," was suggested in *Universal Weekly*,

Figure 13.2 A natural for exploitation.

in which "Exploiteer [Ralph] Ravenscroft has devised a throwaway card series" punning on the title until it is revealed to be a movie.[36]

Movie star Laura La Plante and her role in *The Last Warning* were also widely exploited. In Syracuse, the local *Herald* newspaper helped promote the "blonde matinee" screening stunt, thought up by Universal exploiteer Lee D. Balsly, in which "the idea was to select the blonde [in the audience] who most closely resembled Miss La Plante." Apparently, nearly 500 blondes attended that screening of *The Last Warning*. The *Herald* encouraged "all blondes between the ages of five and 50" to attend through an invitation evidently written by La Plante. As filmgoers entered the lobby, "the judges were busy selecting a group of 11, two of which were finally chosen as most closely resembling Laura La Plante."[37]

A newspaper in New Haven, meanwhile, assisted in a dress-designing contest "using Laura La Plante's figure" which received more than 1,500 responses. Reportedly, the window where the winning drawings were displayed blocked traffic all day. The theater, meanwhile, cold-called townspeople with the message, "Olympia Theatre Calling. This is the 'Last Warning,'" and then hung up. This strategy was combined with radio programming, lobby hangers, and 5,000 ballots distributed door to door to publicize the film.[38]

Finally, genre aspects of the film were exploited as well. In Pittsburgh, the Stanley Theater "devised the gag of having the fans write the dialogue for six silent scenes in the picture" for cash prizes. The *Pittsburgh Press* played along, running the contest all week along with stills from *The Last Warning*.[39] The

Film Daily noted "a gag used on Universal's mystery film, *The Last Warning*," was a jury ballot given to audience members as they entered, containing pictures of the film's cast with corresponding numbers. "The idea is to turn on the house lights at the point in the film where the theater is closed for five years and ask the audience to vote who committed the murder." It was recommended that prizes be offered for the correct answer. Exhibitors were assured that

> the stunt has proved inexpensive as well as exciting because very few patrons light on the real murderer. The ballot requests patrons keep the solution a secret, which stimulates word-of-mouth publicity. The name and address on the ballot is valuable for the theater's mailing list.[40]

Such varied exploitations—playing on the film's title, involving the audience in directly or tangentially related activities and contests, even threatening lawbreakers and, apparently in one case, theater owners—constituted an important aspect of *The Last Warning*'s marketing, along with newspaper advertising, posters, and the familiar elements of the film to draw audiences. This exploitation was prevalent and commonplace as part of film exhibition publicity, even as it struck a slightly desperate note in attempting to attract audiences through publicity and relied at times only loosely on the film's content as a source of exploitation.

Yet by 1929, *Motion Picture News* was among a number of industry trade publications losing patience with the term. "Exploitation, in this industry, is a

Figure 13.3 Jury ballot to be given to patrons.

much-abused term. The word itself has come to be a bromide, because it has been employed to cover almost everything that has to do with many angles of the business," wrote *Motion Picture News*'s William Johnston, who also noted that exploitation had come to include virtually all the means a theater manager "actually employs to attract the public to his house."[41] Reading between the lines of this exasperation, however, it is possible to glean a growing desire to distance the industry from the associations exploitation implied, arriving, as it did, from a long tradition of entertainment "ballyhoo" dating to carnival barkers, nineteenth-century showmen, and the attractions of the midway. Indeed, "exploitation" was a term whose legacy carried with it class and taste associations Hollywood was becoming eager to leave behind.

Even as *The Last Warning* and most other releases of 1929 enjoyed the exploitation efforts of studios, press agents, and especially theaters, a *Motion Picture News* feature article reported on the decline of what it called the "This is No Bull" school of ballyhoo. The journal insisted instead that in successful movie promotion, "certain standards of good taste figure as importantly in the results obtained as the novelty of the basic idea on which the stunt or the campaign is built." Elaborating on the distinction and hinting at the direction the industry more broadly wished to proceed, the article dryly noted:

> The theatres themselves are so far removed from the circus wagon idea of flash that yokel ideas of what constitutes news or spectacle fail utterly to increase the immediate returns of a picture theatre resorting to them in an effort to drum up trade.[42]

In the realm of exploitation, *The Last Warning* was again straddling a transition in film history. It was released into an environment in which theaters still controlled not only a widely varied range of screening conditions and contexts but also much of the publicity, exploitation, and ballyhoo for promoting a film. Exploitation would again transform and expand as a Hollywood practice following industry upheavals and uncertainly about audiences in the 1950s and again in the 1970s, eventually becoming an internalized part of New Hollywood filmmaking. Exploitation in this sense is not a label, but rather a logic. Aspects of *The Last Warning*'s production foreshadow Hollywood's internalization of this logic.

TYPE

It is not an accident that there remains something very familiar about *The Last Warning*, even upon first viewing. For filmgoers at the time, this familiarity was the result and intention of Universal's presentation of the film to its public. For viewers today, this familiarity is a sign of the legacy of the film's influence on later productions.

At the time, the film would have been familiar to those viewers who had helped make Leni's 1927 film *The Cat and the Canary* a box office success. As one profile noted,

> *The Cat and the Canary* was so successful that it quite naturally paved the way for another Universal mystery containing the same elements of interest. *The Last Warning* has packed these elements thick and fast to an exciting climax.[43]

Magazine ads described the film as "The picture of a thousand thrills—and even better than *The Cat and the Canary*," and emphasized it was "Directed by Paul Leni. With Laura La Plante and a great cast. Supervised by Carl Laemmle, Jr."[44] The intention was confirmed in ads taken out by Universal presenting Carl Laemmle's direct address to exhibitors:

> You know how *The Cat and the Canary* took everybody by surprise—and maybe you are one of those unfortunates who missed out on it! You remember how *The Phantom of the Opera* caught you unaware. Don't let it happen in the case of *The Last Warning* because this is destined for bigger things than the other two pictures rolled into one.[45]

The Last Warning was to be one of a type. Elements of interest were being drawn from Universal's previous, successful films, not only Leni and La Plante's work on *The Cat and the Canary*, but also the earlier theater-house spooky mystery *The Phantom of the Opera* (1925). Elements that were thought to have held viewers of those films in sway apparently included a particular conjuncture of mystery, setting, and creepy thrills along with an emerging director, a certain leading lady, and a studio associated with all of these. These factors began to coalesce into a recognizable, particular type of film.

Blending "elements of interest" into recognizable, standard narrative forms—film types, or genres—was rapidly becoming a strategy of studio production. Offering "an increasingly clear-cut variety of styles," as David Puttnam noted, became an important method of marketing films so that "despite the common features of the system as a whole, individual movies began to acquire a clearly identifiable 'brand identity' which greatly facilitated their marketing and advertising."[46] *The Last Warning* was from the start a Paul Leni film, building on his previous successes yet developing beyond unique stylistic traits of a director into something of a genre, even if that genre had not yet fully settled under a consistent label. For all the indeterminate language as to the film's type—it was often referred to as a dark mystery or shivering suspense at the time—it is today recognizable immediately to modern viewers for its display of so many trappings of the early horror film. Indeed, *Motion Picture News* described *The Last Warning* as "Universal's Spook and Horror Film"[47] even though horror was not yet necessarily a term in wide use to describe a movie type. Universal was nevertheless becoming increasingly associated with this type, however it was labeled. Within a few short years, Universal's monster movies, combining monstrous anti-heroes with moody, Leni-esque atmospherics, would come to define the studio and the genre of horror for decades to come.

Film scholars today see the film in this light, generally agreeing with Rick Worland that "*The Last Warning* was another Ufa-style comedy thriller set backstage in a Broadway theater. Between *The Phantom of the Opera* and the films of Paul Leni, Universal had demonstrated major interest and success with stylish mystery-horror."[48] Lotte Eisner slyly implied that *The Last Warning*'s horror roots may even be traced back at least as far as E. T. A. Hoffmann, remarking that "in Leni's *The Last Warning* . . . Erasmus Spikher seems to have gained a brother, a frightened little man who hops around like an automaton."[49]

While evoking descriptions of thrills, suspense, humor, and mystery at the time, *The Last Warning* is now understood as part of the early history of the then-nascent horror genre. It can be retrospectively constructed this way because it was intentionally composed of the same "elements of interest" as a number of earlier films and then built upon them so that audiences and exhibitors alike would understand the appeals of this film and seek it out. In both its contemporaneous presentation to the public and its lasting legacy as an early iteration of the horror genre, it was not merely these elements of interest, but a particular, combined use of them that made the film readily marketable to both exhibitors (who Universal needed to book the film) and audiences (who Universal and the exhibitors needed to pay to see the film).

The Last Warning's *mise-en-scène* and cinematography combined imaginative art direction and a playfully mobile frame into a kind of witty, over-the-top Hollywood take on Expressionism, signifying mystery, creepiness, and a touch of humor. Charles D. Hall's art direction, informed by Leni's vast experience in the field, heightened the spectacular use of the film's locations. Taking place within an abandoned Broadway theater, scenes were filled with deep, dark shadows, menacing corridors and corners, covered in ropes and cobwebs, and scattered with trap doors, hidden passages, and fragilely secured props. Movie magazines described this as part of the fun: "Trap doors yawn, panels slide, ghastly hands are thrust from the wall, two murders are committed all for the sake of persuading a stubborn old man to tear down the theater and build a skyscraper in its place."[50] Without the forced perspective of German Expressionism from a decade earlier, the camera captured these spaces from unusual angles and was free to move through the set, often with abrupt and surprising mobility. Along with cinematographer Hal Mohr, Leni had the camera duck under falling curtains, dodge hanging staircases, zoom toward suspicious and unsuspecting characters alike, even to swing on ropes through the theater spaces.

This overall look was in service of a plot in which a theater company is apparently haunted while attempting to put on a show five years after their lead actor was mysteriously killed during a performance of the very same production in the very same theater. The film essentially transported a haunted house mystery to a spooky, abandoned theater. This simple hook was made all the more familiar and appealing for the references it immediately recalled. For its story, villain, settings, and atmosphere, it was frequently if not always favorably compared to Universal's immensely popular *The Phantom of the Opera*. In addition, newspaper as well as trade press advertisements, lobby cards, and movie posters emphasized the film's connection to Leni's *The Cat and the Canary* by displaying images of Laura La Plante, star of both films, under terrifying threat from a shadowy figure.

Taken together, these elements of *The Last Warning* could work to form the basis of an emerging genre and also, not coincidentally, to make the film easier to market and sell. A consistent, recognizable look combined with a variation and twist on a familiar narrative situation telling an easily summarizable story based on successful and familiar source materials as well as a studio, director, and star who had found success with recent films sharing similar elements of interest. In fact these elements foreshadow aspects of what Justin Wyatt has

Figure 13.4 The look, the horror.

described as the "look, hook, and book" of New Hollywood "High Concept" filmmaking.[51] This is not entirely accidental as in both cases—Universal's filmmaking of the era and Wyatt's much later, post-classical notion of high concept filmmaking—the film is designed foremost to be readily marketable. For Wyatt, high concept films are "differentiated through the emphasis on style in production and through the integration of the film with its marketing." His "look, hook, and book" summarize a particular set of priorities for producing readily marketable films through "the look of the images, the marketing hooks, and the reduced narratives."[52] This implies an institutional strategy that, rather than undertaking the marketing of films produced, prioritizes the production of films that already fit with marketing criteria, streamlining the production process in line with the needs of marketing and promotion.

The point is not that *The Last Warning* somehow presciently embodies specific "high concept" practices from a later historical era, but rather that *The Last Warning* is an apt demonstration of the extent to which these practices (which continue to adhere today in various forms) have long been part of the DNA of Hollywood filmmaking. Historically, they have surfaced and transformed at moments when extreme uncertainty about the audience and its response to filmmaking has been impossible to otherwise manage, control, or ignore. It is clear that Carl Laemmle saw in Paul Leni a skilled film director who could embrace innovation and add style and aesthetic creativity to films whose primary purpose was to exploit marketing techniques and secure audiences amid growing concerns about Universal's status, the transition to sound, widely varying exhibition practices, and the consolidation of the film industry.

THE END

The Last Warning occupies a pivotal position in the history of film, caught up in a time of major transitions in film technology, the exhibition and marketing of films, and the Hollywood studio system itself. Provoked by the extreme uncertainty these transitions occasioned, the production, exhibition, and marketing of *The Last Warning* signal both the end of an era and the emergence of strategies and practices that Hollywood would continue to nurture, grow, and harvest.

Paul Leni, meanwhile, never made another film. He died of sepsis on September 2, 1929. Months before his death, he told reporters, "I do not plan to make more mysteries. They are interesting to make. They mean dark corners, and people do not know what goes on in the dark. But for my next picture? It will be different."[53] We will never know what might have become of the next film he was reported to be making, *The Bargain in the Kremlin*, based on a Philip Gibbs story about a Russian violinist and set to star Joseph Schildkraut.

It is likely, in any event, that his legacy would have remained tied at least in part to the mystery-horror genre, as it is today, as was Universal's. A decade after *The Last Warning*'s release and Leni's death and four years after the Laemmles (father and son) lost financial control and were ousted from Universal, Universal's director of "advertising-publicity-exploitation" looked back and considered the new management that replaced them at Universal: "Under these officials, a new policy was inaugurated, calculated to make pictures from the standpoint of those who exhibit them and in this way to get as close as possible to the demands of the theater-going public."[54] The uncertain pursuit of the movie audience continued.

NOTES

1. Universal bought the screen rights in June 1927 for $15,000, apparently with the idea of a follow-up to *The Cat and the Canary* for Leni to direct. See Richard Koszarski, "Moving Pictures: Hal Mohr's Cinematography," *Film Comment* 10, no. 5 (September–October 1974): 48.
2. William Paul, "The K-Mart Audience at the Mall Movies," *Film History* 6, no. 4 (Winter 1994): 488.
3. Laemmle quoted in "No Let Down on 'Silents' Says Laemmle," *Motion Picture News*, August 11, 1928.
4. Donald Crafton, *The Talkies: American Cinema's Transition to Sound, 1926-1931* (Berkeley: University of California Press, 1999), 170.
5. Carl Laemmle, "Sees Field for Silent and Sound," *Film Daily*, May 20, 1929.
6. *The Man Who Laughs* was released with Movietone sound effects and music with dialogue added after the film was complete to accommodate the sudden audience demand for sound films.
7. Leni quoted in Gertrude Warburton, "Watch Paul Leni!" *Universal Weekly*, January 12, 1929.
8. Crafton, *Talkies*, 171.
9. Mohr quoted in Koszarski, "Moving Pictures," 49.
10. Josef Berne, "In the Realm of Sound—Reviews and Previews," *Sound Waves*, January 15, 1929; "The Last Warning," *Variety*, January 9, 1929; "The Last Warning," *Film Daily*, January 13, 1929; Mordaunt Hall, "The Screen," *New York Times*, January 7, 1929; *New York Evening Journal* quoted in "Newspaper Opinions," *Film Daily*, January 13, 1929.
11. "Scary Drama Made More Scary," *Exhibitors Herald and Moving Picture World*, December 29, 1928.
12. "*The Last Warning* (PT)—with Laura La Plante," *Harrison's Reports*, January 12, 1929.
13. "The Last Warning," *Variety*; "Current Pictures in Review," *Motion Picture*, February 1929.
14. Richard Koszarski, *An Evening's Entertainment: The Age of the Silent Feature Picture, 1915-1928* (Berkeley: University of California Press, 1990), 89.
15. Koszarski, *An Evening's Entertainment*, 86.
16. Interoperability was a much discussed point of contention in 1928 and 1929 as the industry played RCA and Western Electric, the largest purveyors of sound on film, against each other for the best price on the licensing of sound technologies. See Douglas Gomery, "The Coming of Sound: Technological Change in the American Film Industry," in *The American Film Industry*, ed. Tino Balio (Madison: University of Wisconsin Press, 1985), 229–52.

17. "Seattle Top Figure is $18,500," *Motion Picture News*, February 9, 1929.
18. "Motion Picture News Weekly Box Office Check-Up," *Motion Picture News*, February 16, 1929.
19. "Motion Picture News Weekly Box Office Check-Up," *Motion Picture News*, February 23, 1929.
20. "Portland, Ore., First Runs Foresee Banner Year's Film Business in '29," *Motion Picture News*, January 19, 1929.
21. Fred Schader, "Broadway Show Reviews," *Motion Picture News*, January 12, 1929.
22. "Exploitation," *Universal Weekly*, November 24, 1928.
23. Koszarski, *An Evening's Entertainment*, 39.
24. For an example, see advertisement for *The Man Who Laughs*, *Variety*, January 16, 1929.
25. Koszarski, *An Evening's Entertainment*, 40.
26. *Exhibitors Herald and Moving Picture World*, "Reichenbach Signs for Full Time Publicity Work on Universal's Pictures," November 17, 1928.
27. David Puttnam, *Movies and Money* (New York: Vintage Books, 1997), 134.
28. "Reichenbach Signs."
29. "Mystery Note (Publicity Stunt) Brings Police to Reichenbach's Door," *Exhibitors Herald and Moving Picture World*, December 8, 1928.
30. Advertisement, *Motion Picture News*, January 5, 1929.
31. Advertisement, *Motion Picture News*.
32. For Universal's full-page ad, see, for example, *Universal Weekly*, January 19, 1929; for the Strand Theater ad, see, for example, "Live Exploitation Tips from Exhibitors," *Motion Picture News*, March 2, 1929. This was, apparently, a global marketing strategy as an ad with the same copy appeared, for example, in the *Otago Daily Times* (New Zealand), September 12, 1929.
33. "Exploitation Hints on All Films," *Motion Picture News*, March 16, 1929.
34. This report elaborated on the audience response to the film as well, noting that "the picture was a real thriller and kept most of the crowd in a shaky uproar. It must be said that the picture was well produced and directing was up to the standard. The plot was so good that the murder was laid to everyone except the actual slayer. Laura La Plante heads the all-star cast." See "Chicago Personalities," *Exhibitors Herald-World*, January 19, 1929.
35. "Exploitation Hints on All Films."
36. "*Last Warning* Gets Big Teaser Play for New Haven Olympia," *Exhibitors Herald-World*, March 16, 1929; "*Last Warning* Offers Wallop in Teaser Campaign," *Universal Weekly*, January 12, 1929.
37. "Blonde Matinee Attracts Crowds to La Plante Film," *Exhibitors Herald-World*, February 9, 1929; "Exploit-O-Grams: Daily Tips Which Mean Dollars for Showmen," *Film Daily*, February 7, 1929.
38. "Exploit-O-Grams," *Film Daily*, June 6, 1929.
39. Harold W. Cohen, "Pittsburgh," *Variety*, February 13, 1929.
40. "Ballot Stops Show," *Film Daily*, February 3, 1929.
41. William A. Johnston, "Announcing Another Important Service for Exhibitor Readers," *Motion Picture News*, February 23, 1929.
42. "Checking Over Exhibitor Exploitation Ideas Used on 1928 Film Crop," *Motion Picture News*, January 12, 1929.
43. Warburton, "Watch Paul Leni!"
44. Advertisement, *Exhibitors Herald and Moving Picture World*, December 8, 1928.
45. Advertisement, *Motion Picture News*.
46. Puttnam, *Movies and Money*, 135.
47. Photo caption, *Motion Picture News*, January 12, 1929.

48. Rick Worland, *The Horror Film: An Introduction* (Malden, MA: Blackwell Publishing, 2007), 55. See also Thomas Schatz, *The Genius of the System: Hollywood Filmmaking in the Studio Era* (New York: Henry Holt, 1988), 89; and Harry M. Benshoff, "The Monster and the Homosexual," in *The Dread of Difference: Gender and the Horror Film*, 2nd edn., ed. Barry Keith Grant (Austin: University of Texas Press, 2015), 135.
49. Lotte H. Eisner, *The Haunted Screen: Expressionism in the German Cinema and the Influence of Max Reinhardt* (Berkeley: University of California Press, 1969), 145.
50. "Current Pictures."
51. Justin Wyatt, *High Concept: Movies and Marketing in Hollywood* (Austin: University of Texas Press, 1994), 20–2.
52. Wyatt, *High Concept*, 20, 22.
53. Leni quoted in James Hood MacFarland, "Leni Likens Film Game to Spirited Tennis Tilt," *Universal Weekly*, January 26, 1929.
54. John Joseph, "Universal Pictures," in *The Film Daily Cavalcade*, ed. John W. Alicoate (New York: Film Daily, 1939), 137.

Filmography

The following filmography lists every known production for which Leni served as director, writer, set designer, costume designer, or performer, or some combination thereof. Many of the films are considered lost, and the ones that survive often contain only partial credit information; therefore, some listings will appear somewhat fragmentary.

Several sources suggest that Leni may have contributed to a few films beyond the ones listed in this filmography. A 1926 piece in the *New York Times* stated that he worked on the E. A. Dupont films *Whitechapel/Die Stadt der Enterbten* (1920) and *Murder Without a Murderer/Der Mord ohne Täter* (1921). A brief article published in a 1927 studio guide also credits him with the set design for *Murder Without a Murderer* and two other Dupont films: *The Green Manuela/Die grüne Manuela: Ein Film aus dem Süden* (1923) and *The Ancient Law/Das alte Gesetz* (1923). In addition, Chuck Schapiro included the 1921 titles *The Ghost Ship/Das Gespensterschiff* and *Comedy of Passions/Komödie der Leidenschaften* in a Leni filmography he compiled for his 1982 CinemaTexas essay on *Waxworks*. David Quinlan and David Thomson, who borrowed from Schapiro's filmography for their Leni entries in *The Illustrated Guide to Film Directors* and *The New Biographical Dictionary of Film*, respectively, repeated the claim. Leni did not complete these two films, however, and his participation in the four Dupont films noted above could not be verified with any other sources. Thus, these six films are not included in the filmography. See "Some Current Productions on Broadway," *New York Times*, July 11, 1926; "Biographical Sketch," *Motion Picture News Booking Guide and Studio Directory*, October 1927, 110; Chuck Schapiro, "Waxworks [*Das Wachsfigurenkabinett*] (1924)," *CinemaTexas Program Notes* 22, no. 1 (February 9, 1982): 43; David Quinlan, *The Illustrated Guide to Film Directors* (Totowa, NJ: Barnes & Noble, 1983), 183; and David Thomson, *The New Biographical Dictionary of Film*

(New York: Alfred A. Knopf, 2010), 575. See also "Projection Jottings," *New York Times*, September 18, 1927.

An Outcast, Part 1: The Young Boss/Ein Ausgestossener, 1 Teil: Der junge Chef (1913)
Continental-Kunstfilm GmbH. Director and screenplay: Joe May. Cinematography: Willy Hameister, Emil Schünemann. Set design: **Paul Leni**. Cast: Ernst Reicher (Hans von R.), Helene Janon (Marguerite Walser), Theodor Burgarth (Guy Walser), Sabine Impekoven (Lucienne Walser), Anton Ernst Rückert, Karl Platen, Fritz Richard, Otz Tollen, Mary Scheller. 3 reels. Released March 14, 1913.

An Outcast, Part 2: The Eternal Peace/Ein Ausgestossener, 2 Teil: Der ewige Friede (1913)
Continental-Kunstfilm GmbH. Directors: Joe May, Arzen von Cserépy [Konrad Wieder]. Screenplay: Joe May. Cinematography: Willy Hameister, Emil Schünemann. Set design: **Paul Leni**. Cast: Theodor Burgarth (Guy Walser), Sabine Impekoven (Lucienne Walser), Vera Häberlin (Lilly Walser), Theodor Rittersberg (Schmidt, a boatman), Hermann Seldeneck, Marie von Bülow, Otz Tollen, Andreas von Horn. 4 reels. Released March 14, 1913.

The Black Triangle/The Mysterious Mansion/Stuart Webbs: Die geheimnisvolle Villa (1914)
Continental-Kunstfilm GmbH. Director: Joe May. Screenplay: Ernst Reicher. Cinematography: Max Fassbender. Set design: **Paul Leni**. Cast: Ernst Reicher (Detective Stuart Webbs), Sabine Impekoven (Lydia Vengar), Julius Falkenstein, Carl Auen, Werner Krauss, Max Landa, Eva May, Mia May, Lupu Pick, Fritz Richard. 3 reels. Released March 13, 1914.

The Man in the Cellar/Stuart Webbs: Der Mann im Keller (1914)
Continental-Kunstfilm GmbH. Director: Joe May. Screenplay: Ernst Reicher. Cinematography: Max Fassbender. Set design: **Paul Leni**. Cast: Ernst Reicher (Detective Stuart Webbs), Max Landa (Lord Thomas Rawson), Olga Engl, Alice Hechy, Eduard Rothauser, Josef Schelepa. 3 reels. Released March 20, 1914.

Trapped by the Camera/Stuart Webbs: Der Spuk im Haus des Professors (1914)
Continental-Kunstfilm GmbH. Director: Joe May. Screenplay: Ernst Reicher. Cinematography: Max Fassbender. Set design: **Paul Leni**. Cast: Ernst Reicher (Detective Stuart Webbs), Wilhelm Diegelmann (Professor). 3 reels. Released May 1914.

The Armored Vault/Stuart Webbs: Das Panzergewölbe (1914)
Stuart Webbs-Film Company. Director: Joe May. Screenplay: Ernst Reicher. Cinematography: Max Fassbender. Set design: **Paul Leni**. Cast: Ernst Reicher (Detective Stuart Webbs), Hermann Picha, Fritz Richard, Arthur Ullmann. 4 reels. Released June 26, 1914.

The Eighth Commandment/Das achte Gebot: Du sollst nicht falsches Zeugnis reden wider deinen Nächsten (1915)
Projektions-AG Union (PAGU). Producer: Paul Davidson: Director: Max Mack. Screenplay: Adolf Lantz, Rudolf Strauss. Cinematography: Max Lutze. Set design: **Paul Leni**. Cast: Rudolph Schildkraut (Block, a speculator), Hanni Weisse (Baroness Lissi Hohenbach), Paul Otto (Erich von Brandem). 3 reels. Released February 25, 1915.

The Catwalk/Der Katzensteg (1915)
Projektions-AG Union (PAGU). Director: Max Mack. Assistant director: Bruno Lopinski. Screenplay: Adolf Lantz, Max Mack, based on a novel by Hermann Sudermann. Dramaturg: Rudolf Kurtz. Cinematography: Max Lutze. Set design: **Paul Leni**. Cast: Wilhelm von Muhr (Baron von Schranden), Georg Lengbach (Boleslav, the Baron's son), Victor Hartberg (Mr. Merkel), Ludwig Trautmann (Felix Merkel, Mr. Merkel's son), Ferdinand Bonn (Mr. Hackelberg), Leontine Kühnberg (Regine, the castle maid), Karl Platen (Minister), Käthe Haack (Helene, the Minister's daughter), Bruno Lopinski, **Paul Leni**. 5 reels. Released April 27, 1915.

The Dead Awaken/Stuart Webbs: Die Toten erwachen (1915)
Stuart Webbs-Film Company/Reicher und Reicher. Director: Adolf Gärtner. Screenplay: Ernst Reicher. Cinematography: Max Fassbender. Set design: **Paul Leni**. Cast: Ernst Reicher (Detective Stuart Webbs), Fritz Richard, Hans Stock, Arthur Ullmann. 3 reels. Released October 1915.

The Ring of Giuditta Foscari/Der Ring der Giuditta Foscari (1917)
Projektions-AG Union (PAGU). Producer: Paul Davidson. Director and screenplay: Alfred Halm. Set design: **Paul Leni**. Cast: Erna Morena (Judith Arens/Giuditta Foscari), Emil Jannings (Count Waldenau/Mr. Lodovica), Harry Liedtke (Count Waldenau's son/Mr. Lodovica's son). 3 reels. Released October 8, 1917.

The Blouse King/Der Blusenkönig (1917)
Messter Film/Projektions-AG Union (PAGU). Director: Ernst Lubitsch. Assistant director: Sally Lastmann. Screenplay: Ernst Lubitsch, Erich Schönfelder. Set design: **Paul Leni**. Cast: Ernst Lubitsch (Sally Katz), Käthe Dorsch

(Seamstress), Guido Herzfeld (Boss), Max Zilzer (Mr. Lippmann). 3 reels. Released November 2, 1917.

Prima Vera/Die Kameliendame (1917)
Projektions-AG Union (PAGU). Producer: Paul Davidson. Director: **Paul Leni**. Screenplay: Hans Brennert, based on a novel by Alexandre Dumas *fils*. Set design: **Paul Leni**. Cast: Erna Morena (Jutta Dirigero), Harry Liedtke (Melchior Grant, a painter), Wilhelm Diegelmann (Canon Rochus). 3 reels. Released December 11, 1917.

Sleeping Beauty/Dornröschen (1917)
Projektions-AG Union (PAGU). Producer: Paul Davidson. Director: **Paul Leni**. Screenplay: Rudolf Presber, based on the fairy tale. Cinematography: Alfred Hansen. Set and costume design: **Paul Leni**. Set construction: Kurt Richter. Cast: Mabel Kaul (Dornröschen), Harry Liedtke (Prince), Käthe Dorsch (Queen), Georg Kaiser (King), Hermann Picha (Old witch), Victor Janson (Marshal), Marie Grimm-Einödshofer (Amme, the old nurse), Paul Biensfeldt, Paul Wegener. 4 reels. Released December 20, 1917.

The Mystery of Bangalore/Das Rätsel von Bangalor (1918)
Pax Film GmbH. Producer: Alexander von Antalffy. Directors: **Paul Leni**, Alexander von Antalffy. Screenplay: **Paul Leni**, Rudolf Kurtz. Set design: **Paul Leni**. Music compilation: Robert Assmann. Cast: Conrad Veidt (Prince Dinja), Gilda Langer (Ellen, the Governor's daughter), Harry Liedtke (Sir Archibald Douglas). 5 reels. Released January 11, 1918.

The Diary of Dr. Hart/Das Tagebuch des Dr. Hart/Der Feldarzt (1918)
Projektions-AG Union (PAGU)/Bild- und Filmamt (Bufa). Producer: Paul Davidson. Director: **Paul Leni**. Assistant director: Hanns Kräly. Screenplay: Hans Brennert. Cinematography: Carl Hoffmann. Set design: **Paul Leni**. Cast: Heinrich Schroth (Dr. Robert Hart), Käthe Haack (Chatelaine Ursula von Hohenau), Dagny Servaes (Jadwiga Bransky), Ernst Hofmann (Count Bronislaw Krascinsky), Adolf Klein (Count Bransky). 4 reels. Released January 21, 1918.

The Rosentopf Case/Der Fall Rosentopf (1918)
Projektions-AG Union (PAGU). Producer: Paul Davidson. Director: Ernst Lubitsch. Screenplay: Ernst Lubitsch, Hanns Kräly. Cinematography: Alfred Hansen. Set design: **Paul Leni**. Set construction: Kurt Richter. Cast: Ferry Sikla (Rentier Klingelmann), Margarete Kupfer (Rosa, his maid), Ernst Lubitsch (Sally, a detective), Trude Hesterberg (Bella Spaketti, a dancer), Elsa Wagner (Mrs. Hintze). 3 reels. Released September 20, 1918.

Mania: The Story of a Cigarette Worker/Mania: Die Geschichte einer Zigarettearbeiterin (1918)
Projektions-AG Union (PAGU). Producer: Paul Davidson. Director and cinematography: Eugen Illés. Screenplay: Hans Brennert. Set design: **Paul Leni**. Cast: Pola Negri (Mania, a cigarette worker), Arthur Schröder (Hans van der Hof, a composer), Ernst Wendt (Painter), Werner Hollmann (Morelli, a wealthy arts patron). 5 reels. Released November 8, 1918.

The Platonic Marriage/Die platonische Ehe (1919)
May-Film GmbH. Producer: Joe May. Director: **Paul Leni**. Screenplay: Richard Hutter, Joe May, based on an idea by Ruth Goetz. Set and costume design: **Paul Leni**. Cast: Mia May (Wealthy woman), Georg Alexander (Destitute nobleman), Albert Paulig, Ferry Sikla, Kitty Dewall, Hermann Picha. 4 reels. Released January 31, 1919.

Veritas vincit (The Truth Triumphs!): A Film Trilogy/Veritas vincit (Die Wahrheit siegt!): Eine Filmtrilogie (1919)
May-Film GmbH. Producer and director: Joe May. Screenplay: Ruth Goetz, Richard Hutter, based on an idea by Michelangelo Baron Zois and Joe May. Cinematography: Max Lutze. Set design: **Paul Leni**. Set construction: Siegfried Wroblewsky. Costume design: F. Diringer. Music: Ferdinand Hummel. Cast, Part 1 (*Rome at the Time of Decius/Rom zur Zeit des Decius*): Mia May (Helena), Johannes Riemann (Lucius), Magnus Stifter (Decius), Emil Albes (Flavius), Wilhelm Diegelmann (Tullulus), Ferry Sikla (Fucius Asinius), Paul Biensfeldt (Digulus), Georg John (Blind senator), Hermann Picha (Sorceress in the Sugura). Cast, Part 2 (*Around 1500/Um 1500*): Mia May (Ellinor), Johannes Riemann (Knight Lutz von Ehrenfried), Leopold Bauer (Master Heinrich the Goldsmith), Lina Paulsen (Ursula), Friedrich Kühne (Florian). Cast, Part 3 (*Modern Times/Neuzeit*): Mia May (Contessa Helene), Johannes Riemann (Prince Ludwig), Bernhard Goetzke (Indian), Adolf Klein (Prince), Olga Engl (Princess), Josef Klein (General von der Tanne), Max Gülstorff (Poacher), Max Laurence (Coroner), Anders Wikmann (Viscount René de Montmorte), Hermann Picha (Master of ceremonies), Emmy Wyda, Maria Forescu. 8 reels. Released April 4, 1919.

Intoxication/Rausch (1919)
Argus-Film. Director: Ernst Lubitsch. Screenplay: Hanns Kräly, based on a play by August Strindberg. Cinematography: Karl Freund, Theodor Sparkuhl. Set design: **Paul Leni**, Rochus Gliese. Cast: Alfred Abel (Gaston, a writer), Grete Diercks (Jeanne), Rudolf Klein-Rhoden (Coroner), Marga Köhler (Henriette's mother), Karl Meinhardt (Adolph), Pola Negri, Asta Nielsen (Henriette Mauclerc), Sophie Pagay (Mother Kathrin), Frida Richard (Housekeeper), Heinz Stieda (The Abbé). 5 reels. Released September 24, 1919.

Prince Cuckoo/Prinz Kuckuck: Die Höllenfahrt eines Wollüstlings (1919)
Gloria-Film GmbH. Producer: Hanns Lippmann. Director: **Paul Leni**. Screenplay: Georg Kaiser, based on a novel by Otto Julius Bierbaum. Cinematography by Carl Hoffmann. Set design: **Paul Leni**, Karl Machus, Otto Moldenhauer. Music: Friedrich Hollaender, J. Polischuk. Cast: Conrad Veidt (Carl Kraker), Niels Prien (Henry Felix), Olga Limburg (Sara Asher), Magnus Stifter (Prince Wladimir Golkow), Max Gülstorff (Master Sturmius), Paul Biensfeldt (Jeremias Kraker), Wilhelm Diegelmann (Farmer Schirmer), Margarete Kupfer (Sanna Kraker), Gertrud Wolle (Mrs. Hauart), Margarete Schlegel (Marchesa's daughter), Anneliese Halbe (Berta), Erik Charell (Tiberio), Marga von Kierska (Liane), Fritz Junkermann, Toni Zimmerer, Max Ruhbeck, Günther Herrmann, Hanna Ralph, Blandine Ebinger, Agnes Wilke, Henri Peters-Arnolds. 6 reels. Released September 26, 1919.

Patience/Patience: Die Karten des Todes (1920)
Gloria-Film GmbH. Producer: Hanns Lippmann. Directors: **Paul Leni**, Felix Basch. Screenplay: E. A. Dupont, based on a Scottish ballad. Cinematography: Carl Hoffmann. Set design: **Paul Leni**. Cast: Conrad Veidt (Sir Percy Parker), Felix Basch (Edward), Adele Sandrock (Ahne), Irmgard Bern (Jane), Wilhelm Diegelmann (Fischer Tom), Karl Platen (Minister), Aenderly Lebius, Loni Nest, Marga von Kierska, Max Winter. 5 reels. Released April 16, 1920.

The White Peacock/Der weisse Pfau: Tragödie einer Tänzerin (1920)
Gloria-Film GmbH. Producer: Hanns Lippmann. Director: E. A. Dupont. Screenplay: **Paul Leni**, E. A. Dupont. Cinematography: Karl Hasselmann. Set design: **Paul Leni**. Set construction: Robert A. Dietrich, Otto Moldenhauer. Costume design: Bruno Köhler. Cast: Grit Hegesa (Marylowna, a dancer known as the "White Peacock"), Hans Mierendorff (Lord Crossin Field), Adolf Edgar Licho (Navratil, "Golden Ball" variety show host), Emil Rameau (Norbert, an old man), Robert Scholz (Czupan, a young Roma), Lore Sello (Maryla, a young woman), Guido Herzfeld, Karl Platen. 5 reels. Released August 12, 1920.

The Guilt of Lavinia Morland/Die Schuld der Lavinia Morland (1920)
May-Film GmbH. Producer and director: Joe May. Assistant director: Robert Wüllner. Screenplay: Joe May, Wilhelm Auspitzer, based on a play by Ernest Vajda. Cinematography: Werner Brandes. Set design: **Paul Leni**, Martin Jacoby-Boy. Set construction: Erich Kettelhut, Erich Zander. Cast: Mia May (Lavinia Morland), Albert Steinrück (John Morland), Alfred Gerasch (Vicomte Gaston de Cardillac), Paul Bildt (Harry Scott), Loni Nest (Lavinia's child), Albert Patry (Dr. Harrison), Otto Treptow (Servant), Kitty Aschenbach, Rosa Valetti, Mien Duymaer Van Twist. 4 reels. Released November 12, 1920.

The Genoa Conspiracy/Fiesco/Der Verschwörung zu Genua (1921)
Gloria-Film GmbH. Producer: Hanns Lippmann. Director: **Paul Leni**. Screenplay: **Paul Leni**, Georg Kaiser, based on the stage play by Friedrich Schiller. Cinematography: Karl Hasselmann, Carl Hoffmann. Set design: **Paul Leni**. Set construction: Karl Görge. Costume design: Ernö Metzner. Music: Hans Landsberger. Cast: Hans Mierendorff (Fiesco, Count of Lavagna), Erna Morena (Leonore, Countess of Lavagna), Fritz Kortner (Gianettino Doria), Maria Fein (Countess Julia Imperiali), Ilka Grüning (Matron), Magnus Stifter (Verrino, a Republican), Wilhelm Diegelmann (Andrea Doria, the Doge of Genoa), Bernhard Goetzke (Calcagno), Max Gülstorff (Lomellino, a courtier), Fritz Beckmann (Old silk dealer), Lydia Potoczakaja (Bertha, Verrino's daughter), Hellmuth Bergmann (Bourgorgnino), Louis Brody (Mulay Hassan, a Moor), Louis Krieger (Zibo), Wilhelm [William] Dieterle, Lia Eibenschütz, Paul Günther, Ludwig Rex. 6 reels. Released February 25, 1921.

Wally of the Vultures/The Vulture-Wally/Die Geierwally (1921)
Gloria-Film GmbH/Henny Porten Filmproduktion. Producers: Hanns Lippmann, Henny Porten. Director: E. A. Dupont. Screenplay: E. A. Dupont, based on a novel by Wilhelmine von Hillern. Cinematography: Karl Hasselmann, Arpád Virágh. Set and costume design: **Paul Leni**. Production manager: Hanns Lippmann. Music: Giuseppe Becce, Bruno Schulz. Cast: Albert Steinrück (Stromminger, a well-to-do farmer), Henny Porten (Wally, his daughter), Wilhelm [William] Dieterle ("Bear" Joseph), Eugen Klöpfer (Gellner-Vincenz), Elise Zachow-Vallentin (Luckard), Marie Grimm-Einödshofer (Head maid), Julius Brandt (Klettenmeyer), Wilhelm Diegelmann (Roserbauer Sr.), Gerd Fricke (Roserbauer Jr.), Grete Diercks (Afra). 6 reels. Released September 12, 1921.

Lady Hamilton (1921)
Richard-Oswald-Produktion. Producer and director: Richard Oswald. Screenplay: Richard Oswald, based on the novels *Love and Life of Lady Hamilton* and *Lord Hamilton's Last Love* by Heinrich Vollrath Schumacher. Cinematography: Carl Hoffmann, Károly Vass. Set and costume design: **Paul Leni**. Set construction: Hans Dreier. Cast: Liane Haid (Emma Lyon, later Lady Hamilton), Conrad Veidt (Lord Nelson), Werner Krauss (Lord William Hamilton), Reinhold Schünzel (Ferdinand IV, King of Naples), Else Heims (Marie Caroline, Queen of Naples), Anton Pointner (Greville), Julia Serda (Adele Nelson), Georg Alexander (George, Prince of Wales), Paul Bildt (Caraciollo, King's Minister), Theodor Loos (George Romney, a famous painter), Hans Heinrich von Twardowski (Joshua Nesbitt, Nelson's stepson), Gertrude Welcker (Arabella Kelly), Adele Sandrock (Diocese head), Käte Waldeck (Jane Middleton), Celly de Rheydt (Phyrne), Hugo Döblin (Dr. Graham, a

quack), Heinrich George (Captain Sir John Willet Payne), Friedrich Kühne (Tug, Sir John's Chief Petty Officer), Louis Ralph (Tom Kid, a sailor), Ilka Grüning (Landlady), Claire Krona (Emma Lyon's mother), Max Adalbert (Lazzarone), Max Gülstorff (Lazzarone), Hans Stürm (Lazzarone), Rudolf Meinhard-Jünger (Barber), Carl Geppert (Another barber), Adolf Klein (Minister of the Navy), Karl Platen (King's valet), Georg John (Jacobin), Karl Römer (Jacobin), Clementine Plessner. 7 reels. Released October 20, 1921.

Backstairs/Hintertreppe (1921)
Gloria-Film GmbH/Henny Porten Filmproduktion. Producers: Hanns Lippmann, Henny Porten. Directors: **Paul Leni**, Leopold Jessner. Screenplay: Carl Mayer. Cinematography: Karl Hasselmann, Willy Hameister. Set design: **Paul Leni**. Set construction: Karl Görge. Production manager: Wilhelm von Kaufmann. Music: Hans Landsberger. Cast: Henny Porten (Housekeeper), Fritz Kortner (Postman), Wilhelm [William] Dieterle (Craftsman), Eugene Dieterle. 4 reels. Released December 11, 1921.

Children of Darkness, 1: The Man from Naples/Kinder der Finsternis, 1: Der Mann aus Neapel (1921)
Gloria-Film GmbH. Producer: Hanns Lippmann. Director: E. A. Dupont. Screenplay: E. A. Dupont, based on an outline by Max Jungk and Julius Urgiss. Cinematography: Karl Freund, Helmar Lerski. Set design: **Paul Leni**. Production manager: Max Reichmann. Cast: Grit Hegesa (Lilian Gray), Hans Mierendorff (Enrico Fiori), Sybil Smolova (Francesca, Enrico's sister), Károly Huszár [Karl Huszar] (Foreman Geone), Marija Leiko (Maria Geone), Otto Tressler (James Pool, captain of the steamship *Heluan*), Adele Sandrock (Maud Gray, Lilian's mother), Friedrich Kühne (James Stone), Fritz Schulz, Bernhard Goetzke, Margarete Kupfer, Paul Westermeier. 5 reels. Released December 30, 1921.

Children of Darkness, 2: Fighting Worlds/Kinder der Finsternis, 2: Kämpfende Welten (1922)
Gloria-Film GmbH. Producer: Hanns Lippmann. Director: E. A. Dupont. Screenplay: E. A. Dupont, based on an outline by Max Jungk and Julius Urgiss. Cinematography: Karl Freund, Helmar Lerski. Set design: **Paul Leni**. Production manager: Max Reichmann. Cast: Grit Hegesa (Lilian Gray), Hans Mierendorff (Enrico Flori), Sybil Smolova (Francesca, Enrico's sister), Károly Huszár [Karl Huszar] (Foreman Geone), Marija Leiko (Maria Geone), Otto Tressler (James Pool, captain of the steamship *Heluan*), Adele Sandrock (Maud Gray, Lilian's mother), Friedrich Kühne (James Stone), Fritz Schulz, Bernhard Goetzke, Margarete Kupfer, Paul Westermeier. 5 reels. Released January 13, 1922.

Women's Sacrifice/Frauenopfer (1922)
Gloria-Film GmbH/Henny Porten Filmproduktion. Executive producers: Hanns Lippmann, Henny Porten. Producer: Wilhelm von Kaufmann. Director: Karl Grune. Screenplay: Imre Frey, based on a play by Georg Kaiser. Cinematography: Arpád Virágh. Set design: **Paul Leni**. Production manager: Max Reichmann. Cast: Henny Porten (Maria, the Painter's wife), Wilhelm [William] Dieterle (Painter), Albert Bassermann (Count), Ludwig Rex (Administrator), Frida Richard (Administrator), Edgar Klitzsch (Art dealer), Adolf E. Licho (Old Bohemian). 4/5 reels. Released February 15, 1922.

The Tragedy of Love/Tragödie der Liebe (1923)
May-Film GmbH. Producers: Joe May, Rudolf Sieber. Director: Joe May. Assistant director: Robert Wüllner. Screenplay: Leo Birinski, Adolf Lantz. Titles: Hachenberger. Cinematography: Karl Puth, Sophus Wangøe. Set design: **Paul Leni**. Set construction: Erich Kettelhut, Erich Zander. Costume design: Ali Hubert. Music: Wilhelm Löwitt. Cast: Mia May (Countess Manon Moreau), Emil Jannings (Ombrade), Erika Glässner (Musette), Vladimir Gajdarov (André Rabatin), Charlotte Ander (Kitty Moreau), Irmgard Bern (Yvonne), Hedwig Pauly-Winterstein (Countess Adrienne Moreau), Ida Wüst (Madame de la Roquére), Rudolf Forster (Count François Moreau), Curt Goetz (Prosecuting attorney), Arnold Korff (Detective Henry Beaufort), Eugen Rex (Jean, the Moreaus' servant), Hermann Vallentin (Police commissioner), Kurt Vespermann (Attorney), Marlene Dietrich (Lucy), Loni Nest (Kitty as a child), Guido Herzfeld (Marcel), Paul Biensfeldt, Karl Gerhardt, Paul Graetz, Ernst Gronau, Hans Kuhnert, Rudolf Lettinger, Albert Patry, Lena Amsel, Fritz Richard, Ferry Sikla, Hertha von Walther, Hans Wassmann. 6 reels. Released September 21, 1923. Note: Some sources list this production as two separate films: *Tragödie der Liebe, Teil* 1 and *Tragödie der Liebe, Teil* 2.

The Countess of Paris/Die Gräfin von Paris (1923)
May-Film GmbH. Producer: Joe May. Directors: Dimitri Buchowetzki, Joe May. Assistant director: Robert Wüllner. Screenplay: Leo Birinski, Adolf Lantz. Cinematography: Karl Puth, Sophus Wangøe. Set design: **Paul Leni**. Set construction: Erich Kettelhut, Erich Zander. Costume design: Ali Hubert. Music: Wilhelm Löwitt. Location manager: Rudolf Sieber. Still photographer: Hans Lechner. Cast: Mia May (Countess Manon Moreau), Emil Jannings (Ombrade), Erika Glässner (Musette), Vladimir Gajdarov (André Rabatin), Charlotte Ander (Kitty Moreau), Irmgard Bern (Yvonne), Hedwig Pauly-Winterstein (Countess Adrienne Moreau), Ida Wüst (Madame de la Roquére), Rudolf Forster (Count François Moreau), Curt Goetz (Prosecuting attorney), Arnold Korff (Detective Henry Beaufort), Eugen Rex (Jean, Moreau's servant), Hermann Vallentin (Police commissioner), Kurt Vespermann (Attorney

general), Marlene Dietrich (Lucy), Loni Nest (Kitty as a child), Lena Amsel, Paul Biensfeldt, Karl Gerhardt, Paul Graetz, Ernst Gronau, Hans Kuhnert, Rudolf Lettinger, Albert Patry, Fritz Richard, Ferry Sikla, Hans Wassmann. 6 reels. Released October 12, 1923. Note: Some sources list this production as two separate films: *Tragödie der Liebe, Teil 3* and *Tragödie der Liebe, Teil 4*.

Waxworks/Three Wax Men/The Three Wax Works/Das Wachsfigurenkabinett (1924)
Neptun-Film AG; distributed by Universum-Film (Ufa). Producers: Alexander Kwartiroff, Leo Birinski. Directors: **Paul Leni**, Leo Birinski. Assistant director: Wilhelm [William] Dieterle. Screenplay: Henrik Galeen, based on a novella by Gustav Meyrink. Dramaturg: Leo Birinski. Set design: **Paul Leni**. Set construction: Alfred Junge, Fritz Maurischat. Cinematography: Helmar Lerski. Props: Paul Dannenberg. Costume design: Ernst Stern. Production manager: Artur Kiekebusch-Brenken. Still photographer: Hans Lechner. Cast: Emil Jannings (Harun al-Rashid), Conrad Veidt (Ivan the Terrible), Werner Krauss (Jack the Ripper/Spring-Heeled Jack), Wilhelm [William] Dieterle (Poet/Assad the baker/Russian prince), Olga Belajeff (Eva/Maimune/A Bojarin), Paul Biensfeldt (Grand Vizier), John Gottowt (Panopticum owner), Georg John (Prisoner), Ernst Legal (Czar's poison-maker), Elizza La Porta, Fritz Alberti, Agnes Estherhazy. 5 reels. Released November 13, 1924.

The Love Letters of Baroness von S. . ./Die Liebesbriefe der Baronin von S . . . (1924)
May-Film GmbH. Producer: Joe May. Director: Henrik Galeen. Screenplay: Henrik Galeen, Paul Reno. Cinematography: Frederik Fuglsang, Ludwig Lippert, Giovanni Vitrotti. Set design: **Paul Leni**. Set construction: Fritz Maurischat. Music: Eduard Prasch. Cast: Mia May (Baroness von S.), Alfredo Bertone (Baron von S.), Ernst Gronau (Marquis Grillon), Memo Benassi (Giovanni, a busker), Desdemona Mazza (Kokotte Jou-Jou/Ginetta). 6 reels. Released December 15, 1924.

A Woman of Forty/Die Frau von vierzig Jahren (1925)
Richard-Oswald-Produktion. Producer, director, and screenplay: Richard Oswald. Cinematography: Jack Hermann, Theodor Sparkuhl. Set design: **Paul Leni**. Set construction: Fritz Maurischat. Costume design: Gerson-Prager-Hausdorff. Music: Willy Schmidt-Gentner. Cast: Diana Karenne (Woman), Vladimir Gajdarov (He), Siegfried Arno (Family friend), Paul Otto (Man), Dina Gralla (Daughter), Harry Hardt, Eva Speyer, Hugo Döblin, Gerti Kutscherra, Mercedes Erdmann. 6 reels. Released April 12, 1925.

The Film in Film: A Look Behind the Scenes/Der Film im Film: Ein Blick hinter die Kulissen (1925)
Richard Hirschfeld GmbH. Producer: Richard Hirschfeld. Director: Friedrich Porges. Screenplay: Friedrich Porges, Stefan Lorant. Cinematography: Stefan Lorant. Scientific advisor: Curt Thomalla. Appearing as themselves: Henny Porten, Emil Jannings, Harry Liedtke, Asta Nielsen, Conrad Veidt, Erna Morena, Max Linder, Albert Bassermann, Charles Chaplin, Ernst Deutsch, E. A. Dupont, F. W. Murnau, Richard Eichberg, Alexander Girardi, Maria Jacobini, Werner Kahle, Werner Krauss, Fritz Lang, Thea von Harbou, **Paul Leni**, Lee Parry, Julius Pinschewer, Waldemar Psylander, Gennaro Righelli, Hanns Schwarz, Paul Ludwig Stein, Paul Wegener, Hanni Weisse, Robert Wiene. 6 reels. Released June 26, 1925.

Somebody's Son/The Farmer from Texas/Der Farmer aus Texas (1925)
May-Film GmbH. Producer and director: Joe May. Screenplay: Joe May, Rolf E. Vanloo, based on the stage play *Pulp Fiction* (*Kolportage*) by Georg Kaiser. Dramaturg: Rudolf Kurtz. Cinematography: Carl Drews, Antonio Frenguelli. Set design: **Paul Leni**. Set construction: Fritz Maurischat. Production manager: Robert Wüllner. Music: Giuseppe Becce. Cast: Mady Christians (Mabel Brett), Edmund Burns (Erik), Willy Fritsch (Akke Appelbloom), Lillian Hall-Davis (Baroness Alice Barrenkrona), Christian Bummerstädt (Count von Stjernenhoe), Clara Greet (Mrs. Appelbloom), Hans Junkermann (Baron Barrenkrona), Pauline Garon (Abby Grant), Frida Richard (Aunt Jutta), Ellen Plessow, Emmy Wyda. 7 reels. Released October 22, 1925.

Dance Fever/Dancing Mad/Der Tänzer meiner Frau (1925)
Fellner & Somlo-Film GmbH (Felsom-Film). Producers: Hermann Fellner, Josef Somlo. Director: Alexander Korda. Screenplay: Alexander Korda, Adolf Lantz, based on a stage play by Paul Armont and Jacques Bousquet. Cinematography: Nicolas Farkas, Curt Oertel. Set design: **Paul Leni**. Assistant producer and production manager: Rudolf Sieber. Cast: Victor Varconi (Edmund Chauvelin), María Corda (Lucille Chauvelin), Lea Seidl (Madame Yvonne Trieux), Livio Pavanelli (Claude Gerson), Willy Fritsch (Max de Sillery), Hans Junkermann (Dance master), Hermann Thimig (Butler), Olga Limburg (Maid), Marlene Dietrich (Dancer), Alexander Choura (Dancer), Raimund Gessner (Himself), John Loder (Dancer). 6 reels. Released November 6, 1925.

Rebus Film Nr. 1 (1925)
Rebus-Film GmbH; distributed by Nemo-Film-Verleih GmbH. Producer and director: **Paul Leni**. Titles: Hans Brennert. Concept: **Paul Leni**. Cinematography: Guido Seeber. 1 reel. Released December 10, 1925.

Cab Nr. 13/Fiaker Nr. 13/Einspänner Nr. 13 (1926)
Sascha-Film/Phoebus-Film AG. Producer: Arnold Pressburger. Director: Mihály Kertész [Michael Curtiz]. Screenplay: Alfred Schirokauer, based on a novel by Xavier de Montépin. Cinematography: Gustav Ucicky, Eduard von Borsody. Set design: **Paul Leni**. Music: Willy Schmidt-Gentner. Cast: Lili Damita (Lilian), Jack Trevor (François Tapin), Paul Biensfeldt (Jacques Carotin), Walter Rilla (Lucien Rebout), Max Gülstorff (Antiquarian), Valeska Stock (Mme. Coco), Sophie Pagay (Linotte, a laundress), Albert Paulig (Ballet master), Carl Ebert (Henri Landon). 6 reels. Released February 5, 1926.

Rebus Film Nr. 2 (1926)
Rebus-Film GmbH; distributed by Nemo-Film-Verleih GmbH. Producer and director: **Paul Leni**. Titles: Hans Brennert. Concept: **Paul Leni**. Cinematography: Guido Seeber. 1 reel. Released February 11, 1926.

Manon Lescaut (1926)
Universum-Film (Ufa). Producer: Erich Pommer. Director: Arthur Robison. Screenplay: Hans Kyser, Arthur Robison, based on the novel by Antoine François Prévost. Cinematography: Karl Freund, Theodor Sparkuhl. Visual effects: Eugen Schüfftan. Camera operator: Robert Baberske. Set and costume design: **Paul Leni**. Music: Ernö Rapée, Jules Massenet. Cast: Lya de Putti (Manon Lescaut), Vladimir Gajdarov (Chevalier Des Grieux), Eduard Rothauser (Military Commander Des Grieux), Fritz Greiner (Marquis de Bli), Hubert von Meyerinck (Vicomte de Bli), Frida Richard (Manon's aunt), Emilie Kurz (Manon's aunt), Lydia Potechina (Susanne), Theodor Loos (Tiberge), Siegfried Arno (Lescaut, Manon's step-brother), Trude Hesterberg (Claire), Marlene Dietrich (Micheline), Olga Engl (Comtesse Germain), Karl Harbacher, Hans Junkermann, Hermann Picha. 6 reels. Released February 15, 1926.

Rebus Film Nr. 3 (1926)
Rebus-Film GmbH; distributed by Nemo-Film-Verleih GmbH. Producer and director: **Paul Leni**. Titles: Hans Brennert. Concept: **Paul Leni**. Cinematography: Guido Seeber. 1 reel. Released March 18, 1926.

Rebus Film Nr. 4 (1926)
Rebus-Film GmbH; distributed by Nemo-Film-Verleih GmbH. Producer and director: **Paul Leni**. Titles: Hans Brennert. Concept: **Paul Leni**. Cinematography: Guido Seeber. 1 reel. Released April 26, 1926.

Rebus Film Nr. 5 (1926)
Rebus-Film GmbH; distributed by Nemo-Film-Verleih GmbH. Producer and director: **Paul Leni**. Titles: Hans Brennert. Concept: **Paul Leni**. Cinematography: Guido Seeber. 1 reel. Released June 15, 1926.

As Once in May/Wie einst im Mai (1926)
Ellen Richter-Film GmbH. Producer: Ellen Richter. Director: Willi Wolff. Screenplay: Robert Liebmann and Willi Wolff, based on the 1913 operetta by Walter Kollo and Willi Kollo. Cinematography: Axel Graatkjær. Set and costume design: **Paul Leni**. Music: Artur Guttmann, Werner R. Heymann. Cast: Ellen Richter (Eugenie de la Roche/Eugenie Schönlein/Charlotte, her granddaughter/Mabel Ward), Adolf Klein (Baron de la Roche), Paul Heidemann (Friedrich Wilhelm Kietz/Fritz, Fred's son), Hugo Fischer-Köppe (Gottlieb Krause), Frida Richard (Auguste Krause), Philipp Manning (Judge Schönlein), Karl Harbacher (Romeo), Trude Hesterberg (Julia), Walter Rilla (Fred W. Kietz), Gyula Szöreghy [Julius von Szöreghy] (Adolph Lemke), Alice Torning (Mrs. Lemke), Hermann Picha (Theophil), Camilla Spira (Minchen Lemke, the daughter). 5 reels. Released August 19, 1926.

The Golden Butterfly/Der goldene Schmetterling (1926)
Sascha-Film/Phoebus-Film AG. Producer: Arnold Pressburger. Director: Mihály Kertész [Michael Curtiz]. Screenplay: Jane Bess, Adolf Lantz, based on a novel by P. G. Wodehouse. Cinematography: Gustav Ucicky, Eduard von Borsody. Set design: **Paul Leni**. Music: Willy Schmidt-Gentner. Cast: Hermann Leffler (Mac Farland), Lili Damita (Lilian, his foster daughter), Nils Asther (Andy, his son), Jack Trevor (Aberdeen, a millionaire), Curt Bois (André Dubois, ballet master), Kurt Gerron (Regular guest), Karl Platen (Headwaiter), Ferdinand Bonn (Theater director), Gyula Szöreghy [Julius von Szöreghy] (Cook). 6 reels. Released August 30, 1926.

Rebus Film Nr. 6 (1926)
Rebus-Film GmbH; distributed by Nemo-Film-Verleih GmbH. Producer and director: **Paul Leni**. Titles: Hans Brennert. Concept: **Paul Leni**. Cinematography: Guido Seeber. 1 reel. Released October 8, 1926.

Rebus Film Nr. 7 (1926)
Rebus-Film GmbH; distributed by Nemo-Film-Verleih GmbH. Producer and director: **Paul Leni**. Titles: Hans Brennert. Concept: **Paul Leni**. Cinematography: Guido Seeber. 1 reel. Released December 28, 1926.

Rebus Film Nr. 8 (1927)
Rebus-Film GmbH; distributed by Nemo-Film-Verleih GmbH. Producer and director: **Paul Leni**. Titles: Hans Brennert. Concept: **Paul Leni**. Cinematography: Guido Seeber. 1 reel. Released January 13, 1927.

The Cat and the Canary (1927)
Universal Pictures Corporation. Presenter: Carl Laemmle. Producer: Paul Kohner. Director: **Paul Leni**. Screenplay: Robert F. Hill, Alfred A. Cohn, based

on the stage play by John Willard. Titles: Walter Anthony. Story supervision: Edward J. Montagne. Cinematography: Gilbert Warrenton. Editing: Martin G. Cohn. Supervising editor: Lloyd Nosler. Set design: Charles D. Hall. Music: Hugo Riesenfeld. Assistant to the director: Robert F. Hill. Cast: Laura La Plante (Annabelle West), Creighton Hale (Paul Jones), Forrest Stanley (Charles Wilder), Tully Marshall (Roger Crosby), Gertrude Astor (Cecily), Flora Finch (Susan), Arthur Edmund Carewe (Harry), Martha Mattox (Mammy Pleasant), George Siegmann (Guard), Lucien Littlefield (Ira Lazar), Hal Craig (Policeman), Billy Engle (Taxi driver), Joe Murphy (Milkman). 8 reels. Released September 9, 1927.

The Chinese Parrot (1927)
Universal Jewel. Presenter: Carl Laemmle. Director: **Paul Leni**. Screenplay: J. Grubb Alexander, based on a novel by Earl Derr Biggers. Titles: Walter Anthony. Story supervision: Edward J. Montagne. Cinematography: Benjamin F. Kline. Directorial assistant: Victor Nordlinger. Cast: Marian Nixon (Sally Phillmore), Florence Turner (Mrs. Phillmore), Hobart Bosworth (Philip Madden/Jerry Delaney), Edmund Burns (Robert Eden), Albert Conti (Martin Thorne), Kamiyama Sôjin (Charlie Chan), Fred Esmelton (Alexander Eden), Edgar Kennedy (Maydorf), George Kuwa (Louis Wong), Slim Summerville (Prospector), Dan Mason (Prospector), Anna May Wong (Nautch dancer), Etta Lee (Girl in gambling den), Jack Trent (Jordan). 7 reels. Released October 23, 1927.

The Man Who Laughs (1928)
Universal Pictures Corporation. Presenter: Carl Laemmle. Producer: Paul Kohner. Assistant Producer: Lew Landers. Director: **Paul Leni**. Screenplay: J. Grubb Alexander, May McLean, Marion Ward, Charles E. Whittaker, based on the 1869 novel *L'Homme Qui Rit* by Victor Hugo. Titles: Walter Anthony. Story supervision: Béla Sekely. Cinematography: Gilbert Warrenton. Editing: Edward Cahn. Supervising editor: Maurice Pivar. Set design: Charles D. Hall, Thomas O'Neil, Joseph Wright. Costume design: Dave Cox, Vera West. Makeup design: Jack Pierce. Historical research consultants: Robert H. Newlands, Hilda Grenier. Elephant wrangler: Elias English. Production staff: John M. Voshell, Jay Marchant, Louis Friedlander. Musical director: Joseph Cherniavsky. Cast: Mary Philbin (Dea), Conrad Veidt (Gwynplaine/Lord Linnæus Clancharlie), Julius Molnar, Jr. (Gwynplaine as a child), Olga Baclanova (Duchess Josiana), Brandon Hurst (Barkilphedro), Cesare Gravina (Ursus), Stuart Holmes (Lord David Dirry-Moir), Sam De Grasse (King James II), George Siegmann (Dr. Hardquanonne), Josephine Crowell (Queen Anne), Edgar Norton (Lord High Chancellor), Károly Huszár [Charles Puffy] (Innkeeper), Carmen Castillo (Dea's mother), Carrie Daumery (Lady-in-waiting), Delmo

Fritz (Sword swallower), John George (Dwarf), Jack Goodrich (Clown), Frank Puglia (Clown), Nick De Ruiz (Wapentake), Louise Emmons (Gypsy hag), Torben Meyer (Spy), Joe Murphy (Hardquanonne's messenger), Henry A. Barrows, Richard Bartlett, Les Bates, Charles Brinley, Allan Cavan, D'Arcy Corrigan, Howard Davies, J. C. Fowler, Charles Hancock, Lila LaPon, Broderick O'Farrell, Lon Poff, Henry Roquemore, Templar Saxe, Allan Sears, Scott Seaton, Louis Stern, Al Stewart, Anton Vaverka, Zimbo the Dog (Homo the Wolf). 10 reels. Released April 27, 1928.

The Last Warning (1928)
Universal Jewel. Presenter: Carl Laemmle. Director: **Paul Leni**. Screenplay: Alfred A. Cohn, Robert F. Hill, J. G. Hawks, based on the novel by Wadsworth Camp and the play by Thomas F. Fallon. Titles: Tom Reed. Story supervision: Edward J. Montagne. Cinematography: Hal Mohr. Editing: Robert Carlisle. Set design: Charles D. Hall. Associate producer: Carl Laemmle, Jr. Musical director: Joseph Cherniavsky. Cast: Laura La Plante (Doris Terry), Montagu Love (Arthur McHugh), Roy D'Arcy (Harvey Carleton), Margaret Livingston (Evelynda Hendon), John Boles (Richard Quayle), Bert Roach (Mike Brody), Mack Swain (Robert Bunce), Burr McIntosh (Josiah Bunce), Carrie Daumery (Barbara Morgan), Slim Summerville (Tommy Wall), Buddy Phelps (Buddy), Torben Meyer (Gene), D'Arcy Corrigan (John Woodford), Tom O'Brien (First detective), Fred Kelsey (Second detective), Charles K. French (Doctor), Francisco Marán (Jeffries), Ella McKenzie (Ann), Harry Northrup (Coroner), Pat Harmon (Cop), Charles McMurphy (Cop). 8 reels. Released December 25, 1928.

Index

Note: *italic* page numbers indicate illustrations

"Absolute Film," 103, 114n22
achte Gebot, Das SEE *Eighth Commandment, The*
Achtung! Welle 505! SEE *Look Out! Wave 505!*
Alraune, 88
Ancient Law, The, 239
Andersen, Hans Christian, 125
Anemic Cinema, 109
Anna Boleyn, 39
Antalffy, Alexander SEE von Antalffy, Alexander
Anthony, Walter, 200, 252
Aristotle, 197
Armored Vault, The, 241
Arpke, Otto, 80n27
Arrival, The, 107
As Once in May, 251
Ausgestossener, 1 Teil: Der junge Chef, Ein SEE *Outcast, Part 1: The Young Boss, An*
Ausgestossener, 2 Teil: Der ewige Friede, Ein SEE *Outcast, Part 2: The Eternal Peace, An*
"Automata, The" (literary work), 74

Babes in Toyland (operetta), 124, 125
Backstairs, xvi, 13, 27, 52–66, *54*, *62*, 206, 246
Baclanova, Olga, 174, *182*, 195, 252
Bacon, Francis, 180
Bagier, Guido, 125
Bahnwärter Thiel SEE *Lineman Thiel*
Balla, Giacomo, 107
Ballet Mécanique, 104, 105, 109, 114n22
Bargain in the Kremlin, A, xix, 25, 213, 235
Barrie, James M., 19
Batman, 196
Bat Whispers, The, 140
Baum, L. Frank, 137n22
Belajeff, Olga, 19, 69, 71, 76, 82, 91, 248
Belova, Valentina, 126, *127*
Berger, Ludwig, 125
Bergkatze, Die SEE *Wildcat*
Berlin: Die Sinfonie der Großstadt SEE *Berlin: Symphony of a Big City*
Berliner Range, The, xiv
Berlin: Symphony of a Big City, 104

Bernauer, Rudolf, xiv, 3
Biedermeier (art style), 86
Biensfeldt, Paul, 74, 90, 91, 242, 243, 244, 247, 248, 250
Biggers, Earl Derr, 22, 23, 252
Birinski, Leo, xvii, 16, 71, 132, 138n48, 247, 248
Black Triangle, The, 240
Blouse King, The, xv, 8, 10, 241–2
Blusenkönig, Der SEE *Blouse King, The*
Boccioni, Umberto, 107
Boles, John, 208, 253
Bonaventura (Ernst August Friedrich Klingemann), 74
Bosworth, Hobart, 22, 252
Brandmal ihrer Vergangenheit, Der SEE *Mark of Their Past, The*
Braque, Georges, 106
Brecht, Bertolt, 74
Brennert, Hans, xvi, xvii, 10, 14, 15, 39, 97, 242, 243, 249, 250, 251
Brenon, Herbert, xvii, 20, 118, 125
Bride of Frankenstein, 217n6, 217n21
Broadway, 205
Bronson, Betty, 125
Browning, Tod, xviii, 26, 116, *117*, 195, 217n6, 227
Buchowetzki, Dimitri, 13, 247
Bufa (Bild- und Filmamt), xv, 9, 32n19, 37, 38, 242
Buster Keaton, der Matrose SEE *Navigator, The*

Cab Nr. 13, 250
Cabinet of Dr. Caligari, The, xvi, 16, 18, 19, 23, 53, 55, 63, 65, 70, 76–7, 79n8, 82–94 *passim*, 124, 134, 153, 163, 174, 209
Camp, Wadsworth, xix, 204, 215, 219, 253
Carpenter, William Benjamin, 161
Carrà, Carlo, 105, 107

Cat and the Canary, The (1927), xviii–xix, 2, 20–2, 28, 34n54, 82, 94, 132–5, 139n57, 140–3, *144*, 145–7, 151–5, 156n13, 156n18, 158–60, 162–4, 166–8, 170n27, 174, 203, 206, 208, 217n14, 223, 232, 234, 236n1, 251–2
Cat and the Canary, The (1939), 140–1, 149–54, *154*
Cat and the Canary, The (stage play), 20, 54, 133, 134, 138n54, 140, 143, 148–53 *passim*, 156n9, 159, 252
Cat Creeps, The, 149
Catwalk, The, 8, 241
Cavalcanti, Alberto, 110, 112
Cavanagh, Raymond, 129, 130, 131
Chaney, Lon, 116, 142, 174, 178, 192–5, 201
Chaplin, Charles, 109, 249
Chaplin, Syd, 120
Charley's Aunt, 120
Children of Darkness, 1: The Man from Naples, 13, 246
Children of Darkness, 2: Fighting Worlds, 13, 246
Chinese Parrot, The, xix, 22, 23, 135, 203, 252
Christensen, Benjamin, 22, 215
Christoph, Paul, 15
"City Symphonies," 104, 110, 111
Clair, René, 104, 105, 109
Clayton, Jack, 159
Coachmen, The (cabaret act), 14–15, 33n34
Columbia, 223
Comedy of Passions, 239
Congress Dances, The, 93
Continental-Kunstfilm GmbH, 6, 240
Corrigan, D'Arcy, 208, 253
Countess of Paris, The, 13, 247–8
Crowell, Josephine, 174, 195, 252
Cuban Corso (cabaret act), 14

Cubism, 14, 28, 103, 105, 106, 109, 115n29, 122
Curtiz, Michael (Mihály Kertész), 32n18, 203, 250, 251

Dada, 28, 103, 108, 109
Dance Fever, 249
Dancing Girls (cabaret act), 14
Dancing Mad SEE *Dance Fever*
D'Arcy, Roy, 208, 253
Davidson, Paul, 9, 10, 241, 242, 243
Davis, Owen, xix, 25
Dead Awaken, The, 241
Deception SEE *Anna Boleyn*
Decorate Your Home! (cabaret act), 14
de Forest, Lee, 138n45
De Grasse, Sam, 174, 252
Delaunay, Robert, 107
de Lorde, André, 24
Delsarte, François, 194
Denny, Reginald, 130, 131
de Putti, Lya, xix, 122, 250
DeRosa, Jerry, 129, 130, 131
Desire, 174
Destiny, 82, 93
Deutsch, Ernst, xiv, 249
"Deutsches Studentenleben in der Fremde" SEE "German Student Life in a Foreign Land"
Devant, David, 161
Diary of Dr. Hart, The, xv, 9, 10, 26, 36–41, *42, 44, 45, 46, 47*, 47–50, 242
Diegelmann, Wilhelm, 125, 240, 242, 243, 244, 245
Dieterle, Wilhelm (William Dieterle), 13, 55, 56, 67n22, 69, 71, 82, 84, 89–92, 201, 245–8
Dietrich, Marlene, 247–50
Dinamismo di un cane al guinzaglio SEE *Dynamism of a Dog on a Leash*
Diskus-Film, xiv

Dix, Otto, 66
Dr. Mabuse the Gambler, 39, 93
Doll, The, 74
Dornröschen SEE *Sleeping Beauty*
Doyle, Arthur Conan, 126
Dracula, 25, 26, 178, 217n6, 217n21
Dreier, Hans, 9, 245
Drei von der Tankstelle, Die SEE *Three from the Filling Station*
Droschkenkutschern SEE *Coachmen, The*
Duchamp, Marcel, 107, 109
Duchamp-Villon, Raymond, 107
Dulac, Germaine, 105, 112
Dumas *fils*, Alexandre, 10, 242
Dupont, E. A. (Ewald André Dupont), xvii, 8, 13, 20, 39, 56, 113n10, 118, 122, 128, 142, 239, 244, 245, 246, 249
Duskes GmbH, 4
Dynamism of a Dog on a Leash (painting), 107

Edison, Thomas, 220
Eggeling, Viking, 104, 105
Ehre, Die SEE *Honor*
1812 Overture (musical composition), 137n20
Eighth Commandment, The, 241
Einspänner Nr. 13 SEE *Cab Nr. 13*
Eisenstein, Sergei, 110, 112, 170n30
Emak-Bakia, 110
Engel, Erich, 74
Entr'acte, 104, 105, 109
Escape in the Marriage: The Big Flirt, 16
European Rest Cure, The, 40
Expressionism, 6, 13, 16–18, 21, 27, 30, 31n5, 52–5, 58–66, 67n33, 69, 70, 76, 77, 79n16, 83, 86, 91–3, 94n1, 97, 102, 103, 134, 143, 152, 160, 173, 178–9, 192, 196, 204–7, 217n21, 219, 233

INDEX   257

Face Behind the Mask, The, 177
Fallon, Thomas F., xix, 204, 217n10, 219, 253
Fall Rosentopf, Der SEE *Rosentopf Case, The*
Fantôme de l'Opéra, Le (literary work), 204
Faraday, Michael, 161
Farmer aus Texas, Der SEE *Somebody's Son*
Farmer from Texas, The SEE *Somebody's Son*
Faulkner, William, 189
Faust, 39
Fejos, Paul, 205, 215, 217n6
Feldarzt, Der SEE *Diary of Dr. Hart, The*
Fenniker, Josef, xiv
Fiaker Nr. 13 SEE *Cab Nr. 13*
Fiesco SEE *Genoa Conspiracy, The*
Film in Film, The, 249
Flucht in die Ehe: Der grosse Flirt, Die SEE *Escape in the Marriage: The Big Flirt*
Foolish Wives, 205
Forbidden Paradise, xvii, 20, 118, 124, 125, 128
Frank, Leonhard, 65
Frankenstein, 207, 217n21, 218n21
Frauenopfer SEE *Women's Sacrifice*
Frau von vierzig Jahren, Die SEE *Woman of Forty, A*
Freaks, 195
Freud, Sigmund, 64, 65, 91, 192
Freund, Karl, 243, 246, 250
Friedrich, Caspar David, 86
Fröhlich, Gustav, 136n5
From Morn to Midnight, 67n33, 91, 94
Futurism, 28, 103, 105–7, 111, 115n29

Galeen, Henrik, 16, 33n38, 73–6, 80n32, 81n44, 81n45, 88–90, 248
"Galley, The" (musical composition), 14

Geierwally, Die SEE *Wally of the Vultures*
Genoa Conspiracy, The, 12–13, 245
Germanin, 43
"German Student Life in a Foreign Land" (prologue), 120
Gespensterschiff, Das SEE *Ghost Ship, The*
Ghost Breakers, The, 158
Ghost Ship, The, xvi, 239
Gibbs, Philip, xix, 25, 235
Gift der Liebe, Das SEE *Poison of Love, The*
Gilbert and Sullivan, xvii
Gloria-Film GmbH, xvi, 244, 245, 246, 247
Goddard, Paulette, 149, 151, *154*
Golden Butterfly, The, 251
goldene Schmetterling, Der SEE *Golden Butterfly, The*
Goldwyn studio, 19, 205
Golem, The, 16, 88
"Gondel, Die" SEE "Gondola, The"
"Gondola, The" (cabaret), xvi, xvii, 14–17, *15*, 33n32, 33n35, 73, 122, 125
Gottowt, John, 71, 80n32, 248
Gräfin von Paris, Die SEE *Countess of Paris, The*
Grand Cheval, Le SEE *Large Horse, The*
Grand Hotel, 218n22
Gravina, Cesare, 172, 252
Green Manuela, The, 239
Griffith, D. W. (David Wark Griffith), 140
Gris, Juan, 105, 106
Grune, Karl, xvii, 32n18, 247
Guilt of Lavinia Morland, The, 244
Gulick, Paul, 132

Hale, Creighton, 150, 166, 252
Hall, Charles D., 205, 209, 217n14, 233, 252, 253
Halm, Alfred, 10, 241
Ham and Eggs (cabaret act), 14

Hands of Orlac, The, 174
Hauff, Wilhelm, xvi
Haunted Spooks, 140
Hauptmann, Gerhart, 58
Haus zum Mond, Das SEE *House on the Moon, The*
Hays, Will, 142
Heimkehr SEE *Homecoming*
He Knew Women, xix
Hemingway, Ernest, 201
Henny Porten Filmproduktion, xvi, 56, 245, 246, 247
Herbert, Victor, 124, 125
Hesperus (literary work), 74
Hintertreppe SEE *Backstairs*
Hoffmann, Carl, 39, 242, 244, 245
Hoffmann, E. T. A., 74, 233
Hoffmanns Erzählungen SEE *Tales of Hoffmann*
Hofmann, Ernst, 9, 242
Holmes, Stuart, 195, 252
Homecoming, 65
Honor (stage play), 59
Hope, Bob, 149, 150, 151
Houdini, Harry, 161, 162
House of Fear, The (literary work), 204, 215, 219
House of Horror, 22
House on the Moon, The, 74
Hugo, Victor, xix, 23, 24, 29, 135, 139n59, 174, 187n4, 189–92, 194, 195, 199, 200, 252
Hunchback of Notre Dame, The, 24, 142, 174, 192, 202, 205
Hurst, Brandon, 174, 195, 252
Hyman, Richard, 119

Imaginary Invalid, The (stage play), 25
"Im Puppenladen" SEE "In the Doll Shop"
Independent Moving Pictures Company, 220
Innocents, The, 159

"In the Doll Shop" (prologue), 124
Intoxication, 243
Invisible Lodge, The (literary work), 74

Jacoby, Georg, 10
James, Henry, 189
Jannings, Emil, 19, 43, 67n22, 69, 82, 83, 89–91, 92, 113n10, 113n11, 122, 137n12, 241, 247, 248, 249
Janowitz, Hans, xvi
Jazz Singer, The, 173, 203, 220
Jessner, Leopold, 13, 27, 32n18, 52, 55, 56, 60, 61, 66, 86, 246
Jolts of a Taxicab (painting), 107
jour se lève, Le, 218n22
Joy, Jason, 142–43
Joyce, James, 189
Julian, Rupert, 205

Kameliendame, Die SEE *Prima Vera*
Kammerspiel, 57, 58, 62, 66
Kammerspielfilm, xvi, 57, 58, 61, 206, 208
Kam Tai Chinese juggling troupe, 116
Karl und Anna (literary work), 65
Katzensteg, Der SEE *Catwalk, The*
Keaton, Buster, xviii, 126
Kellar, Harry, 162
Kertész, Mihály SEE Curtiz, Michael
Kiewa, Iwanka Jana, 15
Kilenyi, Edward, 129
Kimmich, Max, 43
Kinder der Finsternis, 1: Der Mann aus Neapel SEE *Children of Darkness, 1: The Man from Naples*
Kinder der Finsternis, 2: Kämpfende Welten SEE *Children of Darkness, 2: Fighting Worlds*
King Amuses Himself, The SEE *roi s'amuse, Le*
King of Jazz, 205
Kipho, 102, 113n16
Klein, César, 80n32

Klingemann, Ernst August Friedrich
    SEE Bonaventura
Koch, Robert, 43, 44
Kohner, Paul, 176, 251, 252
Kolportage SEE *Pulp Fiction*
Komödie der Leidenschaften SEE *Comedy of Passions*
Kongress tanzt, Der SEE *Congress Dances, The*
Kortner, Fritz, 13, *54*, 55, 59, 60, 66, 74, 245, 246
Kräly, Hanns, 39, 242, 243
Krauss, Werner, 19, 43, 67n22, 69, 70, 82, 89, 240, 245, 248, 249
Kroyt, Boris, 137n20
Kuleshov, Lev, 110
Kurtz, Rudolf, xvii, 6, 11, 13, 14, 26, 30, 31, 70, 102, 103, 105, 114n19, 114n25, 241, 242, 249
Kwartiroff, Alexander, xvi, 14, 16, 248
Kyser, Hans, 125, 127, 250

Lady Hamilton, xvi, 8–10, 245–6
Laemmle, Carl, xviii, 19, 20, 28, 117, 128–35 *passim*, 137n33, 138n36, 142, 159, 173, 176, 187n4, 203, 205, 206, 217n20, 219–21, 224, 227, 232, 235, 251, 252, 253
Laemmle, Carl, Jr. ("Junior Laemmle"), 219, 220, 232, 253
Landers, Lew, 176, 252
Lang, Fritz, xvii, 39, 82, 136n5, 249
La Plante, Laura, 24, *144*, 159, 208, *226*, 229, 232, 234, *234*, 252, 253
Large Horse, The (sculpture), 107
Last Laugh, The, 84
Last Performance, The, 205, 217n6
Last Warning, The, xix, 22, 24, 29, 30, 31n10, 34n59, 113n12, 135, 136, 139n60, 203–6, *207*, 208–10, *210*, 211–16, 217n9, 217n14, 218n24, 219–25, *226*, 227–36, *229*, *230*, *234*, 237n34, 253

Laugh, The (painting), 107
Laughton, Charles, 201
Laun, Friedrich, 74
Leben und Treiben in den böhmischen Bädern Marienbad, Karlsbad, Franzensbad SEE *Life and Times in the Bohemian Baths of Marienbad, Karlsbad, Franzensbad*
Léger, Fernand, 104, 105, 109
Leidenschaft SEE *Passion*
Leni, Paul
    costume designs, xiv, xvi, 3, 8, 16, 20, 72, 91, 117, 121, 124, 127, 136n1, 138n48, 239, 242, 243, 245, 250, 251
    death of, xix, 1, 26, 30, 114n19, 203, 216, 235, 236
    early career of, xiii–xv, 3–6, *4*, 102
    "Gondola" cabaret and, xvi, 14–16, 17, 33n32, 33n35, 73, 121–2, 125
    graphic designs, xiii, xvi–xviii, 2–6, 3n5, 38, 71, 102, 104, 121–2, 131
    military service in World War I, xv, 9–10, 33n32, 45
    poster designs by, xvi, 3–7, 31n5, 31n10, 102
    prologues, xvii, xviii, 20, 28, 34n60, 113n10, 116–18, 121–36, 137n16, 137n20, 159, 224
    set designs, xiii–xviii, 3–17, 19–21, 24, 30, 31, 38, 55–66 *passim*, 70, 71, 73, 74, 75, 79n12, 80n32, 83, 86, 91, 97, 102–3, 112, 117, 121–33 *passim*, 136n1, 138n48, 142, 203–4, 212–14, 239–51
    SEE ALSO individual film and prologue titles; Brennert, Hans; Dupont, E. A.; Expressionism; Laemmle, Carl; Lubitsch, Ernst; May, Joe; Kurtz, Rudolf; Sello, Leonore "Lore"; Universal; Veidt, Conrad
Leroux, Gaston, 204
Lerski, Helmar, 85, 246, 248
Leschnitzer, Georg, 104

L'Étoile de mer, 110
Levi, Moses Hirsch, xiii, 3
Levi, Rosa Mayer, xiii, 3
L'Herbier, Marcel, 105
L'Homme à la Pipe SEE *Man with a Pipe*
L'Homme Qui Rit (literary work), 252
Liebesbriefe der Baronin von S . . ., Die SEE *Love Letters of Baroness von S . . ., The*
Liedtke, Harry, 10, 241, 242, 249
Life and Times in the Bohemian Baths of Marienbad, Karlsbad, Franzensbad, 40
Lineman Thiel (literary work), 58
Liszt, Franz, 126
Little Match Girl, The, 125
Lloyd, Harold, 140
Look Out! Wave 505! (stage revue), xvii, 122
Lorre, Peter, 177, 178, 186
Lost World, The, xviii, 126, 127
Love, Montagu, 208, 253
Love Letters of Baroness von S . . ., The, 6, 248
Lubitsch, Ernst, xiii, xv, xvii, xix, 8, 10, 19, 20, 39, 74, 90–1, 94, 118, 124, 142, 203, 241, 242, 243
Ludendorff, Erich, 37
Lugosi, Bela, 178, 186, 217n6
Lumière, Auguste and Louis, 39

Macbeth (stage play), xiv
Mack, Max, 8, 241
Mädchen mit den Schwefelhölzern, Das SEE *Little Match Girl, The*
Mad Love, 178
Madame DuBarry, 39
Manhatta, 111
Mania, 243
Man in the Cellar, The, 240
Manon Lescaut, xviii, 9, 10, 127, 128, 138n48, 250

Man Who Laughs, The, xix, 22, 23–4, 29, 59, 135, 139n60, 172–86, *176*, *182*, 187n1, 187n5, 189–202, 202n4, 203, 204, 208, 216n2, 217n14, 226, 236n6, 252–3
Man with a Guitar (painting), 106
Man with a Pipe (painting), 106
Mark of Their Past, The, xiv
Martin, Karlheinz, 67n33, 74, 91, 244
Maskelyne, John Nevil, 161, 162, 163, 169n20
Mattoni, André, 128
Mattox, Martha, 162, 252
May, Hans, xvi, 14
May, Joe, xv, xvii, 6, 8, 10, 13, 16, 32n15, 65, 73, 86, 101, 132, 240, 241, 243, 244, 247, 248, 249
Mayer, Carl, xvi, 55–6, 64, 246
Mayer, Rosa SEE Levi, Rosa Mayer
May-Film GmbH, 6, 243, 244, 247, 248, 249
Meinhard, Carl, xiv, 3
Méliès, Georges, 161, 169n20
Mendeleev, Dmitri, 161
Merry-Go-Round, 142
Messmer, Otto, 100
Metropolis, 136n5
Meyrink, Gustav, 33n36, 73, 74, 248
MGM, 203, 205
Mikado, The (operetta), xvii
Mohr, Hal, 222, 233, 253
Molière, xix, 25
Mord ohne Täter, Der SEE *Murder Without a Murderer*
Moss, B. S. (Benjamin S. Moss), 224
Motion Picture Patents Company, 220
Mr. Smith Goes to Washington, 218n22
müde Tod, Der SEE *Destiny*
Münsterberg, Hugo, 161
Murder Without a Murderer, 239

Murnau, F. W., xiii–xiv, xvii, 16, 39, 65, 67n22, 82, 88, 142, 174, 203, 209, 216n3, 249
Mysterien eines Frisiersalons SEE *Mysteries of a Barbershop*
Mysteries of a Barbershop, 74
Mysterious Mansion, The SEE *Black Triangle, The*
Mystery of Bangalore, The, xv, 10–13, 187n2, 242

Nachtwachen SEE *Night Watches, The*
Navigator, The, xviii, 126, 127, 128, 135, 137n24
Nazi Agent, 178
Negri, Pola, 124, 243
Neptun-Film AG, xvii, 16, 80n32, 248
Nevinson, Christopher Richard Wynne, 107
Nibelungen, Die, 39
Night Watches, The (literary work), 74
Nixon, Marian, 22, 252
Nosferatu, 16, 65, 82, 84, 86, 88, 93, 209
Nosler, Lloyd, 156n18, 252
Novembergruppe (artists' collective), 103, 104
Nugent, Elliott, 150

O'Brien, Willis, 126
Old Dark House, The, 140, 158, 207, 217n21
One Exciting Night, 140
Opfer, Das SEE *Sacrifice, The*
Orlacs Hände SEE *Hands of Orlac, The*
Oswald, Richard, xvi, 8, 74, 245, 248
Oumansky, Alexander, 120, 121, 122, 124–7
Outcast, Part 1: The Young Boss, An, xv, 6, 240
Outcast, Part 2: The Eternal Peace, An, 240

Outside the Law, xviii, 20, 34n60, 116, 117, 129, 130, 133

Pabst, G. W., 43
Päch, Gertrud, 15
Panizza, Oskar, 74
Paracelsus, 43
Paramount, 19, 128, 140, 149–51, 154, 156n9, 203, 205
Passion (1913), xiv
Passion (1919) SEE *Madame DuBarry*
Path that Leads to Damnation, The, 136n5
Patience, 12, 187n2, 244
Paul, Jean, 74
Paul, Robert W., 161
Paul-Leni-Film GmbH, xvi, 16, 73
Pax Film GmbH, 10, 242
Pechstein, Max, 3, 104
Peter Pan, xvii, 20, 34n60, 118, 125, 126, 128, 137n22
Phantom of the Opera, The, 25, 142, 174, 195, 204, 205, 232–4
Philbin, Mary, 24, 25, 172, 195, 252
Picabia, Francis, 104, 109
Pick, Lupu, xvii, 240
Pierce, Jack, 175, *176*, 186, 252
Pinschewer, Julius, 102, 249
Platonic Marriage, The, 12, 243
platonische Ehe, Die SEE *Platonic Marriage, The*
Pleasant, Mary Ellen, 156n9
Poacher, The, 126
Poison of Love, The, xiv
"Police Sergeant's Story, The" (prologue), xviii, 116, *117*, 118, 129, 130, 133, 135, 136n1
Polish Blood, xix
Pommer, Erich, 85, 93–4, 250
Porten, Henny, 13, *54*, 55–7, 60, 62, 65, 245, 246, 247, 249
Porter, Edwin S., 40

Prévost, Antoine François, 127, 250
Prima Vera, xv, 10, 38, 242
Prince Cuckoo, xvi, 12, 187n2, 244
Prinz Kuckuck: Die Höllenfahrt eines Wollüstlings SEE *Prince Cuckoo*
Projektions-AG Union, 9, 241, 242, 243
prologues, xvii, 20, 28, 34n60, 113n10, 116–27, 129–36, 137n16, 137n24, 139n57
Provinzonkel, Der SEE *Wiener in Berlin, Ein*
Pulp Fiction (stage play), 249
Puppe, Die SEE *Doll, The*
Puzzles, 35n68

Rachmann, Sam, 120, 121, 122, 125, 136n6
Rapée, Ernö, 120, 121, 124–7, 137n24, 250
Rätsel von Bangalor, Das SEE *Mystery of Bangalor, The*
Rausch SEE *Intoxication*
Ravenscroft, Ralph, 229
Ray, Man, 75, 105, 109, 112
Rebecca, 218n22
Rebus film series, xvii, 28, 30, 32n15, 73, 97–112, *101*, *108*, 113n9, 137n16, 249, 250, 251
Rebus-Film GmbH, xvii
Rebus Nr. 1, 98–101, *101*, 104–11, *108*, 113n16, 137n16, 139n60, 249
Rebus Nr. 2, 250
Rebus Nr. 3, 113n3, 250
Rebus Nr. 4, 250
Rebus Nr. 5, 250
Rebus Nr. 6, 251
Rebus Nr. 7, 251
Rebus Nr. 8, 251
Reichenbach, Harry, 227
Reimann, Walter, 63
Reinhardt, Max, xiv, 55, 57, 58, 67n22
Return of the Phantom, The, 25
Rhythmus 21, 104, 114n22
Rhythmus 25, 105

Richter, Hans, 104–5, 112, 114n24
Richter-Berlin, Heinrich, 104
Rien que les heures, 110
Rigoletto (opera), 24, 25
Rinaldo Rinaldini (literary work), 33n37, 89
Ring of Giuditta Foscari, The, xv, 10, 241
Rippert, Otto, 136n5
Risata, La SEE *Laugh, The*
RKO, 205, 225
Robert Koch, 43, 44
Robison, Arthur, xviii, 9, 82, 127, 250
Röhrig, Walter, 63
roi s'amuse, Le (stage play), 24
Rolling Home, xviii, 20, 118, 130, 131, 134, 135
Rosentopf Case, The, 242
Ruttmann, Walter, 104, 111, 112

Sacrifice, The, 10
Savage, Jack, 129
Scared Stiff, 158
Schatten – Eine nächtliche Halluzination SEE *Warning Shadows*
Scherben SEE *Shattered*
Schildkraut, Joseph, 235
Schmücke dein Heim! SEE *Decorate Your Home!*
Schroth, Heinrich, 9, 242
Schüfftan, Eugen, 250
Schuld der Lavinia Morland, Die SEE *Guilt of Lavinia Morland, The*
Schumacher, Heinrich Vollrath, 8, 245
Schünzel, Reinhold, 95n9, 245
seeber, Guido, xvii, 32n18, 97–9, 102, 104, 107, 111, 113n16, 115n38, 249, 250, 251
Sehnsucht SEE *Desire*
Seiter, William, 118
Sekely, Béla, 176, 252
Seldes, Gilbert, 1

Sello, Leonore "Lore," xvi, xviii, xix, 20, 129, 244
Servaes, Dagny, 9, 242
Seven Footprints to Satan, 140
Shattered, 58
Shaw, George Bernard, 19
Sheeler, Charles, 111
Sheridan, Thomas, 194
Siegmann, George, 179, 252
Siodmak, Robert, 216
Sjöström, Victor, 19
Sleeping Beauty, xv, 10, 242
Smith, George Albert, 161
Sobbalzi di carrozza SEE *Jolts of a Taxicab*
Sôjin, Kamiyama, 22, 252
Somebody's Son, 6, 249
Souvenir de Moscou (musical composition), 137n20
Stanley, Forrest, 159, 252
Steiner, Rudolf, 194
Steinhoff, Hans, 43
Stern, Ernst, 80n32, 248
Stewart, Billy, 139n57
Stiller, Mauritz, 203, 215, 216n3
Strand, Paul, 111
Strike, 170n30
Strindberg, August, 243
Stuart Webbs: Das Panzergewölbe, SEE *Armored Vault, The*
Stuart Webbs: Der Mann im Keller SEE *Man in the Cellar, The*
Stuart Webbs: Der Spuk im Haus des Professors SEE *Trapped by the Camera*
Stuart Webbs: Die geheimnisvolle Villa SEE *Black Triangle, The*
Stuart Webbs: Die Toten erwachen SEE *Dead Awaken, The*
Student of Prague, The, 86
Sudermann, Hermann, 59, 241
Sullivan, Pat, 100
Sumurun, 91

Surrealism, 103, 109
Sylva, Toni, xiv
Symphonie Diagonale, 104, 105

Tagebuch des Dr. Hart, Das SEE *Diary of Dr. Hart, The*
Tales of Hoffmann, 74
Tangokönigin, Die SEE *Tango Queen, The*
Tango Queen, The, xiv
Tänzer meiner Frau, Der SEE *Dance Fever*
Tchaikovsky, Pyotr Ilyich, 137n20
Tenniel, John, 195
Thalberg, Irving, 142
1001 Nights (cabaret act), 14, 15, 16, 17, 83, 125
Three from the Filling Station, 93
Three Wax Men, SEE *Waxworks*
Three Wax Works, The SEE *Waxworks*
Titan (literary work), 74
Tonight at 12 (stage play), xix, 25
Torrence, Ernest, 125
Tour Eiffel (painting), 107
Tragedy of Love, The, 6, 8, 247
Tragödie der Liebe SEE *Tragedy of Love, The*
Trapped by the Camera, 240
"Tremendous Trifles" (prologue), xviii, 118, 130, 131, 133, 134, 135
Tress, Sylvia, 139n57
Trier, Walter, xvi
Tucholsky, Kurt, xvi, 14

Ufa (Universum-Film Aktiengesellschaft), xvii, xviii, 10, 16, 37, 38, 50, 56, 69, 93, 99, 103, 118, 120–9, 132, 233, 248, 250
Unatonable, 10
Uncanny Stories (literary work), 74
Unheimliche Geschichten SEE *Uncanny Stories*
United Artists, 223

Universal, xviii, 19, 20–30 *passim*,
    31n10, 35n75, 37, 50, 116–18, 128,
    129, 130–4, 137n33, 138n45, 140,
    142, 147, 149, 156n18, 159, 160,
    173–5, 187n7, 192, 202n4, 203–7,
    213, 215, 216n2, 217n6, 217n21,
    219–21, 223–35 *passim*, 236n1,
    237n32, 251, 252, 253
Universum-Film Aktiengesellschaft
    SEE Ufa
unsichtbare Loge, Die SEE *Invisible
    Lodge, The*
Unsühnbar SEE *Unatonable*

Valentino, Rudolph, 128, 201, 227
Varieté, xvii, 20, 39, 113n10, 118, 122, *123*,
    124, 126, 128, 135, 137n12, 137n16,
    139n60
Veidt, Conrad, xiv, xv, xix, 19, 24–6,
    29, 32n25, 69, 70, 82, 87, *87*, 89,
    172–5, *176*, 177, 178, 184, 186,
    187n8, 189, 192, 193, 194, 197,
    201, 202, 242, 244, 245, 248,
    249, 252
verbotene Paradies, Das SEE *Forbidden
    Paradise*
Verdi, Giuseppe, 24
Veritas vincit, 6, 243
verlorenen Welt, Die SEE *Lost World, The*
Verschwörung zu Genua, Der SEE *Genoa
    Conspiracy, The*
Vertov, Dziga, 110
Vignola, Robert, xix
Virgin of Stamboul, The, 227
Vitascope, xiv, 4
voluntad del muerto, La, 149
von Antalffy, Alexander, 10, 11,
    32n25, 242
von Harbou, Thea, 249
von Möllendorff, Else, 125
Von morgens bis mitternachts SEE *From
    Morn to Midnight*

von Stroheim, Erich, 205
Vulpius, Christian August, 33n37, 89
Vulture-Wally, The SEE *Wally of the
    Vultures*

Wachsfigurenkabinett, Das SEE *Waxworks*
Wally of the Vultures, 8, 56, 245
Waltz Dream, A, 125
Walzertraum, Ein SEE *Waltz Dream, A*
Warm, Hermann, 63
Warning Shadows, 18, 82, 84
Warrenton, Gilbert, 34n54, 252
Wasser schweigen, Die SEE *Waters Are
    Silent, The*
Waters Are Silent, The, xiv
Wax Figure, The (literary work), 74
Waxworks, xvii, xviii–xix, 1, 2, 16, 17,
    18, 19, 20, 27, 33n37, 33n38, 33n40,
    59, 61, 69–78, 79n6, 79n8, 79n12,
    80n18, 81n39, 82–94, *87*, *92*, 104,
    117, 125, 128, 129, 132, 134, 137n33,
    138n48, 142, 173, 174, 203, 209,
    239, 248
Wegener, Paul, 16, 67n22, 88, 242, 249
Weisse, Hanni, xiv, 241, 249
*Weisse Pfau: Tragödie einer Tänzerin,
    Der* SEE *The White Peacock*
Wells, H. G., 19
Whale, James, 207, 217n6
White, Peggy, 122, 124, 125
Whitechapel, 239
White Peacock, The, xvi, 8, 244
Wie einst im Mai SEE *As Once in May*
Wiene, Robert, xvii, 16, 53, 65,
    82, 249
Wiener in Berlin, Ein, 99
Wieniawski, Henryk, 137n20
Wildcat, 91
Wilderer, Der SEE *Poacher, The*
Willard, John, xviii, 20, 133, 140, 148,
    150, 151, 153, 156n9, 159, 252
Wizard of Oz, The, 191

Wodehouse, P. G., 251
Woman of Forty, A, 248
Women's Sacrifice, 247
Wonderful World of Oz, The (literary work), 137n22
Wong, Anna May, 22, 34n60, 135, 252
Woolf, Virginia, 189
Woolworth, F. W., 130, 224
World War I, 9–10, 26–7, 33n32, 36–50, 52–3, 65–6, 68n43, 94, 142
Worsley, Wallace, 205
Wright, Jack, 139n57
Wumba-Wumba (cabaret act), 14, 33n32
Wünsche, Alfred, 3
Wynne, Arthur, 112n1

EU representative:
Easy Access System Europe
Mustamäe tee 50, 10621 Tallinn, Estonia
Gpsr.requests@easproject.com

www.ingramcontent.com/pod-product-compliance
Lightning Source LLC
Chambersburg PA
CBHW050211240426
43671CB00013B/2294